WILKIE COLLINS, LE FANU
AND OTHERS

S. M. ELLIS

WILKIE COLLINS
LE FANU
AND OTHERS

Essay Index Reprint Series

 BOOKS FOR LIBRARIES PRESS
FREEPORT, NEW YORK

First Published 1931
Reprinted 1968

LIBRARY OF CONGRESS CATALOG CARD NUMBER:
68-29203

PRINTED IN THE UNITED STATES OF AMERICA

CONTENTS

LIST OF ILLUSTRATIONS TO WILKIE COLLINS, LE FANU, AND OTHERS

WILKIE COLLINS

' The windy trouble of the western sky
    Has all died out, save one long line of fire.
And hark ! the brooding north sweeps sadly by,
    And moans about the poplar's gusty spire.'

THUS one of Wilkie Collins's contemporaries, writing in
Tinsley's Magazine, might have claimed to picture the
fateful scenic background for the literary methods of the
Master of Suspense who compelled awe-inspiring ' atmosphere ' to his purpose. For the romances of Wilkie
Collins cannot be disassociated from their setting : all his
effects are built up from some preliminary expectation of
mystery and doom, and the atmosphere for this state of
mind in both the author and his reader is created by impressive scenery and the forces or phenomena of Nature.
A hot sultry night, with summer lightning playing
vividly on the horizon, and a sense of deep oppression
in the air ; a lonely moon-lit heath, with the wind
soughing amid the fir-trees like the far wailings of the
damned ; a haunted, derelict ship, with the waves
booming in the rocks and caverns near by ; the dreary
rain beating on the dim window panes ; the sun setting
redly over the reedy wastes and waters of a Norfolk
Broad, or breaking through the white clouds of an
autumn afternoon in a Cumberland church-yard—all
prepare the way and attune the mind for impending
scenes of sensation and the workings of Fate :

' The peacefulness of the lonely country was over-shadowed
and saddened by the influence of the falling year . . . the sunset
was near at hand. The clouds had parted ; the slanting light
fell mellow over the hills. The last of the day was cold and
clear and still in the quiet valley of the dead. . . . '

E.W.C.   A

'The shadow of a swiftly-deepening darkness swept over the sky. The pattering of the rain lessened with the lessening wind. There was a momentary hush of stillness. Then on a sudden, the rain poured down like a cataract, and the low roll of thunder came up solemnly on the dying air.'

What a command of simple but vivid language is here. Sky effects painted in words with an avalanche of suggestion of coming fateful and direful experiences. And when Allan Armadale comes upon the tragic cabin what a sense of premonition is conveyed :

'In his terrible ignorance of the truth, he put his head into the doorway, and looked down, laughing, at the place where his murdered father had died. "Pah!" he exclaimed, stepping back suddenly, with a shudder of disgust. "The air is foul already—and the cabin is full of water."'

In the main, Collins's stories are preoccupied with suggestion and imaginative excitement : only occasionally does he present a visible supernatural being, or even an actual murder, though at the outset all the omens point to violent death or doom dogging the footsteps of his characters. His heroes and heroines, however shocking and terrible their experiences, generally survive to marry and live happy ever after (*Basil* is one of the exceptions), while the villains, Count Fosco, Sir Percival Glyde, Miss Gwilt, Godfrey Ablewhite, and the rest, meet with appropriate retribution and death. In this respect, Collins's artistry is hampered and standardised by the conventions of novel writing of his period : even his greater contemporaries, Dickens and Thackeray, ended their stories in like pattern manner, foreign though it be to the sad realities of life, where the roses of romance fade after a few years of marriage and the wicked flourish like the green bay-tree.

With the reservation just mentioned one may otherwise delight in the novels of Wilkie Collins by reason of their ingenuity in plot, their vivid description of scenery and exciting incidents and events, and power of imaginative suggestion. They may be theatrical and melodramatic—no drawback, in my opinion, if all we seek is a good, stirring, dramatic tale. For if we find one of our greatest pleasures in the theatre and pay 14s. 6d. for a seat as an auditor, why should the correlative adjective when applied to a book be a term of opprobrium or supercilious criticism? Wilkie Collins's main claim for himself postulated that he was a good story-teller. He said, ' I have always held the old-fashioned opinion that the primary object of a work of fiction should be to tell a story ; and I have never believed that the novelist who properly performed this first condition of his art was in danger, on that account, of neglecting the delineation of character.'

To the detractors of Wilkie Collins's methods who think his characters mainly puppets designed to carry out the purpose of the incidents—a criticism I do not in the least agree with—I would admit that Collins's place in literature might be adumbrated as somewhat akin to that of the scene-painter in the higher ranges of the theatre at its best ; for he had all the skill of the greatest theatrical producers and creators of stage effects. As he himself said : ' Believing that the Novel and the Play are twin sisters in the family of Fiction ; that the one is a drama narrated, as the other is a drama acted ; and that all the strong and deep emotions which the Play-writer is privileged to excite, the Novel-writer is privileged to excite also, I have not thought it either politic or necessary, while adhering to realities, to adhere to every-day realities only.'

One of his contemporary novelists, Anthony Trollope, dealing with Collins as a novelist of construction, a fictional method he had not himself practised, remarked : ' Of Wilkie Collins it is impossible for a true critic not to speak with admiration, because he has excelled all his contemporaries in a certain most difficult branch of his art.' While, with the same critical reservation, Thomas Hardy truly observed [1] of Wilkie Collins : ' He probably

[1] In a letter to Mr. A. Compton-Rickett, 1912.

stands first, in England, as a constructor of novels of complicated action that depend for their interest on the incidents themselves and not on character. Yet while he was writing he was scandalously ridiculed by the same critical papers that twenty years afterwards praised second-rate imitations of his methods.' He is indeed a thousand times better and more readable than his imitators. What later detective story can approach the literary skill, knowledge, and distinction of *The Moonstone* ?

I have suggested Wilkie Collins as the theatrical scene-painter of literature, and the pictorial comparison is not perhaps amiss, for his imaginative gifts and perception of scenic and natural beauty were strengthened and vividly coloured by his complementary talents as a painter with pigments. As a young man he had seriously intended to follow the profession of Art. One of his landscapes was exhibited at the Royal Academy in 1849, and he has depicted artistic life in *Hide and Seek* and in portions of *After Dark*. He had been brought up in the artistic tradition and environment, for he was the elder son of the distinguished painter, William Collins, R.A., who excelled in landscape and subject pictures ; and his christian name came from his godfather, the even more famous genre painter, Sir David Wilkie, R.A. His grandfather, William Collins, senior, was a picture dealer, and author of *Memoirs of a Picture* (1805) and a *Poem on the Slave Trade*.

William (a name he later entirely dropped) Wilkie Collins was born on January the 8th, 1824, at No. 11 New Cavendish Street, Marylebone.[1] His sponsor, Sir

---

[1] In the memoir of Wilkie Collins in *The Dictionary of National Biography* it is stated, I do not know on what authority, that he was born in Tavistock Square. But as his father, William Collins, had lived at 11 New Cavendish Street since 1815, took his wife there when he married in 1822, and is still mentioned as the occupier of the house in *Boyle's Court Guide* for 1824, 1825, and 1826, it seems reasonable to conclude that the child would have been born there in 1824. Wilkie Collins was baptised in St. Marylebone Church, the parish church for New Cavendish Street : Tavistock Square is in the parish of St. Pancras.

David Wilkie, was a confirmed bachelor and altogether
ignorant of domestic matters ; so, when he saw his infant
godson for the first time, calling to mind his recollections
of the ways of kittens and puppies, he exclaimed with
astonishment and pleasure to the proud father, ' Why,
the child's eyes are *open !* He *sees* already ! ' Like his
younger brother Charles also, Wilkie Collins was much
under the influence, until her death, of his strong-minded
Scotch mother, born a Geddes. Both brothers lived
with her, as a widow, until they were middle-aged men ;
and in their early years it was owing to her views that
neither of the boys was sent to school. Wilkie was
educated privately at Highbury.

His later boyhood and youth were spent, when in
London, at Bayswater ; 20 Avenue Road, Regent's Park ;
85 Oxford Terrace, and at the adjoining No. 1 Devon-
port Street. But in his childhood he was more often at
Hampstead, for this was the period when William
Collins occupied cottages at The Green and, later, at
North End, and delighted in painting the charming rural
scenery which, as he told Bernard Barton, when inviting
him to Hampstead, ' notwithstanding its proximity to
the " Great Babel " is acknowledged to have many and
peculiar beauties.' Its varied aspects were limned in
many of his pictures, and David Wilkie writing to William
Collins, in 1841, from Jerusalem observed : ' Sacred as
this place is, yet here the rain rains and the sun shines
much as it does at home ; and Woodburn will often
talk of a " *Collins sky* " behind the Mount of Olives,
the same as if he saw it behind Hampstead, which this
Mount of the Ascension, though greatly higher, much
resembles.'

Hampstead Heath was then very wild and lonely, and
lovely tree-ful country lay beyond Hendon and Golders
Hill. The influence of Hampstead was very strongly
impressed upon Wilkie Collins's plastic mind in boyhood.
The Heath was for him the Realm of Romance, and a
quarter of a century after he conveyed its magic to others

by the power of his suggestive gifts.   The great opening
scene of *The Woman in White* is on Hampstead Heath, and
the cottage whence Hartright set forth on that sultry
night to meet his vast adventure was doubtless the one
where Wilkie Collins had lived in youth at North End—
probably one of those at Wildwood :

' It was nearly midnight when the servant locked the garden-
gate behind me.   I walked forward a few paces on the shortest
way back to London ; then stopped and hesitated.   The moon
was full and broad in the dark blue starless light sky ; and the
broken ground of the Heath looked wild enough, in the
mysterious light, to be hundreds of miles away from the great
city that lay beneath it. . . . '

Again, in *Armadale*, that fateful Sanatorium, where
Miss Gwilt met her death, was on the London side of the
Heath, no doubt in the Belsize district, and seldom has
the aspect of a rural suburb destroyed by the speculative
builder been more forcibly depicted.   Here the ruin is
linked up with the lowering atmosphere of the story in
the manner so entirely the secret of Collins :

' Fairweather Vale proved to be a new neighbourhood,
situated below the high ground of Hampstead, on the southern
side.   The day was overcast, and the place looked very dreary.
We approached it by a new road running between trees, which
might once have been the park-avenue of a country house.   At
the end we came upon a wilderness of open ground, with half-
finished villas dotted about, and a hideous litter of boards,
wheelbarrows, and building materials of all sorts, scattered in
every direction.   At one corner of this scene of desolation
stood a great overgrown dismal house, plastered with drab-
coloured stucco, and surrounded by a naked unfinished garden,
without a shrub or a flower in it—frightful to behold. . . .
The bell, when the cabman rang it, pealed through the empty
house like a knell ; and the pallid withered old man-servant in
black, who answered the door, looked as if he had stepped up
out of his grave to perform that service.   He let out on me a
smell of damp plaster and new varnish ; and he let in with me a
chilling draught of the damp November air. . . .   I remember
that I shivered as I crossed the threshold.'

In September, 1836, when he was a boy of twelve, Wilkie accompanied his parents and young brother to Italy, where they remained for nearly two years. William Collins accomplished much good painting, while the lovely Italian scenery, the varied impressions and experiences and ever-changing panorama of Continental life were of inestimable benefit to the opening, imaginative minds of his young sons. Wilkie, in particular, was impressed by Rome, and he stored up memories and notes which a few years later found expression in his first romance, *Antonina, or the Fall of Rome*. The Italy the Collinses saw in 1836-8 retained much of the picturesqueness of the eighteenth century in days before Lazzaroni and Gondolieri had become respectable and taken to English dress. The numerous priests, too, were often as immoral as the Abbé Da Ponte ; in fact, some were murderers. At Naples the Collinses witnessed the trial of a monk for the murder of a woman, while another priestly assassin employed a forerunner of Sweeny Tod the Barber :

' The visits of a priest to the wife of a person of consideration being discovered by the husband, who expressed himself strongly upon the subject, the priest engaged a barber, who knew the habits and person of the injured husband, to murder him, for the sum of a hundred ducats : which he did ! '

One of William Collins's models in Rome was a young boy of wonderful beauty, who was painted as Christ in Collins's picture of ' Our Saviour with the Doctors in the Temple,' purchased by the Marquis of Lansdowne for the Bowood Collection. This boy ' had sat to every one for cupids, angels, and whatever else was lovely and refined ; and who was in " private life " one of the most consummate rascals in Rome—a gambler, a thief, and a *stiletto* wearer at twelve years of age.' All this was very exciting, and as godfather David Wilkie wrote from England, ' I shall answer for this—the young gentlemen have no dislike for Travelling, with all its inconveniences.

Pray have they begun to *parler* or to *parlare* ? ' In
Naples there was an English friend, Major Thew, who
was very kind to the Collins boys, ' who swear by the
Major ; he brings them swords, colours, hoops, and
other heart-winning things.'   At Venice they had for
cook and guide and gondolier Beppo, who had been a
cook of Byron's, though he said of the poet, ' he eat
little but biscuits and fruit.'   But all the interesting
things the family saw and heard in Italy must be read in
Wilkie Collins's *Memoirs* of his father.

In the summer of 1842 Wilkie Collins accompanied his
father to Scotland, first to Edinburgh, and thence by
steamer to Wick and Shetland, where William Collins
executed his beautiful illustrations for the Abbotsford
edition of *The Pirate*.   Here they rode the sturdy Shetland ponies, got lost in the mist on the solitary moors,
and were given hospitality for the night at a lonely house
quite in the appropriate manner of a Waverley novel.
Thus Wilkie Collins describes his father at work :

' Most of the painter's studies in his northern sojourn were
produced under unpropitious skies ; and he and his party
would frequently have formed no bad subject for a picture in
themselves, when they halted on a bleak hill-side.   Mr. Collins,
with one knee on the ground, steadying himself against the
wind ; his companion holding a tattered umbrella over him,
to keep the rain off his sketch-book ; the guide standing by,
staring at his occupation in astonishment ; and the ponies
browsing near their riders, on the faded grass, with mane and
tail ever and anon floating out like streamers on the gusty
breezes that swept past them.'

Hitherto, it will be observed, Wilkie Collins's youth
had mainly been devoted to happy and congenial com-
panionship with his father, who was now to suffer fast-
failing health.   The boy, after a period of apprenticeship
to Antrobus and Co., Tea Traders, finally decided he
would prefer to be trained for the profession of the Law.
He entered Lincoln's Inn in May, 1846, at the age of
twenty-two, and was called to the Bar in November, 1851.

No particulars survive of his gifts as a barrister, but the training and experience of human nature thus acquired provided him with much knowledge for his future books. His father's death in 1847 was the indirect cause of his turning to literature. A memorandum by William Collins was found, expressing the hope that ' my dear son, William Wilkie Collins, may be tempted to furnish the world with a memoir of my life.' The son fulfilled the aspiration ; he immediately commenced the work, and *Memoirs of the Life of William Collins, R.A.*, was published in November, 1848, twenty-one months after the artist's death. It was an extremely creditable and well-executed piece of work for a young man of twenty-four, who had no previous experience of biography, or, indeed, very little of any kind of writing. It is of interest to observe in this book the first essays in the author's subsequent characteristic style—the minute detail, the scenic effects. Thus the Colosseum at Rome :

' It was evening ; the friars had retired, after singing before the little chapels placed round the interior of the mighty ruin ; darkness was approaching. Beneath the tall crucifix in the middle of the arena, knelt a peasant woman, prostrate in adoration, and a Carmelite monk beating his breast—the two last-left worshippers at the holy symbol. At some distance from them stood a penitent—his face covered with a hood pierced with two apertures for the eyes—looking spectral, as his veiled, motionless form half disappeared in the gathering gloom. The glorious arches of the Colosseum, showing doubly mysterious and sublime in the dim, fading light cast down on them from the darkening sky, alone surrounded this solemn scene, whose tragic grandeur is to be painted but not to be described.'

I think it will be granted that the scene witnessed by a boy of thirteen and thus described by him ten years later is finely done, and shows a strongly developed sense of the picturesque.

The success of his biography of his father decided Wilkie to look up and utilise the rough drafts of the story he had commenced as a boy in Rome. So he set

to work on what became *Antonina*.[1]   In the meanwhile
he was also pursuing his legal training and painting, for
as I have said he exhibited a picture at the Royal Academy
in 1849.   He was encouraged in his pursuit of Art by a
friend eight years his senior, E. M. Ward, destined to
become a distinguished historical painter and Royal
Academician (in 1855).   As far back as 1841, William
Collins, alluding to his seventeen-year old son Wilkie,
notes : ' Willie would have been dull enough by himself—as it was he was amused, for I had asked Mr. Ward
to spend the evening with us,'—at 85 Oxford Terrace.
The two became the most intimate of friends, and it was
Wilkie Collins who stage-managed the romantic run-
away marriage of E. M. Ward a few years later.   For
Collins in his youth was full of romantic ideas together
with a keen sense of humour and fun—in marked contrast to the cynicism and pessimism of his latter years.
E. M. Ward had fallen in love with a precocious and
talented young girl, Henrietta Ward, a member of
another (but not traceably related) artistic family of his
name.   She was only fourteen when he proposed and
was accepted.   Her parents naturally said she was too
young to be married, and that the lovers must wait two
years.   But they decided that they would not delay, and
taking Wilkie Collins into their confidence he advised
an immediate clandestine wedding.   My dear old friend,
Mrs. E. M. Ward, used to tell her romantic story thus :

' We were at the Royal Academy one day, and settled our
plan of campaign in the Octagon Room. . . .   Wilkie Collins
played an important part in our plot ; he impressed great
caution and secrecy, as he planned out the whole affair with zest
and enjoyment.   My sister-in-law, wife of Charles Ward, was
another conspirator who fell in with his arrangements for unit-
ing our destiny.   My sister-in-law gained permission for me to
spend a day with her at her home in Grove End Road, St. John's

[1] According to a writer in *The Athenæum*, Wilkie Collins, as a
youth, wrote an earlier tale, weird and savage, of life in the South
Pacific, which never found acceptance by a publisher.   As a small
boy he often invented ghostly tales to amuse his companions.

Wood ; she called for me, and we walked to the Church of All Souls', Langham Place. It was May 4th, 1848, and I was not yet sixteen years of age. The first person we saw was Edward, gaily attired in bridal array—wearing a conspicuous white waistcoat and a lovely gardenia in his coat. . . . Wilkie Collins arrived soon after, well in his element. The spice of romance and mischief appealed to him ; he gave me away to the best of men with a hearty good-will. . . . My sister-in-law and Wilkie Collins saw us into a cab for her home, and off we started. The cab was held up for some time by a crowd surrounding a belated May-Day " Jack-in-the-Green," a man dressed in fantastic attire with green boughs and leaves, and walking on stilts. He looked into our window and grinned with delight as we waved him away, in our anxiety to escape notice, and at last we arrived at my sister-in-law's house.' [1]

Wilkie Collins must have delighted in the bizarre figure of ' Jack-in-the-Green ' as the finishing touch to his romantic arrangements. One conjures up the scene and it seems a glimpse of the far past, for a man on stilts to-day in the rushing motor race of Langham Place would be—what would he be ? After a dinner in Grove End Road at which the Collins brothers and the bride's parents were present—the latter quite unaware, of course, that she *was* a bride—Henrietta Ward returned to her home, 31 Fitzroy Square. It was not until three months later that she ran away to join her husband. She went through the garden of Fitzroy Square, of which she had a private key, early one morning ; her husband was waiting in a cab on the east side of the Square ; she threw the key of the gate into the garden as she entered the cab, and so away to Iver, near Slough, ' for our honeymoon, to rooms which Wilkie Collins, who played the part of fairy godmother, had found for us.'

Naturally Wilkie Collins was asked to be godfather to the first child, Alice Ward, born of this marriage he had so materially arranged. He celebrated the occasion, and was in an hilarious state at the christening. Peering at his goddaughter as she lay in the clergyman's arms, he

[1] *Memories of Ninety Years*, by Mrs. E. M. Ward (Hutchinson).

said : ' The baby sheems moving in a very odd way, and is making funny faces.   Why, 'pon my soul, the baby's drunk ! the baby's drunk ! '   Wilkie Collins was never a family man, and he observed to E. M. Ward when the next child was born : ' When you have a few more children I shall cease to congratulate you : I find married men look as if their feelings were hurt when you flatter them about large families.'   But, as is often the way with bachelors, he was fond of certain selected children, one being this second child of the Wards, Leslie—the future cartoonist ' Spy,' of *Vanity Fair*. He would send his love to ' my goddaughter and L. Ward of the medieval countenance.'   And R. C. Lehmann has described him years later as still devoted to certain children :

' Wilkie—we never called him by any more formal name, even when we were little fellows . . . to us boys and to our sister soon grew to be what he ever afterwards remained ; not merely the grown-up and respected friend of our parents, but our own true companion and close associate.   He took our young imaginations captive with stories of Tom Sayers, with whom he had often conversed, whose face-destroying hand he had shaken, whose awful arm he had felt.   " He hadn't any muscle to speak of in his fore-arm," said Wilkie, " and there wasn't any show of biceps ; but when I remarked on that, he asked me to observe his triceps and the muscle under his shoulder, and then I understood how he did it." '

After the death of William Collins in 1847, his widow and two sons removed to 38 Blandford Square, where they lived for two years.   It was a time of much pleasant friendship, for the E. M. Wards were living close by at 33 Harewood Square, and Charles Collins used to bring home his artistic friends, Millais, the Rossettis, Holman Hunt, Frith, and the rest of the bright spirits of that active young time.   Wilkie Collins and E. M. Ward delighted in getting up and acting in amateur theatricals of quite an ambitious description ; the Theatre Royal Back Drawing-Room, Blandford Square, witnessed productions of Goldsmith's *Good-natured Man* and *The*

WILKIE COLLINS
From an unpublished drawing by Leslie Ward (*Spy*) made in 1862 when the
artist was eleven years old
By permission of the Misses Ward

Rivals by Sheridan.   Blandford Square is described as
' Baregrove Square ' in *Hide and Seek*.[1]

Millais has preserved the aspect of Wilkie Collins in
these early days, a solemn-looking young man, with a
large head,[2] wearing spectacles, several rings and Glad-
stonean collar, and with his finger-tips pressed close
together as he cogitates some intricate tale or plot.   For
by now, February, 1850, his first romance, *Antonina, or
the Fall of Rome*, was published.   It was written frankly
in imitation of his favourite author, Bulwer-Lytton, but
neither the subject nor the period—the fifth century—
was the right medium for him.   It was a *ballon d'essai*,
and its characteristics were not repeated in future books.
Nevertheless the story attracted attention, and made
Collins known.   Describing a civic banquet later in this
year, 1850, he relates to Ward :

' An awful crowd at the Mayor's last Thursday, stewards
with names of distinguished individuals on private printed
lists—charged to make civil speeches to all authors and artists,
made hideous mistakes instead : Cardwell taken for Bulwer,
your humble servant taken for a P.-R.B., and asked whether the
author of *Antonina* was there that night.   Gallons of cider-cup
in a vessel like a gold slop-pail, out of which the company
drank like horses out of a trough.   Seedy next morning, and

---

[1] If the numbering has not been changed since 1849, No. 38 still
survives on what is now the only remaining side of Blandford
Square—the north side, which forms a row of drab, forlorn houses,
with narrow windows looking out upon the premises of the Great
Central Railway, at whose coming the rest of Blandford Square was
destroyed.   It is difficult to realise that this sad little miry cul-de-sac
was once, at No. 38, the cheery meeting-place of so many ardent and
talented people.   Harewood Square, where the E. M. Wards lived,
has entirely disappeared, and the site is covered by Marylebone
Station and the Great Central Hotel.

[2] Describing Wilkie Collins at this period, Holman Hunt says that
he had an impressive head, the cranium being noticeably more prominent on the right side, an inequality which did not amount to a
disfigurement, ' perhaps indeed it gave a stronger impression of
intellectual power.'   He states that Wilkie was a man of slight
build, about five feet six inches in height.

miserably unfit to be in the house of a virtuous man whose
servant had never heard of Brandy and Soda Water in the whole
course of his life.   I met Bulwer at a party on Monday night.
He is looking Bright and Plump.   Now is the time to take his
portrait.'

It was probably the success of *Antonina* that brought
Wilkie Collins to the attention of Dickens.   They met,
through the intermedium of Augustus Egg, the artist,
in 1851, and were immediately and mutually attracted by
each other.   On May 16th of that same year Collins
played the part of Smart in Bulwer-Lytton's comedy of
Not So Bad As We Seem, produced at Devonshire House,
in the presence of the Queen and the Prince Consort, by
the famous Amateur Company, headed by Dickens, in
aid of the Guild of Literature and Art.   As is well known,
Dickens was ardently interested in this scheme, and in the
following year, 1852, he took his company of Splendid
Strollers to play in various provincial cities and earn
more money for the Guild.   Wilkie Collins was of the
company, and in addition to his original part he acted in
the old comedy of *Used Up* and as Lithers, a landlord, in
Mr. Nightingale's Diary by Dickens and Mark Lemon.
He was an excellent actor, and Dickens wrote, ' You
have no idea how good Tenniel, Topham, and Collins
have been in what they had to.'   And Forster adds,
' The last of them, Mr. Wilkie Collins, became, for all the
rest of the life of Dickens, one of his dearest and most
valued friends.'   Wilkie Collins henceforth was a principal factor in the affairs of Dickens and the record of
their constant association and trips abroad and theatricals
and amateur acting can be read in Forster's *Life* and in
The Letters of Charles Dickens to Wilkie Collins (published
in 1892).   Dickens seems to have enjoyed the society
of Collins more than that of any other man, for he regarded Forster as his mentor and guide, but with Collins
he could forget he was a genius and celebrity and give
himself up unrestrainedly to the jollities of life, and go
off with Wilkie alone on those ' Lazy Tours of Two Idle

Apprentices ' which were, perhaps, the happiest hours
of Dickens's crowded and troubled life.

Further, Wilkie Collins was one of the few authors
who definitely influenced Dickens's literary work.
Oliver Twist and *Barnaby Rudge* were written to a certain
extent in imitation of the great romantic-criminal
successes of Ainsworth and Bulwer, but far more pronounced were the influences of Wilkie Collins, with his
wealth of details and mysterious machinery of plot, on
the later Dickens of *Our Mutual Friend* and other work of
that period. This, however, is in years to come, and at
first it was Dickens who influenced Collins, for Wilkie's
second novel, *Mr. Wray's Cash Box*, published in January,
1852, was ' A Christmas Sketch ' distinctly in the
Dickensian method. *Basil*, which followed in November
of this year, a powerful and sombre ' Story of Modern
Life,' [1] was the first indication of the real style of Wilkie
Collins with its interplay of natural phenomena and
scenery upon the actions and experiences of the characters.
Indeed, he never did anything better than the symbolical
thunderstorm and moaning wind which accompany
Basil's first interview with his foe, Mannion ; and the
later descriptions of the visions seen by Basil in delirium
are impressively and powerfully presented. Despite
some absurdities arising from the conventions of the
period he was living in—such as the caricature of the
implacable Victorian father and the horror expressed by
Basil's family that he should have *married* a linen-draper's
daughter instead of merely seducing her—*Basil* is a
tragic and moving tale. It has also historical value, for
it accurately pictures the manners and modes of 1850
even to the gaudy furnishings of the drawing-room of a
vulgar but prosperous shopkeeper in a new glaring
house of a square in the then outer and unfinished suburb

---

[1] Wilkie Collins was undecided as to the best sub-title for his
story. The original manuscript has these variations : *Basil ; a
Young Man's Confession. Basil ; or Leaves from the History of a Young
Man's Life. Basil ; or the Love Secret.*

of the Regent's Park Road district. *Basil* was much criticised by a section of the press for its alleged impropriety in alluding to certain facts and aspects of life—a hypocritical charge which the author effectually disposed of in the introduction to the 1862 edition of the book. However, Millais thought *Basil* 'very clever,' and Dickens wrote to the author at the outset, highly praising the story for its 'admirable writing and many clear evidences of a very delicate discrimination of character.' While Swinburne in his essay on Wilkie Collins says of *Basil*: 'Violent and unlovely and unlikely as it is, this early story had in it something more than promise—the evidence of original and noticeable power to constrain and retain attention of a more serious and perhaps a more reasonable kind than can be evoked by many later and more ambitious and pretentious appeals.'

Wilkie Collins was now definitely embarked on a literary career, and says in February, 1853, that 'I am overhead and ears in work,' and a few months later that 'I blush to own that I shall be at work on Sunday ! ! ! ' His new tale, *Hide and Seek*, 1854, only marked time, for it was mainly concerned with painters and painting, showing considerable acquaintance with contemporary Art and no small measure of critical ability. Some readers thought Collins still under the Dickensian influence, but as Dickens himself wrote to his sister-in-law, Georgina Hogarth :

'Neither you nor Catherine [his wife] did justice to Collins's book. I think it far away the cleverest Novel I have ever seen written by a new hand. It is much beyond Mrs. Gaskell, and is in some respects masterly. . . . Nor do I recognize much imitation of myself.'

Hide and Seek was dedicated to Dickens ' as a token of admiration and affection.'

In October, 1853, Wilkie Collins accompanied Dickens and Egg on that expedition of two months through Switzerland and Italy of which Forster provides such an amusing account. Collins thus visited again the places he had been so well acquainted with as a boy fifteen years earlier. On the voyage from Genoa to Naples the steamer was terribly overcrowded. On the first night the three friends had to sleep on deck—on the bare planks—and were drenched by a tropical rain storm. The next evening a state-room was found for Dickens, who says :

' The store-room down by the hold was opened for Collins and Egg ; and they slept with the moist sugar, the cheese in cut, the spices, the cruets, the apples and pears, in a perfect chandler's shop—in company with what a friend of ours would call a hold gent ; a cat ; and the steward, who dozed in an arm-chair, and all-night-long fell head foremost, once every five minutes, on Egg, who slept on the counter or dresser.'

Augustus Egg, earlier on the trip, had nearly been killed by a falling block of stone when with Dickens and Collins on the Mer de Glace in the Swiss Alps.

More theatricals followed in 1855, when on June 19th was presented at Dickens's home, Tavistock House, in ' The Smallest Theatre in the World,' *The Lighthouse*, a Domestic Melo-Drama in two acts by Wilkie Collins. The author and Dickens, billed as ' Mr. Crummles,' played the two lighthouse keepers ; and both appeared in their original parts in the after-piece, *Mr. Nightingale's Diary*. The two friends paid several visits to France together during these years. Writing on March 18th, 1856, from 63 Avenue Champs Elysées, Paris, Collins relates to E. M. Ward :

' I have got a most perfect little bachelor Apartment ; a " Pavilion " like a house in a Pantomime ; and the most willing, pleasant concierge and wife, in the world, to wait on me. Here my luck has stopped. I caught a chill a fortnight ago, which, while it lasted, seriously interfered with Paris pleasures, and put me back sadly in some work I had to finish. Some things, how-ever, I have seen of the interesting sort—two charming little plays at the Gymnase acted to perfection, and a very fine portrait of Dickens by Ary Scheffer. I went expecting to be disappointed

—and came away amazed.[1]   This picture is to be exhibited in the rooms of the corrupt Institution to which you belong.

' In the way of imposters, add to *our* former experiences here the name of *Madame Ristori*,[2] the Italian actress about whom they have been going mad in Paris.   Perfect conventionality of the most hopelessly stage kind—walk, attitudes, expression, elocution, all nothing but commonplace in a violent state of exaggeration.   We saw her in a play of Alfieri's exhibiting the unnatural beastiality of a daughter in love with her own father in long classical speeches.   Virtuous females of all nations, sitting in balloons of crinoline petticoat, observed the progress of this pleasant and modest story with perfect composure.

' I am to be taken to-day to see Mr. Leighton's [3] new triumph in Art—Orpheus playing the fiddle.   Adelaide Kemble is said to have been the model, more or less, for every man, woman, and child in the composition.   Surely an amusing " canvas " must be the result of this.'

Also during these years Dickens, of course, gladly welcomed in his periodical, *Household Words*, contributions by Wilkie Collins, such as *Sister Rose* and *The Yellow Mask* in 1855,[4] which were included the

[1] Dickens wrote on this matter : ' Scheffer finished yesterday ; and Collins, who has a good eye for pictures, says there is no man living who could do the painting about the eyes.   As a work of art I see in it spirit combined with perfect ease, and yet I don't see myself.'   Dickens was staying at 49 Champs Elysées.

[2] Adelaide Ristori was born in 1821.   In Paris, at the time Collins saw her, she was succeeding Rachel as the greatest actress of the time, and was thought to excel as Medea, Lady Macbeth, and Adrienne Lecouvreur.   Dickens agreed with Collins's verdict against Ristori (see Forster's *Life*, Book Seventh, v.).

[3] Frederic Leighton was at this date twenty-six years old, and had won attention recently with his picture ' Cimabue's " Madonna " carried through the Streets of Florence,' exhibited at the Royal Academy in 1855.   Adelaide Kemble (Mrs. Sartoris) was a mature lady over forty.   She was the daughter of Charles Kemble by his Viennese wife, Marie Thérèse De Camp, and the niece of Mrs. Siddons.

[4] For *The Holly-tree Inn*, the Christmas Number of *Household Words*, 1855, Wilkie Collins wrote the powerful dream story entitled *The Ostler*.

In the early summer of 1857 Wilkie Collins was at Gad's Hill when

following year in the volume of collected short stories entitled *After Dark*. One of these tales, *A Terribly Strange Bed*, is admirable. The idea was given to the author by W. S. Herrick, the artist, and it was, I fancy, the first story of the kind, relating the process for murdering travellers in an inn by means of a bed tester, which, working by mechanism above, comes down and suffocates the sleeper. Probably Joseph Conrad obtained from Collins's details the idea for his own supreme tale of terror, *The Inn of the Two Witches*. Wilkie's story, *A Rogue's Life*, relating to illegal coining appeared in *Household Words* in 1856 (though it was not published in book form until 1879); and then, in the same periodical, Wilkie Collins took possession of his kingdom with *The Dead Secret*, which had serial publication from January to June, 1857; in the latter month it was issued in two volumes by Bradbury and Evans. This is the first of

Hans Andersen came on a visit to Dickens, and concerning this time Sir Henry Dickens has given me an amusing recollection of his own boyhood :

' A strange, gaunt, angular, and eccentric person was Andersen, who spent most of his time in cutting out beautiful and weird figures in paper of fairies, elves, and what not,—beautifully executed and strangely reminiscent of his wonderful stories. On one occasion when Wilkie was wearing a very large wide-awake hat, Andersen managed, quite surreptitiously, to crown this hat, while it was on Wilkie's head, with a chain of daisies. Seeing him thus decorated, we small boys wickedly encouraged Wilkie to come for a walk with us through the village. So we trotted him out, when Wilkie, being quite unconscious of the garland, appeared to be somewhat astonished at the pleasant, not to say laughing, reception which he met with on our way ; but it amused us young folk amazingly.

' I remember in my young days coming to the conclusion that a beard did not go well with snuff taking, because Wilkie's beard was generally more snuffy than was altogether pleasing to the eye.

' I am glad you are writing a memoir of Wilkie whose work I have always greatly admired. I hope the public read him still. If so, they must recognise the extraordinary power of *The Moonstone* and *Armadale*, even if all other books are eliminated. I have heard my father say that he regarded the description of the Woman in White's first appearance on the Hampstead Road as one of the most dramatic bits of descriptive fiction that he knew.'

Wilkie Collins's four great stories of mystery and sensation, though curiously enough four years more were to
elapse before the author reached universal success with
The Woman in White. As Dickens had perspicaciously
perceived, *The Dead Secret* is an excellently told tale of
engrossing interest, which keeps the reader's attention
throughout, even though he may perceive what the dénouement will be; and those who assert that Wilkie
Collins could not create living characters might with
profit study again Sarah Leeson and Uncle Joseph, with
his beloved musical-box which played Mozart's ' Batti,
Batti.' Collins related that two of the characters, Rosa-
mond and Uncle Joseph, ' had the good fortune to find
friends everywhere who took a hearty liking to them.
A more elaborately drawn personage in the story, Sarah
Leeson, was, I think, less generally understood. The
idea of tracing, in this character, the influence of a heavy
responsibility on a naturally timid woman, whose mind
was neither strong enough to bear it, nor bold enough to
drop it altogether, was a favourite idea with me at the
time, and is so much a favourite still, that I privately
give Sarah Leeson the place of honour in the little
portrait-gallery which my story contains.' The scenic
setting of *The Dead Secret* in a wild part of Cornwall was
well done, for the author described country he had seen
during a walking-tour in 1850. The same trip had provided materials for his book, *Rambles Beyond Railways, or
Notes in Cornwall Taken Afoot*, published in 1851, with
excellent illustrations by the friend, Henry C. Brandling,[1]

---

[1] Henry Brandling was a son of W. R. Brandling, of Low Gos-
forth, Northumberland, who had spent much money in support of
the invention of George Stephenson. Henry Brandling was a
fellow student of Charles Collins at the Academy School, and his
sister, Emma, married the 4th Lord Lilford, and was painted by
Watts at the height of her beauty. Her sons are the present Lord
Lilford and the Honourable Stephen Powys. Henry Brandling,
after his marriage about 1871, seems to have given up the pursuit of
Art and to have lost sight of his early friends of the Collins circle.
He died in 1897.

who accompanied him. Collins supplies an interesting account of the scenery of Cornwall and a lively picture of its primitive social conditions in those days when tourists were few. The friends, with their knapsacks and atrudge on foot, were taken for pedlars, tramps, or 'mappers' forerunning the threatened railway. One good old woman, on seeing them, moaned out, ' Ah ! poor fellows ! poor fellows ! Obliged to carry all your baggage on your own backs; very hard ! poor lads ! very hard indeed ! ' Nobody would believe that they were walking for pleasure, so Collins and Brandling ' soon gave up any idea of affording any information at all, and walked through the country comfortably as mappers, trodgers, tradesmen, guinea-pig mongers, and poor back-burdened vagabond lads, altogether, or one at a time, just as the peasantry pleased.' They were only just in time, too, for an inspection of Cornwall unspoiled by railway, for in the following year the iron horse penetrated there. The wild, rocky coast of Cornwall, between Land's End and Penzance, also furnished the scene for the tragic end of Mannion in *Basil*—in ' The Devil's Throat ' near Kynance Cove.

All through these years, since 1849, of mounting the steps of Fame, Wilkie Collins was living with his mother and brother at 17, Hanover Terrace, a pleasant house overlooking Regent's Park, and where many pleasant people were entertained. The two brothers were ever delightful hosts, and old Mrs. Collins was a great character who did not object to tobacco smoke in her drawing-room. Sir Leslie Ward says ' she was a quaint old lady who wore her kid boots carefully down on one side and then reversed them and wore them down on the other. She had a horror of Highlanders because they wore kilts, which she considered scandalous. . . .' And to Mrs. E. M. Ward, as a young artist, Mrs. Collins gave the opinion that she ought to devote all her energies to domestic matters, tend and cook for her husband, and make her children's clothes, and then there would be no

time for painting—strange advice from the mouth of the
sister and wife and mother of successful painters.   And
Millais would proclaim that he was in love with old Mrs.
Collins, and ask her to name the day, to which she would
reply with amusing repartee, for she was a woman of
humour, and the good-looking and talented young artist
was a privileged favourite with all.   Millais wrote in
1852 to Mr. Combe :

' You ask me to describe the dance of Mrs. Collins.   I truly
wish you had been there.   It was a delightful evening.
Charlie (Collins) never got beyond a very solemn quadrille,
though he is an excellent waltzer and polka dancer.   Poor
Mrs. Collins was totally dumb from a violent influenza she
unfortunately caught that very afternoon.   She received all her
guests in a whisper and a round face of welcome.   There were
many lions—amongst others the famous Dickens, who came
for about half an hour and officiated as principal carver at
supper.   Altogether there were about seventy people.'

Holman Hunt, too, says nothing could exceed the
jollity of small dinners with the Collins family : ' Edward
Ward and his pleasant wife would sometimes be of the
party. . . .   We were all hard-worked people enjoying
one another's society, and we talked as only such can.'
He proceeds to give Wilkie Collins's conversation on the
Art situation of that time, and concludes : ' Wilkie
Collins had knowledge of the interests of Art for more
than one past generation ; thus he spoke with authority
on the matter.'   So in addition to his rising literary fame,
Wilkie's views on painting were highly regarded by his
artist friends.

At this date also Percy FitzGerald met him at dinner
with Dickens, and relates in his *Memoirs of an Author* that
Collins was ' a rather brilliant young man, pleasant,
lively in talk, of much industry and enthusiasm in his
calling.   Dickens was very partial to him, and found
great enjoyment in his company.   They were constantly together, dining or foraging in the City, making
expeditions over the country. . . .   I was struck by the

cheery, exuberant tone of Collins's talk ; he seemed to *pose* as a conversationalist, and to take the lead in describing in his fluent, dramatic way how he was subject to a curious ghostly influence, having often the idea that someone was standing behind him, and that he was tempted to look round constantly,'—which reminds one of Leech's illustration for *The Haunted Man* of Dickens.

The year 1857 had commenced with more Dickensian theatricals at Tavistock House, when on Twelfth Night was produced ' An entirely new Romantic Drama, in Three Acts, by Mr. Wilkie Collins, called *The Frozen Deep.*' The scenery was painted by Clarkson Stanfield and Telbin, and John Forster spoke the Prologue. Thackeray waxed merry over the announcements of ' God Save the Queen,' and ' That carriages may be ordered at half-past eleven.' Dickens, Wilkie Collins, Mark Lemon, and Miss Hogarth, all acted in *The Frozen Deep* and in the after-piece of *Animal Magnetism.* Further performances took place in the country, and the proceeds were invested for an income that was paid to the unmarried daughter of Douglas Jerrold.[1]   *The Frozen Deep* was put on at the Olympic Theatre some nine years later, November 27th, 1866, when the professional cast included Henry Neville (in Dickens's original part), H. J. Montague (in Wilkie Collins's original part), Horace Wigan, and Lydia Foote.   E. L. Blanchard says the piece went slowly.   He had liked better the professional production of *The Lighthouse* at the Olympic Theatre on August 1st, 1857, when he reported, ' Delighted with it, most effectively got up.'   On this occasion, Dickens's part was played by the celebrated Robson.   One would have liked to have seen another powerful melodrama mentioned by Blanchard on October 13th, 1858 : ' To Olympic, see Wilkie Collins's extraordinary drama, *The Red Vial*; acting of Mrs. Stirling wonderfully fine.'

[1] There was also a special performance—not for the Jerrold Fund —at The Gallery of Illustration, 14 Lower Regent Street, on July 9th, for Queen Victoria, who particularly wished to see this play.

Robson played in his own inimitable style Hans Grimm, a half-wit. The piece was a failure, and Collins many years later, 1880, turned it into his novel, *Jezebel's Daughter*. The original manuscript of the play bears the note in his holograph that at its first representation at the Olympic Theatre on October 11th, 1858, it was ' damned. Mrs. Stirling and Addison both admirable. Poor little Robson did his best. The rest is silence.'

When *The Red Vial* was converted into *Jezebel's Daughter*, the name of the lunatic, Hans Grimm, was changed to Jack Straw. The story deals with madness, poisoning, and recovery from a death trance. The great scene in the Frankfort Deadhouse is immense, and in the character of the drunken watchman, Schwartz, Collins essayed a creation in the style of the sexton Alan in Harrison Ainsworth's *Rookwood*, who was much given to the chaunting of what Thackeray called Ainsworth's ' churchyard ballads of the sepulchral school of poetry.' So too Wilkie Collins's Watchman warbles :

> ' Any company's better than none I said :
> If I can't have the living, I'd like the dead.
> In one terrific moment more,
> The corpse-bell rang at each cell door,
> The moonlight shivered on the floor—
>   Poor me !
>
> The curtains gaped ; there stood a ghost,
> On every threshold, as white as frost,
> You called us, they shrieked, and we gathered soon ;
> Dance with your guests by the New Year's moon !
> I danced till I dropped in a deadly swoon—
>   Poor me ! . . .
>
> And, oh, when I lie in my coffin-bed,
> Heap thick the earth above my head !
> Or I shall come back, and dance once more,
> With frantic feet on the Deadhouse floor,
> And a ghost for a partner at ever door—
>   Poor me ! '

In September, 1857, Dickens and Wilkie Collins went

off on an eventful expedition to Cumberland (where Collins gathered up scenic impressions for his future use in *The Woman in White*), Lancashire, and Yorkshire. They climbed Carrock Fell, 2174 feet high, when in the words of Dickens, ' rain terrific, black mists, darkness of night.' He himself, a strong, expert walker, was ' confident,' the guide uneasy, and poor Wilkie ' a long way down in perspective, submissive.' Collins was always a delicate man, cursed with ill-health, and he was quite unfitted for a strenuous scramble of this kind. They got lost on the sombre fells and wandered about, the guide having altogether missed his way. Finally Dickens suggested they had better follow the course of a ' thundering, roaring watercourse . . . subject to all gymnastic hazards,' downwards. ' Leaps, splashes, and tumbles, for two hours. Collins lost. C. D. whoops. Cries for assistance behind. C. D. returns. Collins with horribly sprained ankle, lying in rivulet.' There was great trouble in getting the victim to the bottom of the mountain, by shoving, shouldering, and carrying in turn. Then he was propped against stones and his injured foot bound up in a flannel waistcoat. After much difficulty a cart was procured. Then Dickens carrying Collins ' melodramatically ' (for he had done the same when they were both acting in *The Frozen Deep*)—everywhere— ' into and out of carriages ; up and down stairs ; to bed ; every step. And so to Wigton, got doctor, and here we are ! A pretty business.' They moved on in time, and at Doncaster poor Collins had so far recovered as to be able, doubled-up, to walk with a thick stick ; in which condition, ' being exactly like the gouty admiral in a comedy I have given him that name.' Dickens was too boisterous and rudely healthy for his companion on foot, but in a literary sense their tour was eminently suitable and successful, for they collaborated and related their experiences and adventures in the series of papers entitled *The Lazy Tour of Two Idle Apprentices*, which appeared in *Household Words*, October, 1857. The ' King's Arms '

inn, Market Street, Lancaster, and the ' Angel ' Hotel,
Doncaster, inspired them both to write mysterious stories
of the first rank.   Dickens wrote the fine ghost story of
The Bride's Chamber, and Wilkie Collins that most
terrifying tale of The Double-bedded Room (which he
reprinted under the title of *Brother Morgan's Story of The
Dead Hand*, in the volume called *The Queen of Hearts*, 1859).
The two friends became even more nearly connected in
1860, when Wilkie's brother, Charles Collins, married
Kate, the younger daughter of Dickens.

By 1859 the pleasant united family life at 17 Hanover
Terrace, with its delightful hospitality, came to an end.[1]
Mrs. Collins and her younger son, Charles, moved to a
house in Clarence Terrace.   Wilkie, owing to ill-health,
was becoming reluctant to go much into society.   And
there were what his memoirist, Thomas Seccombe, in
The Dictionary of National Biography discreetly calls ' in-
timacies.'   Consequently after some temporary residence
at 124 Albany Street and 2A New Cavendish Street,
Wilkie Collins formed an establishment at 12 Harley
Street, where he was destined to write three of his
greatest novels.   *The Woman in White* commenced to
appear in Dickens's new periodical, *All the Year Round*,
on November 26th, 1859, where it immediately followed
the completion of *A Tale of Two Cities*, with this
Dickensian intimation in between :

' We purpose always reserving the first place in these pages
for a continuous original work of fiction. . . .   The second
story of our series we now beg to introduce to the attention of
our readers.   It will pass into the station hitherto occupied by
A Tale of Two Cities.   And it is our hope and aim, while we
work hard at every other department of our journal, to produce,
in this one, some sustained work of imagination that may
become a part of English Literature.'

The pious hope was soon realised in this tale of which
even the title was good, for as Dickens wrote to the

[1] A later occupier of 17 Hanover Terrace was the late Sir Edmund
Gosse, who lived here for many years.

author, ' I have not the slightest doubt that *The Woman in White* is the name of names, and the very title of very titles.' The intensely effective commencement of the story had a foundation in fact, as related in *The Life of John Everett Millais*, by his son :

' One night in the 'fifties Millais was returning home to 83 Gower Street from one of the many parties held under Mrs. Collins's hospitable roof in Hanover Terrace, and, in accordance with the usual practice of the two brothers, Wilkie and Charles, they accompanied him on his homeward walk through the dimly-lit, and in those days semi-rural, roads and lanes of North London. . . . It was a beautiful moonlight night in the summer time, and as the three friends walked along chatting gaily together, they were suddenly arrested by a piercing scream coming from the garden of a villa close at hand. It was evidently the cry of a woman in distress ; and while pausing to consider what they should do, the iron gate leading to the garden was dashed open, and from it came the figure of a young and very beautiful woman dressed in flowing white robes that shone in the moonlight. She seemed to float rather than to run in their direction, and, on coming up to the three young men, she paused for a moment in an attitude of supplication and terror. Then, suddenly seeming to recollect herself, she suddenly moved on and vanished in the shadows cast upon the road.

' " What a lovely woman ! " was all Millais could say. " I must see who she is, and what is the matter," said Wilkie Collins, as, without another word, he dashed off after her. His two companions waited in vain for his return, and next day, when they met again, he seemed indisposed to talk of his adventure. They gathered from him, however, that he had come up with the lovely fugitive and had heard from her own lips the history of her life and the cause of her sudden flight. She was a young lady of good birth and position, who had accidentally fallen into the hands of a man living in a villa in Regent's Park. There for many months he kept her prisoner under threats and mesmeric influence of so alarming a character that she dared not attempt to escape, until, in sheer desperation, she fled from the brute, who, with a poker in his hand, threatened to dash her brains out. Her subsequent history, interesting as it is, is not for these pages.' [1]

[1] Quoted by permission of Mr. John G. Millais from his book, *The Life and Letters of John Everett Millais*, published by Methuen and Co.

It is open to conjecture if this Woman in White so
gallantly rescued by Wilkie Collins was the same lady
who henceforth lived with him. I understand that
Dickens's daughter, Kate, who married Wilkie Collins's
brother, Charles, used to intimate that it was so. In
such case, the romantic origin of the ' intimacy '
might well have cozened the virtuous British Matrons
of the time to overlook the irregularity, in the same way
as a blind eye was turned to the immoral manner in
which George Eliot conducted her domestic life. But
they were not to be persuaded in the case of Collins, and
but few ' respectable ' females passed the threshold of the
houses in Harley Street and elsewhere that he, later, resided
in, though the famous author himself, *alone*, was gladly
welcomed to the dinner-tables of his censorious friends.

In his romance, Wilkie Collins placed the scene of the
meeting with The Woman in White at that portion of
the Finchley Road where it is bifurcated by West End
Lane and Frognal Lane :

' I had now arrived at that particular point of my walk where
four roads meet—the road to Hampstead, along which I had
returned ; the road to Finchley ; the road to West End ; and
the road back to London. I had mechanically turned in this
latter direction, and was strolling along the lonely high-road
. . . when, in one moment, every drop of blood in my body
was brought to a stop by the touch of a hand laid lightly and
suddenly on my shoulder from behind me. . . .   There, in the
middle of the broad, bright high-road—there, as if it had that
moment sprung out of the earth or dropped from the heaven
—stood the figure of a solitary Woman, dressed from head to
foot in white garments ; her face bent in grave inquiry on
mine, her hand pointing to the dark cloud over London. . . . '

What a story, and what a situation on that lonely road
and in the dead of night for its commencement ! I
wonder if the prosperous dwellers in the comfortable
flats and houses which now line and surround the spot
ever look out of their windows when it is full moonlight and recover that romantic conception which has
made reality of fiction.   The story describes the Finchley

Road as it was seventy years ago. There were no houses until the wayfarers arrived at Swiss Cottage, which was then still separated from London by a toll-bar gate—' We had reached the first houses, and were close on the new Wesleyan College . . . we came within view of the turnpike at the top of the Avenue Road,' the Avenue Road, where, at No. 20, Collins had lived as a youth. So he ever wound and wove in his own experiences with his fictional creations.

The Cumberland scenes are infinitely picturesque, and seldom has a dramatic episode been presented so powerfully as when Walter Hartright sees Laura, Lady Glyde, standing by the white tombstone beneath which he believed her to be buried.

There never was such a success as *The Woman in White* achieved, for as Dickens wrote, ' In character it is excellent, the story is very interesting, and the writing of it admirable.' [1] Thackeray is said to have sat up all night in order to read the exciting tale he could not put down. Swinburne delighted in Count Fosco and pronounced Marian Halcombe to be ' a glorious woman.' Edward FitzGerald, in discussing Fielding and Jane Austen thought ' *The Woman in White*, with her Count Fosco, far beyond all that ' ; and in 1867 he wrote that he had ' to my great sorrow finished *The Woman in White* for the third time, once every last three Winters. I wish Sir Percival Glyde's Death were a little less of the minor Theatre sort ; then I could swallow all the rest as a wonderful caricature, better than so many a sober Portrait. I really think of having a Herring-lugger I am building named *Marian Halcombe*, the brave Girl in the Story.' There were numerous publicity triumphs too, all through 1860, for every possible commodity was labelled ' Woman in White.' There were ' Woman in White ' cloaks and bonnets, ' Woman in White ' per-

[1] As a writer in *The Times* observed nearly thirty years later : ' *The Woman in White* is the first of English novels of plot and situation. Count Fosco is a creation almost of the first order.'

fumes and all manner of toilet requisites, 'Woman in White' Waltzes and Quadrilles. Wilkie Collins deserved his sudden fame, for he had written his book in a spirit of inspiration and tremendous enthusiasm. He wrote on January 7th, 1860, from 2A New Cavendish Street to E. M. Ward, who had been one of the first of his friends to congratulate him on the opening chapters in *All the Year Round*:

'I am honestly glad to hear you like the opening of *The Woman in White*, because I know that you have an eye for detecting what is really genuine and good in literary workmanship. I do hope and believe the story *will* be the best I have written yet. It is on a much larger and much more elaborate scale than anything I have done hitherto—and, as far as it has gone, it has certainly made itself felt pretty strongly not only in England, but in America as well. The effort of keeping it going week after week is (in the reporter's famous phrase) "more easily imagined than described." When I approach the glass in the morning to brush my hair, I am quite agreeably surprised to find that it has not turned grey *yet*.'

Then, as the story neared its serial completion and was about to be published, in three volumes, by Sampson Low, in September, 1860, the author gave a dinner in celebration of the event, following the pleasant custom established by Dickens on the completion of *Pickwick* some twenty-two years earlier. In inviting Ward to 12, Harley Street, and writing on the 3rd August, 1860, he says:

'My dear Ned. I have done! (except my *varnishing days*, in respect of proof sheets which publishers and translators are still bothering about). We dine here at ½ past 6, on Thursday the 9th to drink success to the book in England, Germany, America (United States), and Canada, in all which places it will be published this month. Will you come? No evening dress —everything in the rough. Hunt[1] and Egg[2] are coming, and

[1] W. Holman Hunt (1827-1910).

[2] Augustus Egg (1816-1863), R.A. Wilkie Collins was greatly grieved when Egg died. Hunt states he rocked himself to and fro, saying, 'And so I shall never any more shake that dear hand and look into that beloved face. Ah! Holman, all we can resolve is to be closer together as more precious in having had his affection.'

Walker ¹—and perhaps Gregory, and Lehmann ² and H.
Bullar.³ Cast respectability to the winds and write me a line
to say you will come.'

History does not record if the original ' intimacy '
of The Woman in White was present at this dinner :
probably not. Doubtless the food was good, for
Wilkie was a sybarite. Holman Hunt relates in his
Pre-Raphaelitism of Collins : ' No one could be more
jolly than he as the lord of the feast in his own house,
where the dinner was prepared by a chef, the wines
plentiful, and the cigars of choicest brand. The talk
became rollicking and the most sedate joined in the
hilarity ; laughter long and loud crossed from opposite
ends of the room and all went home brimful of
good stories.'

All through 1860 The Woman in White was selling in
vast quantities, and at the end of October ⁴ the author
wrote to his publisher, Edward Marston :

' If any fresh impression of *The Woman in White* is likely to be
wanted immediately, stop the press till I come back. The
critic in *The Times* is (between ourselves) right about the mistake in time. Shakespeare has made worse mistakes—that is
one comfort, and readers are not critics who test an emotional
book by the base rules of arithmetic, which is a second consolation. . . . They are going to dramatise the story at the Surrey
Theatre, and I am asked to go to law about *that*. I will
certainly go and *hiss* unless the manager makes a " previous
arrangement " with me.'

¹ Frederick Walker (1840-1875), at this period a young book-
illustrator and on the threshold of his career as a painter.

² Frederick Lehmann.

³ Henry Bullar, a barrister on the Western Circuit, and a member
of a family who were old friends of the Collinses. Doctor Joseph
Bullar was medical attendant to William Collins, R.A., and John
Bullar was his executor. Wilkie Collins dedicated his *My Miscellanies* to Henry Bullar in 1863.

⁴ The second edition of *The Woman in White* was published a month
after the first, that is in October, for the publisher's List dated
November 1st, 1860, announces ' *The Woman in White*, 3 volumes,
post 8vo., Second Edition, 31/6.'

I am not aware of the fate of this proposed unauthorised version of the story, but it was not until October 9th, 1871, that Wilkie Collins's own dramatisation of *The Woman in White* was produced, at the Olympic Theatre, with the following cast :

Anne Catherick and Laura Fairlie -	*Ada Dyas*
Marian Halcombe - - - -	*Mrs. Charles Viner*
Sir Percival Glyde - - - -	*John Billington*
Walter Hartright - - - -	*Wybert Reeve*
Professor Pesca - - - -	*F. Robson*
Count Fosco - - - -	*G. Vining*

It was for this production that Fred Walker executed his magnificent poster design of The Woman in White passing from a black doorway into the starry night. He made the original sketch on September 6th, 1871, at Charles Collins's house, 10, Thurloe Place—what he called ' a dashing attempt in black and white.' On the 14th Wilkie Collins came to see the picture at the artist's studio, 3, St. Petersburgh Place, when, Walker notes, ' Wilkie Collins has just been and expresses himself *delighted* with what I have done . . . it strikes me we shall make a good thing of it.' This was the first poster drawn by an eminent artist in England, and pictorial advertisements of the kind were then rare for the theatre. The original drawing was exhibited at the Dudley Gallery in 1872 and 1876, and it is now at the Tate Gallery, but stored away and not easy to see.

The Woman in White brought a great deal of money to Collins, and he was able to make even better terms for his next book, *No Name*. It appeared serially in *All the Year Round* from March, 1862, to January, 1863, when it was published in three volumes by Sampson Low, who paid £3000 for the copyright. *No Name* was not so good a story as its predecessor, but the publishers did not lose by their speculation and, indeed, made some profit. As Marston says,[1] ' It was a great risk forced

---

[1] *After Work*, by Edward Marston, 1907.

THE WOMAN IN WHITE
From the poster design by Fred Walker, 1871

upon us by very vigorous competition,' though Charles
Reade put the matter to him more bluntly :

' I take a much simpler view of your transactions with Mr.
Collins. *Woman in White* was a great book, *No Name* is not.
The independent public bought the former largely because it
was well worth buying. *No Name* you forced in even greater
numbers on the libraries, and the libraries forced it on their
slaves the genteel public. But the great public are not crushed
under machinery, and they had a judgment and a will of their
own.'

However, most of Wilkie Collins's admirers were delighted with *No Name* ; Dickens, as usual, said he had
read the tale ' with strong interest and great admiration ' ;
and the author in April, 1862, told E. M. Ward :

' I am really and truly delighted to find that the opening
chapters have taken so strong a hold on your interest and Mrs.
Ward's. It is " half the battle " to begin well, in cases where
periodical publication is concerned—and, I am glad to say,
that readers in general seem to be of your opinion. Results at
All the Year Round (as stated by the publishers) are already very
encouraging. I thought certain old memories of ours would
be roused by that chapter about the private theatricals. I read
The Good-natured Man and *The Rivals* again while I was writing
it, and saw you once more in " Croaker " as plainly as I see
this paper. I have been engaged in far more elaborate private
theatrical work since that time—but the real enjoyment was at
the Theatre Royal, Blandford Square.[1]
' Between work and weather I am feeling a little jaded, and
am going to try for a breath of sea air this month.'

He was not at all well this year, and often had to
cancel engagements. He says in June :

' The plain truth is (though I keep it concealed from the
doctor, in the hope of being able to do without him this time)
that my old enemy, whose name is *Liver*, has been attacking me
lately. I went to bed on Tuesday with a bad pain in my right
side, when I ought to have been enjoying myself at your party,
and as pills and diet don't seem to do alone, I am going into the
country to try change of air. . . . !'

[1] See *ante*, page 12.

And in December :

' I am far from well (though I don't tell my mother so) and I
am refusing most of the dinner invitations which reach me.
But your kind note is irresistible, and I shall be only too glad
to see another glimpse of those happy old times at your always
pleasant table. . . . '

' One line to say which day it shall be, and what hour, and
whether I walk in (as I did last time) in my morning costume,
to take up my knife and fork at your ordinary dinner, will
receive (as the tradesmen say) the strictest attention.   . . .
My best love at home.   I shall be almost afraid to look at my
goddaughter.   Is she A Young Lady yet ?   And has she got
taller than a certain middle-aged gentleman who answered for
her at the baptismal font ? '

When Wilkie Collins stated in April, 1862, that he was
going to try some sea air, it may be safely concluded that
it was the air of Aldeburgh, in Suffolk, he tried, for in
the August numbers that same year of *All the Year
Round* the setting of *No Name* was suddenly transferred
to Aldeburgh as ' The Fourth Scene ' ; and a very complete description of that quaint and ancient little marine
town is given, though by some mischance its name is
continuously misspelt as Aldborough.   Like Meredith
over forty years later, Collins was fascinated by the
melancholy qualities of the flat place, but a few feet from
the angry waves of the North Sea ; the sandy heaths and
pine-woods ; and the decayed quay of Slaughden, where
the river Alde turns to reach the marsh-lands and reedy
water-ways at the back of the town.   Here were por-
tentous atmospheric effects and low red sunsets glower-
ing through the mists as though specially designed for
the romantic needs of Wilkie Collins :

' It was a dull, airless evening.   Eastward was the grey
majesty of the sea, and hushed in breathless calm ; the horizon
line invisibly melting into the monotonous misty sky ; the idle
ships shadowy and still on the idle water.   Southward, the
high ridge of the sea dyke, and the grim massive circle of a
martello tower, reared high on its mound of grass, closed the
view darkly on all that lay beyond.   Westward, a lurid streak

of sunset glowed red in the dreary heaven—blackened the fringing trees on the far borders of the great inland marsh—and turned its little gleaming water-pools to pools of blood. Nearer to the eye, the sullen flow of the tidal river Alde ebbed noiselessly from the muddy banks ; and nearer still, lonely and unprosperous by the bleak water-side, lay the lost little port of Slaughden, with its forlorn wharfs and warehouses of decaying wood, and its few scattered coasting vessels deserted on the oozy river-shore. . . . Now and then, the cry of a sea-bird rose from the region of the marsh ; and, at intervals, from farm-houses far in the inland waste, the faint winding of horns to call the cattle home, travelled mournfully through the evening calm.'

So he attuned the mind for the mournful experiences of Magdalen, leading to the great scene of the story where she is only saved from suicide by a self-imposed hazard of Fate, where the scene is set on the Aldeburgh sea at dawn. There is also a scene at the neighbouring and historic Dunwich, a place which has been depicted in many fine pieces of literature, from the poems of Swin-burne to William De Morgan's powerful romance, *An Affair of Dishonour*. *No Name* contains some excellent characterisation in the figures of Captain Wragge, Mrs. Lecount, Magdalen Vanstone, and Miss Garth—one of the pre-eminent governesses of fiction, though she was to be surpassed by Collins's later creation, Miss Gwilt, who appeared in his next romance, *Armadale*, which in merit of sustained interest and marvellous, intricate plot and power of suggestion is second only to *The Woman in White*.

The author devoted great care and thought to his new story, and two years elapsed before the opening chapters appeared in *The Cornhill Magazine* in 1865. It was issued in two volumes, by Smith, Elder, with illustrations by George Housman Thomas, who originally engraved bank notes, who also illustrated Trollope's *The Last Chronicle of Barset*, 1867, and who died in the following year at the early age of forty-four. Few sensational novels have had such an effective *mise en scène* as that

portion of *Armadale* which passes on the haunted, derelict ship, wrecked in the Sound between the Isle of Man
and the Islet of the Calf. Fit location indeed for the
Dream which forms the subsequent motif of the tale
were those restless waters beating against the great rocky
headlands jutting into the sea—the aerie of thousands of
sea-birds uttering shrill and plaintive cries. For later
scenes of *Armadale* the author determined to return to
the reed-lands and water-ways of East Anglia which had
so fascinated him at Aldeburgh. This time he determined
upon Norfolk and the Broads. He wrote from The
Victoria Hotel, Great Yarmouth, on August 6th, 1864 :

'I am down here cruising at sea, and studying localities
(inland) for my new book. On Wednesday I go away for a
short visit to Yorkshire—but return here on the Saturday
following.'

And in the book itself he told his ' readers, who may
be curious on such points, that the Norfolk Broads are
here described after personal investigation of them.'
He was accompanied on these excursions by his brother
Charles, and the particular broad which is depicted in
Armadale as ' Hurle Mere ' is Horsey Mere. Admirable
is the description of the country as seen on the drive
from Thorpe Ambrose—which is possibly Aylsham if
not Thorpe, the suburb of Norwich—and then from the
boat :

' The reeds opened back on the right hand and the left, and
the boat glided suddenly into the wide circle of a pool. Round
the nearer half of the circle, the eternal reeds still fringed the
margin of the water. . . . The sun was sinking in the cloud-
less westward heaven. The waters of the Mere lay beneath,
tinged red by the dying light. The open country stretched
away, darkening drearily already on the right hand and the
left. And on the near margin of the pool, where all had been
solitude before, there now stood, fronting the sunset, the figure
of a woman. . . . '

So, again, was the sombre scenery all vocal with the
premonition of Fate and doom, for the figure was that

of the woman who was to plot murder and herself meet
with death in strange guise. O rare Wilkie Collins ! !

Armadale was dedicated to John Forster partly ' in
affectionate remembrance of a friendship which is associated with some of the happiest years of my life,' which
was a kindly gesture, for Forster never liked Collins ;
that is to say he was resentful and extremely jealous of
the affection and jolly friendship entertained by Dickens
for Wilkie. Collins was the gentlest and most kind-
hearted of men, without a spark of jealousy, but he did
permit himself to deliver the *mot* in after years on
Forster's *Life of Dickens* (wherein his great intimacy and
congenial friendship with Dickens was dismissed with a
few perfunctory words and without any quotation from
Dickens's letters to Collins) that it was ' *The Life of John
Forster*, with occasional anecdotes of Charles Dickens.'

In all the books of Collins can be found adaptations of
recent events and of people who had figured in the
public press and eye. Thus, in *Armadale*, Mrs. Older-
shaw, the proprietress of the Ladies' Toilette Repository
in Diana Street, Pimlico, was suggested by the case of
the notorious Madame Rachel, who at her Beauty
Parlour, 47A, New Bond Street, professed to make
' Beautiful for ever ' foolish women who were prepared
to pay Madame's exorbitant prices for baths, perfumes,
and unguents, and incidentally to run the risk of being
blackmailed. Madame Rachel had recently been in the
Law Courts with the case of Mrs. Carnegie, and at the
time Wilkie utilised her she was at the height of her
prosperity with her box at the Opera and her advertisements that she was ' Purveyor to the Queen.' But she
came to grief a few years later in the famous case of Mrs.
Borradaile and Lord Ranelagh, and in 1868 was sentenced
to five years' penal servitude. Again, in *The Moonstone*,
Collins made use of certain aspects of the Road Murder
of June, 1861, when Constance Kent brutally killed her
little brother. She did not confess until 1865, and important evidence at her trial concerned a blood-stained

shift and a washing-book. So, in *The Moonstone*, the detectives were interested in a washing-book and a paint stain on the dress or nightdress of one of the witnesses, while the strained relations existing between Superintendent Foley and Inspector Whicher in the Road Case were undoubtedly reflected in the attitudes to each other of Superintendent Seegrave and Sergeant Cuff. The famous Whicher, who all along was convinced of the guilt of Constance Kent, retired from the Force in 1863, but he returned to active service in order to assist the Tichborne family in their tremendous case. It is of interest, therefore, to study his methods and personality as adapted by Wilkie Collins to the character of Sergeant Cuff, who was a great favourite with Swinburne. The admiration of the poet for *The Moonstone* ' was considerable. " A wonderful story ! " he said, and commented on the extraordinary skill with which the various narratives are taken up by different persons. He went on to talk about the rose-loving Inspector Cuff as if he had been a personal friend, comparing him with another favourite character of his—Inspector Bucket. Each, he said, was excellent in his way, and yet Collins's character owed nothing at all to Dickens's vivid creation.' [1] In *The Moonstone* also, Godfrey Ablewhite is inveigled to a house where he is attacked, and the mysterious house is in Northumberland Street, Strand, which had been the scene of the terrible affray in 1861, when Major Murray was induced to go to some chambers there and was murderously assaulted by a man named Roberts, who was however killed by the Major in self-defence.

In general estimation *The Moonstone* is placed first in merit in the list of its author's writings, though personally I rank it third, after *The Woman in White* and *Armadale*, but at the same time I lay stress on the admirable skill of this greatest of ' detective ' stories. Collins was at his best of his sombre descriptive power in the scenes at the Shivering (quick) Sand on the coast of Yorkshire,

[1] Mr. A Compton-Rickett in *The Bookman*, June, 1912.

a locality he had examined for his purpose in August, 1864, when he went there from Great Yarmouth :

'As I got near the shore the clouds gathered black, and the rain came down, drifting in great white sheets of water before the wind. I heard the thunder of the sea on the sand-bank at the mouth of the bay. A little further on, I passed the boy crouching for shelter under the lee of the sand-hills. Then I saw the raging sea, and the rollers tumbling in on the sand-bank, and the driven rain sweeping over the waters, like a flying garment, and the yellow wilderness of the beach with one solitary black figure standing on it—the figure of Sergeant Cuff.'

That is a pictorial passage which might have found a place in the great description of the storm at sea in *David Copperfield*. Most excellent too is the character drawing in this story—old Gabriel Betteredge, whose philosophy and touch-stone of life were all based on *Robinson Crusoe* ; and Miss Clack, 'the Evangelical Hag' as Swinburne called her, she is one of the author's surest and most amusing creations, an admirable burlesque of the pious, tract-distributing people who typified the second Puritan reaction, in this case from the racket and riot of the Regency period in which they were born and reared, and who finally found their full expression in the Mildmay Movement and in the prognostications of the prophet Baxter. 'Oh, be morally tidy ! Let your faith be as your stockings . . . both ever spotless,' said Miss Clack, as a presiding genius of The Servants'-Sunday-Sweetheart-Supervision-Society. Miss Clack was certainly a near relation of Stiggins and the Chadbands, and again to quote Swinburne :

'Though Dickens was not a Shakespeare, and though Collins was not a Dickens, it is permissible to anticipate that their names and their works will be familiar to generations unacquainted with the existence and unaware of the eclipse of their most shining, most scornful, and most superior critics.'

Although *The Moonstone* is notable for its humour, the story was written for *All the Year Round* during 1868, a period when the author was suffering much both in mind and body, for in his own words, in a later Preface to the book :

‘ While this work was still in course of periodical publication . . . and when not more than one-third of it was completed, the bitterest affliction of my life and the severest illness from which I have ever suffered, fell on me together. At the time when my mother lay dying in her little cottage in the country, I was struck prostrate, in London ; crippled in every limb by the torture of rheumatic gout. Under the weight of this double calamity, I had my duty to the public still to bear in mind. . . . I held to the story—for my own sake, as well as for theirs. In the intervals of grief, in the occasional intervals of pain, I dictated from my bed that portion of *The Moonstone* which has since proved most successful in amusing the public—“ The Narrative of Miss Clack.” Of the physical sacrifice which the effort cost me I shall say nothing. I only look back now at the blessed relief which my occupation (forced as it was) brought to my mind. The Art which had been always the pride and the pleasure of my life, became now more than ever “ its own exceeding great reward.” I doubt if I should have lived to write another book, if the responsibility of the weekly publication of this story had not forced me to rally my sinking energies of body and mind—to dry my useless tears and to conquer my merciless pains.’

Wilkie Collins was thus again under the influence of Dickens in sharing his troubles with the public. But his grief at the loss of the mother who, from his infancy to his mature age, had been a forceful factor of his life was profound and touching. *The Moonstone* was inscribed, ‘ In Memoriam Matris.’ During the last years of her life Mrs. Collins lived at Bentham Hill Cottage, Southborough, near Tunbridge Wells. She became seriously ill in January, 1868, when Charles Collins wrote to E. M. Ward :

‘ My mother is suffering—among many other sufferings— from nervous excitability of a most painful kind, and the Doctor has said that seeing even old and valued friends is a thing not to be thought of. She has an excellent nurse, who attends to her comfort in every way, and even Wilkie and I only see her at occasional intervals and for a short time. Poor soul, she is staunch to the last, and when she is herself is as unselfish, and as thoughtful about us and our comforts, as ever. It is enviable to have such a life, as hers has been, to look back upon.'

And Wilkie himself wrote a few days later, January 21st :

' You will be grieved, I know, at the miserable news which I have to tell you. My dear old mother is dying. She is perfectly conscious, perfectly clear in her mind. But the internal neuralgia, from which she has suffered so long, has broken her down—and, at her great age, there is now no hope. Charley is with me here. All that *can* be done to soothe her last moments *is* done. The end may be deferred for a few days yet—but it is now only a question of time. I can write no more.'

There is something strangely moving in this last glimpse of these two distinguished and middle-aged men grieving by the death-bed of the old mother with whom all their earlier memories were intwined—the happy childhood days on Hampstead Heath, the momentous travels in Italy in boyhood, the exciting years in Blandford Square when both the sons were achieving success, and the jolly parties there and in Hanover Terrace when the complete battle was won.

When Wilkie Collins, in sorrow and pain, imagined in 1868 he might not live to write another book after *The Moonstone*, he little thought that he was to survive to write some fifteen more novels and many shorter stories. But it is a fact that *The Moonstone* was his last great book. With it he crested the hill, and then descended on the other side into the valley. He had left behind the high realms of sensation and mystery, and in the future was to be concerned more with the novel of propaganda which aimed at redressing some wrong or exposing some social or legal injustice, which was his last reaction to the influence of Dickens. But he was not equipped with the universality of Dickens or his sudden turns into the byways of broad humour which enabled him to conduct a crusade without boring his readers. Collins took his evangelisation much more seriously, with the result that his propaganda novels show but little of the sense of fun and satire which lit up *The Moonstone* and *Poor Miss Finch*. At the same time, the early and great stories were novels with a purpose, although most of their armies of readers were unaware of the fact. A rude guest at the dinner-table of W. P. Frith once said to Wilkie Collins, ' Your books are read in every back-kitchen.' The author was entirely unruffled by the remark, for if he knew it was true, he knew also that his books were read in every drawing-room and library of the kingdom.[1] But probably few, either below-stairs or up-stairs, perceived that Wilkie was a novelist who sought to convey science and pathology skilfully mixed with the draught of romantic fiction, even though he had indicated in the preface to *Armadale* that the story had overstepped, in more than one direction, the narrow limits to which some readers would like to restrict the range and development of modern fiction. In *The Woman in White* he had presented a study of insanity and morbid criminal pathology. In *The Moonstone* he presented the criminal effects of laudanum. While in *Armadale* he presented the terrifying influences of heredity and the psychology of crime and its reaction to love. The author's love of chemistry also comes into this book, and he prided himself upon the professional accuracy with which he described the episode of the Purple Flask and the strange mechanism whereby Miss Gwilt came by the death she had planned

---

[1] William Tinsley relates : ' During the run of *The Moonstone* as a serial there were scenes in Wellington Street that doubtless did the author's and publisher's hearts good. And especially when the serial was nearing its ending, on publishing days, there would be quite a crowd of anxious readers waiting for the new number, and I know of several bets that were made as to where the moonstone would be found at last. Even the porters and boys were interested in the story, and read the new number in sly corners, and often with their packs on their backs, but *The Woman in White* was, I think, rather over the heads of these boys and men.'

for Allan Armadale. Wilkie Collins was always interested in the subject of gases; I have a letter of his
asking for particulars of a portable form of gas lighting
which had surprised the Londoners of 1853. In a later
book, *Poor Miss Finch* (1872), he, in addition to relating
the after effects on the skin of nitrate of silver as a
specific for epilepsy, adumbrated a theory which in our
time has received much scientific attention, namely the
power of unconscious memory and early suggestion,
arising from some shock or fright in infancy, to cause
mental trouble in adult years. Despite these rather for-
bidding subjects for a novel, *Poor Miss Finch* is a most
delightful story set in the South Down country near
Lewes, the scenic aspect being most excellently conveyed.
The character drawing shows Collins at his best, from
the diminutive but progenitive 'Reverend Finch,' with
his booming bass voice, to the altogether amusing
German oculist, Herr Grosse. 'How goot of Gott,'
he remarked, 'when he invented the worlds to invent
eatings and drinkings too. Ah!' sighed Herr Grosse,
gently laying his outspread fingers on the pit of his
stomach, 'what immense happiness there is in THIS!'
And again: 'For me, I go to smoke my tobaccos in the
garden. . . . When Gott made the womens, he was
sorry afterwards for the poor mens—and he made
tobaccos to comfort them.'

If Herr Grosse had been created—just as he is—by
Dickens, he would have been one of the celebrated
figures of fiction and his sayings quoted as Household
Words, like those of the Wellers and all the rest of the
Boz philosophers. As it was, the original readers of *Poor
Miss Finch* took Herr Grosse as a very real person, and
Collins received letters from several people suffering from
eye trouble, who requested the address of this wonderful
oculist with the view of consulting him. But the author
had to point out that Grosse was not drawn from any
actual prototype. 'Like the other Persons of the
Drama,' he said, 'in this book and in the books which

have preceded it, he is drawn from my general observation of humanity. I have always considered it to be a
mistake in Art to limit the delineation of character in
fiction to a literary portrait taken from any one sitter.'

About 1865 Wilkie Collins left Harley Street and lived
for a time at 9 Melcombe Place, Dorset Square, before
moving into 90 Gloucester Place, when he told Ward,
' Try and remember Portman Square in connection with
my Gloucester Place. Say to yourself, " I once went to
Paris with Wilkie ; he took a PORTMANteau ; the first
two syllables spell *Portman* ; Wilkie lives near PORTMAN
Square." ' In Gloucester Place Collins remained for many
years. He finished *The Moonstone* there. In 1867 for the
Christmas Number—the last there was—of *All the Year
Round*, Wilkie Collins collaborated with Dickens in
writing *No Thoroughfare*, a rather too sentimental piece
which Collins also adapted as a play, produced at the
Adelphi in December of the same year, with Fechter as
Obenreizer, and Benjamin Webster, Henry Neville,
Carlotta Leclercq, and Mrs. Alfred Mellon, also in the
cast. E. L. Blanchard was much pleased with the play,
but Shirley Brooks ' went home howling at myself for
sitting out such unmitigated wrott.' Wilkie Collins had
a much more brilliant theatrical success in the dramatic
version of his novel, *Man and Wife* (1870), a story dealing
with the curious marriage laws of the kingdom. It was
produced on February 22nd, 1873, at the old Prince of
Wales's Theatre, near Tottenham Court Road, and was
the dramatic event of the season. The Bancrofts, John
Hare, Coghlan, and Lydia Foote, all performed in the
piece ; and it was the first new play this management put
on after the famous series of comedies by Tom Robertson.
Seats for the first night were at a premium ; speculators
obtained five guineas for a stall and two guineas for a
place in other parts of the house. When the eventful
evening arrived, an atmosphere of intense excitement
pervaded the theatre, which was filled with representatives of every art and calling, in addition to distinguished

members of Society and all the celebrities of the time. 'Literary and artistic London was present in unusual force, and an audience more representative of the intellect of the time has seldom been gathered within the walls of a theatre.'[1] Bancroft says that Wilkie Collins remained almost throughout the evening in the actor's dressing-room in a state of nervous terror painful to see, but that his sufferings were relieved now and then by loud bursts of applause from the front of the house. 'Only for one brief moment did he see the stage that night, until he was summoned by the enthusiastic audience to receive their plaudits at the end of the play. Ever modest, ever generous, he largely attributed his success to the acting, and was loud in his admiration.' While Collins himself relates :

'It was certainly an extraordinary success. The pit got on its legs and cheered with all its might the moment I showed myself in front of the curtain. I counted that I had only thirty friends in the house to match against a picked band of the " lower orders " of literature and the drama assembled at the back of the dress circle to hiss and laugh at the first chance. The services of my friends were not required. The public never gave the " opposition " a chance all through the evening. The acting, I hear all round, was superb ; the Bancrofts, Lydia Foote, Hare, Coghlan, surpassed themselves ; not a mistake made by anybody.'

Man and Wife was played one hundred and thirty-six times ; it was a great favourite with the Prince and Princess of Wales, who came to see the piece thrice, bringing on one occasion the future Emperor and Empress of Russia. In the provincial tour of this play, the principal parts were performed by Charles Wyndham and Ada Dyas. *Man and Wife* was revived, at the Haymarket Theatre in March, 1887, when much interest was aroused by Mrs. Brown-Potter as Annie ; as Geoffrey ' E. S. Willard was almost too powerful ' ; while Charles Collette and H. Kemble were most excellent.

[1] *The Bancrofts : Recollections of Sixty Years.*

Although Swinburne wrote of Collins's new phase as a propaganda novelist,

> ' What brought good Wilkie's genius nigh perdition ?
> Some demon whispered, " Wilkie ! have a mission ! " '

the author had no reason to complain of the success of *Man and Wife* and his subsequent ' missionary ' novels, for his old public was faithful to him and read whatever he wrote. *Man and Wife*, in addition to its main theme, voiced Wilkie's protest against the growing cult of athleticism, which he thought was brutalising the young men of England. The story was ' Affectionately dedicated to Mr. and Mrs. Frederick Lehmann,' at whose Highgate house a good deal of it was written. Their son, R. C. Lehmann, has preserved an impression of Collins at this period in his *Memories of Half a Century* :

> ' I can see him now as I used to see him in those early, unforgotten days ; a neat figure of a cheerful plumpness, very small feet and hands, a full brown beard, a high and rounded forehead, a small nose not naturally intended to support a pair of large spectacles, behind which his eyes shone with humour and friendship ; not by any means the sort of man imagination would have pictured as the creator of Count Fosco and the inventor of the terrors of *Armadale* and the absorbing mystery of *The Moonstone*.'

The same characteristics were noted, though in a less kindly manner by Julian Hawthorne,[1] who saw Collins about 1870 :

> ' I found him sitting in his plethoric, disorderly writing-room : there are two kinds of bachelors, the raspingly tidy sort, and the hopelessly ramshackle ; Wilkie was of the latter. Though the England of his prime had been a cricketing, athletic, outdoor England, Wilkie had ever slumped at his desk and breathed only indoor air. He was soft, plump, and pale,

[1] In *Shapes that Pass* (1928). Neither of these descriptions of Collins mentions his habitual attitude in his study. He would sit clasping his knees with both hands, while rocking himself backwards and forwards, gazing through his spectacles at his visitor solemnly or humorously as the conversation tended.

suffered from various ailments, his liver was wrong, his heart weak, his lungs faint, his stomach incompetent, he ate too much and the wrong things. He had a big head, a dingy complexion, was somewhat bald, and his full beard was of a light brown colour. His air was of mild discomfort and fractiousness ; he had a queer way of holding his hand, which was small, plump, and unclean, hanging up by the wrist, like a rabbit on its hind legs. He had strong opinions and prejudices, but his nature was obviously kind and lovable, and a humorous vein would occasionally be manifest.'

It is true that Collins was now suffering from chronic ill-health, and to deaden his discomfort and pains took an amazing quantity of opium daily, as much, in fact, as would have been the medical prescription for twelve persons to use. Sir Squire Bancroft tells a story in proof of this fact, related by Frederick Lehmann in connection with a visit he and Collins once paid to Coire, and in further confirmation Bancroft states that at a dinner-party at his own house, when Wilkie Collins was present, Mr. Critchett, one of the guests, put this question, with Collins's consent, before Sir William Fergusson, the eminent surgeon : ' The novelist had confided to him the quantity, which he named, of laudanum which he swallowed every night on going to bed, and which Critchett had told him was more than sufficient to prevent any ordinary person from ever awaking. He now asked Sir William if that was not well within the truth. Fergusson replied that the dose of opium to which Wilkie Collins had long accustomed himself was enough to kill every man seated at the table.'

1873 was a notable year in the theatre for Wilkie Collins, for while *Man and Wife* was in the midst of its successful run at the Prince of Wales's, a dramatic version of his new novel, *The New Magdalen*, was produced at the Olympic on May 19th, two days after the book was published. The story had been running serially through *Temple Bar*, and it was a favourite tale of Matthew Arnold's, though he as a rule was not addicted to the reading of sensational fiction. The play also attracted much attention, and it was revived in January, 1884, at the Novelty Theatre with great success, Ada Cavendish then playing the part of Mercy Merrick and Fred Kerr that of Ignatius. In this story the author attacked the problem of the fallen woman, a theme he returned to in *The Fallen Leaves* (1879), one of the least successful of his works.[1] Indeed, the scenes where the hero rescues the young prostitute from her haunts and takes her back to his rooms *en preux chevalier*—his name is Mr. Goldenheart!—are pitched altogether in the wrong key, in the very worst style of super Dickensian sentiment. Yet impossible as the main theme is, Collins's old merits flash out at times. The description of the rough street market is well done, and the death of Mrs. Farnaby, from strychnine, horrifying. Old Toff, the French servant, is his typical creation. While the account of the Community of Primitive Christian Socialists at Tadmor, Illinois, has some interest, as it is probably based on the Community of the Brotherhood of the New Life at Brocton (Salem-on-Erie), where Laurence Oliphant spent some years and much of his money. Wilkie Collins may have visited Brocton when in America, on his Reading Tour, in 1873-1874. Another echo of his time in America is his story *The Dead Alive*, which appeared in *The New York Fireside Companion*, 1873, based

---

[1] Wilkie Collins dramatised versions of some of his other stories in addition to those I have already mentioned. Thus *No Name* in 1863 (partly the work of W. B. Bernard) and 1870; *Armadale* in 1866, and *Miss Gwilt* in 1875; *Black and White*, A Love Story in Three Acts, produced at the Adelphi in March, 1869, with Fechter as de Layrack; *The Dream Woman* in 1873; *The Moonstone* in 1877; and *Rank and Riches*, produced at the Adelphi in June, 1883. In the last-named play George Alexander had the part of Cecil and Mrs. Billington that of Lady Sherlock. G. W. Anson was the Mr. Dominic, and when there were some hisses he ' sought to play the pedagogue to the audience . . . and exceeded its patience ' (H. G. Hibbert).

In 1865, overcoming for once his constitutional shyness, Wilkie Collins presided at the General Theatrical Fund Dinner—' good chairman and excellent speech,' Blanchard reports.

on the trial which had taken place that year of Jesse and Stephen Boorne for the murder of Russell Colvin at Manchester, Vermont.

Percy FitzGerald says that Wilkie Collins was not at his best as a reader of his own work—he was ' without emphasis or dramatic effect. He read in a very low tone, but was apparently quite satisfied with himself and the performance.'

I must not stay to comment on the various stories which were published in *Miss or Mrs?* (1873) and *The Frozen Deep* (1874), or on the longer tales of *The Law and the Lady* (1875), wherein the author vented another legal injustice protest, and *The Two Destinies* (1876), but pass on to *The Haunted Hotel*, which appeared in *Belgravia*, with illustrations by A. Hopkins, in 1879 before publication at the close of the same year in book form together with *My Lady's Money*. The latter story was also issued by Tauchnitz in 1879 with *The Ghost's Touch*, one of the rarest items of Collinsian bibliography, for it seems to have had no other publication, at any rate in England. For once I am not in agreement with Swinburne when he terms *The Haunted Hotel* a ' hideous fiction.' It is a macabre story of the supernatural, and in its own genre very well done.

The decade of the seventies was a sad one for Wilkie Collins. Age was creeping upon him and his chronic physical suffering made him older than his actual years. And the old ties were breaking fast. Dickens died in 1870, Charles Collins in 1873, and his oldest friend, E. M. Ward in 1879. To the son, Leslie Ward, of the last named he wrote on January 20th, 1879 :

' No ordinary engagement would prevent me from paying the last tribute of affection to my dear lost friend. Illness alone makes it impossible for me to join those who will follow him to the grave to-morrow. I am suffering from rheumatism —and in the present state of the weather the doctor's advice obliges me to give up the hope of being with you.

' I first knew your father when I was a boy—forty years

since—and it is no figure of speech, it is only the sad truth, to say that I do indeed share in your grief, and feel the irreparable loss that you have suffered as, in some degree at least, my loss too.   I do not venture to intrude so soon on your mother's sorrow, after the dreadful calamity that has fallen on your household.   I only ask you to assure her of my heartfelt sympathy, when it is possible for her to think of old friends.'

In 1881 appeared one of the best of Collins's later stories, *The Black Robe*, which, although it was a propaganda work aiming to expose the machinations of the Jesuits, displays much of the author's original descriptive power.   The early scene of the duel in the fog on the sands of Boulogne is vivid, and Father Benwell, the machiavellian and materially-minded Jesuit, is an excellent character sketch in Collins's gallery of portraits. But for serious purposes Wilkie Collins was a little late in his campaign against Roman aggression.   If he had written *The Black Robe* thirty years earlier in the days of Manning and Pusey agitations he would have achieved a tremendous success, for novels on this subject were then greatly in demand by publishers.   Frank Smedley most amusingly satirised this point in *Lewis Arundel* (1852), where Mr. Nonpareil, a publisher, makes £600 out of a novel called *Ambrosius, or the Curate Confessed.*   Then he says :

' Shortly after that, the Rev. Clerestory Lectern, one of the very tip-top ones, went to Rome, and took his three curates, a serious butler, and the family apothecary with him.   This made a great sensation, convulsed the public mind fearfully, and brought on a general attack of the ultra-protestant epidemic. Accordingly, I sent for the author of *Ambrosius*, offered him terms he was only too glad to jump at, shut him up in the back shop, with half a ream of foolscap and a bottle of sherry, and in little more than a week we printed off 5000 copies of *Loyoliana, or the Jesuit in the Chimney-corner.*   The book sold like wild-fire. A second edition was called for and went off in no time. . . . '

In his next novel, *Heart and Science*, 1883, Wilkie Collins attempted another propaganda campaign, in a nobler cause—that of revolting public opinion against

the abominations of vivisection. It is to be feared he
did not accomplish much, and though he did not take
his readers beyond the threshold of the laboratory, the
sounds and sights he pictured even there were not con-
ducive to the success of a novel. Nevertheless his plea
for helpless and suffering animals was a fine gesture.[1]
He was devoted to dogs, and one of his pets appears in
My Lady's Money, ' Tommie,' a Scotch terrier, whose
appetite was truly wonderful—' nothing comes amiss to
him, from pâté de fois gras to potatoes.'

Collins's next book was *I Say No*, published in 1884,
followed by *The Evil Genius* in 1886, the latter story,
dedicated to Holman Hunt, being interesting with the
exception of the improbable dénouement of two divorced
persons remarrying. This same year, too, he wrote
The Guilty River for *Arrowsmith's Christmas Annual*,
and despite his sixty-two years was working as hard as
in his prime, for as he told Mrs. Lehmann :

' You know what a fool I am—or shall I put it mildly and say
how " indiscreet " ? For the last week while I was finishing
the story, I worked for twelve hours a day, and galloped along
without feeling it, like the old post-horses, while I was hot.

[1] In his Preface, Collins stated to his readers : ' It encourages me
to think that we have many sympathies in common ; and among
them that most of us have taken to our hearts domestic pets.
Writing under this conviction, I have not forgotten my responsibility towards you and towards my Art in pleading the cause of the
harmless and affectionate beings of God's creation. From first to
last, you are purposely left in ignorance of the hideous secrets of
vivisection.'

One of the incidents of his book describes how a vivisector
obtains a monkey for his purposes, and Wilkie Collins was here
again alluding to a recent topical matter—the appearance at Bow
Street Police Court, in November, 1881, of David Ferrier, Professor
of Forensic Medicine at King's College, charged with performing
experiments calculated to give pain to two monkeys in violation of
the restrictions of the Vivisection Act. The proceedings were
brought by the Victoria Street Society for the Protection of Animals,
and evidence was given that the experiments in question had caused
paralysis in one monkey and total deafness in the other : Sir James
Ingham, the magistrate, dismissed the summons.

Do you remember how the fore-legs of those post-horses quivered and how their heads drooped when they came to the journey's end?'

An apt simile, for when at his own journey's end his head drooped, to rise no more, he was still working. *The Legacy of Cain* appeared in 1888, and when he died on September 23rd, 1889, his last story, *Blind Love*, was running serially and weekly in *The Illustrated London News*. He knew he would not live to complete the work, so he sent a message to Walter Besant asking him 'to finish it for me.' He had had an attack of paralysis: yet his old orderly methods of literary composition were continued to the end. When Besant received the material for the posthumous obligation he had undertaken, he found a detailed scenario for the completion of the tale, with every incident, however trivial, minutely noted, while fragments of dialogue were inserted to guide Besant in the realisation of the author's conceptions. Thus completed, *Blind Love* was published in January, 1890, three months after Collins's death. As of old, he had summoned scenic effects to his aid and the pale moonlight lit up for the last time the last act of Collinsian drama and the last mile-stone of his life:

'The wind rose a little ... and the threatening of rain had passed away ... Low and faint, the sinking moonlight looked its last at the dull earth ... She looked back and discovered the mile-stone ...'

And then his mind went back to old times and he wrote for his last book a chapter, with a tragic happening, entitled, 'On Hampstead Heath,' the Heath where he had walked hand in hand with fearsome romance in his childhood and where, or near by, he had later placed some of the most dramatic scenes of his own literary creation. Wilkie Collins died at 82 Wimpole Street, where he spent the last few years of his life after leaving 90 Gloucester Place.[1] He was thus consistently faithful to

[1] No. 82 Wimpole Street has been entirely rebuilt since Collins's time.

Marylebone, for he was born there and baptised in its parish church. Indeed, nearly all his life, apart from the sojourns in Hampstead and Italy and France, passed in Marylebone or its immediate neighbourhood—Oxford Terrace, Avenue Road, Blandford Square, Hanover Terrace, Albany Street, New Cavendish Street, Harley Street, Melcombe Place, Gloucester Place, and Wimpole Street. In most of his books scenes are laid near the Regent's Park and in St. John's Wood, and in that district he had found the romance of his life. The ' intimacy ' was with him until the end and so his latter life was that of a recluse so far as social entertainment in his own house was concerned. Perhaps for this reason he left directions that his funeral at Kensal Green Cemetery should be of the simplest description. Among those present at the interment on September 27th, 1889, were Holman Hunt, Squire Bancroft, Hall Caine, Oscar Wilde, A. W. Pinero, Edmund Yates, Edmund Gosse, and Miss Blanche Roosevelt.[1] His memorial stone fittingly records that he was ' Author of *The Woman in White* and other works of fiction.'

NOTE.—I do not append a bibliography of the works of Wilkie Collins as this is already available in expert form in Mr. Michael Sadleir's *Excursions in Victorian Bibliography* (1922). Some few details not given in his book will be found in my memoir above, and I may add I have come across some unrecorded short stories by Wilkie Collins, such as *A Fatal Fortune*, in *Lotos Leaves*, 1875 ; *How I Married Him*, in *Belgravia*, 1882 ; and *Royal Love*, in the Christmas Number, 1884, of *Longman's Magazine*, illustrated by T. Graham, R.S.A. At a sale, in December, 1923, of many of Wilkie Collins's manuscripts the catalogue mentions the following items which have not been seen by me in printed form : *The Captain's Last Love*, 15 pages ; *The First Officer's Confession*, 20 pages ; *Who Killed Zebedee*, 19 pages ; *The Poetry Did It*, 19 pages; *The Clergyman's Confession*, 19 pages ; *Fatal Fortune*, 14 pages ; *Your Money or Your Life*, 22 pages ; *The Air and the Audience : Considerations on the Atmospheric influence of Theatres* ; *Recollections of Charles Fechter*, 1882 ; *Reminiscences of a Story Teller* ; and the original skeleton draft of *Love and Liberty*, ' date of the story say 1870.'

[1] Author of *Stage Struck* (1884), *The Life and Reminiscences of Gustave Doré* (1885), *The Copper Queen* (1886), *Hazel Fane* (1891).

CHARLES ALLSTON COLLINS

It is perhaps inevitable that the gentle, sensitive personality of Charles Collins should be roughly shovelled
under the turf of oblivion, for Fate never was friendly
to him, and if a man voluntarily leaves his own light
under a bushel it is but seldom that his contemporaries
or posterity remove it to the appropriate candlestick.
In life and letters he was always overshadowed by his
more famous brother, Wilkie Collins, and he was so
fastidious and retiring in his attitude to Art and Literature that, as Forster truly remarks (in his *Life of Charles
Dickens*), 'No man disappointed so many reasonable
hopes with so little fault or failure of his own, his difficulty always was to please himself, an inferior mind
would have been more successful in both the arts he
followed.' For Charles Collins was distinguished alike
as artist and author. He had hereditary claims to both
avocations. He was the second son of William
Collins (1788-1847), R.A., and his mother, Harriet
Geddes, was a sister of Mrs. Carpenter, the portrait
painter,[1] and a near relative of Andrew Geddes (1783-

[1] Mrs. Collins and Mrs. Carpenter were the daughters of Captain
Geddes, of Salisbury. Harriet, later Mrs. Collins, was very pretty
in youth, and Holman Hunt relates that once at an evening party
Samuel Taylor Coleridge had singled her out and talked to her in
the highest strains of poetical philosophy, of which the girl understood not one word. Hunt suggests that a portrait of Harriet in
youth painted by her sister Margaret would explain the cause of the
poet's partiality. The sister, Margaret Geddes (1793-1872), settled
in London as a professional portrait painter when only twenty-one,
but she came with the patronage of her neighbour at Salisbury, the
Earl of Radnor, and her portrait of his son, Lord Folkestone,
exhibited at the Royal Academy in 1814, immediately brought her
many commissions for similar work. Her portraits of John Gibson,

1844), A.R.A., and Dr. Alexander Geddes (1737-1802), the theological writer. His second name came from his godfather, Washington Allston, the American historical painter, who was elected an Associate of the Royal Academy, and for whom William Collins had the highest regard. Writing in 1843, at the time of Allston's death, he said : ' His name was always before me ; for in my high estimation of his character, I had, by proxy, fifteen years ago, ventured to connect him with my family, as godfather to my second son ; who has been christened Charles Allston. And it is perhaps not unworthy of remark that he, having been left entirely to his own choice as regards a profession, has determined to follow that of a painter ; and is now carrying on his studies at the Royal Academy—I desire no better thing for him, than that he may follow the example of his namesake, both as a painter and as a man.' The parental aspiration was granted.

Charles Allston Collins was born on January the 25th, 1828, at Hampstead Green (near Pond Street). This was the period I have already described, when William Collins, delighted with the rural beauties of Hampstead, had fixed his residence near the Heath. The young Charles inherited his mother's Scotch colouring, and at three months old is described by his father as ' a little blue-eyed, red-haired bairn.' He was delicate and highly-strung, so, as he grew to boyhood, he was mercifully spared the rough and hard régime of the schools of his period. He received his education privately at home. As I have related in my Memoir of Wilkie Collins, little Charles also accompanied his family to Italy in 1836, when he was eight years old. In Naples he had a fall, which caused an illness of some weeks' duration. The Italian scenes stimulated his innate taste for the beautiful

R.A., and R. P. Bonington are now in the National Portrait Gallery. Margaret Geddes married, in 1817, W. H. Carpenter (1792-1866), a London bookseller, who was Keeper of the Prints at the British Museum, 1845-1866, and author of a Memoir of Vandyck.

which he evidenced even as a child. He early displayed a talent for drawing, and his brother's godfather, Sir David Wilkie, pronounced that he *must* be a painter. Accordingly at the age of fifteen he became a student at the Royal Academy School, a remarkable looking boy, of graceful figure, deep blue eyes, aquiline features, and a mop of bushy red hair. With his sensitive shyness, he resented the attention which his flaming hair received, and he asked Holman Hunt's advice in the matter of some specific for reducing the blaze of his hirsute beacon. At seventeen he painted a portrait of his father, who notes in his Journal of 6th January, 1846 : ' Sat to Charley nearly all day, for a drawing of my head.' Portraits of friends followed. William Collins writes on January 24th, 1846 :

' Yesterday and to-day a letter each from Mr. Bullar and his son, Dr. Joseph Bullar, to Charley, with their most gratifying commendations upon the drawing of the three children of Mrs. John Bullar. Their hopes respecting his moral and religious duties and privileges, I most sincerely thank them for. God grant he may always " first seek the kingdom of Heaven and its righteousness " ; the rest, by God's blessing and gift, will surely follow. I most fully and sincerely believe that, if this boy does justice to the genius with which he is endowed, and with the blessing of health—which most fervently I pray the Giver of all good to bestow upon him—he will, with his tact and taste, produce most satisfactory and popular works. 25th. Dear Charley's birth-day. God be praised for having brought him to this his eighteenth birth-day.'

William Collins was devoted to his two gifted sons, and it would indeed have rejoiced his heart could he have lived to know that both won an abiding place of distinction in the literary and artistic records of their generation.

Charles Collins was still a youth when he exhibited at the Royal Academy his pictures of ' Eve ' and ' Ophelia.' Then under the influence of his brother's great friend, E. M. Ward, he painted an historical subject, Charles II in exile, but as suddenly revolted to the new school of the Pre-Raphaelites with his ' Berengaria.' Ever ready to change his views of Life and Art as the stream bore him along, he took for his guides Millais and Holman Hunt, who were respectively his junior and senior by one year, and at first it was supposed that he would succeed to the place of James Collinson as a full member of their Brotherhood, which was founded in 1848.

Charles Collins was scarcely of age when thus he became an associate of the newly-formed Pre-Raphaelite group of painters, and, at first, had his share of the 'critical' abuse that was showered upon Holman Hunt, Millais, and the rest of the band. Thus *The Athenæum*, reviewing the Royal Academy Exhibition of 1850, said: 'Another instance of perversion is to be regretted in "Berengaria's Alarm for the Safety of her Husband," by Mr. Charles Collins.' But the following year, when 'Convent Thoughts' was exhibited, it was conceded that 'Mr. Charles Collins is this year the most prominent among the band. There is an earnestness in this work worth a thousand artistic hypocrisies which insist on the true rendering of a buckle or a belt while they allow the beauties of the human form to be lost sight of.'

He reached his highest success with 'May in the Regent's Park,' 1852, that floral year of Art, when, in response to a casual suggestion by Ruskin, the Academy galleries blossomed with pictorial hawthorns and other flowering shrubs. It is not clear why the Pre-Raphaelites decided to ignore Collins's claim to be elected a full Brother, but they did pass him over in favour of another painter—apparently because he was 'very much of a conventional man'; the decision cut Collins to the quick, and may have had some force in shaping his decision to abandon Art for the pen. When discussing Charles Collins's career in his *Pre-Raphaelitism*, William Holman Hunt says that his friend, in spite of original gifts and high yearnings, was doomed to be turned back on the threshold of Success by want of courageous confidence. He became perplexed, could not make up his mind, and lost heart, so that he, finally, was disenchanted

with the pursuit of painting. The real reason, of course,
for his comparative failure, was his temperamental
nervousness—in the actual sense of the word—and his
sensitive fastidiousness, which caused him to regard his
work as failure inasmuch as it never rose to the heights
of his fine ideal. Also it may be that Charles Collins in
his artistic achievement suffered from his early family
environment, where it was taken for granted that he
would be a great painter. He never had to fend for
himself or feel the spur of want to speed his steed of
ambition. There was no distant paradise of the elect
and famous for him to strive to reach, for he was there
from infancy as he said :

'I was already enjoying the brightness and glory of the
haven where the crowned ones were resting, talking of the race
they had run as only part of their youth. I was dandled on
their knees. I took to drawing from mere habit, and they all
applauded my efforts. I looked upon the diadem as a part of
manhood that must come, and now I begin to doubt and fear
the issue.'

Charles Collins also lived on terms of intimacy with
the leaders of the Pre-Raphaelites, particularly with
Millais, for the two friends were together in the summer
of 1850 at Botley, near Oxford, when Millais painted his
picture of 'The Woodman's Daughter' in Wytham
Park, the seat of the Earl of Abingdon, and Collins executed his excellent portrait of an old man named Bennett,
uncle of Mrs. Combe (wife of Thomas Combe, of the
Clarendon Press at Oxford). At this time, too, Millais
made the charming drawing of the youthful Collins which
is here reproduced. On their return to London in
November Millais stayed for a few days with the Collins
family at 17, Hanover Terrace, Regent's Park, from which
address he wrote to Mrs. Combe : 'I scribble this at
Collins's house, being totally incapable of remaining at
my own residence after the night's rest and morning's
"heavy blow" of breakfast. The Clarendonian visit,
the Botleyonian privations, and Oxonian martyrdoms

CHARLES ALLSTON COLLINS
From the drawing by J. E. Millais, 1850
By permission of Mr. J. G. Millais

have wrought in us (Collins and myself) such a similar
feeling that it is quite impracticable to separate '—the
privations and martyrdoms having been the scanty,
rough fare provided for the young artists by Mrs. King,
at whose cottage they had lodged in Botley. A little
while later he tells of walking to Hanover Terrace on a
night so cold ' that horses should wear great-coats.
Upon arriving there I embrace Collins, and *vice versa* :
Mrs. Collins makes the tea, and we drink it ; we then
adjourn upstairs to his room and converse till about
twelve. . . . Every Sunday since I left Oxford, Collins
and I have spent together, attending Wells Street Chapel.
. . . I am ashamed to say that late hours at night and
ditto in the morning are creeping on us again. . . . I
think I shall adopt the motto, " *In cœlo quies,*" and go over
to Cardinal Wiseman, as all the metropolitan High
Church clergymen are sending in their resignations.
To-morrow (Sunday) Collins and myself are going to
dine with a University man whose brother has just
seceded, and afterwards to hear the Cardinal's second
discourse. . . . The Cardinal preaches in his mitre and
full vestments, so there will be a great display of pomp as
well as knowledge.' [1]

Millais was flippant, but Charles Collins at this date
had become sincerely attracted by the high ritual of both
the Roman and extreme Anglican churches. An ascetic
and monastic frame of mind was attune with his passing
mournful mood, for he was in love with Maria Rossetti,
but had become imbued with the religious melancholy
of the Rossetti sisters who both resigned the idea of
marriage on earth for the consolations of the Spiritual
Bridegroom. So it was, Christina Rossetti resigned
James Collinson and Charles Cayley. Maria Rossetti resigned Charles Collins and John Ruskin ; she entered
an Anglican sisterhood as her brief years drew to an end,
while Charles Collins turned from the practice of Art,
in the form of ' Convent Thoughts,' to Literature, and

[1] *The Life and Letters of John Everett Millais,* by John G. Millais.

was destined to marry the daughter of a very famous author ; and his friend Millais married the woman John Ruskin had wedded, with unhappy sequel, in lieu of Maria Rossetti.[1]   Charles Collins's conventual habit of mind, while it lasted, was very earnest and sincere despite the obstreperous chaff of his friends.   Millais said, ' He is as good a little chap as ever lived, with no nonsense about him, except, perhaps his new inclination to confession and fasting,' and that was owing to his being ' hipped in love.'   On one occasion at dinner, Charles Collins having, for ascetic reasons, declined to partake of blackberry pudding, Millais consumed his portion as well as his own, and soundly lectured his friend on this absurd rule of supererogation, saying, ' I have no doubt you will think it necessary to have a scourge and flagellate yourself for having had any dinner at all.'   And later Millais observed to Holman Hunt : ' We must cure him of this monkish nonsense.   It is doing him a great deal of harm, taking away the little strength of will he has.'   Wilkie Collins, too, was much perturbed by his brother's High Church discipline and fasting, for he knew his delicate health was unsuited to such rigours, but he begged Charles's friends not to comment too persistently upon the boy's eccentricity, which he hoped would prove to be only a passing absurdity.   So Millais moderated his chaff, for indeed he had the greatest affection for Charles, who, Millais's son states, ' was much to him in these early days when men open their hearts to

[1] Maria Francesca Rossetti (1827-1876) was the author of *A Shadow of Dante* (1871).   She entered the Anglican Sisterhood of All Saints' Home, Margaret Street, in 1873-1874.   A brief acquaintance with John Ruskin ' had engaged her warm heart,' but she decided that ' such mere tastes and glimpses of congenial intercourse on earth wait for their development in heaven.'   Maria Rossetti died in November, 1876, and was buried in that same Brompton Cemetery where her early lover, Charles Allston Collins, had preceded her three years before.   Christina Rossetti wrote of her sister's funeral : ' Flowers covered her, loving mourners followed her, hymns were sung at her grave, the November day brightened, and the sun (I vividly remember) made a miniature rainbow in my eyelashes.'

each other, discussing their doubts and fears with candour
born of mutual sympathy and mutual striving after the
ideal.' And when Millais advised his friends, the
Combes, to purchase for £150 a picture ('Convent
Thoughts') by Charles, he said :

'I feel it my duty to render you my most heartfelt thanks for
the noble appreciation of my dear friend Collins's work and
character. I include character, for I cannot help believing,
from the evident good feeling evinced in your letter, that you
have thought more of the beneficial results the purchase may
occasion him than of your personal gratification at possessing
the picture. You are not mistaken in thus believing him
worthy of your kindest interests, for there are few so devotedly
directed to the one thought of some day (through the medium
of his art) turning the minds of men to good reflections, and so
heightening the profession as one of unworldly usefulness to
mankind. *This is our great object in painting.* . . . '

The blackberry pudding episode took place at Worcester Park Farm, between Kingston and Ewell, during
that happy summer and autumn of 1851, when Millais,
Holman Hunt, and Charles Collins were lodging there
in artistic fraternity and doing great work, as may be
read in Hunt's *Pre-Raphaelitism and the Pre-Raphaelite
Brotherhood*[1] and in *The Life of Millais*. Their farm
lodging, approached by a glorious avenue of elms (still
to be seen in part in Holman Hunt's picture, 'The
Hireling Shepherd'), had been a hunting-box attached
to Nonsuch Park in the time of the Duchess of Cleveland,
the strumpet of Charles the Second. All around lay
woodlands, green meads, and gentle hills. Now, to-day,
this pleasant countryside is disappearing before the
invasion of the suburban builder, and its pastoral quiet
is defamed by the rush and roar of mechanical traffic on
a new by-pass road. But let us remember that here,
eighty years ago, great painters found inspiration for
works that are now immortal. In a turn of the little
river Ewell Millais knew a pool with flowering rush and

[1] Published by Macmillan and Company.

water-lily, o'erhung with dog-roses and other blossoming shrubs, which he painted for the scene of his ' Ophelia ' (the model being Elizabeth Eleanor Siddal, who later married D. G. Rossetti), while the ivied wall in the background of ' The Huguenot ' was painted exactly from one at Worcester Park Farm, at the bottom of the garden. Holman Hunt by the side of another reach of the Ewell river found a hut abandoned by the powder workers— for there were gunpowder mills on the way to Surbiton— and here was the scene for ' The Light of the World,' for ' on the river side was a door locked up and overgrown with tendrils of ivy, its step choked with weeds. I stood and dwelt upon the desolation of the scene, and pictured in mind the darkness of that inner chamber, barred up by man and nature alike.'

There was pleasant store of ghosts also at Worcester Park Farm.   The great elm avenue was haunted ; and one evening when Hunt was returning from Ewell station, in the company of the station-master, they encountered a most mysterious white figure of gigantic size, apparently of a supernatural nature, for its identity was never solved despite close inquiries.   These matters made Charles Collins extremely nervous, and he dreaded crossing the dark fields after night-fall.   However he had to go up to London one day to see his mother in Hanover Terrace, which would involve a return to Surbiton station by the last train.   He was irresolute when he thought of the lonely walk back to the farm, and Millais cried, ' What do you fear most, ghosts or foot-pads ? ' ' Both, perhaps,' replied poor Charley. So his friends promised they would come and meet him at the station when he returned.   ' Good-bye, old Timidity,' shouted Millais as he went off, ' hurry up, or you'll have all Tam O'Shanter's troupe after you.   Give my love to Harriet, and tell her that I shall soon want her to fix the day for the wedding.'   Collins held up his hands deprecatingly at this customary reference to his mother [1] and

---

[1] See *ante* page 22.

departed, ' advancing daintily one foot before the other in a straight line as though he were walking on a tight-rope.' Hunt kept his promise to meet him on his return, and taking his lantern set forth into that dark murky night of October 19th, 1851. But he was late, and Collins's train was in before he reached the station. He heard a sound of timid feet rustling on the other side of the road, so he crossed and turned the light of the lantern on the face of the wayfarer. It was Collins, in a breath-less state of fear, for he had been terrified by the ad-vancing light, thinking of hob-goblins and jack-a-lanterns. 'I gave myself up for lost,' he gasped. . . . ' What I have suffered is beyond conception.'

But this nervousness of temperament was caused en-tirely by excess of imagination and a too-delicately strung organism, for in a real emergency he could evince courage. As Millais said, he had the ' unflinching resolve of the conductor of a storming-party. . . . He can act on sudden resolve, and yet withal he is as fearful as a mouse,' which is confirmed by Hunt's description of Charles Collins's personal appearance at this period : ' He was slight with slender limbs, but erect in head and neck, and square in the shoulder . . . having beautifully cut features, large chin, a crop of orange-coloured hair, and blue eyes that looked at a challenger without sign of quailing.' Altogether a charming youth, both in looks and nature.

Charles Collins seems to have been of what may be described as a donnish nature as he grew older—pedantic, precise, and entertained by small jokes. Percy Fitz-Gerald said he dwelt too much on trifles, and used to expound at great length a cure he had conceived for sea-sickness—namely to fill a tumbler to the brim with water, raise it to the eyes and gaze at it fixedly without spilling a drop. This he would attempt to demonstrate with much gravity and scientific detail, to the enjoyment of his friends, who would rally him unmercifully on his system, he accepting the chaff with his habitual gentle

humour.   FitzGerald adds that Collins at one time held
a post at one of the Museums for the collection of specimens of all the newspapers published in the United
Kingdom.   In this odd pursuit his mild sense of fun
was much tickled by the often quaint names of the
journals he procured.   He gave the palm for a combina-
tion of stately sonorousness and bathos to *The Skib-
bereen Eagle*, which he could never name without a burst
of refined laughter.   His quaint sense of humour enabled
him to laugh at his own constitutional weakness and
nervousness.   Mrs. E. M. Ward used to tell how he was
coming to dine with her one night in London which
happened to be the occasion when the crowds were
celebrating the Declaration of Peace with Russia, after
the conclusion of the Crimean War in 1856.   The crush in
the streets was immense, and there was an unprecedented
display of fireworks.   Charles Collins managed to struggle
half way to the house where he was expected when he got
swept off his feet by the crowd.   He returned home
dinnerless and alarmed.   The next day, by way of apology,
he sent to Mrs. Ward a sketch of himself transfixed in a
precarious position on the railings of a house.

Charles Collins did not accomplish great work, like
that painted by Millais and Hunt, during the stay at
Worcester Park Farm, but he was engaged all the time
on the background of a picture he had in mind.   He
painted a picturesque old shed he had discovered in the
neighbourhood, with the sunlight streaming through its
broken roof and sides, and, outside, trees swaying in the
summer breeze.   Finally he decided to make the shed
the scene of an old French legend telling how an outcast
family had taken refuge therein and were ministered to
by a saint.   But the picture was never finished, though,
as will be seen presently, the artist's dream of it remained
with him until the end.

The year 1851 was now at the fall, the avenue of elms
' snow down leaves all day long . . . .   Collins still fags
at the shed, Hunt at the orchard, and I at the wall,'

wrote Millais on November 22nd ; ' right glad shall we
be when we are having our harvest home in Hanover
Terrace, which we hope to do next Tuesday week.'
So the happy and eventful time by Ewell river ended.
The three friends intended to have many such sojourns
together for work in the future, but the future never
repeats the present, and long years after Holman Hunt
regretfully recalled :

' We took leave of the farm household and came up to town
in December, parting from one another where the Waterloo
Road and Strand met, thinking that we should often again
enjoy such happy fellowship, but alas ! no two dreams are
alike. Never did we live again together in such daily spirit-
stirring emulation. I feel this deeply in my old age when I
alone am left of the band who worked together with so much
mutual love and aspiration.' [1]

All through 1852 Charles Collins was thinking about
his picture of the Shed and the Saint, but he did not make
much progress, and in February, 1853, Millais says he is
desponding about the quantity of work he would have
to accomplish if he was to finish in time for the Exhibition, while Wilkie Collins writes to Ward :

' My mother has been laid up with influenza, and is only just
out of bed. Charley goes on slowly—slowly—with his picture. We are all sick and sorry together, but as patient as
righteous Job, and as cheerful about " the good time coming "
as Mr. Henry Russell, the eminent vocalist. Millais has been
ill in bed, to complete the *partie carré*. He has only just got to
work again.'

In the autumn of 1854 Charles Collins accompanied
Millais, Mike Halliday, and John Luard on a visit to
Scotland, and, after the other two men left, he and
Millais went on a further walking tour to the neighbourhood of Fort William. It was here Millais made a
number of sketches which show the peculiar garments
worn by Charles, for ' in the kindness of his heart Collins
looked rather to the necessities of his tailor than to his

[1] *Pre-Raphaelitism and the Pre-Raphaelite Brotherhood.*

skill, with results quite appalling to the worshippers of fashion.' In the following year when Millais was painting ' The Rescue,' inspired by the bravery of fire-men he witnessed at the great fire at Meux's Brewery, and was at work until late at night for several days before sending in to the Royal Academy, Charles Collins sat up with him and painted the fire-hose so that the picture could be completed in time, this being one of the very rare occasions when Millais permitted anyone to touch his work. For this exhibition of 1855 Collins actually succeeded in finishing a picture of his own—not the one he had commenced at Worcester Park Farm, but a work begun years before and entitled ' The Good Harvest.' This was the last picture Collins ever exhibited, for hence-forth his vacillation and dissatisfaction with his art had become an obsession with him. He would commence a new painting and before it was half-finished he would doubt its worth, become disgusted, and cast the unlucky canvas on a heap of its elder discarded brethren, though his delicate touch with tone and tint was ever exquisite. But at last a fiasco over a portrait this same year, 1855, seems to have caused him to throw away his brush finally in despair. Millais had married, in July, Euphemia Gray—the former Mrs. Ruskin—and after their honey-moon they returned to Perthshire, where one of their first visitors at Annat Lodge was Charles Collins. He wanted to paint Mrs. Millais's portrait, so she sat to him every day for a fortnight. ' Then, seeing that the picture made very slow progress, and that she was pre-sented as looking out of the window of a railway carriage —a setting that would have vulgarised Venus herself— she refused to sit any longer, and the picture was never finished.' [1]

He found some consolation in the fact that he could do literary work with pleasurable facility, and prompt acceptance of it owing to his family friendship with Dickens, which extended to Dickens's children and Miss

[1] *The Life and Letters of John Everett Millais*, by J. G. Millais.

Hogarth. He is generally to be seen in those photographic groups taken on the lawn or in the porch of Gad's Hill Place.

When he laid aside the brush for the pen, Charles Collins commenced his literary career and his association with Dickens by contributing to *All the Year Round*, in 1859, his sketches of travel humour entitled *A New Sentimental Journey*, which was re-issued at the end of the same year, together with two illustrations by the author, by Dickens's publishers, Chapman and Hall. Collins was at that date living in Clarence Terrace, Regent's Park. In the following year he wrote for the same journal his series of papers called *Our Eyewitness*, duly reprinted, and for the Christmas Number of 1866, *Mugby Junction*, his contribution was the excellent tale of a ghostly nature entitled *The Compensation House*. In the summer of 1860, Charles Collins was married to Kate Dickens,[1] the younger daughter of the novelist. Holman Hunt was best man, and the guests included Wilkie Collins, Henry Chorley, Charles Kent, Edmund Yates, the Willses, the Lehmanns, Percy FitzGerald, Miss Marguerite Power (niece of Lady Blessington), Miss Mary Boyle, and Fechter, the actor. The ceremony took place in the little church near Gad's Hill, when in honour of the event all the villagers turned out, triumphal arches were erected in the lanes, and the blacksmith exploded a *feu de joie* by means of two small cannon outside his forge. As for the sensitive bridegroom, ' I doubt,' says Forster, ' if the shyest of men was ever so taken aback at an ovation.' While of the new Mrs. Collins, Hunt relates, as the ladies left the Gad's Hill dining-room after the wedding-breakfast, ' no more graceful leader of a

---

[1] In the same year as her marriage, Kate Dickens had sat to Millais for the woman in the artist's great picture of ' The Black Brunswicker.' In 1874, the year following Collins's death, his widow married Charles Edward Perugini (1839-1918), a Neapolitan by birth, and an artist of some distinction. Mrs. Perugini died in 1929 at the age of nearly ninety.

wedding band could have been seen than the new bride.'
A billowing, rustling procession the ladies must have
made in their silk dresses, for 1860 was the year when
crinolines were at their fullest expanse.   The honeymoon
was spent in France, and the places there seen were described in the book Charles Collins commenced to write
on his return to London.   This was *A Cruise Upon
Wheels* (1862-1863), now the author's best remembered
work—that minor classic and most humorous odyssey of
Fudge and Pinchbold, the two Londoners who travelled
along the post roads of France in a horsed carriole,
meeting with divers strange and laughable adventures.
This story was a favourite of the neglected genius, John
Payne, as he recorded in a poem to be found in his volume
called *Carol and Cadence* :

> ' Collins, the credit which thou mightest claim,
>   Hadst thou on honour's bede-roll stood alone,
>   Was shadowed by a brother better known,
> Though less deserving than thyself of name,
> And more yet by the world-involving fame
> Of one to whom thou stoodst, though not his own,
> In son's stead : he who dwelleth near the throne
> Must needs be cast in shadow by its flame.
> But I that am " a borrower of the night," [1]
> And more to those that shun the garish light
> Incline than those who in the full noon-sheen
> Of public favour bask, too oft by chance,
> With thee " on wheels " to wander love and e'en
> A-horseback through the wilder ways of France.' [2]

Charles Collins and his wife were living at 5 Hyde
Park Gate South at the time Thackeray died so tragically
during the night preceding Christmas Eve of 1863.   His
house at Palace Green was near to their own, and it was

---

[1] An allusion to the insomnia of Payne.

[2] Mr. Thomas Wright, in his biography of Thomas Payne, says
that ' by the books of C. A. Collins (Dickens's son-in-law) he was
strangely fascinated, and in conversation with me he often referred
to them, praising particularly *A Cruise Upon Wheels, A New Sentimental Journey,* and *The Bar Sinister.'*

to the Collinses that Thackeray's distracted daughters at once sent for aid on making the terrible discovery in the morning. Charles Collins and his wife went over at once and were constantly there until the funeral.

In 1864, Charles Collins produced two novels, *The Bar Sinister*, where again the scene was mostly laid in France, and *Strathcairn*, a remarkable and delicately told story of frustrated love and resulting suicide, with picturesque scenic descriptions of the Highlands. *At the Bar*, 1866, is a tragic tale of poisoning, with a long account of the accused woman's trial. Collins also contributed *Some Chapters on Talk* to *The Cornhill Magazine*, and in 1861-1862, to *Macmillan's Magazine* articles with such titles as *Beggars* and *The Morning Paper*.

Towards the close of his short life, Charles Collins reverted to the pencil and supplied the designs for the covers of the monthly parts of his father-in-law's last work, *The Mystery of Edwin Drood*, those pictures which ever cause such agitation to Dickensians who worry and argue over the solution of this unfinished tale ; though why some disputants should contend that Drood was not murdered is equally a mystery, for to any one with a spark of imagination it must be obvious that the atmosphere of the story is electrical and charged with gloom and doom, and that all the clues to the mystery are darkened by the hovering wings of Death. It is sufficient for my own opinion that Dickens's sister-in-law, Miss Georgina Hogarth, assured me that from what Dickens had said on the subject in his own house it was clearly in his mind that Drood had been murdered ; and this point is further substantiated by Sir Luke Fildes's statement that Dickens definitely informed him that Drood was to be strangled by Jasper and that an illustration of a condemned cell would be required ; and there is also Forster's assertion that the story was to relate the murder of a nephew by an uncle. However, Charles Collins's drawing of a figure in a vault, discovered by the lamp of a mysterious stranger, will doubtless provide

conjecture for all time concerning Dickens's ultimate
intentions when winding up his sensational story.
Dickens said that Charles Collins had ' designed an
excellent cover,' and he had wished his son-in-law to
furnish the other interior illustrations ; but for some
reason not clear Millais advised against the employment
of his old friend (just as, twenty years earlier, he had been
the partial cause of Collins's rejection as a Pre-Raphaelite
Brother). Millais liked some drawings in *The Graphic*
done by a then unknown and young artist of twenty-five
named Luke Fildes, who accordingly, on Millais's recommendation, executed the interior illustrations for *Edwin
Drood* (1870). Six of Charles Collins's rejected illustrations for *Edwin Drood* were reproduced in the Summer
Number, 1929, of *The Dickensian*. Unfortunately, the
writer of the accompanying article, Professor Lehmann-
Haupt, advanced a theory that would deprive Collins
even of the credit of the completed form of the cover
designs of *Edwin Drood*. He stated : ' When visiting
Sir Henry and Lady Dickens in October, 1926, I was
shown by Lady Dickens, in the Memorial Room at their
home, the original drawing made by Charles Collins for
the cover of *Edwin Drood*. . . . This cover design did
not entirely agree with the cover as published.' And
he proceeded to quote a subsequent letter from Lady
Dickens, who wrote : ' I *did* tell you that Charles Collins
made the first drawing for the cover of *Edwin Drood*, but
he fell ill and did not finish it. Luke Fildes continued
and finished the drawing with several alterations.' This
is a startling assertion, and entirely at variance with the
statement of Collins's widow, Mrs. Perugini, who attributed the cover design entirely to her first husband. I
asked, in *The Dickensian*, if there were any documentary
proofs for this new claim, and if the final form of the
cover drawing was signed or even initialled by Fildes ?
No answer was forthcoming, so the theory remains un-
substantiated. Sir Luke himself never claimed or admitted any share in this cover drawing, or hinted that he

had aught to do with it. On the contrary, he wrote to me in reply to certain questions I put to him on the subject many years before this new claim was made :

'11, MELBURY ROAD, KENSINGTON,
' 29*th* November, 1914.

' DEAR SIR,
' I had better not attempt any explanation of the design of the cover of the monthly parts of *Edwin Drood*, as it was *not made by me*. It is the work of the late Charles Collins, *done before I came on the scene*, and I doubt if Collins himself quite knew the meaning of many of the incidents he depicted.

' Dickens, for obvious reasons, was not very communicative about the story. It was a " mystery " which he naturally wished to sustain. . . . One could not collaborate with a writer like Dickens without receiving some hints as regards the story, notwithstanding his desire to maintain the "mystery" as long as possible.

' I rather agree with you there is very little if any foundation for the local theory that Drood was thrown from the Cathedral tower. It sounds rather absurd. . . .
' Yours faithfully,
' LUKE FILDES.'

I have italicised the words emphasising the fact that Fildes was speaking of the cover design in the form it was published. It seems reasonable to assume that the original drawing by Charles Collins, now in the Memorial Room at Sir Henry Dickens's house, was a trial design by the artist, and that he later elaborated it into the published version. Other illustrators of Dickens made initial sketches which were not used, such as Phiz's manifold studies of Mr. Dombey.

Charles Collins was thus always fated to be unfortunate and superseded. He never asserted himself or proclaimed his own merits, and, as I have said, he was too sensitive and highly-strung and nervous for success in the battle of life. And now, in addition, ill-health of long standing developed to the stage of acute suffering. The disease was not diagnosed during life, but a *post-mortem* revealed cancer of the stomach. So Fate never

ceased to wound this harmless victim, whose last years
were little less than martyrdom, when 'paroxysms of
anguish were followed by profound prostration.' Yet,
as the same pen goes on to record, 'Never was excru-
ciating pain borne more patiently—his friends recall to
mind those pale and delicate features, expressive of the
sweetest good-nature and of a silent and noble endur-
ance.' The fatal access of agony came upon him on
April the 5th, 1873, and lasted until the 9th, when he
mercifully sank into unconsciousness, and breathed his
last towards early morning. Holman Hunt had seen
him (in the company of Millais) only a short time before,
and noted his increased feebleness of gait, though the old
humorous perplexity and quaint philosophy of his long-
time friend were just the same. A few days later, Hunt
stood beside the death-bed of Charles Collins and made
that remarkable sketch of the dead face which he gave to
Wilkie Collins. On the bed lay the canvas of the
picture Charles had commenced in the old days, over
twenty years ago, at Worcester Park Farm, when he
painted the beautiful background of Ewell scenery for
the legendary conception he never finished. But the
dream was with him at the end of his baffled life. He
died at 10 Thurloe Place (where now stands the Rem-
brandt Hotel), South Kensington, and it was not until
six days after the event that a bare announcement
appeared in the obituary column of *The Times*. There
was, apparently, no biographical information available
to relate the artistic and literary achievements of a gifted
and notable man, himself the son-in-law of Dickens whose
death less than three years previously had filled the land
with grief and the newspapers with pages of encomium.
At last, on April the 21st, twelve days after his death,
The Times reprinted verbatim from *The Athenæum* an
appreciation of Collins, written evidently by a friend who
had known and loved him well.

    Charles Allston Collins is buried in Brompton Ceme-
tery, that most melancholy necropolis where the dead lie

packed like sardines and where to read a memorial stone one has often to tread upon a dozen other graves before reaching the desolate ' resting ' place. His grave is covered by a flat granite slab on which it is just possible to decipher his name and the dates of his birth and death. There is no text or inscription to record who he was or what he did : inadequate recognition in death as in life.

LIST OF WORKS BY CHARLES ALLSTON COLLINS

1. A New Sentimental Journey. Published by Chapman and Hall, London, 1859. With two engravings on steel after drawings by the author. Preface from Clarence Terrace, Regent's Park, dated November, 1859. Pink glazed boards.

The story had appeared in *All the Year Round*, June and July, 1859.

2. The Eyewitness : His Evidence about Many Wonderful Things. By Charles Allston Collins. Published by Sampson Low, Son, and Co., 47 Ludgate Hill, 1860. Vignette by R. Young. Orange cover.

Dedicated to Chauncy Hare Townshend : Letter dated 6th August, 1860, Calais.

These papers had appeared in *All the Year Round* during 1859 and 1860, and described current sights and topics.

3. A Cruise upon Wheels : / The / Chronicles of Some Autumn Wanderings among the / Deserted Post Roads of France by / Charles Allston Collins, / author of ' The Eyewitness,' etc. With illustrations by the author. Published by Routledge, Warne & Routledge. 2 vols. 1862. Maroon covers.

This book was re-issued in 1926, by Peter Davies, London, with new illustrations by Andrew Johnson.

4. The Bar Sinister, A Tale. Published in two volumes by Smith, Elder, London, 1864. Grey-purple cloth.

5. Strathcairn. Published in two volumes by Sampson Low, London, 1864. Mottled maroon cloth.

6. At the Bar, A Tale. Published in two volumes by Chapman and Hall, London, 1866.

MORTIMER COLLINS

' As a poet, I am below Browning in insight, above him in lyrical powers, and a trifle above Tennyson in both. As a novelist, I am less successful than Thackeray, because I take less pains, but far superior to your Trollopes and Wilkie Collinses.'

Thus Mortimer Collins announced his position in contemporary letters of 1868, and though he wrote half humorously he really believed these words to be true. He would indeed be indignantly amazed could he know that to-day he is almost forgotten, even by people who profess to be literary, and that his name is unknown to, probably, ninety per cent. of the younger generation of readers, while the five authors with whom he compared himself are all sure of lasting fame—at any rate for another century.

Collins is a fairly common name, and there have been several members of the clan who have distinguished themselves in literature ; but the chief luminary, Wilkie Collins, has monopolised most of the limelight, particularly obscuring thereby his contemporaries, Charles Allston Collins and Mortimer Collins, vaguely supposed by many people to have been his sons or near relations. Charles Allston Collins, as we have seen, was the brother of Wilkie, but Mortimer Collins was in no way related to them. He came of Devonshire stock, his father being Francis Collins, a solicitor and mathematician, author of *Spiritual Songs* (1824) and his mother a Branscombe, a well-known Devon family ; his maternal grandmother was a Mortimer of Dorset.

Mortimer Collins was born at Plymouth on June 29th, 1827. He was only twelve years of age when his father died ; and he was then sent to a boarding-school in the distant county of Hertfordshire, Totteridge Park, a house occupied a few years later by Bunsen, who delighted in its extensive park and lovely grounds with spreading sylvan prospects, for he wrote, in 1848, with ecstasy of the ' grand trees ; those lofty firs, the pride of Totteridge ; the fine terrace, the charming garden.'   Probably the place had its share of influence in forming Mortimer Collins's life-long predilection for woodland scenery, his love of trees in near proximity to his dwelling-place and for the birds and wild life in the woods.   He gives a glimpse of what he was like as a school-boy in his auto-biographical novel, *Sweet Anne Page*, when describing little Stephen at school :

' He had a good memory, and learned his lessons easily.   He was popular among the boys, for they soon discovered his tale-telling faculty, and he spun them interminable yarns in the bed-room.   He was averse from athletic sports, and used to wander about the country in dreary loneliness.   The boys were not kept within bounds. . . .   But Stephen lived apart from all their robust fun, and dreamed his dreams, and saw weird phantoms, and told strange tales when the moonlight poured through the casements upon their little beds.'

' You cannot destroy the past.   Experiences such as those of Stephen Langton's boyhood are indelible.   They pass into the imagination ; they photograph themselves upon the retina of the mind's eye.'

He later was at a school at Westbury, in Wiltshire, where is the lesser White Horse cut out of the turf of the downs, and his early facility for telling tales here com-menced to bring reward, for some poems and sketches he sent to *Punch* and *Fraser's Magazine* were accepted. He used to relate that one day when a cheque for £3 had reached him, in payment for one of these contributions, he expended his honorarium in purchasing hot-cross buns and ginger-beer for his school mates when the boys were out for a long walk on a Good Friday.   He early dis-played his love for archæology, so marked a feature of his adult life, by offering to fight one of the school-boys

whom he detected in chipping off a fragment of Stone-
henge.   When his school-days ended as a pupil, Mortimer Collins became a youthful tutor in a small seminary,
as again is pictured in *Sweet Anne Page*.   Soon after this
period he had a holiday (1846) in the Lake District, and
his resulting poem, *On Windermere*, was dedicated to
' Christopher North,' who pronounced the young author
to be ' a very clever boy.'   Perhaps it was John Wilson
who provided Mortimer Collins with a letter of introduction to Wordsworth ;   at any rate the young poet
visited, in 1848, the supreme poet of Nature at Rydal
Mount and walked with Wordsworth in that garden
which looked upon the chain of hills and lakes, and saw
the noble laurel trees reared by Wordsworth from the
slips taken from the trees planted by Petrarch over
Virgil's tomb.   The youth was favoured with many
noble words, ' pregnant with meaning.'   Wordsworth,
' speaking as if he were an old Roman senator dressed
like an English farmer,' discanting on the beauties of his
Lake scenery, observed :   ' Height of hill and movement
of water are health-giving.   They are associated with
primeval soil, and an air fresh and stimulant.   If you
want to judge of the truth of this, look at the obituary
notices in *The Westmorland Gazette*.' [1]

Mortimer Collins married early, in 1849, soon after he
came of age, Susannah Crump (daughter of John
Hubbard), a widow, by whom he had a daughter,
Mabel Collins, born in 1851 [2] in Guernsey, where her
father was at that time Mathematical Master of Elizabeth

---

[1] Over twenty years later he acted on Wordsworth's suggestion,
and wrote to the editor of *The Westmorland Gazette*. The statistics he
obtained were evidence of remarkable longevity in that district and
furnished Mortimer Collins with material for his essay, *Long Life in
Lakeland*.

[2] A poem by Mortimer Collins was entitled *Mabel's Birthday* :

    ' Well do I love September : best for this—
        A daughter's kiss
    First knew I in that pleasant time,

College. Here he completed a little volume of poems entitled *Idyls and Rhymes*, published in 1855 and styled by a reviewer in *The Dublin University Magazine*, ' fine, rich, musical lyrics.' Thus encouraged, he resolved to devote himself entirely to literature. He fortunately had independent means, because, though he left Guernsey in 1856 to pursue his new calling, his next book of poems, *Summer Songs*, did not appear until four years later. He was then editor of *The Plymouth Mail* and living at Lara, Plymouth; he wrote for Disraeli's paper, *The Press*, and in 1860 joined the staff of *Temple Bar*. In 1861 he came to London to carry on his journalistic work, and resided at Granville Road, Southfields, Wandsworth. At the close of 1862 he found an additional and ideal home in a small house on the Bath Road at Knowl Hill, near Twyford in Berkshire. Here there was abundance of trees and the birds that he ever loved, and inspiration came in full measure; he poured forth a stream of novels, poems, articles, squibs, glancing with sharp persiflage at every event and foible of the day in a clever style that almost justifies Mr. Arthur H. Elliott's suggestion that Mortimer Collins ' was indeed incomparably our ablest master since the incomparable author of *Don Juan*.'

He wrote for *The Owl*, that curious little intermittent paper of four pages, price sixpence, which lasted from 1864 to 1869 under the conduct, it is believed, of super-superior Government clerks; he supplied *vers de société* and his *Adversaria* weekly to *The St. James's Chronicle*; and held a prominent position on *The Globe*. The best of Collins's serious poetry (his lyrics were greatly admired by Longfellow) will be found in *The Inn*

First saw beneath September's skies
    My Mabel's eyes,
Full often sung in careless rhyme. . . .
Ah ! Mabel mine, some sorrow comes to all,
    Some shadows fall
On every path, however fair.'

of Strange Meetings (1871).   His songs were often attuned
to a sad and wistful key, and he had a penchant for
unexpectedly introducing an unusual word or rhyme :

> ' Lo, song and sleep I love.
>   For song's susurrus
> Is the soul's wine throughout the weary days :
>   And silent sleep, restorer of decays,
> Smooths from the fretted brow the deepening furrows ;
>   'Tis the true Fountain of Jouvence, unfound
> By knight or troubadour in the far forest ground.
>
> Death is the ocean of immortal rest :
>   And what is sleep ? a bath our angel brings
> Of the same lymph, fed by the selfsame springs :
> Dip in it, and freshen the despondent breast,
>   And taste the salt breath of the great wide sea,
> Where shines 'mid laughing waves a far-off isle for me.
>
> .   .   .   .
>
>   ' Yes, I long to float on a haunted lake,
>   And the weary past forget,
>   And the thirst of my restless heart to slake
>   With the songs of Amoret.'

He delighted, contrariwise, in writing humorous
scraps of verse and nonsense rhymes.   His letters were
nearly always garnished with *jeux d'esprit* of this kind :

> ' As for me, I will plague you with banter
>   And plenty of rascally rhymes,
>   And frequently fill the decanter
>   And drink just a little sometimes.'

Or in sending a valentine, say, to his cousin, Henry
Frowde, then London manager of the Oxford University
Press, he would commence :

> ' Harry, in Holy Land of Bible and Book of Prayer,
>   Of course a Valentine's a libel, and spoils the air.'

Or to Frederick Locker-Lampson he would write in
Austin Dobson style :

'Dear Locker, 'Tis an idle night,
    I have been resting from my labours ;
And a pet book shelf caught my sight,
    Where Praed and you are next-door neighbours.
So in these days of maudlin rhyme,
    When half our poets are Empirics,
I've read for the five hundredth time
    His *Characters*, your *London Lyrics*.
Trifles in truth, no passion there,
    No frightful advent of sensation,
But a most calm and classic air,
    A grace and beauty quite Horatian. . . . '

Again in a style that suggests Austin Dobson he
addressed a girl who had, for mischief, removed his
beloved volume of Horace from his writing-table, a book
that was his inseparable companion :

'Who stole my Horace ?   Naughty girl !
When next you come I'll steal that curl
    That hangs above your shoulder.
Your heart I'm sure will palpitate
To think of such a frightful fate,
    Ere you're a fortnight older.

No ! I forgive you.   When I see
How Chloë, Lydia, Lalage,
    Asterië, plagued their poet,
I think my Lady, flower and gem
Of ladies, may outrival them. . . .
    . And, faith, she seems to know it.'

These quaint lines of verse also crop up in his novels
in the most unexpected places.   At the slightest excuse
of allusion, off he would go on some tangential expedition of rhyming.   Thus in *Marquis and Merchant*
(1871), speaking of ' The Capital of Berkshire,' Reading,
he recalls that it was here Bunyan came to preach disguised as a waggoner and that here, too, Coleridge, the
future poet, was discovered as Trooper Silas Comber-
back, of the Fifteenth Light Dragoons, aged twenty-one :

'At Reading, too, when trial was warmest,
Bunyan, that sturdy Nonconformist,

Whose *Pilgrim's Progress* is the raptest
Of books, came preaching at the Baptist
Chapel, in the frock of a waggoner.
—Time passes : lo, who draws his flaggon here ?
Who, in a tap-room vowed to Bacchus,
Lovingly reads Horatius Flaccus ?
How came that queer fish to arrive at
The level of a cavalry private ?
Who shall, in magic, irresistible,
Hereafter clothe the tale of *Christabel* ;
And make his *Ancient Mariner's* glistening
Eye compel the world to listening.'

During 1861-1868 Mortimer Collins was a prominent
figure in the Bohemian and journalistic world of London,
and well-known in the rowdy nights of song and drink
beloved by the denizens of those recondite regions.   He
possessed the gift of being able to work while at play,
that is to say he could write his ' copy ' or verse in any
circumstances of noise, and with a dozen people talking
and laughing round him.   A friend thus describes him :

' He was tall in stature.   His head was high, broad, and
compact, covered by a goodly crop of brown hair.   The eyes
were grey, expressive of thought, but at times lit up by the fine
fire of genius.   The complexion was pale, or rather sallow ;
the features even and well-defined.   His neckerchief, of buff,
hung loosely in long ties over his breast.   At that time, " in
his green and salad days," as he afterwards styled them, we
. . . . predicted for him the literary success which he afterwards
—though not to the full—achieved.   Superior to most of his
compeers in polite learning on the London press, his company
was courted ; but in a large number of the lesser lights he
excited a maddening jealousy.'

Tom Taylor has left a vivid impression of Mortimer
Collins's striking personality, and how the big man with
the leonine head would stride into the old-fashioned
tavern, in Fleet Street or near by, he frequented, and
shout in stentorian tones : ' Waiter ! Steak and Oyster
Sauce.'   ' Yes, Sir.'   ' And   Waiter ! '   ' Yes,   Sir.'
' OYSTERS GALORE ! '

MORTIMER COLLINS
From a contemporary photograph
By kind permission of *The Bookman*

His clothes were ultra Bohemian, and in his later years always followed the same style—a black or brown velvet coat, a white waistcoat, a shirt with wide open collar, no tie, light brown trousers, and a battered old straw hat with a red ribbon. This costume never varied in summer or winter, save that his coats by continual exposure to all kinds of weather soon turned to all the colours of the spectrum. Owing to this carelessness of convention and of public opinion, indifference to the susceptibilities of those he met, and absolute fearlessness in what he said or wrote—as will be seen presently he made the most amazing allusions to living people in his novels—it is clear that he formed many enemies. But, on the other hand, among those who comprehended his gifts and sterling, sensitive nature—for it is always those who are most sensitive who have a faculty for wounding others by personalities and dubious humour—he had many faithful friends. Among the most intimate of his Bohemian period in London were James Hannay and Bertrand Payne (1833-1898),[1] of The Grange, Brompton, manager of Moxon's publishing business at 44 Dover Street, who in 1866 had abandoned the publication of Swinburne's *Poems and Ballads* following the public outcry aroused by the hypocritical reviews of John Morley and E. S. Dallas.

On January 10th, 1867, Mortimer Collins and Bertrand Payne were involved in a typical fracas of that rackety time of London night life. They had dined together, and at 11.45 decided they would go on to the Alhambra and see some of the fair coryphées who, to the number of 400, were dancing in the great ballets produced by

[1] Mortimer Collins mentions Bertrand Payne by name in one of his characteristic personal digressions, in *Sweet Anne Page* (1868) : ' There is good old blood in Corsica. The Buonapartes, comparatively *novi homines*, seem to have been there A.D. 947—and my friend, Mr. Bertrand Payne, can only trace the progenitors of Millais, the painter, back to 1331. For me, I can trace no further than Ralph de Mortimer, *tempore* William I. ; but my friend, James Hannay is the fellow for genealogy.'

Milano, such as ' The Beauties of the Harem,' the company being headed by Mademoiselle Anais Tourneur, of
the Châtelet Theatre, Paris.   As a member of the staff of
The Globe newspaper, Mortimer Collins had a pass check
entitling him to entrance by the stage door in Castle
Street ; but on presenting this, the stage-door keeper
said it was too late and they could not enter.   The ladies
of the ballet were just leaving the stage, so the bon-
vivant twain apparently tried to force their way in, when
the Cerberus of the stage-door and an assistant—' two
fellows like garrotters,' as Collins described them in
Court—seized and assaulted them, struck and kicked
them, and thrust them into the street.   Collins said he
was struck full in the face, and but for the fact that his
hand had been hurt in the melée he would have been able
to give a better account of the man who had assaulted
him.   Payne fared worse, for he received three severe
blows, one blackening his eye, and a dangerous kick on
the spine from his assailant, a man named Thomas
Palmer.   A policeman was called, and he and another
witness in their subsequent evidence tactfully advanced
that ' Mr. Payne was not exactly drunk, but Mr. Collins
more so.'   When the case was heard at Marlborough
Street Police Court, and John Barnet, a check-taker at
the Alhambra, charged with assaulting the literary
gentlemen, the defendant who appeared was not the man
required though Payne said he was.   The charge was
dismissed, and the magistrate observed, ' Mr. Payne, you
have placed yourself in a very awkward position.   You
have rendered yourself liable to an action, and, you may
depend upon it, the matter will not rest here.'   However,
that was apparently the end of it, for nothing further
transpires except that Mortimer Collins wrote in his next
book, ' Some men hear the music of the Spheres ; others,
deaf to that sublime harmony, are delighted with what
they get at the Alhambra.' [1]

[1] I understand that Tennyson commemorated the affair in a
poetical epigram of four lines.

In 1868, Mortimer Collins got into trouble of another kind on the publication of the extraordinary novel in question, *Sweet Anne Page*, which was largely autobiographical and related his experiences as a schoolboy and as a tutor in Wiltshire. 'Idlechester' is Salisbury and 'Kingsleat' is Southampton. The nomenclature of the characters was too intimate; the principal people in the story were called Branscombe, the maiden name of the author's mother; while such names as the Duke of Axminster ('who assumed that there was something in poetry when Lord Byron condescended to write it . . . and if he had lived to see the Earl of Derby translating the *Iliad* he would have patronised Homer') and Beau Séjour seemed near to suggesting Beaufort and Badminton. What really caused trouble, however, was an amazing scene of a tickling match, witnessed by the little boy, Stephen, between two young women as they disrobed for the night, the ladies in question being Claudia Branscombe and Mrs. Bythesea, wife of the Bishop of Idlechester—Idlechester, from the description given, being easily identified with a Cathedral city in Wessex. Also notable living people were alluded to by their own names, such as the first Earl of Lytton—and when quoting a line from Owen Meredith he adds, 'As, however, he seems to have borrowed everything he ever said, I suppose the remark really belongs to somebody else.' And of Henry Taylor, author of *Philip van Artevelde*, he remarks, 'Unhappily Mr. Taylor is not a poet, and nothing is more painful than to see a man straining himself to appear something which he is not and cannot be.'[1] Further, there were certain love passages which were not suitable for print in the subscription libraries of 1868, so consequently *Sweet Anne Page* was

---

[1] Mortimer Collins did not think much of the majority of his contemporary poets. He carried on a frequent correspondence with Frederick Locker, who stated after his friend's death that 'the letters almost entirely consist of criticism of living Poets, so they are not ripe for publication.'

withdrawn from circulation before the year was out. It reappeared some years later in a one volume form.

Mortimer Collins was not allowed to forget this early indiscretion by the reviewers of his later books, and he replied in 1875 :

' When I see London journalists raking up an old book of mine (which had its follies) I am simply amused. Let them laugh at me : why not ? A lustrum and more has passed. . . . I am no more ashamed of having written a certain book, which these people bring up against me at intervals, than Mr. Gladstone is of *The Church in its Relations with the State* (1838) or Mr. Disraeli of *Vivian Grey* (1826). A man whose youth has no follies will in his maturity have no power. *Sic itur ad astra.* Sow your wild oats, and grow the wheat of wealth on the glorious grapes of genius.'

He could hardly expect his reviewers to like him, for he had written in *Sweet Anne Page* : ' Everybody ought to be educated. In which case, who is to cart dung and criticise novels ? ' Then quoting a verse by Wynyard Powys, he comments : ' I don't know whether my poor little friend Powys, who has tried so hard to revenge himself on me in the *Pall Mall* and the *Saturday*, thinks that's poetry ; but I can assure him it isn't. A poet needs back-bone ; he has none.'

Despite its *bêtises*, *Sweet Anne Page* is an extremely interesting and lively story, though with black tragedy at the close. The period is the reign of William the Fourth, and there are vivid glimpses of the London life of the period, such as a *bal masqué* at the Clarendon Rooms (which were situated in Burlington Gardens, somewhere near the site of the London University Buildings), as well of the Wiltshire and Berkshire country. Collins was at his best in picturing the hostelry life of the time ; whether it be the old Chapter House by St. Paul's Cathedral or the little inn at Maidenhead Thicket or one near Salisbury Plain, the scene is alive with warmth, firelight, and steaming punch-bowl inside for the tired passengers alighted from the mail or gig :

' They reached the cross roads.   The mare had gone like
the wind ; it wasn't half-past one, and the mail came by at two.
They knocked up the land-lord of the little inn, and the
kitchen fire was resuscitated, and something hot and strong
prepared Ralph Branscombe for his ride over the great plain.
Oh ! those old country inns, with their generous kitchens,
their strong home-brewed ale, their great flitches always ready
to be sliced and broiled, their fresh eggs, their wholesome,
neat-handed waitresses.   Steam has annihilated them ; and I
am one of those who find no consolation in the gaudy coffee-
rooms of the Magnificent Hotel (Limited).
   But there are the lamps of the Salisbury Mail.'

   In this book Collins gave rein to his penchant for using
a rare word rather than the one, meaning the same thing,
in general use :   thus ' ligneous sinciput,' ' astucity,'
' patulous elms,' ' gonoph,' ' adyta.'   On the other hand,
it is strange to find the word ' pyjamas ' used in 1868, and
a young girl of that time, addicted to slang, already
saying that she felt ' seedy,' was ' spoons ' on a young
man, and that she might as well ' shut up.'
   Mortimer Collins's first novel, *Who is the Heir ?* (1865),
had appeared serially in *The Dublin University Magazine*.
This journal, some years later, 1878, was edited by
Keningale Cook, the author of *Love in a Mist*, *The Guitar
Player*, and other works.   Collins's daughter Mabel had
married Keningale Cook in 1871.   Mabel Collins was a
beautiful woman both physically and in personality.   She
inherited all her father's love for birds and animals, and
had been educated at home on original lines planned and
carried out by Mortimer Collins.   She later devoted her
life to the cause of ameliorating the sufferings of helpless
animals.   She founded the Incorporated Parliamentary
Association for the Abolition of Vivisection, and was
ceaseless in her activities against the practice.   She was
also a Theosophist, mystic, and occultist, and was the
first to put forward the belief that hunting people and
sportsmen, after death, will be confronted and tormented
by the astral bodies of the animals they slaughtered on
earth merely for their own perverted pleasure.   She was

the author of many books, such as *Light on the Path*,
Through the Gates of Gold, *Pleasure and Pain*, dealing with
the interests of her life, and also of some novels.   She
died in 1927.   Julian Hawthorne, in his *Shapes that Pass*,
mentions how he went to see Mabel Collins and her
husband, Keningale Cook, soon after their marriage, in
connection with an article on the Fourth Dimension they
wanted him to write for *The Dublin University Magazine*.
It was to a modest little house in a Bloomsbury side
street that he went, and ' met my host—a plain, bearded,
candid, and kindly little man in black ; and, beyond my
expectation, his wife, beautiful, vivid, eager, animated . . .
sensitive, restless, yearning for esoteric wisdom.'

Mortimer Collins's wife (the mother of Mabel) died
in 1867, and in the following year he married Frances
Cotton, a lady who for some time had acted as his secretary.   ' She is a *jewel*.   She is an amethyst.   You know
the virtue of that gem,' he wrote of her.   The marriage,
for the eight years of its duration, was probably unique,
for until his death he was passionate and chivalrous lover
as well as husband.   On certain anniversaries of each
year, Valentine's Day, New Year Day's, and so on, he
would write verses to his wife and post them to her at the
village office.   They were in this romantic style :

> ' Oh, touch that rosebud ! it will bloom,
>   My lady fair.
> A passionate red in dim green gloom,
> A joy, a splendour, a perfume,
>   That sleeps in air.
>
> You touched my heart ; it gave a thrill
>   Just like a rose
> That opens at a lady's will ;
> Its bloom is always yours until
>   You bid it close.'
>
> ' One time there is, one only time,
>   'Twixt birth and death, from sorrow free,
> And that, O lady of my rhyme,
>   I passed with thee.'

'Fast falls the snow, O lady mine,
    Sprinkling the lawn with crystals fine,
    But by the gods we won't repine :
        While we're together,
    We'll chat and rhyme, and kiss and dine,
        Defying weather.

So stir the fire and pour the wine,
    And let those sea-green eyes divine
    Pour their love-madness into mine :
        I don't care whether
    'Tis snow or sun or rain or shine
        If we're together.'

Mortimer Collins, after his second marriage, was ever
complimentary to women, as could be cited from any
and all of his works : ' To make a man good and great
there is nothing but the love of a good woman ' ; ' Without a woman a poet is inconceivable ' ; ' Women were
not designed to be the mere physical comrades of men ;
they were also meant to be their intellectual and poetical
associates.' But he was not uxorious. He was both
called The Master in his home and acted as such ; and he
expressed his real views of women and their right
destiny when discussing the campaign of ' Rights for
Women ' : ' The great mass of gentlewomen look upon
the movement with indifference or contempt, aware that
woman's highest destiny is to marry—to be merged in
her husband, and complete his character.'

So it was with Collins himself, for it was after his
marriage and settlement altogether at Knowl Hill in
1868 that he accomplished his best work. He gave up
the riotous night life of London, and settled down to a
healthy country existence, glad to forget the tighted-legs
of the ballerinas of the Alhambra in

' A straggling village round a pleasant hill,
    Whence Windsor's ancient towers the eyesight fill.
    Life in a town is something I detest—
    Even in London, of all towns the best.
    I have grown tired of noisy streets and squares,
    Of lovely ladies with their numerous airs,

> Of theatres where dancers show their limbs,
> Of Parliament where men parade their whims :
> These I have seen and heard—would rather see
> A sunset—hear a thrush upon a tree. . . . '

The amount of work he now carried on was immense, for in addition to books, produced at the rate of two or more a year, he was writing regularly for a number of papers, *The Globe*, *The Press and St. James's Chronicle* (wherein, as by ' Cæcilius,' appeared his weekly *Adversaria*), *The World*, *Temple Bar*, *The Pictorial World* (where his papers were written under the pseudonym of ' The Loiterer '), and *Punch* (for the last two years of his life). He would work habitually until two o'clock in the morning—his Sonnets at Midnight, in *The Inn of Strange Meetings*, were actually composed at that hour, while beside him was his ' Big-Dog,'—' a mighty Pyrenean wolf-hound lies beside me while I work, or think, or dream ' :

> ' Let the hot noon with all its pomp and splendour
>   Revel in sunlight rich as golden wine,
>   Making the lover strong, the lady tender,
>   Filling the wide green glades with dreams divine,
>   Bringing a calm to which we all surrender
>   Like halcyon brooding on the hyaline :
>   Yet midnight's mine.
>
> Is it for work ?   There comes no fool to bore us :
>   Midnight intoxicates the human swine.
>   Ay, they are uttering now the snore sonorous—
>   Such folk drink heavily when'er they dine.
>   I, pen in hand, with all the gods for chorus,
>   Write then my clearest thought, my noblest line.
>   Midnight is mine.'

He said : ' A supreme sunrise is more frequent than a supreme sunset. I often enjoy a sunrise just before going to bed.'

He only needed a few hours of sleep, and by eight o'clock he would be up and out in the garden, feeding the pigeons and other birds. In summer time he would work out on the lawn, and on his table sat a tortoise who

knew well his master, and would put out his head to be
stroked. Mortimer Collins had a cup of tea with his
letters and the morning papers ; at eleven he partook of
breakfast or ' prandium,' as he called it. Then he would
make notes, watch his dogs and birds until twelve, when
he settled down to writing, which would continue (with
an interval for a walk) until seven, when he dined.
Conversation followed until ten, when he went upstairs
to work until two A.M. This programme was unfail-
ingly continued for eight years, and only varied when
friends were staying in the house. Then he put aside
his night work, and would keep his guests up till three
in the morning with brilliant talk and humour : at eight
o'clock he was in their bedrooms playing all manner of
school-boy tricks, stealing their clothes, pelting them with
flowers or birdseed. No wonder, as one of the guests,
R. H. Horne, said, every delight could be had at the
Knowl Hill cottage except sleep. But on the other hand,
the guests were not allowed to work either, for Horne
says Collins ' used to follow me from one place to
another to prevent my writing ; and after promising he
would not speak to me, or come to me, he went into the
garden, and after passing and repassing the window
where I was at work, eventually came to a stand right in
front, with an owl on his shoulder, and pretending to an
equal gravity and profundity of thought.'

In ' The Book of Knowl Hill Rhymes,' an elaborate
volume in which all the guests had to make an original
contribution in verse, they voiced the pleasure they had
enjoyed. As their host put it :

' These rhymes of Poet's Cottage at Knowl Hill
 May possibly in time a volume fill.
 Our notion in this cottage far from town,
 Where incomes don't go up though friends come down,
 Is just to chronicle the happy life
 Led by a lazy author and his wife :
 Who like to meet their various friends at home,
 And sometimes think their friends are glad to come.'

They were, and ever left with regret. As one youth put it :

> ' It has often seemed to me
> As I've started full of glee
> From the station to the cottage at Knowl Hill,
>   That soft sunshine never glowed
>   On as sweet a bit of road
> As that on which fond memory lingers still.
>
> But when on Monday morn
> I took my way forlorn
> From " Poet's Cot " to catch the early train,
>   I could not bear to see
>   Each gloomy flower and tree,
> But that I hoped ere long to come again.'

To which Mortimer Collins replied :

> ' We are very glad, dear Jack,
> That you like the Knowl Hill track
> That leads you to the lawn beneath the limes,
>   Where the musical shy birds
>   Have a song more sweet than words,
> Where we hope that we shall meet you many times.'

Collins's capacity for work was tremendous. In addition to his main literary avocations he could find time to write these rhyming letters to his friends and even for his servants. Thus his garden boy one birthday received a present from the local post-mistress and village-shopkeeper. So Mortimer penned these lines to be sent in acknowledgment to Miss Avery :

> ' To the Major Sub-Postmistress Tom returns thanks,
>   For her beautiful tie and good wishes,
> Now he's fifteen years old 'tis with her that he banks,
>   And her sweets he considers delicious.
>
> He hopes in reply that a fortune she'll make
>   By savings-banks, orders, and letters,
> Retire by-and-by, and not bother to bake,
>   But set up a coach like her betters.'

As I have said, he could write under any circumstances of interruption, and at short notice, as evidence of which gift I will relate a story told to me by Richard Bentley, the last of the famous publishers of that name. One day Mortimer Collins was off to enjoy a summer's-day, punting on the Thames. As the train was just rolling out of Paddington station a newspaper-devil rushed up to the carriage window with a letter. 'Confound you,' said Collins, shoving the missive into one pocket, while from the opposite pocket he extracted with his other hand a fine cigar. Settling himself comfortably in a corner seat he travelled down to Windsor, where he secured a punt and went afloat in the lovely sunshine. Nearly an hour passed lazily by when he chanced to— SNEEZE ! His hand diving hastily into a pocket in search of a handkerchief whipped out instead the forgotten letter. 'What's this ?' quoth he, in surprise, tearing the envelope open.

' LEADING ARTICLE ON . . . URGENTLY REQUIRED AT ONCE ' (doubly underlined) : ' MUST BE IN THE OFFICE BY FOUR O'CLOCK TO-DAY.'

His stipend, a handsome one, depended upon it. A dig at his watch, and perspiration on his brow. Punt pole went lustily to ground, and in a few moments he landed at the picturesquely named inn, 'The Bells of Ouseley' (called originally after the bells of Oseney Abbey), and shouted, 'WAITER ! Four mutton chops and three tankards of stout—QUICK ! ' Then came a great feat of chemistry. The chops and stout were TRANSLATED within an hour into one of those famous leaders that he could reel off on occasion. The up fast train was caught at Windsor, and the 'copy' was deposited in Fleet Street office not many moments after Saint Bride's clock had struck four. Mortimer Collins had written one of his best articles on paper-bills of 'The Bells of Ouseley.'

There was always a personal touch in the work of Collins ; some of his critics thought there was too much of him. Thus his third novel, *The Ivory Gate* (1869) contained a description of the author's personal appearance and cottage at Knowl Hill. *Miranda, A Midsummer Madness* (1873) is perhaps the best example of the author's wild, almost mad, novels. *From Midnight to Midnight* (1876) is also a very odd story, written to confute a critical friend who objected to Collins's habitual digressions and begged him to compose a story wherein the action would be confined to the duration of a month. 'That is too easy,' laughingly replied Mortimer, 'I will restrict the whole period of the story to twenty-four hours.' This tale was the successful result, and certainly there was no lack of exciting incidents, which range from adventures in a menagerie of wild beasts in London, attempted murder on a train, two suicides, to a midnight marriage at Clifton. It is a story of life in London over fifty years ago—those vanished days of hansoms and 'mighty draughts of claret,' when men before a railway journey still breakfasted on 'lobsters, prawns, kidneys *aux fines herbes*, light wines, both still and sparkling,' and when the motto for the prosperous was 'The faster you hurry through the disasters of the world, the more of them you are likely to endure. Loiter. Laze. Leave the troubles of existence to come at their own time.' This story was published originally with *Blacksmith and Scholar*, and in its first form a Calibanian character was called the Duke of Albany. As this was an actual title borne by members of the Royal Family (it was revived five years later in the person of Prince Leopold, the youngest son of Queen Victoria), no doubt remonstrances were made to the author, for in a new one volume edition of the tale the title in question was changed to Duke of Albery. *Blacksmith and Scholar* also contained curious personal and entirely irrelevant remarks such as :

'I also have seen the mulberries of Ashow and the oaks of Stoneleigh, and heard the strange legend how the late Lord Leigh, gentlest and kindest of men, established his claim to the estates by a series of murders.'

More permissible and amusing were his strictures on the successful female novelists of his time, Rhoda Broughton and Miss Braddon :

' It is perchance the worst evil of modern novel-writing (and I fearlessly accuse George Eliot as chief offender) that the favourite heroine is the silly girl—somebody who cometh up as a flower, or throweth her husband down a well.'

But Mortimer Collins's most reprehensible introduction of a living person into one of his books was his travesty of Swinburne as ' Swynfen ' in *Two Plunges for a Pearl* (1871-1872) :

' Mr. Swynfen, favourite poet of the ladies and the Pre-Raffaelites, a little man built like a grasshopper, but with energy enough to inform the bodies of both Anak and Chang. It was hard to criticise Swynfen's face, for the vast amount of bright yellow hair which he wore wherever hair would grow ; but his eyes were small and deep-sunk, were of an intense blue, like the first flame of a lucifer match. Swynfen firmly believed himself the greatest living poet ; and his fury if anybody ventured to doubt this was exquisitely amusing. His excitable brain could stand but little wine ; a pint of claret made him as mad as the Atys of Catullus. His poems, gentle reader, you may have read or tried to read, deal with effeminate heroes and somewhat masculine heroines, Rizzios and Messalinas. . . . He wore a violet velvet morning-coat, cravat and ruffles of lace, a waistcoat of white silk, buckskin breeches, and top-boots. Thus accoutred he had ridden to Lepel's on a piebald horse. . . . He was smoking honeydew from a wonderful meerschaum with certain choice carvings of Aphrodite and Adonis. He always smoked honeydew, though it invariably made him ill. . . . " Be assured," said Mr. Reginald Swynfen, " that nothing worthy of fame is done by men not of good family. All the rarest poets have had good blood. There is no one worth naming in this century save Byron, Shelley, and one other." " Yourself, I suppose ? " struck in the Honourable Geoffrey. " Why not," he exclaimed defiantly, springing from the ottoman on which he was lounging, while his bright hair and beard streamed like a meteor on the smoky air. " Why not ? " '

Apparently this attack passed unnoticed during the anonymous serial appearance of *Two Plunges for a Pearl* in

London Society in 1871, but directly the book was published a reviewer in *The Athenæum* wrote :

' There is one grave blot to which we much regret to have to call attention. If the reprehensible sketch of an epicene poetaster, whose name we think it well to withhold, be really . . . intended as a personal onslaught on a living individual, so gross an offence against good feeling must destroy all the pleasure we have experienced in reading what in other respects we regard as a successful story.'

On the same day, D. G. Rossetti wrote to Swinburne :

' Extreme irritation is unavoidable when one experiences such an elaborately spiteful outrage as the one you allude to, and it is quite natural that at first only others and not oneself should see that complete contempt is the only possible answer to it. I do not mean to say that a life-long training in the use of fists or the horse-whip might not inevitably lead to another course of action, but in reality it is well that you should not give the cur even this kind of immortality. One thing is that everyone knows you to be a high-spirited man, and no one doubts that he is already a dead dog, and these are two classes which are not usually expected to come into collision. . . . The real origin of the thing is doubtless twofold. Firstly— however little you may have been aware of it—you doubtless failed to suppress your contempt when you met the creature ; and secondly he is an intimate of the other thing called Bertrand Payne.'

Rossetti goes on[1] to recall, incorrectly, the fracas at the Alhambra I have already related, but he does not seem to have perceived that the attack by Collins on Swinburne was a spontaneous if reckless demonstration of friendship for Payne, who had refused to go on with the publication of Swinburne's *Poems and Ballads* in 1866, after the attacks made upon both the book and the poet by Morley and Dallas, thereby incurring the hatred and objurgations of Swinburne and his friends. A small piece of evidence in support of this view is that Mortimer Collins's and

[1] The full letter will be found in Mr. T. J. Wise's privately printed pamphlet, *Letters from Dante Gabriel Rossetti to Algernon Charles Swinburne, Regarding the attacks made upon the latter by Mortimer Collins* (1921).

Bertrand Payne's nick-names for each other were Chang and Anak, names of giants whom Collins had mentioned in the attack on Swinburne, quoted above.[1] Rossetti's allusions to fisticuffs and horse-whippings were rather unfortunate, for these remedies were the last in the world that the fragile Swinburne could be expected to apply to the gigantic and muscular Collins.   It is pleasant to add that after a time Swinburne expressed no resentment towards Collins for the gross affront he had received, and, as will be seen presently, the two men met on most amicable terms at a Mansion House dinner some four years later.

Mortimer Collins had also, at an earlier date, addressed Swinburne directly by name in his now very rare pamphlet of rhyme, *A Letter to the Right Honourable Benjamin Disraeli*, published in 1869 by the curious publisher, J. C. Hotten. But in this ' eccentric libellus,' as the author called it, there are no crude personalities, and the reference to Swinburne's poetry is on the whole complimentary :

' Swinburne, a singer perfect as the birds,
 Poet spontaneous, demigod of words,
 Too fond, no doubt, of blood and filth and foam,
 With the hetaira far too much at home,
 Yet rises to the height of the highest bard
 Pourtraying Mary with her Chastelard.
 Learned historians, prodigies of toil,
 Ne'er touched his picture of the Harlot Royal.
 They could not know her chamber's faint perfume,
 Or how lamps flickered in that amorous room,
 Or how she kissed, or how white throat and breast
 Throbbed through the midnight's exquisite unrest,
 Or how her serpent nature, sensuous, cruel,
 Made of what men call love a deadly duel—
 Wherein the opponent always fell we know,
 Dauphin or Darnley, Bothwell, Rizzio.
 Heartless and shameless, perfect form and face,
 The poison-blossom of the Stuart's wild race,
 Knowledge of her was Swinburne's fame and fate,
 Behold I crown him Mary's Laureate.'

[1] See also page 97.

Browning is alluded to thus :

' If he were only English ! if he could
But think in English it would do him good . . .
He tells a tale whose actors would delight
Charles Reade or Wilkie Collins, men of might,
A Tale the Adelphi would receive with joy—
And makes it longer than the tale of Troy.'

.   .   .   .   .   .

' Is Tennyson no poet ?   Yes, indeed,
" Miss Alfred's " are delicious books to read. . . .
Ethics of Dr. Watts', Colenso's creed,
Those nice green volumes give you all you need.'

Morris is described as ' the husband of Chaucer's
widowed Muse,' and Collins refers to his own personal
friend—

' Locker, whose Muse is " just the Period's Girl, a pretty
creature,"
In whom no tragic impulse ever rankles,
Who always says her prayers and shows her ancles.'

There is an amusing couplet about the publishing firm
his friend, Bertrand Payne, managed—

' I don't care much to see Apollo's oxen
Herded through Dover Street by Muddling Moxon,'

while Mortimer Collins's final opinion on contemporary
poetry is summed up in the line, ' Since Byron died, the
Muses have been dumb.'

Sweet and Twenty (1875) contains a picture, as ' Canon
Tremaine,' of the Rev. R. S. Hawker, the famous vicar
of Morwenstow, who had died that year.   Apropos of
this book he wrote to R. D. Blackmore, whom he
admired above all other men, and to whom he had
dedicated *The Vivian Romance* (1870) as a fellow ' Poet
and Gardener ' :

' MY DEAR BLACKMORE,
You have not told me if like *Sweet and Twenty*.   I
think *Alice Lorraine* charming . . . specially the grocery and
the idyls of the cherry orchard.   You ought to have given

Alice a lover at an earlier date. You are in a second edition, I
see, while my publisher tells me my book is moving slowly. . . .
I honestly think your work too good for popularity. . . . Shall
we ever see you here again ? [1]

> " Golden lads and lasses must,
> Like Chimney Sweepers, turn to dust."

And as I write on Chimney Sweepers' Day, it is just as well to
remark that before we both crumble into dust we might as
well have a confabulation.
' Thine,
Bohemia.'

' My wife fancies from your letter that you think she does
not appreciate *Alice Lorraine*. By Jove, Sir, doesn't she ? She
made me quite jealous as she read it by exclaiming,

" Delicious ! "
" Idyllic ! "
" Heroic ! "
" Poetic ! " etc., etc., etc.

' She thinks nothing of my stuff after it. I'm out in the cold.
I mean to write something ultra-diabolical next time. Lovely
weather. Thrush shouting. Blackbird hatched from young
'uns. New servants to-day. Happy thought.'

His old friend, Bertrand Payne, was ever a welcome
guest at Knowl Hill, and to him, in 1871, Mortimer
Collins writes,[2] addressing him by the name of the giant
who had been exhibited at the Egyptian Hall and made a
fortune by investing the money thus earned in the tea
trade :

' MY DEAR CHANG,
I shall look forward with infinite satisfaction to your
coming down here, and of course shan't at all object to a

[1] Blackmore used to drive by road from Teddington to Knowl
Hill, taking about three hours for the journey. On October 28th,
1868, he notes in his diary : ' Drive M. Collins to Henley through
Wargrave—Henry Kingsley's house.' The two friends played much
chess in the evenings.

[2] This letter to Bertrand Payne is now in the possession of his son,
Mr. de V. Payen Payne, by whose courtesy it is quoted here.

case of the widow's or to some of your giant weeds.   For my-self, I chiefly smoke cigarettes ; my wife having developed a genius for making them.

Glad you like *Marquis and Merchant*.   There's a novel of mine (anonymous) called *Two Plunges for a Pearl* in *London Society*.   The first part of it was writ two or three years ago, but I think the finish will be tolerable.

The Shelley is a charming book in spite of the editor's weak-ness.[1]   Rossetti is a thorough believer in Shelley's greatness, which is all right enough : but he had no ear for rhythm, and no knowledge of English literature, and by those defects is betrayed into ludicrous errors. . . . '

' I want to go in for a one vol. novel, my tendency being to terseness and condensation.   Ye *Owl* will hoot again next Wednesday, I believe.

' Yours sempiternally,

' ANAK.'

One of the visitors to Knowl Hill, R. H. Horne (1803-1884), was a link with an earlier period of writers, for his epic poem, *Orion*, and his virulent abuse of Bulwer Lytton and ' Ingoldsby ' in *The New Spirit of the Age*, had appeared some thirty years before.   He was now an old man over seventy, far from his adventurous youth in Mexico with its shipwrecks and sharks, fire and fever. At Knowl Hill one evening he was playing the guitar, but suddenly stopped because he thought his host was inattentive.   Mortimer Collins placated the irritable senex, and persuaded him to renew his strains on the light guitar.   While Horne played, Collins in about five minutes wrote these lines :

> ' O dreamer of Orion ! Back again,
>   Thou hast returned from the far Southern life,
>   The glory and the suffering and the strife,
>   A wondrous burial, but not in vain.
>
>   For thou bring'st home to us the ancient strain,
>   And our small school with poetasters rife
>   Shudders at satire cutting like a knife,
>   Wonders at music diamonds dropped like rain.

---

[1] The edition of Shelley's Poems edited by W. M. Rossetti appeared in 1870.

I love the echo of thine ancient youth,
I love thy second youth, o'erfilled with power.
I love the joyous tone of thy guitar.
Revive, O Poet, full of strength and truth !
Astonish rhymers of a weaker hour !
We hail the radiance of thy evening star.'

The sonnet was read aloud, and the ancient Horne, entirely restored to good humour by the flattering lines, immediately improvised both with words and music, a reply on his guitar, his song commencing ' O Quinbus Flestrin ! Quinbus Flestrin ! '—the name he had bestowed on Collins in allusion to his great size. Horne said Collins reminded him of one of the Homeric heroes who had just put off his armour and was thinking of his oxen at the plough and of his golden cornfields.

Another septuagenarian friend, who like Horne survived Mortimer Collins by several years, was Grantley Berkeley, the author in the long ago of the eccentric novel, *Berkeley Castle* (1836) and of the savage flogging of the publisher of *Fraser's Magazine* which caused the death of that unfortunate man. Collins dedicated to him his novel, *Marquis and Merchant*, with the adage, ' Whom the Gods love die young,' which presumably he did at the age of eighty-one.

One of Collins's novels, *Mr. Carington* (1873), was written under the pseudonym of ' Robert Turner Cotton,'—Cotton being the name of his wife's family. His publishers, King and Co., had become a little fearful of the critics whom Collins had offended, and they imagined the new novel would be judged on its merits and not made the vehicle for personal attacks on the author if it appeared as the work of an apparently unknown writer. However, those familiar with Collins's individual style could not fail to read through the subterfuge, for here were all the old, delightful digressions on every subject, the personal idiosyncrasies, the love of Nature ; Collins portrayed himself in both the school-boy Frank Noel, and his uncle, Canon Lovelace. The scene opens at Salisbury, this time the city being mentioned by its own name and not as ' Idlechester.'

Next of Mortimer Collins's most remarkable books, in a different vein, was *The British Birds : A Communication from the Ghost of Aristophanes* (1872). This satire in the metres of his favourite Greek poet gave him opportunity both for the ' word-coinage ' he liked—many of the archaic words he used in all his books were old English which he wished to preserve or revive—and to tilt at persons and movements he disliked. Thus the Chorus comments on Positivism :

> ' Life and the universe show spontaneity :
> Down with ridiculous notions of Diety.
>   Churches and creeds are all lost in the mists :
>   Truth must be sought with the Positivists.
>
> Wise are their teachers beyond all comparison,
> Comte, Huxley, Tyndall, Mill, Morley, and Harrison :
>   Who will adventure to enter the lists
>   With such a squadron of Positivists ? . . .
>
> There was an ape in the days that were earlier ;
> Centuries passed and his hair became curlier ;
>   Centuries more gave a thumb to his wrist—
>   Then he was MAN—and a Positivist.'

His novel, *Transmigration* (1874), also struck an unusual note for him, and he explained its origin in the Preface.

' Writers of what have been called Utopian romances need not accuse their rivals of plagiary, since they are all treading in the track of giants like Aristophanes and Swift. But it may be well to state that I had not read *The Coming Race* until these volumes were passing through the press, and that I have never seen *Erewhon*.

The idea of an experience of metempsychosis has dwelt in my mind since walking with one of England's great poets on the terrace of Rydal Mount,[1] in full sight of that " aerial rock " which he loved to greet at morn and leave last at eventide, he answered an inquiry of mine with the immortal words on my title-page.'

[1] See *ante* page 76.

The words in question were from Wordsworth's *Ode*, ' Our birth is but a sleep and a forgetting.'

Some of Mortimer's last novels, *Blacksmith and Scholar*, *You Play Me False*, and *The Village Comedy*, were written in collaboration with his wife, Frances Collins. He died before he had completed his share of *The Village Comedy*, and he was working at it until within a few days of his death. It related the life of Knowl Hill village as ' Copse Hill,' and in earlier years it would have developed into a charming rustic idyll: but unfortunately an epidemic of gossip and slander had later attacked the place, and Collins and his wife being some of the victims of this malicious talk, they were embittered towards certain neighbours they had of yore lived in amity with and liked. This attitude is reflected in *The Village Comedy* and detracts from its charm ; there is always matter for regret when a book preserves an atmosphere of trivial ill-feeling long after all the actors in the scene have passed away. All the characters in the story were drawn from life. Mortimer Collins himself figures as ' Manly Frowde,' where he again uses a family name, for he had cousins of that cognomen. There is also a character named Henry Branscombe. ' Sir Herbert West ' was Sir Gilbert East, of Hall Place, Maidenhead ; ' Nugent ' is said to represent Mr. Sturges, a vicar of Wargrave, and ' Bonfellow ' the Rev. A. H. Fairbairn, a former vicar of Knowl Hill, much liked by Collins. Thus some of the characters were pleasantly introduced. But the new and youthful vicar of Knowl Hill, the Rev. Gilbert Royds, who had come from a curacy at Doulting, Somerset, had incurred the dislike of Mortimer Collins and his wife, and is depicted in the book as ' Mr. Viper Voyd.' Miss Avery, the gossiping village shopkeeper, is presented as ' Miss Tattleton,' while the landlord of the ' Seven Stars ' inn, a hostelry near to Collins's cottage and with its name changed to the ' Pleiades,' had also some cause for complaint in his translation. Collins quite expected to have his windows broken as the result of this tale, for in

addition the author had incurred the ill-will of neighbouring farmers by preventing, or attempting to prevent,
their snaring of birds, and putting the police on to the
offenders.[1]   However, nothing so disagreeable as violence
occurred, and Collins's sudden death cancelled, it is to
be hoped, all ill memories for, after all, the man was finer
than his books and he had dearly loved Knowl Hill.   He
was so big (over six feet in height) and strong, yet gentle
and tender-hearted despite his trenchant pen, and very
merciful to birds and animals ; a great pedestrian and
athlete ; so jovial, a lover of old ways, old customs, old
houses, old wine, good food—' the noble title of epicure
—the second in the world, poet being first,' as he
said ; an old-fashioned Tory, stout defender of Church
and State, yet styled ' The King of the Bohemians '
—but a rural Bohemian in his last years, for after he
settled at Knowl Hill in 1868 he rarely left that loved
haven and home, except for walks, until the all too
early end came eight years later.   He has several times
described his careless personal appearance, bearded and
clad in velvet jacket, as he leans over the white
railings of his garden waving welcome or adieu to the
friends he delighted to entertain at his rural paradise
—' The Mount Hybla of Berkshire,' as it came to be
called :

' Some thirty miles from Megalopolis,
    Miles also from the shrieking, grinding rail,
    On a high-road where once the four-horse mail
Flashed gaily past—so placed my cottage is :
    Roars merrily now the wind tall limes between,
Which guard my quiet lawn a triangle scalene.

And you may see me, if you pass this way,
    Lean on my gate and looking into the road,
    And listen to the skylark's joyous ode—
Thoughtful, not oft cigarless.   Will you say,

[1] Edmund Yates said it was astonishing how, in his last years,
Mortimer Collins would dwell upon and worry over these petty
rural commotions.

Who wears that velvet coat, a trifle tattered,
That curious cool straw hat which wind and rain have
     battered ?

Sometimes there comes a friendly visitant,
     Brimmed with the life o' the town, rewarding me
   Well for my mutton and my Burgundy ;
And so we laugh together at fraud and cant,
     While everywhere is heard a flutter of wings,
And winter's chorister, the unwearying redbreast sings.

O, but one visitant, the nightingale.
     Throb, throb, wild voice, through passionate twilight
        hours.
   Love is thy gift from the Eternal Powers ;
Yet in thy song there seems a tragic wail,
     Because in Argos, ages long ago,
A poet turned thy lyric wooing into woe.'

His house, of two low stories, at Knowl Hill was very
picturesque, standing in an acre of grounds and completely surrounded by trees.[1]   He had an ideal study and
book-room, long and low-pitched, with bay windows
opening on to the lawn, bounded by a row of tall lime
trees, the haunt of the thrushes :

> ' Ah ! never may thy music die.
> Sing on, dear Thrush, amid the limes.'

He had three dogs, ' Big-Dog,' the wolf-hound ;
' Growl,' a Scotch terrier ; ' Fido,' a Skye terrier ; and
he would romp with them like the eternal boy he ever
was.   As an old Berkshire labourer remarked one day
to Collins when the latter was playing with one of his
noisy canine friends, ' You be a pair, you be.'   ' Fido '
died in October, 1874, to the grief of his master : ' I shed
some tears. . . . With my own hands have I buried
my dear friend beneath the yellowing limes.   Shall
I meet his spirit again ?   Ah who can solve that

---

[1] The house was later called ' Springfield,' and occupied for some
years by R. Caton Woodville, the war artist.

problem ? ' ' Big-Dog ' went in April, 1875, when
Collins wrote :

' It is very sad, as I have lately proved, to lose by old age a
dog that was yours in its youth.   When a dog has been thirteen
or fourteen years your friend you have melancholy pleasure in
tending his old age.   " Put him out of his misery," says some
well-meaning friend.   I cannot see it.   " The whole duty of a
dog," said Christopher North, " is to love man and to keep his
commandments."   It is clear that man should act with God-
like tenderness towards his dogs.'

And then only three months later the last of the loving
trio, ' Growl,' was laid beneath the limes and poor
Collins was sorrowful indeed, for ' Growl ' dated back
to the old days at Wandsworth and had come to Knowl
Hill with his master in 1862 :

' I was present at his birth and christened him " Growl,"
because his first act was to growl at his mother for bringing
him into the world without his leave.   Poor old boy, he has
growled through life, always most at those he loved best, as is
the way with some human cynics, and when he let me touch
him without growling I knew he was in a bad way. . . .   He
has walked with me through many counties of England, sometimes doing forty miles a day with ease ; and once, when
walking through Buckinghamshire, we met Mr. and Mrs.
Disraeli, and just such another little dog, and, although neither
he nor I had been introduced, he commenced a conversation at
once.   That night we stayed at the " George " at Aylesbury,
where I amazed the waiter by eating seven consecutive mutton
chops, " Growl " devouring the bones.   Ay, we have had
joyous times together, poor little dog ; and it is satisfactory to
know that while you shared my gaiety, you had no share in
those multitudinous troubles to which man is born.'

He himself was to die a year later, in the prime of
manhood and strength, and so the happy years at
Knowl Hill vanished with a sigh as suddenly as the
setting sun sinks below the horizon in a wide flat
country.

In May, 1876, a few weeks before his death, Mortimer
Collins made a remarkable and brief reappearance in

London.   His wife was a relative of the Lord Mayor of that year, Sir W. J. Richmond Cotton,[1] and Collins was persuaded to emerge from his rural retirement and, with his wife, spend a few days at the Mansion House, where he was present at the dinner given in honour of literary men.   At this function he met Browning, who observed to him, ' We sympathise on Greek Subjects.'   ' Yes,' replied Mortimer, ' but we differ often.'   ' Never mind the difference,' returned Browning, ' it is the *in*difference I object to.'   Swinburne was there also, and unhappy thoughts of *Two Plunges for a Pearl* all forgotten, he and Mortimer Collins found that they liked each other and shared mutual interests.   They had a tremendous conversation on the Greek poets—' Euripides was a cad, Sir,' spluttered the excited Algernon.   Thereupon the Lady Mayoress remarked, ' If some one does not separate those two gentlemen, they will talk Greek poets all night.'   Among others present were Lord Houghton, Locker, Sala, and William Tinsley, the publisher, who years after recorded his horror at the unconventional dress worn by Collins at this banquet amid the blaze of Civic State and Plate, for the recluse of Knowl Hill was ' attired in light coloured trowsers, white waistcoat, and short-cut brown velveteen jacket—and seemed to revel in an act of very bad taste.'   Tinsley was unaware that, when he accepted the invitation to the Mansion House dinner, Collins stipulated that he should be exempted from wearing evening-dress and could appear in his usual Bohemian clothes, and the Lady Mayoress very gladly assented.   The banquet was held on a Saturday night, and the next morning Collins was up at seven o'clock and out, the only human being on London Bridge, for ' I wanted to see what the City looked like early on Sunday morning.'   Later that morning he drove with the Lord

[1] The Lord Mayor was of literary tastes—author of *Imagination and Other Poems*, and of *Smash, A Sketch of the Times.* ' Musis Amicus,' Mortimer Collins styled him when dedicating to him *A Fight with Fortune.*

Mayor in state and the splendid civic equipage with
hanging footmen—Mortimer wearing his battered old
straw hat with the red ribbon—to the re-opening service,
after restoration, of the church of St. Andrew Under-
shaft ; and on Monday morning he was present with the
Civic company when the colours of the 77th Regiment,
which Picton commanded at Waterloo, were handed to
the Lord Mayor on the steps of the Mansion House and
by him deposited in St. Paul's Cathedral, a ceremony
which intensely moved Collins, now at the close of life
and literary pursuit.   He wrote :

'Never have I been more impressed by any solemnity.
When I saw those torn flags of many victories placed upon the
shrine of everlasting peace, I wished to be young again, that I
might choose another vocation, and use the sword rather than
the pen in defence of religion and loyalty.'

He seemed full of health and high spirits during this
visit to the Mansion House.   He romped with the Lord
Mayor's children, played with them blind man's buff and
battledore, when he smote the shuttlecocks so high that
they lodged on the cornice of the great ball-room, where
they presumably remained until the next cleaning of the
chamber.   There was further meeting with the Civic
Cottons a month later, for, early in June, the Lord Mayor
and Lady Mayoress, with the Sheriffs and other officers,
after attending state banquets at Bristol, Bath, and
Reading, travelled from the last-named town to visit
Mortimer Collins at his Knowl Hill cottage.   The party
arrived by coach with four horses, and took tea on the
lawn to the amazement of the villagers, who had always
regarded Collins with some contempt as a poor devil
who had to earn his living ' by writing for the papers.'
Mortimer Collins had gone into Reading the previous
morning to meet the Lord Mayor, and he returned there
again in the evening to attend the dinner given by the
Mayor of Reading in honour of the London Civic party.
Evidently the strain of these expeditions and entertain-

ments affected his health for it was noticed at Reading
that he was extremely pale and obviously unwell. Some
years before he had suffered from a bad attack of rheumatic fever, and now he was troubled by difficulty of
breathing which prevented his lying down and consequently deprived him of sleep. As soon as it was day-
light in those early July mornings he would go and sit
by his window and read the *Noctes Ambrosianae* of his
boyhood's admiration, Christopher North, the wistaria
framing his head as he sat there in the summer dawn. . . .
He thought he was in for consumption, but his malady
was hereditary weakness of the heart.

The last visitor to Knowl Hill was a little eight-year-
old boy, the son of Collins's friend, Edward Draper.
He left on July 22nd ; on the 26th Mortimer Collins
went to Richmond, to the house of his daughter and son-
in-law, Keningale Cook, in the hope that change of air
would be of benefit. . . . On the last day at Knowl Hill,
when the time for departure came, his wife found the big,
once-strong man in the book-room with a favourite robin
by his side, the last of his birds he was ever to see. The
journey to Nightingale Hall (now the New Star and
Garter Hotel), at Richmond, was made by road, and on
arriving Mortimer Collins was taken to a room overlooking a lovely reach of the river with Petersham and
Ham in the foreground. The sun was setting behind
the trees, leaving a long soft glowing line of colour. The
red afterglow gradually died away from the water, and
as the moon rose, her pale light became reflected there.
He lay a long time gazing at the wonderful changing
lights and the fading trees, thinking perhaps of the lines
he had written in active days before strange weariness
had overcome him :

> ' Stern hours have the merciless Fates
> Plotted for all who die :
> But looking down upon Richmond's aits,
> Where the merles sing low to their amorous mates,
> Who cares to ask them why ?

We'll have wit, love, wine,
'Ere thy days divine
   Wither, July . . .
Swift Life's stream flows,
But alas ! who knows
   Whither, July ? '

Two days later, on July 28th, 1876, he died, ' looking down upon Richmond's aits,' at the age of forty-nine. He was not afraid of death, for he had written :

' No : I shall pass into the Morning Land
   As now from sleep into the life of morn ;
   Live the new life of the new world, unshorn
Of the swift brain, the executing hand ;
   See the dense darkness suddenly withdrawn,
   As when Orion's sightless eyes discerned the dawn . . .

O virgin world ! O marvellous far days !
   No more with dreams of grief doth love grow bitter,
   Nor trouble dim the lustre wont to glitter
In happy eyes.   Decay alone decays :
   A moment—death's dull sleep is o'er ; and we
   Drink the immortal morning air, Earine.'

But that is not all.   He was full young to leave this beautiful world he had loved so well, and the dear things of home.   Again and again he had protested in his work that the coming of death at the unknown hour was horrible and unspeakably cruel.   His death in the prime of life and his literary powers was a great shock to his friends.   R. D. Blackmore writes in his diary that the first intimation he had was the notice of the funeral, which he at first disbelieved, but ' find it too true.   Much shocked.'   He walked over to the funeral of his friend in Petersham churchyard, which was very simple.   No black was worn, and a white pall was used.   The widow and daughter did not attend.   Others present, in addition to Keningale Cook, were Tom Taylor, the editor of *Punch* ; Frederick Locker ; Percival Leigh ; Edward Legge ; Vizetelly, the publisher ; Henry Campkin, Librarian of the Reform Club ; and R. H. Horne.   A strange experience occurred to another person who chanced to be present—the Irish novelist, ' Owens Blackburne ' (Elizabeth Casey). She had never met or even seen Mortimer Collins in his life-time, but during the committal service she whispered to the friend she had come with : ' Who is that mysterious tall, broad-shouldered man walking about rather rapidly ? He has on a velvet coat, and is very big in the shoulders, and long in the legs ; he has a brown beard and moustache. He is going about from one person to another, and seems very troubled that no one will speak to him or take any notice of him.' ' Why, how amazing,' replied her friend, ' I see no one here answering to your description, and no one is walking about : but you have described Mortimer Collins exactly as he was in life.'

Many notable people lie interred near his grave— Vancouver, the discoverer ; Agnes and Mary Berry, the ' wives ' of Horace Walpole ; the Duchess of Lauderdale —at Petersham, which another wistful poet, Roden Noel, has sung—its ' little church, with golden vane aglister in the sun, ancient, rich, red, and weather worn,' amid an ecstasy of hawthorn and chestnut tree in spring-time. A lovely and peaceful resting-place would say those unmindful of the unthinkable horrors of death : for, though the surroundings are lovely, this churchyard is damp and sadly neglected, with many of the older tombs overgrown and falling to decay. Indeed, a search on several occasions has failed to discover the grave of Mortimer Collins, who lies there forgotten ; and if there is a stone to his memory, the inscription is probably illegible from the corroding effects of atmosphere. So, if spirit and memory can escape from the tomb, would one fain fancy the shade of poor Mortimer Collins embarking in a phantom boat from Petersham Meadow and sailing in the misty moonlight on and up to a higher reach of Thames ; past the green ' enamelled meadows and filagree hedges ' of Walpole's Strawberry Hill ; past Hampton Court and Datchet Meads and the glorious pile of Windsor Castle ; past haunted Hurley, and so to Wargrave, and back to Knowl Hill and dear home, where in the long, low bookroom the wide windows stand open to the lawn, with the scent of the tall lime trees, with its memories of good friends and birds and romping dogs and happy—oh ! happy—*life*.

Knowl Hill is only a place of shadowy memories now, for Mortimer Collins's cottage is entirely demolished. The garden palings and some of his trees remain, and perchance the far descendants of his birds. There is no echo of the vibrant life and laughter poured forth there sixty years ago—except for those with the ear of Phantasy.

LIST OF WORKS BY MORTIMER COLLINS

1. IDYLS AND RHYMES / By / Mortimer Collins / Dublin : J. McGlashan, 50 Upper Sackville Street / W. S. Orr and Company, London / Stephen Barbet, Jun., 25 High Street, Guernsey / MDCCCLV.   Orange-red cover with gold lettering.

' These Poems are dedicated to my little daughter, Minna Mabel Collins.'

2. SUMMER SONGS / By / Mortimer Collins / [Design (S) Sans Changer] London / Saunders, Otley, and Co., Conduit Street / 1860.   Magenta cover.

Preface from Lara, Plymouth, 1860, alludes to various criticisms of his earlier book of verse, *Idyls and Rhymes*.

' This volume is dedicated to the Right Honourable the Earl of Mount Edgcumbe, whom I venerate as the Inheritor of an Ancient Name and as a resolute Vindicator of Constitutional Principles.'

This was the third Earl of Mount Edgcumbe (1797-1861).

3. WHO IS THE HEIR ? / A Novel / by / Mortimer Collins / In Three Volumes / London / John Maxwell and Company, 122 Fleet Street / 1865.   Magenta covers.

' To Joseph Sheridan Le Fanu, Esq., I dedicate this Story in gratitude for friendly encouragement and in sincere admiration for his power as a writer of romance.'

This story had appeared serially in *The Dublin University Magazine*, which was owned and edited at that date by Le Fanu.

4. A / SELECTION FROM / THE WORKS / OF / SIR WALTER SCOTT, Bart. / EDITED BY MORTIMER COLLINS / Ward Lock and Co. / London, Warwick House, Salisbury Square.   One of the series of Moxon's Miniature Poets.

Preface from Knowl Hill, 1865, of twenty pages.   Mortimer Collins claimed to publish, in this volume, for the first time Scott's last verses, written in Miss Wordsworth's album on 22nd September, 1831, and they were copied for him by Miss Priscilla Wordsworth.

5. SWEET ANNE PAGE / By / Mortimer Collins / In Three Volumes / London / Hurst and Blackett, Publishers / 13 Great Marlborough Street / 1868.   Magenta covers.

6. THE IVORY GATE / By Mortimer Collins / In Two Volumes /London / Hurst and Blackett / . . . / 1869.   Red covers.

' To Lord Sussex Lennox this story is dedicated in Remembrance of days of political conflict and evenings of pleasant converse.'

Lord Sussex Lennox (1802-1874) was a son of the fourth Duke of Richmond.

7. A LETTER / TO THE / RIGHT HONOURABLE BENJAMIN DISRAELI, M.P. / Forti nihil difficile / London / John Camden Hotten, 74 and 75 Piccadilly / 1869.   8vo.   28 pages.

This was written in verse couplets : 276 lines.

This very rare pamphlet is not, apparently, in the British Museum, but the Bodleian Library has a copy (Press Mark : 280.g.6.3).

8. THE VIVIAN ROMANCE / By / Mortimer Collins / In Three Volumes / London / Hurst and Blackett, Publishers / . . . / 1870.   Maroon covers.

' To Richard Doddridge Blackmore, Poet and Gardener.'

9. THE / INN OF STRANGE MEETINGS / and other Poems / By Mortimer Collins / London / Henry S. King and Co., 65 Cornhill / 1871.   Brown cover.

Fourteen lines of Dedicatory verse ' To my Wife ' in this style :

> ' Spring's youngest sister art thou, Lady mine,
> Child who has love for every thing
> Of earth and air. A moment now I linger—
> Linger and think of thee, and give thee this
> Love gift of rhymes made when my spirit was free.
> If thou wilt touch it with a white forefinger—
> Nay, if the volume thou wilt deign to kiss—
> Surely my verse shall live, Earine.'

10. THE / SECRET OF LONG LIFE / London / Henry S. King and Co., 65 Cornhill / 1871. Blue cover with gold design. A book of Essays.
' To Lord Saint Leonards, one of the foremost of the Illustrious Brotherhood who possess the Secret of Long Life.' (He died in 1875, at the age of ninety-four.)

11. MARQUIS AND MERCHANT / By / Mortimer Collins / In Three Volumes / London / Hurst and Blackett, Publishers / . . . / 1871. Maroon covers.
' To the Honourable Grantley Fitzhardinge Berkeley, who, both in Life and Literature, shows the true meaning of the Adage, " Whom the Gods love die young." '

12. TWO PLUNGES FOR A PEARL / By / Mortimer Collins / In Three Volumes / London / Tinsley Brothers, 18 Catherine St., Strand / 1872 (November, 1871). Red covers.
' To Josephine Mason : More charming (as I think) than her charming seven sisters.'
This story appeared serially in *London Society*, January to November, 1871, as *Two Plunges for a Pearl* / A New Novel by a Popular Author / With ten illustrations by F. W. Lawson.

13. THE BRITISH BIRDS / A Communication from the / Ghost of Aristophanes / By / Mortimer Collins / London / The Publishing Company, Limited, 7 Quality Court, Chancery Lane / MDCCCLXXII (April). Quarto. Brown covers. Bright blue end papers.
' To Miss Louisa Court of Castlemans.'

> ' Lady, whose eyes oft deign to look
> Over my careless rhyming words,

> Use as you will this tiny book,
> In which I treat of British Birds ;
> Some plumaged dusk, some bright of hue,
> And never one so fair as you.
>   M.C.'

Second Edition.

Title as above / Second Edition / London / Richard Bentley and Son / 1878. Red cover with design of birds in black.

14. THE PRINCESS CLARICE / A Story of 1871 / By / Mortimer Collins / Two Volumes / London / Henry S. King and Co., 65 Cornhill / 1872. Red-terra cotta covers.

' To Arthur Cook, of the Albany, and Sir William Robert Clayton, Baronet, of Harleyford.'

15. SQUIRE SILCHESTER'S WHIM / By / Mortimer Collins / In Three Volumes / London / Henry S. King and Co., 65 Cornhill / 1873 (February). Red covers.

' To Frederick Locker, Poet and Friend of Poets.'

Scenes at the ' Cheshire Cheese,' London, and at Lechlade.

16. MIRANDA / A MIDSUMMER MADNESS / By / Mortimer Collins / In Three Volumes / ' Why this is very midsummer madness,' etc. / London / Henry S. King and Co., 65 Cornhill and 12 Paternoster Row / 1873 (July). Green covers.

' To Henry Campkin, Poet and Archaeologist, "Mihi nemo est amicior." '

Scenes in Wiltshire, London, and Sark.

17. MR. CARINGTON / A Tale of Love and Constancy / By Robert Turner Cotton / In Three Volumes / Henry S. King and Co. / 65 Cornhill and 12 Paternoster Row, London / 1873 (October). Blue decorated covers.

18. TRANSMIGRATION / By / Mortimer Collins / Author of *Marquis and Merchant* / ' Our birth is but a sleep and a forgetting,' etc. / In Three Volumes / London / Hurst and Blackett, Publishers / 13 Great Marlborough Street / 1874. Blue covers. Preface from Knowl Hill, 1873.

19. FRANCES / By / Mortimer Collins / In Three Volumes / London / Hurst and Blackett, Publishers / . . . / 1874. Red-brown covers.

' To Harry Frowde :

    F rances, dear Harry, is a name that we
    R ank above common names, for is not she
    A perfect woman, if such thing there be ?
    N o problem puzzles her, no bore will vex,
    C almly she takes the troubles of her sex.
    E ach man she meets is tried by touchstone true,
    S o who can wonder she is in love with you ? '

20. SWEET AND TWENTY / By / Mortimer Collins / ' Then come kiss me . . .' / In Three Volumes / London / Hurst and Blackett / . . . / 1875 (April).   Green covers.

' To Charles Dinham : With three verses of dedication in this style :

    ' Yet there's another reason, this above,
    Why I assail you with a Dedication :
    'Tis that you love the lady whom I love—
    " To love her is a liberal education." '

21. BLACKSMITH AND SCHOLAR / and FROM MIDNIGHT TO MIDNIGHT / By Mortimer Collins / In Three Volumes /London / Hurst and Blackett, 13 Great Marlborough Street / 1876 (November, 1875).   Orange-red covers.

' To Sir Gilbert Augustus Clayton East, Baronet, of Hall Place, Berkshire.'

Blacksmith and Scholar occupies Volume I and part of Volume II., where *From Midnight to Midnight* commences, the latter story comprising also the whole of Volume III.   In a subsequent one volume edition of *Blacksmith and Scholar* the title-page states it is by Mortimer and Frances Collins.

FROM MIDNIGHT TO MIDNIGHT /A Story / By Mortimer Collins / A New Edition / London / Chatto and Windus, Piccadilly / 1883.   In pictorial yellow boards.

22. A FIGHT WITH FORTUNE / By / Mortimer Collins / In Three Volumes / London / Hurst and Blackett / . . . / 1876 (April).   Brown covers.

' To the Right Honourable William James Richmond Cotton, M.P., Lord Mayor of London. *Princeps Municipalis : Musis Amicus.*

23. YOU PLAY ME FALSE / A Novel / By Mortimer and Frances Collins / Miranda : ' Sweet Lord, you play me false. . '

The Tempest / In Three Volumes / London / Richard
Bentley and Son / 1878.   Dove-grey covers.
' To Percy Cotton this book is dedicated in gratitude and
love.'

24. THE VILLAGE COMEDY / By / Mortimer and Frances Collins / In Three Volumes / London / Hurst and Blackett,
Publishers / 13 Great Marlborough Street / 1878.   Green
covers.
' To Mrs. Byron Blewitt this book is dedicated.'

25. MORTIMER COLLINS : HIS LETTERS AND FRIENDSHIPS /
With Some Account of his Life / Edited by / Frances
Collins / In Two Volumes / London / Sampson Low,
Marston, Searle, and Rivington / 1877.   With Photo-
graphic portrait of Collins.   Maroon covers.
This work is largely composed of Mortimer Collins's letters in
prose and rhyme and of extracts from his published works.

25. PEN SKETCHES / FROM A VANISHED HAND / From the
Papers of the late Mortimer Collins / Edited by Tom
Taylor / With Notes by the Editor and Mrs. Mortimer
Collins / In Two Volumes / London / Bentley and
Son / 1879.   With photographic portrait of Collins.
Brown covers with floral design.
The Introduction contains some recollections of Collins
by Tom Taylor.
' To Rose May Crawshay, of Cyfarftha Castle, in recogni-
tion of many acts of kindness, this book is dedicated by
Frances Collins.'

26. THOUGHTS IN MY GARDEN / By / Mortimer Collins /
Edited by / Edmund Yates / With Notes by the
Editor and Mrs. Mortimer Collins / In Two Volumes /
London / Richard Bentley and Son / 1880.   Floral
covers, brown backs.
The Introduction contains some recollections of Collins by
Edmund Yates.
' To Charles Reade, Dramatist and Novelist, This book is
dedicated by Frances Collins.'
' The animosities perish : the humanities are eternal.'
The quotation refers to a regrettable affair in which Mortimer
Collins and his wife and Charles Reade were concerned in 1873.

Upon the publication of Reade's story, *The Wandering Heir*, in *The Graphic*, Mortimer Collins, writing as ' Caecilius,' his usual pseudonym, in *The Press and St. James's Chronicle*, and Frances Collins as ' C.F.' in *The Athenaeum*, accused the author of plagiarism from Swift. Reade replied to the charge in *Once a Week*. An account of the matter can be read in *Charles Reade*, by Malcolm Elwin, pages 244-247. Evidently mutual regret and forgiveness were expressed by Mrs. Collins and Charles Reade at some date following the death of Mortimer Collins.

27. ATTIC   SALT / or / Epigrammatic   Sayings / Healthy Humorous and Wise / In Prose and Verse / Collected /From the Works of / Mortimer Collins / By / Frank Karslake / London / B. Robson and Co. / 43 Cranbourn Street, Leicester Square / 1880.

Preface.   Frontispiece of classical subject repeated on greystone covers.

' To Frances Collins this Collection of Sayings so wise and so worthy of preservation to all Time is dedicated.'

28. SELECTIONS FROM THE POETICAL WORKS OF MORTIMER COLLINS / Made by F. P. Cotton / London / Richard Bentley and Son / 1886.

29. SELECTION FROM THE POETICAL WORKS OF MORTIMER COLLINS / Edited by T. W. Littleton Hay / 1891. In the Poets and Poetry of the Century.

R. D. BLACKMORE

It is difficult for me to realise that the author of *Lorna Doone* was born over a hundred years ago—when George the Fourth was King and Napoleon dead but four years. Because I knew Blackmore in my boyhood, when he by no means seemed an old man, but was, on the contrary, a hale, sturdy, square-built figure, with a fresh high colour, suggestive of the prosperous agriculturist or horticulturist, which indeed he ever was by preference rather than the man of letters. But time—alas !—goes by so quickly, and I realise upon reflection that it is thirty-six years since I met him, though I can still see him in his loosely-cut grey clothes, soft hat and pink shirt, and with his Victorian white whiskers reaching from ear to ear round his chin. It was Blackmore's curious literary fate to write fourteen excellent novels and to be extolled and remembered only as the author of one. Yet as Mr. Eden Phillpotts has truly said :

' He enriched the language with many great works, works inspired by his own wealth of head and heart, proceeding from his own abundance as an artist and a man. There was in his broad sweep, like the roll of an ocean wave, something Elizabethan. His manliness, insight, glorious humour were a tonic to the mind. . . . '

Richard Doddridge Blackmore was born on June 7th, 1825, at Longworth, in the romantic country of the White Horse in Berkshire, and not far from Oxford. His father, the Rev. John Blackmore, was curate of the parish, and he had married Anne, daughter of the Rev. Robert Knight, vicar of Tewkesbury. Blackmore was thus a descendant, through his mother, of Sir John Knight, ' the Elder ' (1612-1683), merchant and Mayor of Bristol, who was active in the persecution of Nonconformists and Roman Catholics. Blackmore's maternal uncle, the Rev. H. Hey Knight, of Nottage Court, Newton Nottage, Glamorganshire, provided further clerical connection, though there was a dissenting strain on the maternal side of the Knight family because their mother was descended from Philip Doddridge (1702-1751), the notable Nonconformist divine and hymn-writer. R. D. Blackmore's second name came from this sturdy forebear. There was a Richard Blackmore, of Parracombe, North Devon, in the seventeenth century. The novelist's grandfather was Rector of Oare, Somerset, so Blackmore had hereditary links with the Exmoor country he was to immortalise.

Blackmore suffered the misfortune never to know his mother, for she died three months after his birth, a victim to typhus fever, which ravaged Longworth in the autumn of 1825. Mr. Blackmore, Senior, removed to a curacy at Ashford, near Barnstaple, in North Devon and remarried. In consequence, the future author spent a good deal of his early life with his maternal grandmother, Mrs. Knight, at Newton House, Glamorganshire. These topographical details have some interest, because it was the country-side round Barnstaple and Porthcawl (divided by the Bristol Channel) that formed the scenic background of some of Blackmore's best romances in later years ; so those early impressions were fine and lasting.

Blackmore went first to a school at Bruton, in Somerset, and then passed to the famous Blundell's at Tiverton, in Devon. It was a hard, rough period for school-boys who were not big and strong, and Blackmore —a shy lad, reserved and proud—had a bad time as a fag. In fact he was so bullied and maltreated that serious results continued in after life, causing attacks of epilepsy. But no trace of bitterness is to be found in his picture of his old school in *Lorna Doone*—a vivid picture, this, of Blundell's, which almost ranks with the inimitable account of Manchester Grammar School, a few years earlier, in Ains-

worth's *Mervyn Clitheroe*—though Blackmore does indi-
cate how ' the great boys vexed the small ones,' and how
the day-boys or ' caddes ' were persecuted. The great
fight in the novel between John Ridd and Robin Snell
and the general blood-thirstiness of their companions
were, probably, actual experiences of Blackmore's which
he ante-dated to the seventeenth century for the purposes
of his story. Anyway, an actual contemporary of his
at Blundell's, Frederick Temple, afterwards Bishop of
London and Archbishop of Canterbury, had to fight
often, and not always victoriously, in the school combats
which took place at the Ironing Box, as the milling-
ground was called. Blackmore, four years his junior,
became the fag of Temple, who was ' a beast and a
brute ' [1] to the young boy in his power. Mr. F. J. Snell
states in his *Blundell's* :

> ' Temple's favourite mode of punishment being to strike
> poor Richard on the head with a brass-headed hammer. When
> both were well on in years, Temple referred to this practice
> with some glee, as if it was a proper subject for humour.
> Blackmore, on the contrary, detested that sort of victimisation,
> and detested Temple, not only then, but always.'

Although he was unhappy at the school, Blackmore
became head boy, and in due course passed on to Exeter
College, Oxford. Like his father before him, he was a
classical scholar ; but his undergraduate pursuits also
included angling and nature study, and chess, which was
a life-long recreation.

In 1847, when with a reading-party at St. Helier, in
Jersey, he met a young Irish lady, Lucy Maguire, whom
he married in 1852, after some trouble with his clerical
relatives over the fact that his bride was a Roman
Catholic, for such religious differences were far more
agitating in those days of Newman and Dr. Pusey than

---

[1] The Archbishop of York has recently related the true version of
the Rugby school-boy's definition of his father. It was not ' He is
a beast—but he is a just beast ' : the words written were ' He may
be a beast and a brute, but he is a fair one.'

in the present latitudinarian times. However, Blackmore's marriage proved an exceedingly happy one, and his wife's death, thirty-six years later, was an abiding grief to the survivor.

In this same year, 1852, Blackmore, intending to follow the profession of the Law, was called to the Bar, and practised as a conveyancer. (Some reflections of his legal time can be traced in his novel *Christowell*.) But owing to the epileptic troubles bequeathed from Blundell's School he was soon compelled to relinquish office work, and turned to the more open-air life of an assistant schoolmaster. Accordingly he and his wife left their lodgings in the north of London for others at Hampton Wick when Blackmore obtained a post at Wellesley House School,[1] situated in the Hampton Road, then (1853) a rural and outlying portion of the scattered parish of Twickenham. The head-master was T. J. Scalé, to whose memory, later on, *Cradock Nowell* was dedicated.

During this period Blackmore commenced his literary career by the publication of two little volumes of poetry. Both appeared in 1854 and were anonymous. The first was entitled *Poems by Melanter*, and the second *Epullia*, which contained, in addition to various verses on the topical Crimean War,[2] the prophetic lines ' To My Pen ' :

> ' . . . Thou shalt be more to me
> Than sword or golden sceptre's reach ;
> With mind, and soul, and heart in thee
> To please, and purify, and teach :
> However poor I be.'

R. D. Blackmore had added his name to the list of notable men who have abandoned the lucrative pro-

---

[1] The house, or the site of it, is now incorporated in the Metropolitan and City Police Orphanage, and the name of the school is preserved in the adjoining Wellesley Road, which runs from Hampton Road to Strawberry Hill station.

[2] It is interesting to note that George Meredith's first published piece of work was also a poem on a topical battle—*Chillianwallah*, which appeared in *Chambers's Edinburgh Journal*, July, 1849.

fession of the Law for the Lily and Rue Paths of Literature—Walter Scott, Disraeli, R. S. Surtees, Harrison
Ainsworth, Wilkie Collins, G. A. Lawrence, Charles
Reade, Sheridan Le Fanu, F. C. Burnand, Rider Haggard,
Shirley Brooks, and George Meredith.

In 1857 Blackmore was able to realise his ambition of
combining literary pursuits with the cultivation of fruit
and flowers, for he inherited this year a substantial legacy
from his mother's Knight estate.[1]   His father died in the
following year.   Accordingly he purchased an estate of
eleven acres, in Teddington, which he had often noticed,
and longed to possess, when taking walks in the vicinity
of Wellesley House School.   His new property was in
an extremely charming and sequestered part of South
Middlesex.   Teddington was then a little hamlet by the
Thames, comprising a tiny church, several fine mansions
in large grounds, and a village shop or two—never
dreaming of the years to come when train and trams
would metamorphose it into a London suburb and
popular river-side resort.   The land purchased by Blackmore was some distance away from the river, and bordered
the Udney House estate.   In the other direction, to the
south-west, it was but a short walk (with no intervening
railway line in those days) to Bushy Park, with its magnificent avenue of chestnut trees, designed for William
the Third by Sir Christopher Wren as a stately approach
to Hampton Court Palace from the London side.[2]

[1] The Knights were related to the Turberville family, and R. D.
Blackmore's brother Henry took the name of Turberville or Turverville.   He died in 1875, with some circumstances of mystery, at
Yeovil.   The bulk of his property, valued at £15,000, he had bequeathed to his executor, Charles Bradlaugh, but a subsequent will,
made a few hours before his death, revoked these provisions and
benefited a local person.   R. D. Blackmore joined with Bradlaugh
in a case to secure a verdict of intestacy against the second will.
The matter was eventually settled in 1876, Charles Bradlaugh receiving £2,500, in addition to his costs.

[2] As I have indicated, there was no railway when Blackmore first
came to Teddington, and it was a great annoyance to him, some

In this truly delightful spot—though but a few miles from London—let us picture Blackmore supervising the planting of his orchards of pears, apples, and standard peaches (a novelty in England then), planting his roses and strawberry beds, building his long vineries and, in the midst, the small, unpretentious but comfortable, mid-Victorian house wherein he was to live for the remainder of his life and to write practically all his novels—in the little south study upstairs, in front, shaded by the great magnolia tree.   He called his home Gomer House, after a dog bearing that name he had owned in his youth. Blackmore wrote *Lorna Doone* and nearly all the other novels on a little knee-hole writing-desk, with tiers of small drawers at each side, a desk which the Victorians called an escritoire.   This one is carefully preserved at Gomer House.

Blackmore's life here was a happy, idyllic one.   He wrote when and as it pleased him, without any financial necessity to do so, and for forty years he witnessed the recurring miracle of spring when his fruit orchards were a vision of loveliness in bloom.   In summer the rich fruits piled his tables.   In autumn the foliage blazed with harmonious colour—' differently coloured torches held up in our woods,' as Meredith would have said.   In winter all the exquisite network and tracery of the bare branches were as a veil across the setting red winterly sun or the crescent moon.   Best of all, Blackmore loved his gardens in their early burgeoning of spring when the trees and shrubs emerged from their long winter sleep

---

years later, when the line from Twickenham to Kingston was made. The Company acquired by compulsory powers a portion of his land on which to build Teddington station and the portion of the track that now runs by Gomer House.   But, no doubt, as time went on, Blackmore appreciated the convenience of the station near his house, enabling his friends to visit him expeditiously.   He rarely went to London himself, or away on visits.   In the spring of 1894 he stayed for a few weeks at Southwold, in Suffolk, and it was there I first met him and his wife's nieces, the Misses Pinto-Leite.

R. D. BLACKMORE
In the garden of Gomer House, from a photograph sent by Miss Pinto-Leite
By kind permission of *The Bookman*

with the promise of glorious summer life. Thus he pictured it in *Cripps the Carrier* :

' Little fluttering, timid things, that meant to be leaves, please God, some day, but had been baffled and beaten so that their faith had shrunk to hope ; little rifts of cover also keeping beauty coiled inside, and ready to open, like a bivalve shell, to the pulse of the summertide, and then to be sweet blossom ; and the ground below them pressing upward with ambition of young green ; and the sky above them spread with liquid blue behind white pillows.'

But *Cripps the Carrier* is sixteen years ahead, and we are still in 1860. In this year Blackmore issued the first work to bear his name on the title page—*The Fate of Franklin*, a poem, the receipts from the sales being given to the fund for erecting a statue of the explorer in his native town of Spilsby. In 1862 there followed *The Farm and Fruit of Old*, an appropriately-named translation of the First and Second *Georgics* of Virgil.

' Indulgence have ye for a gardener's dream,
 (A man with native melody unblest),
 How patient toil and love that does its best,
Clouds though there be, may follow the sun-beam :
But yonder to my amethysts and gold,
 So please you—grapes and apricots constrain
 These more accustomed hands : unless you deign
To tend with me the " kine and bees of old." '

He was disappointed with the response to his appeal, yet nearly ten years later he issued translations of the Third and Fourth *Georgics* prefaced with an ' Apology ' :

' Ten years of trouble and mistaken scope,
 Since first I dared the " Farm and Fruit of Old,"
 O'er me and my unfruitful farm have roll'd
To prune audacity, and weed out hope. . . . '

But during that decade he had been writing novels and was about to join hands with great and abiding fame in *Lorna Doone*.

Blackmore's first novel, *Clara Vaughan*, appeared

anonymously in 1864. It was—and remains—an excellent example of the sensational romance of murder and ' ghosts,' the scene being laid in Gloucestershire. It was the decade when sensational novels of this type were most in demand. Wilkie Collins set the fashion with *The Woman in White* (1860), followed by *Armadale* and *The Moonstone*; Sheridan Le Fanu rivalled him during 1862-1864 with *The House by the Churchyard*, *Wylder's Hand*, and *Uncle Silas*; Miss Braddon was not far behind, in 1862, with *Lady Audley's Secret*—indeed she was the pioneer of the series when she blazed the trail with the first form of *The Trail of the Serpent*; Mrs. Henry Wood leaped to fame with *East Lynne* in 1862; Dickens supported and supplied the sensational demand with *Great Expectations* (1860-1861), and more so with *The Mystery of Edwin Drood*; and even the hypercritical George Meredith, as reader to Chapman and Hall, advised Thomas Hardy, in 1868-1869, to write a novel with a *sensational* plot, which Hardy duly produced in the form of *Desperate Remedies*.

Concerning *Clara Vaughan*, Blackmore in after years told Mrs. Alfred Hunt : ' I think you have never seen my fundamentally Corsican story—*Clara Vaughan*. . . . It was my first work in prose ; and of course is full of faults, as indeed the rest are.'

Blackmore did not continue in this particular popular vein, for his next novel, *Cradock Nowell* (1866), a tale of the New Forest, was remarkable chiefly for its formality and erudition with much classical allusion. It contained a charming heroine in Amy Rosedew, and John Rosedew was a portrait of the author's uncle, the Rev. H. H. Knight. The name Cradock Nowell was suggested by that of a former owner of Nottage Court ; Blackmore, as a child, used to gaze at this worthy's monument in Newton Church, Glamorganshire, to beguile the tedium of long services.

Now comes *Lorna Doone* (1869), the one book by which Blackmore is remembered by the majority of his countrymen. As has been the case with many masterpieces, this

story was declined by several publishers at the outset—
' all the magazines rejected her, and Smith and Elder
refused to give £200 for the copyright,' as Blackmore
himself related. Happily, wiser publishers were found
in Sampson Low and Marston ; but the first edition, in
three volumes, was a failure. Nearly two years went by,
until in 1871 Princess Louise (daughter of Queen Victoria)
married the Marquis of Lorne. Someone started the
idea that the book called *Lorna Doone*, which made some
mention of an Earl of Lorne, concerned the family of the
noble bridegroom of the moment. There was a rush of
orders for the novel ; the one volume edition of 1872
was brought out ; *The Saturday Review* at long last condescended to review it ; and the publisher came down
post haste to Teddington to announce to Blackmore that
Lorna Doone was going to have ' a run.' It has ' run '
ever since—for sixty years—and has appeared in count-
less editions. Blackmore always rather resented the
popular fame of this one novel to the exclusion of his
numerous other books ; perhaps his artistic sense was
offended by the fact that this really fine romance only
secured belated recognition by the chance association of
its name with a royal marriage. Anyway, he said to his
friend, Mr. James Baker : ' It's a pity the book was ever
written, a pity it cannot be destroyed.' [1] And on
another occasion he wrote : ' There is something rather
childish in *Lorna Doone*. I think, perhaps, taken altogether, *Alice Lorraine* is the best.' It is perfectly true
that Blackmore by no means considered *Lorna Doone* his
best novel. In addition to *Alice Lorraine* he also placed
before it, in his own estimation, *The Maid of Sker* and
Springhaven. And in literary merit he reckoned first his
early translation from Virgil, *The Farm and Fruit of Old*,
for he wrote :

' That translation of the " Georgics " (from which I never
got a penny, but paid myself for the venture) is the best thing
I ever did. It is not perfect, I needn't say that, but it is full of

[1] R. D. *Blackmore* ; *The Fortnightly Review*, May, 1904.

good work and lucky turns, and true love of the subject. . . . In none of my books have I satisfied myself.'

Of course, Blackmore's later verbal strictures upon *Lorna Doone* must not be taken too seriously. At the bottom of his heart he appreciated the book's deserved success, and the money it brought him repaid the losses on his fruit-growing. He had no training or aptitude for business, and the fruit generally involved him in an exorbitant annual loss, although at one time he had a stall at Covent Garden Market for its disposal. He said he had tried to sell fruit for thirty years, and 'lost some £20,000 which might have saved me from the ink-bottle.' So in the preface to the sixth edition of *Lorna Doone* (1873) Blackmore wrote :

'Nothing has more pleased me than the great success of this simple tale . . . any son of Devon may imagine, and will not grudge, the writer's delight at hearing from a recent visitor to the West, that *Lorna Doone*, to a Devonshire man, is as good as clotted cream almost.'

Further, a quarter of a century later, in his penultimate book, *Tales from the Telling House* (1896), Blackmore returned to his famous subject and offered a story called *Slain by the Doones*. What's in a name ? A great deal. As Miss Edith Shackleton has truly said :

'*Lorna Doone* ! How Blackmore must have whooped with joy when he evolved that super-romantic name. It is a potted ode, containing the echo and essence of the most glamorous phrases in our language.'

The glamour of romance is indeed the misty veil of *Lorna Doone*. It is pre-eminent for its description of the wild and beautiful scenery of Exmoor, which Blackmore even elaborated by the power of his perceptive imagination. Visitors to Exmoor have expressed disappointment at the inadequate hollow which is pointed out to them as ' The Doone Valley,' for it is by no means commensurate with the great spaces and romantic glooms of

the outlaws' retreat in the novel. Further, too strong a
faith in the actual existence of the lawless Doones of the
seventeenth century had better not be entertained,
because the historians *will* shatter all romantic beliefs in
these days—if they can. Over twenty years ago Mr.
E. J. Rawle explored the legends of Exmoor, and proved
that a first attempt to collect them was made in 1834, the
chief source of information being a reputed witch, an old
woman named Ursula Johnson. In 1857 there appeared
an article in *Fraser's Magazine* relating the legend of the
Doones seizing an infant and eating it, and the tale of
the highwayman, Tom Faggus, and his strawberry horse.
In September-October, 1863, a crude short story was
published in *The Leisure Hour* under the title of *The
Doones of Exmoor*. The period was 1642. This was
read by Blackmore, who acknowledged that he ' obtained
in it the clue for the weaving of his own romance and
which caused him to study the details on the spot,' and,
further, weave romance round Dunkery Beacon for all
time. There have been claimants to descent from the
Doones of Oare [1] and Badgworthy ; but Mr. Rawle declined to accept them and asserted that Doone was simply

[1] Not long after Blackmore died, a lady named Ida Marie Stuart
Browne (' Audrie Doone ') arrived on Exmoor, and announced that
she was seventh in descent from Sir Ensor Doone, the grandfather
of Lorna. She stated that the Doones or Dounes were a Scotch
family descended from James V., and that a certain branch, following
a family feud, settled on Exmoor in exile. Further, that one, Rupert
Doone, of Braemuir, fought for the cause of Prince Charles Edward
in 1745, and that in his journal two years later he recorded a visit to
' a place called Oare, where our people came after their cruel treat-
ment at the hands of Earl Moray.' There was produced a pistol
bearing the inscription, ' C. Doone, 1681,' no doubt the weapon
with which Carver Doone shot Lorna on her wedding-day ! Yet
Blackmore said, ' When I wrote *Lorna Doone* I had not the least idea
it would ever be heard of in Oare parish, for my books had hitherto
obtained scarcely any notice.' This was in explanation to an actual
Nicholas Snow, living in Oare, and Blackmore added he would
never have used the name had he known : ' It is too late now to help
it, and I can only say that I am very sorry, and hope that now you
know the truth, you will forgive such a trespass on your manor.'

a corruption of Dane, and that memories of the ancient Danish marauders of the Bristol Channel shores were still handed down in the seventeenth century and adapted to local romance and local romantic scenery.

Despite his sudden fame, Blackmore's life and tastes did not change. Some fifty-five years ago, Julian Hawthorne was living at Twickenham, and he relates in his *Shapes that Pass* how he went over to Teddington with an idea of interviewing Blackmore, though that ' art ' was then in its infancy :

' All I wanted was to see my enchanting author and hear his voice. . . . But I felt afraid, and he was as shrinking as the sensitive plant which stood beside us as we tried to talk ; and I didn't remember to speak of *Lorna Doone*, which I was so full of, nor he of *The Scarlet Letter*, of which, in his confusion, he may have thought I was the author. . . . He, a homely man of about fifty, looked in his shirt-sleeves more like a gardener than the Oxford scholar, barrister, and romancer that he was. He said that gardening came easier to him than writing—" though when I get into a story it's hard to get out. But I like to put some garden truck in my waggon and drive in at dawn to Covent Garden Market. . . . " I saw him at a Lord Mayor's dinner a few years later, and admired the good luck that enabled him to avoid making a speech ; he contrived to insinuate Black, who sat beside him, into the breach, and the toast-master, getting the names mixed, passed over Blackmore.

Blackmore followed his great romance with another excellent novel, *The Maid of Sker* (1872), which combined memories of the two districts where he spent his boyhood, Newton, near Porthcawl, and Barnstaple, together with a vivid presentment of life in the Navy. The character of the child Bardie and her quaint sayings were suggested by Mrs. Blackmore's little niece, Eva Pinto-Leite.[1] *Alice Lorraine*, a tale of Steyning and the South

---

[1] On one occasion, when Eva Pinto-Leite was a tiny girl, she went up to Blackmore's study (where he generally liked to have her with him). He said, ' You must be very quiet to-day, as I have to write something very important.' Upon which the child seized a piece of paper and began scrawling scribbles and dashes, saying, ' I can yite also, like you's doing.'

Downs in the time of the Peninsular War, followed in
1875 ; *Cripps the Carrier*, which has some scenes in
Oxford, came in 1876 ; *Erema, or My Father's Sin*, in
1877 ; and *Mary Anerley* in 1880.

Erema was not very well received, and Blackmore
seems to have had some difficulty in obtaining satisfactory terms for his next book, *Mary Anerley*, for he
wrote to Mr. Marston, in January, 1879 :

' *Mary Anerley* seems, as you say, to be at a discount without
anybody having seen her, and I suppose *Erema* (which was
mauled by some of the critics) has pulled down my value. . . .
The story is cast on a large scale and written with more than
my usual care. A page a day is my maximum. It is a very
quiet tale so far, but will have plenty of incident. It will bear
more resemblance to *Lorna Doone* than my other works. I
take to the poor thing all the more for her evil fortunes. But
for you, *Lorna Doone* might never have seen the light. . . .
Thank Heaven, I have plenty of self-confidence, simply because
I know good work when I see it, and pretty soon condemn
work—though my own—when it is scampish. . . . And I
certainly do sympathise with unmitigated defiance—the which
I hereby hurl at all who despise *Mary Anerley* without seeing
her.'

In *Christowell* (1882) can be found some aspects of
Blackmore himself as ' Captain Larks '—with his ' shaggy
eyebrows, soft blue eyes . . . his back was as straight as
a soldier's in drill ; his legs were stout and steadfast,' as
were the author's. The early description of the long
vinery might well be that of the one at the back of Gomer
House. *The Remarkable History of Tommy Upmore* (1884)
contains a portrait of Blackmore's greatest friend, Sir
Richard Owen. *Springhaven* (1887), a tale of the Great
War with Napoleon, is one of the author's best novels,
and in it he expressed his life-long interest in Nelson.
Springhaven—presumably Newhaven—pictures the coast
of Sussex between Beachy Head and Selsey Bill. The
edition of 1888 contained a number of delightful illustrations by Alfred Parsons and Fred Barnard. In his
preface Blackmore commented on the absence of material

or stories relating to the threatened invasion of England by Napoleon in the first years of the nineteenth century : he had overlooked *The Trumpet-Major*, by Thomas Hardy, which appeared in 1880, and the same writer's *A Tradition of Eighteen Hundred and Four*. Blackmore received £900 for *Springhaven*, which he thought poor pay. He wrote : ' I have laboured for three years at *Springhaven*, getting up my subject with great mental sweat ; and the English maximum for three years' labour is to be £900.' He wanted £1200 for the English and American serial rights of a story at this date.

Springhaven, as I have indicated, is a fine historical novel which deserves resuscitation, and so, for other reasons, does *Kit and Kitty* (1890), a tale of West Middlesex, for in this book Blackmore gives the most complete portrait of himself as ' Uncle Corny,' the market gardener and peach-grower. This is the novel that reflects the author's greatest interest in life, and though the scene is laid principally at Sunbury, all the country round Teddington—from Hanworth and Halliford to Twickenham and Turnham Green—comes into it. *Perlycross* appeared in 1894, and the clergyman in it pictures Blackmore's father at Culmstock, in Devon, where he held a curacy at one time and where Frederick Temple, the future Archbishop, was his pupil. *Fringilla*, a book of verse, was published in 1895 ; and Blackmore's last novel, *Dariel* (1897) described Surrey and the alien land of the Caucasus.

Such was the varied literary work of R. D. Blackmore, but, as I have pointed out, he ever considered it secondary to his skill as a horticulturist and fruit-grower. Writing to his publisher, Mr. Edward Marston, he said :

' My vines are going on gloriously, white bunches hang like water-spouts, and black ones like far thunder clouds. All things know my hand, and surely how much better is the grape than the gall, the fruit of the vine than the famine of the pen. . . . Anyone looking at my vines would say, " This is your rôle, my good fellow, stick to it. Any ass can write novels (at least in the opinion of the publishers) ; but to make a vine needs intellect." '

He seems to have been dissatisfied with his great achievement in literature for he used to say that when a boy his grandfather warned him, ' Story telling never answers in the end ' : and he would humorously add, ' Oh ! how could he thus foresee my fate ! '

Mr. Marston, in his *After Work*, gave a charming picture of Blackmore at home in his garden. The publisher with his son and grandchildren spent the day at Gomer House :

' It was a time when his beautiful gardens and lawns were at their best, with fruit trees laden with apples and pears, strawberries and cherries in luscious abundance, apricots and peaches as plentiful as blackberries. . . . Here it was, in the midst of all these glories, that Mr. Blackmore romped with the children on the lawn. He had a beautiful little pony, and it was a sight to see him mounting the children one by one . . . and leading them about and all round the grounds. He seemed to be perfectly happy, and he made us all happy.'

Blackmore was always attached to children and animals ; to women his manner was gentle and chivalrous, though his was a self-centred, somewhat autocratic nature. He was caustic and shrewd in humour. He had a humorous dislike for printers and printers' readers whom he would term his ' inveterate foes '—' of such is the kingdom of fools . . . see my remarks which are much too mild. I cut off strong language from bottom last time, *stet* everything beginning with a D now.' For reviewers his dislike had more justification in view of the fact that not one, apparently, perceived the future fame of *Lorna Doone*. He said there ' are no critics now,' only reviewers : ' It is amusing to see how flatly they contradict one another, saving their author the trouble of reply ; and above all, in my case, exalting to the skies a book themselves, or their fathers, had not a good word for, when it had to be transported to Botany Bay for want of a friend in England.'

He was not a man of wide male friendships and he knew but few of his great literary contemporaries.

Thomas Hardy, however, on one occasion, about 1875, visited him at Gomer House. Blackmore had some skill with the lathe, and he made several sets of chess, his favourite game. His mornings were always devoted to his garden and fruit trees, and when he wrote it was in the afternoon. His favourite reading included the works of Virgil, Homer, Shakspere, Matthew Arnold, and Thackeray. There is not much evidence in his own books to show he took any profound interest in the mystic and occult : yet one night, in the winter of 1878, he had a remarkable dream a few days after attending the funeral of a very dear relative, his aunt, Mrs. Gordon (née Knight). He dreamed he was again at this funeral, and he heard the mourners sing a curious dirge-like hymn. Contrary to the usual experience with dreams, he clearly remembered the words of the hymn on awaking. There were four verses in this strain :

> ' In the hour of death, after this life's whim,
> When the heart beats low, and the eyes grow dim,
> And pain has exhausted every limb—
> The lover of the Lord shall trust in Him.
>
> .   .   .   .   .   .
>
> When the last sigh is heaved and the last tear shed,
> And the coffin is waiting beside the bed,
> And the widow and child forsake the dead,
> The angel of the Lord shall lift his head.' [1]

Blackmore's last years were saddened by loss and pain. The death of his wife in 1888 was a terrible blow. He wrote to Mr. Marston :

' At present I am lost and wandering, having nothing to live for. . . . I am cast into the wilderness at 62. . . . all the spring of my mind seems gone.'

He suffered from sciatica, and could only write with great pain. He was threatened with paralysis and lost

---

[1] See *The Athenæum*, July 3rd, 1909. Blackmore sent a copy of the lines to Keningale Cook (son-in-law of his friend, Mortimer Collins), with permission to print them—' only please not to put my name beyond initials or send me money for them,' he wrote.

the use of his left arm in 1887 ; but his late wife's nieces took every care of him, and he recovered to spend some happy years in their society.   In 1894 (the year he stayed in Southwold), he wrote to Mr. Marston : ' The finest fellows in London told me that I should never walk again, a year and a half ago, but lo, though not like you, I can " feel my feet again ".'

> ' What thumping fees they charged.   Oh, laws !
>   For " best advice procurable,"
> But now my hopes revive, because
>   I am pronounced incurable.'

In his final illness his terrible sufferings were patiently borne.   R. D. Blackmore died at Gomer House on January 20th, 1900—the same day as Ruskin (who was six years his senior)—and was buried in the cemetery at Teddington.   Later, a memorial window in Exeter Cathedral was unveiled by Mr. Eden Phillpotts.   The tablet underneath, in addition to names and dates, bore this appropriate quotation from ' Cradock Nowell ' :

' He added Christian courtesy, and the humility of all thoughtful minds, to a certain grand and glorious gift of radiating humanity.' [1]

A few years ago I revisited Gomer House at Teddington.   Many inevitable changes have taken place there ; the eleven acres of fruit orchards have dwindled to three, and little suburban red villas now press and peep in on two sides where once was absolute seclusion.   But once again it was spring, in early May, with the fruit trees snowing exquisite blossom—though he who planted and

---

[1] The memorial tablet to the commemoration of R. D. Blackmore in the sequestered little church of Oare, Exmoor, which was put up in 1928, in addition to these words bears the following tribute from the pen of his friend, A. J. Munby :

> ' Story and Humour, and the Rhythmic Roll
> Of antique lore, his fertile fancies swayed,
> And with their various eloquence arrayed
> His sterling English, pure and clean and whole.'

loved them has been gone from the scene for more than thirty years. And I remembered a sentence from a letter written by Blackmore twenty-eight years agone to the actual day : ' The prime of the pear-bloom is past, and the walks snowed over with petals '—sad symbol of Life's brief day of beauty and joy.

LIST OF WORKS BY R. D. BLACKMORE

By the courtesy of my friend, Miss Pinto-Leite, the following particulars are taken from Blackmore's personal copies of the first editions of his books which are still preserved at Gomer House, Teddington.

1 POEMS / by / MELANTER / London / Robert Hardwicke, 38, Carey Street / 1854. Limp maroon cover.

CONTENTS :

Eric and Karine, A Swedish Drama.	TRANSLATIONS.
Mount Arafa, A Moslem Legend.	*Hylas.*
St. Paul at Athens.	*Cyclops.*
Poor Englishman !	*Clouds.*
The Fleet at Spithead.	*Love.*
Epitaph on a Tortoise.	From Shakespeare.
	Song.
	From Milton.

In this copy Blackmore has written ' For Lorna Melanter Armstrong's copy :

' On this 29th day of November, my dear,
You will have beholden the light for a year ;
As your shadow extends, may no shadows arise,
But the light of intelligence grow in your eyes,
Until, with those gentle eyes gazing above,
Yourself are the light, and the life, and the love.
November, 1883.'

Poems by Melanter is a very scarce work. A copy presented by the author to a former school-master of his and inscribed, ' Rev. H. Sanders. With compts. of a former alumnus of Tiverton School,' was on sale (1930) at £38.

2. EPULLIA / By the Author of / ' Poems by Melanter ' London / Hope and Co., 16, Great Marlborough Street / 1854. Paper cover, rebound in dark blue cloth.

The original binding is dark green limp cloth, lettered in gold, *Epullia, 1854.*

CONTENTS :

Lyril Mohun, A Tale of Torbay.	*A Harvest Song,* 1854.
Lita of the Nile.	*A Cuckoo Song.*
A November Dream.	*Hero and Leander*—A Transla-
The Fleet at Spithead, 1853.	tion (from Musæus).
(7 verses).	*The Battle of the Alma.*
The Fleet in the Black Sea, 1854.	*To My Pen.*

3. THE / BUGLE OF THE BLACK SEA / OR / THE BRITISH IN THE EAST / by / Melanter / [Latin line] / London / Robert Hardwicke, 26, Duke Street, Piccadilly / 1855. Yellow pictorial boards.

Contents comprise twenty-one Poems, including reprints of the topical *The Fleet at Spithead* (with three additional verses) and *The Fleet in the Black Sea,* and *The Battle of the Alma.*

Inscribed : ' Lucy Blackmore, Jany. 10, 1855.'

4. THE / FATE OF FRANKLIN / By / Richard Doddridge Blackmore / of Exeter College, Oxon, M.A., and of the Middle Temple / [Two Greek lines] / In Aid of the / Spilsby Fund for Erecting a Statue of Franklin / in his Native Town / London / Robert Hardwicke, 192, Piccadilly / 1860. Price Half a Crown. Green cardboard cover. This is a poem.

In the Preface it is observed : ' If the candid purchaser finds nothing to please him in this little Work, let him fall back upon a purer thought, that he has contributed to the honour of the brave.'

5. THE / FARM AND FRUIT OF OLD / A Translation in Verse of the / First and Second Georgics / of Virgil / By a Market-Gardener / London / Sampson Low, Son and Co. / 47, Ludgate Hill / 1862. Grey-green paper cover.

' Preface ' in verse : ' C—— Garden, 1862.'

In later years this work was reissued as

THE / GEORGICS OF VIRGIL / Translated by / R. D. Blackmore, M.A. / Coll. Exon, Oxon / Author of *Lorna Doone,* etc. / London / Sampson Low, Sons, and Marston / Crown Buildings, Fleet Street / 1871. This includes, in addition to the original work, Translations of the Third and Fourth Books. ' Apology ' in verse, 1871. Black cover with gold design.

' To the Rev. Charles Williams, D.D., Principal of Jesus College, Oxford, this little work is, under kind permission, dedicated by a grateful admirer of his scholarship and learning.'

Cheaper edition, 1886, has red cover.

6. CLARA VAUGHAN / A Novel / In Three Volumes / London and Cambridge / Macmillan and Co. / 1864.   Blue covers.

7. CRADOCK NOWELL / A Tale of the New Forest / By / Richard Doddridge Blackmore / Author of *Clara Vaughan* / [Line from *As You Like It*] / In Three Volumes / London / Chapman and Hall, 193, Piccadilly / 1866.   Green covers.

' To the Memory of my dear Friend, Thomas James Scalé. This work (in which, from month to month, he took the kindest interest) is in gratitude affectionately dedicated. R. D. B.'

8. LORNA DOONE / A Romance of Exmoor / By R. D. Blackmore / Author of *Cradock Nowell* / [Four lines of Greek] / In Three Volumes / London / Sampson Low, Son, and Marston / Crown Buildings, 188, Fleet Street / 1869.   Blue watered covers.   Preface, 1869.

There have been, of course, many subsequent editions of *Lorna Doone*, some of them finely illustrated, the thirty-ninth appearing in 1893.   The Preface to the twentieth edition of 1882 is of interest.

9. THE / MAID OF SKER / By / R. D. Blackmore / Author of . . . / In Three Volumes / William Blackwood and Sons / Edinburgh and London / 1872.   Blue covers.

Inscribed to ' Lucy Blackmore, Withypool, August 2nd, 1872.'

10. ALICE LORRAINE / A Tale of the South Downs / By / Richard Doddridge Blackmore / Author of . . . / [Two Lines of Greek] / In Three Volumes / London / Sampson Low, Marston, Low, and Searle / Crown Buildings, 188, Fleet Street / 1875.   Blue covers.

' To Professor Owen, C.B., F.R.S., With the Writer's gratitude, for words of true encouragement and many acts of kindness, this Work most heartily is dedicated.   April, 1875.'

11. CRIPPS THE CARRIER / A Woodland Tale / By / Richard Doddridge Blackmore / Author of . . . / [Four lines of Greek] / In Three Volumes / London / Sampson Low, Marston, Searle, and Rivington, Crown Buildings, 188, Fleet Street / 1876.   Light green covers.

12. EREMA, OR / MY FATHER'S SIN / By / R. D. Blackmore / Author of . . . / [Two lines of Greek] / In Three Volumes / London / Smith, Elder, and Co., 15, Waterloo Place / 1877.   Light grey-brown covers.

Inscribed, ' Lucy Blackmore,
From her affectionate husband.
Sept. 29th, 1877.   Bridlington Quay, Yorkshire.'
This story appeared in *The Cornhill Magazine*, November, 1876-November, 1877.
Illustrated by F. D. (Dicksee).

13. MARY ANERLEY / A Yorkshire Tale / By / R. D. Blackmore / Author of . . . / [Four lines of Greek] / In Three Volumes / London / Sampson Low, Marston, Searle, and Rivington / Crown Buildings, 188, Fleet Street / 1880.   Blue covers.

' To my old and valued friend, Arthur Joseph Munby, M.A., F.S.A., of Lincoln's Inn, Barrister-at-Law, and of Clifton Holme, near York, this book, owing much to his kind aid, is gratefully dedicated.'

A. J. Munby (1828-1910) was the author of *Verses New and Old*, 1865, and *Dorothy*, 1880, works much praised by Browning for good craftsmanship.

14. CHRISTOWELL / A Dartmoor Tale / By / R. D. Blackmore / Author of *Mary Anerley* / ' Splendide mendax ' / In Three Volumes / London / Sampson Low, Marston, Searle, and Rivington / 1882.   Dull red covers.

15. THE REMARKABLE HISTORY / OF SIR THOMAS UPMORE, BART., M.P. / FORMERLY KNOWN AS / ' TOMMY UPMORE '/ [Two lines in Latin] / In Two Volumes / London / Sampson Low, Marston, Searle, and Rivington / Crown Buildings, 188, Fleet Street / 1884.   Blue covers.   The second and similar edition was published in the same year.   Although the author's name does

not appear on title-page or covers, the Preface is signed
R. D. Blackmore.

An edition in one volume followed on March 1st, 1885.

16. SPRINGHAVEN / A Tale of the Great War / By Richard
Doddridge Blackmore / Author of . . . / [One line of
Greek] / In Three Volumes / London / Sampson Low,
Marston, Searle, and Rivington / Crown Buildings,
188, Fleet Street / 1887.   Pale green-grey covers with
pictorial design.

' To the Memory of my revered friend, Paul Hamilton
Hayne, Poet, Patriot, and Philanthropist.'

P. H. Hayne was the author of *Legends and Lyrics*, 1872, and
Poems, 1882, both published in America.

The edition of 1888 has charming illustrations by Alfred
Parsons and Fred Barnard.

17. KIT AND KITTY / A Story of West Middlesex / By / R. D.
Blackmore / Author of . . . / ' Si tu Caia, ego Caius ' /
In Three Volumes / London / Sampson Low, Marston,
Searle, and Rivington, Limited / St. Dunstan's House,
Fetter Lane, Fleet Street, E.C. / 1890. . . .   Pale blue
green covers with butterfly design.

18. PERLYCROSS / A Tale of the Western Hills / By / R. D.
Blackmore / Author of . . . / In Three Volumes /
. London / Sampson Low, Marston and Company /
Limited / St. Dunstan's House, Fetter Lane, Fleet
Street, E.C. / 1894.   Grey-green covers.

19. FRINGILLA / Some Tales in Verse / By Richard Doddridge Blackmore / Pictured by Louis Fairfax Muckley /
With 111 Drawings / by James Linton / [Three lines
of Latin] / London / Published by Elkin Mathews /
In Vigo Street / MDCCCXCV.   Grey pictorial cover.

Blackmore has written in this copy: 'Received from Mr.
Mathews, June 12th, 1895, supposed to be the date of publication.'

Also 25 large paper copies on hand-made paper, bound in
full vellum.

20. TALES FROM THE / TELLING HOUSE / By / R. D. Blackmore / Author of *Lorna Doone* / London / Sampson

Low, Marston and Company, Limited / St. Dunstan's House / 1896. Light brown decorated cover.

CONTENTS :

Slain by the Doones.   *George Bowring.*
Frida ; or the Lover's Leap.   *Crocker's Hole.*

21. DARIEL / A Romance of Surrey / By / R. D. Blackmore / Author of *Lorna Doone* / With Drawings by Chris Hammond / William Blackwood and Sons / Edinburgh and London / 1897. Blue cover.

An American edition was published the same year by Dodd, Mead, and Company, New York. Red cover.

JOSEPH SHERIDAN LE FANU

THE outstanding characteristic of Le Fanu is his amazing literary versatility. As Mr. Edmund Downey has well put it, ' Sober, orderly historical romance ; stories charged with boisterous fun and frolic ; stories of the supernatural, which of their kind have no equal ; stirring ballads ; lyrics full of sweetness and sympathy ; tender love stories ; novels with plot and purpose and passion, alive with creatures of flesh and blood—all were creations of the same brain.' In England, Le Fanu's fame rests upon his stories of the supernatural and of murder, but other aspects of his work are almost unknown. In Ireland he is remembered for his ballads of national aspirations and studies of native character and types. To understand these latter phases of his literary expression it is necessary to look back to the author's origin and boyhood.

The Le Fanu family was of Huguenot race, and the subsequently Irish branch settled in Dublin about 1730. A certain Reverend Thomas Philip Le Fanu had for his mother Alicia Sheridan,[1] sister of Richard Brinsley Sheri-

---

[1] Alicia Sheridan, Mrs. Le Fanu, was the author of the comedy, *Sons of Erin*, 1812, concerning which Lady Morgan wrote :

> ' Dame Comedy so dull hath grown
> She made the town in sadness moan,
> Now to her native spirit true
> She treats us to a LAUGH ANEW.'

The two last words are a pun on the pronunciation by the lower classes in Ireland of Le Fanu as Laffanew.

A niece of this Alicia Le Fanu was also Alicia Le Fanu, daughter of her sister, Elizabeth Sheridan, who married Captain Henry Le Fanu. The younger Alicia was the author of *Strathallan*, 1816, *Leolin Abbey*, 1819, and other novels, and the rather inaccurate *Memoirs of Mrs. Frances Sheridan*, 1824.

dan, and consequently his son, Joseph Sheridan Le Fanu, the future novelist, was a great-grandson of the old actor, Thomas Sheridan, who undoubtedly transmitted to his descendant those histrionic qualities so evident in *The House by the Churchyard*, *Uncle Silas*, and many another dramatic tale—though it is worthy to note in passing that, curiously enough, despite their tragic qualities the books of Le Fanu have but very seldom been dramatised for stage production. The novelist was born on August the 28th, 1814, at the Royal Hibernian Military School in Phœnix Park, Dublin, where his father was at that time Chaplain. His early impressionable years were spent amid most romantic surroundings and traditions, which he was to recall and re-present years later in *The House by the Churchyard*, and the historic sense was implanted in him from the outset. Soldiers still wearing their Waterloo uniforms of a decade before paraded on the Fifteen Acres near his father's house, and duels were still fought here. Even as a boy, despite his high spirits and delight in practical jokes, he showed signs of a reserve and desire for seclusion that in his last years made him a recluse. Although an active, strong boy, he never cared for games and field sports as did his younger brother William, but was of a lonely temperament and preferred nothing better to being left alone to his own devices. Sometimes, when he was unwilling to see visitors, he would retire to a sanctum he had on the roof of the house only to be reached by a ladder, which he would draw up after him, and so be free from all intrusion or pursuit, and at liberty to write down his romantic imaginings, for naturally he essayed to write at a very youthful age.

In 1826, when Joseph Le Fanu was twelve years of age, the family removed to Abington, in the county Limerick, of which place his father had become rector, in addition to holding the Deanery of Emly. Joseph was ever a lover of practical jokes, and one of the earliest perpetrated by himself and his brother, William, occurred at Abington Rectory. There was a huge watch-dog there of uncertain temper ; one time he would be playful as a kitten, and another as ferocious as a lion. One day when the dog's mood was mild, the boys decided to dress him up in some ancient garments they had discovered in a cupboard. Accordingly Carlo was attired in an old blue cloth tail-coat, ornamented with brass buttons, while a green cocked-hat was placed on his head. Enjoying the joke, the dog pranced up and down in his finery, but when the boys tried to divest him of his clothes he showed fight and turned on his savage mood, for all the world like a canine Jekyll and Hyde. Finally he set himself down by the front steps, snarling, and there the boys had to leave him. Some time later, the Dean, chancing to look out of one of the front windows, noticed that a large number of people were assembled outside the gate, all gazing in the direction of the hall-door, and laughing heartily. He went out, and found the masquerading dog to be the cause of the excitement, but all his efforts to remove the animal were in vain. Both lost their tempers, and the Dean's annoyance was increased by the fact that every idler of the neighbourhood was assembled to witness the contest. The dog won, and remained on the steps in his fancy dress for days, having much the appearance of a dishevelled reveller from a ball shut out from his own door. As Le Fanu used to say, when telling this story, the vain hound of Abington set the fashion for a philosophy of clothes long before Carlyle's Teufelsdröckh evolved his system.

The Le Fanu boys used to play all manner of jokes upon their good-natured father. On one occasion Joseph, who was always habitually late for morning prayers, did not appear until ten o'clock, when his father, taking out his watch, said to the young delinquent, ' I ask you very seriously, Joseph, is this right ? ' ' No, Sir,' replied his son, ' I'm sure it must be fast.' It was Joseph, too, who added a postscript, imitating his handwriting, to a letter written by his father, causing Curry, the Dublin bookseller, to endeavour to procure for the

Dean an entirely imaginary and non-existent volume entitled Dodd's *Holy Curate*.   But what delighted the boys
most of all was a mis-adventure which befell their father
in Dublin.   The Dean, arrayed in knee-breeches, shovel
hat, and apron, was walking home one Sunday from the
Chapel Royal at Dublin Castle, where he had preached.
It was a winter's day of hard frost, and as he passed along
the foot-path around St. Stephen's Green, where in
frosty weather boys always made slides, the stately cleric
accidentally stepped on the icy way, slid along it, and
came down on his knees, bursting his breeches in a
critical portion.   An old woman, who was passing,
admonished him in indignant tones : ' Isn't it a shame for
you, you old blackguard, to be making slides to knock
decent people down ?   You ought to be took up by the
police.'   A story which William Le Fanu told in later
years to Thackeray, who used it in *Punch* with a little
drawing of his own.

Typically Irish adventures and vituperative language
were common in those days, and another experience dear
to the Le Fanus was one that befell Anthony Trollope
when he was in Ireland, and which he thus related to
William :

About 1845 he had been ordered to proceed to a
remote village in the west, to make inquiries respecting
some irregularities in the post-office there.   After a
tiring journey, he arrived late in the afternoon at his
destination, where he had to put up at a small inn, the
only place of the kind that the village possessed.   His
bedroom was approached by a flight of steps, half stairs,
half ladder.   The room was scantily furnished, but it
contained two beds close together.   Weary after his long
coach journey, Trollope retired early ; he tried to fasten
his door, but found it had neither lock nor bolt.   He
went to bed, feeling nervous and uncomfortable in this
remote, wild place, and strange bedroom.   At last he
fell into an uneasy, restless doze.   Suddenly he was
aroused by the sound of stealthy footsteps approaching

him. Frightened and only half awake, Trollope sprang
from his bed, seized the intruder, and found himself
grappling with a powerful man, clad, like himself, only
in a night-shirt, whom he grasped so tightly by the
throat that he could not speak. In the struggle they came
to the open door, where Trollope thrust out his an-
tagonist, who stumbled and fell down the ladder-stairs.
Aroused by the noise of the combat, the inmates of the
inn rushed into the lower room with a light, when Trollope heard his landlady cry out : ' Oh, boys, that
murderin' villain upstairs has killed his Raverence.'
' We'll soon settle the bloody sassenach,' cried the men,
rushing to the steps ; and but for the intervention of the
half-strangled priest, who had by now somewhat recovered, Trollope would no doubt have been murdered.
When peace was established, explanations made, apolo-
gies offered and accepted, it transpired that the parish
priest had been to a remote part of his cure, and being
benighted had decided to remain at the inn for the rest
of the night. Hearing that an English gentleman was
occupying the other bed in the only guest-chamber, the
priest went up and undressed as noiselessly as possible.
He was creeping very quietly to his bed when Trollope
awoke, with the consequences related. Fortunately the
genial priest was not injured by his fall, and he and
Trollope became fast friends.

At Abington, where, as I have said, Joseph Le Fanu
spent most of his boyhood, there was constant excitement, and often danger, when, in 1831, came the Tithe
troubles. Both Le Fanu's sister and brother were stoned,
and the Rectory people were well armed. One day
William Le Fanu and a cousin, Robert Flemyng, when
out riding were saluted by a considerable crowd with
cries of ' Down with the Orangemen ! Down with the
Tithes ! ' A cart was pushed across the road, but the
boys drew their pistols and got away under a shower of
stones. A quarter of a mile further on they came upon
another band of the disaffected who flung volley after

volley of stones. The boys were covered with blood, but fortunately were not stunned. Then, as William Le Fanu relates in his *Seventy Years of Irish Life*, one of the men armed with a spade ' made a tremendous blow at me ; it missed me, but struck the horse just behind the saddle. The spade was broken by the violence of the blow. Down went the horse on his haunches, but was quickly up again, and on we went. Had he fallen, I should not have been alive many minutes ; he brought me safely home, but never recovered, and died soon afterwards.'

Despite these unpleasant experiences, Joseph Le Fanu loved and sympathetically understood the lawless, wild peasantry around his home, and the peasants loved him and his family when not led astray and blinded by political passion. One of these Limerick boys, who had been fishing attendant to the Le Fanus, was anxious to emigrate to America, and when William sent him a few pounds towards his passage money, he received the following reply :

' Honoured Sir, God bless you for what you sent me. If I gets on I'll send as much back : but if I dies, plaze God I'll meet you in the Lizzum fields, and pay your honour then. But any way you always have the prayers of your humble servant,   MICHAEL BRIEN.

P.S.—Is there any one here that ever done anything to injure or offend you, that your honour would like anything to be done to ? I'd like to do something for your honour before I goes, to show how thankful I am.'

However, William Le Fanu did not engage the sanguinary services of this youth, who was the same I fancy who replied to a gentleman, when asked how his sick father was : ' Ah, my poor father died last Wednesday, your honour.' ' I'm sorry to hear it,' replied the other. ' It must have been very sudden. What doctor attended him ? ' ' Ah, sir,' said the boy, ' my poor father wouldn't never have a doctor ; he always used to say he'd like to

die a natural death.' Which is capped by another story
of the man in Limerick who went to the undertaker to
order a coffin for Pat Connell. 'Dear me, I'm sorry,'
said the undertaker; 'is poor Pat dead?' 'No, he's
not dead yet,' answered the messenger, 'but he'll die
to-night, for the doctor says he can't live till morning,
and he knows what he gave him.'

Such were the quaint and plaintive people, passionate,
often treacherous and murderous, yet often lovable and
faithful, among whom Le Fanu spent some of his most
impressionable years, whose qualities of mind and
character he grew to understand more truly perhaps than
any other author who has sought to present his humble
fellow-countrymen in poetry and prose. Thus it came
about that in the first phase of his literary career Le Fanu
interpreted the lives and aspirations of the Irish peasantry,
particularly those of Limerick and the neighbouring
counties; and no better vantage ground for his observation could have been found than his home at Abington [1]
in the seething Thirties. Here the faction fights and the
superstitions of the peasantry were of immense interest
to the Le Fanu boys, and here they heard much of—and
perhaps saw—a famous outlaw named Kirby, whose
escapades were the inspiring cause of Joseph Sheridan
Le Fanu's famous ballad of *Shamus O'Brien* in later years.
All through his life he had an innate deep sympathy for
the wild, unruly elements of the Irish character, and at
heart he was ever a Nationalist, though he deprecated
any public movement of reaction tending to violence in
political affairs. His interest in the patriots of his native
land was fostered in early life by his mother (a daughter
of the Rev. W. Dobbin, D.D., of Dublin). She had

[1] The scenery round Abington was, of course, described by Le
Fanu in many of his stories, particularly in *Sir Dominick's Bargain*.
Concerning Le Fanu's humorous sketches of Irish character, such
as *Jim Sulivan's Adventures in the Great Snow*, *The Quare Gander*, and
Billy Malowney's Taste of Love and Glory, Dr. J. S. Crone, President of
the Irish Literary Society, has observed truly, 'they are bubbling
over with true Irish fun and laughter-making episodes.'

known personally some of those who had been executed
for their participation in '98, including the brothers
named Sheares, and she possessed the actual dagger—
venerated by her as a sacred relic—with which Lord
Edward FitzGerald had killed Captain Ryan in that
terrible scene of his capture in Thomas Street, Dublin.
In an apostrophe to the sleeping Muse of Erin, entitled
The O'Donoghue, written when he was about fourteen
years of age, the youthful Joseph Le Fanu cried in this,
one of his earliest, poems :

' Muse of Green Erin, break thy icy slumbers ;
 Strike once again thy wreathed lyre ;
Burst once more and make thy tuneful numbers
 Kindle again thy long-extinguished fire.
Long hast thou slept amidst thy country's sorrow ;
 Darkly thou sets't amid thy country's woes ;
Dawn yet again to cheer a gloomy morrow ;
 Break with the spell of song that long repose.

Fallen thy fair castles, past thy princes' glory ;
 Thy tuneful bards were banished or were slain ;
Some rest in glory on their death-beds gory,
 And some have lived to feel a foeman's chain.
Yet for the sake of thy unhappy nation,
 Yet for the sake of Freedom's spirit fled,
Let thy wild harp-strings, thrilled with indignation,
 Peal a deep requiem o'er thy sons that bled.'

A little later came the ballad on Lord Edward Fitz-
Gerald, which opens with all the poignant pathos of a
Jacobite lament from Scotland :

' The day that traitors sould him and inimies bought him,
The day that the red gold and red blood was paid—
Then the green turned pale and trembled like the dead
 leaves in autumn,
And the heart an' hope iv Ireland in the could grave was
 laid.'

In *Shamus O'Brien*, which was written when Le Fanu
was twenty-six, how finely he voices the point of view

of the young Nationalist, when Shamus replies to the Judge :

‘ My Lord, if you ask me if in my life-time
I thought any threason or did any crime
That would bring to my cheek as I stand alone here
The hot blush of shame or the coldness of fear,
Though I stood by my grave to receive my death blow
Before God and the world I would answer you—No !
But, if you would ask me, as I think it is like,
If in the Rebellion I carried a pike,
An’ fought for ould Ireland from the first to the close
An’ shed the heart’s blood of her bittherest foes,
I answer you—Yes ! An’ I tell you again,
Though I stand here to perish, it’s my glory that then
In her cause I was willin’ my veins should run dhry,
An’ now for her sake I am ready to die.’ [1]

The same sentiments are to be found in Le Fanu’s other great ballad, *Phaudhrig Crohoore*—frankly the Irish version of *Young Lochinvar* :

‘ In his arms he took Kathleen, an’ stepped to the door ;
And he leaped on his horse and flung her before ;
An’ they all were so bothered, that not a man stirred
Till the galloping hoofs on the pavement were heard.

Then up they all started, like bees in the swarm,
An’ they riz a great shout, like the burst of a storm,
An’ they roared and they ran, and they shouted galore ;
But Kathleen and Phaudhrig they never saw more.

But them days are gone by, an’ he is no more ;
An’ the green grass is growin’ o’er Phaudhrig Crohoore,
For he couldn’t be aisy or quiet at all ;
As he lived a brave boy, he resolved so to fall.

And he took a good pike—for Phaudhrig was great—
And he fought, and he died in the year ninety-eight.
And the day that Crohoore in the green field was killed,
A sthrong boy was sthretched, and a sthrong heart was
    stilled.’

[1] The opera based on *Shamus O’Brien* was produced in 1896, the composer, Sir Charles Villiers Stanford, being a cousin of Le Fanu’s wife.

Concurrently with his interest in the peasantry of Ireland, Le Fanu had naturally, being an imaginative boy, from his earliest youth found an equal pleasure in the wild legends, the superstitions, and ghost stories of his native land.   As he said, ' In my youth I heard a great many Irish traditions, more or less of a supernatural character, some of them very peculiar, and all, to a child, at least, highly interesting ' ;   and he goes on to picture the appropriate setting in which he heard these mysterious tales—' the old-fashioned parlour fire-side and its listening circle of excited faces, and, outside, the wintry blast and the moan of leafless boughs, with an occasional rattle of the clumsy old window-frame behind shutter and curtain, as the blast swept by. . . .'

Only a few years were to elapse after his boyhood passed before he wrote down and embellished with supreme artistry these aural tales he had loved in his childhood ;   and then, with increasing power of composition, he went on to the creation of some of the greatest stories of mystery and the supernatural ever written in any language.   As in the case of most imaginative authors, Le Fanu owed a great deal to his irregular education and escape from the hide-bound moulds and individuality-slaying codes of boarding-schools.   He was taught English and French by his father, and the rest of his education was left to the eccentric services of an elderly clergyman named Stinson, who devoted most of his time and attention to piscatorial pursuits, leaving his two pupils to their own devices.   Joseph Le Fanu, having a desire for knowledge on his own lines, read largely and without restriction in his father's well-stocked library, where he found good store of old tomes on demonology, occult and curious lore, which confirmed and cultured his natural inclination to such subjects.   So he passed, in 1833, to Trinity College, Dublin, and his first published ghost story, *The Ghost and the Bone-setter*, appeared in *The Dublin University Magazine*, for January, 1838, when he was twenty-three years of age.   During the next three years this same magazine published twelve further contributions from his pen. *The Fortunes of Sir Robert Ardagh* and *Schalken the Painter* were the first forms of themes, demoniac visitation and Satanic possession, he often returned to in later stories. *Sir Robert Ardagh* is also the first example of Le Fanu's rather curious predilection for presenting a story in successive forms of short, medium, and full length, for he used the theme again in *Sir Dominick's Bargain* and *The Haunted Baronet* (1870). *Passage in the Secret History of an Irish Countess* was the original short form of a story which later was enlarged to *The Murdered Cousin* and finally made a full length appearance as the famous *Uncle Silas*. In the same way, *A Chapter in the History of a Tyrone Family* was years later extended into the novel entitled *The Wyvern Mystery* ; while *Some Account of the Latter Days of the Hon. Richard Marston of Dunoran*, which appeared in *The Dublin University Magazine* in 1848, became somewhat longer as *The Evil Guest* in 1851, and reached three-volume form as *A Lost Name* in 1868. In *The Dublin University Magazine* also appeared Le Fanu's ballads and studies of Irish life. All these early contributions were anonymous, and purported to be transcripts of actual narratives related, by reason of his ghostly office, to Father Francis Purcell, a parish priest of Drumcoolagh, in the south of Ireland, and by him recorded in his private papers. This form of literary hoax was just then much in vogue owing to the brilliant polyglot work of Francis Mahony—figuring as ' Father Prout.' Two other clever Irishmen, William Maginn and Edward Kenealy, also adopted this form of pseudonymous literary contributions ; and in England, Thackeray and Ainsworth wrote under various disguises in their earlier years.

The original ingenuous deception concerning the authorship was elaborated in the eighth Purcell Paper— *Scraps of Hibernian Ballads*—by the introduction of a character named Michael Finley, an Irish minstrel, to whom Le Fanu chose to attribute the authorship of his ballads, including the popular *Phaudhrig Crohoore*, which was here printed for the first time in June, 1839. In so far as Finley had a prototype it was Paddy O'Neill, a fiddler and bag-pipe player, who composed his own songs for the amusement of the passengers on the steamer plying between Limerick and Kilrush ; Le Fanu found much pleasure in the peregrinating Bard's society and songs when staying at Kilkee during summer holidays. *Phaudhrig Crohoore* was written for the author's brother William, who was much given to reciting and asked for 'an Irish *Young Lochinvar*.' For the same purpose Joseph Le Fanu wrote his most famous ballad, *Shamus O'Brien* in 1840. He scribbled it down on scraps of paper which were passed on to William, who as soon as he had learned the song by heart lost the original script. So when, later on, a copy was required for publication it rested with him to write out the ballad from memory, for the author, with typical Irish insouciance, had forgotten his own immortal work. *Shamus O'Brien* was first published in *The Dublin University Magazine* for July, 1850. When Samuel Lover visited America in 1846 he had also obtained a copy of the ballad from William Le Fanu, and he recited it with the greatest success during his reading tour. But he took an unwarrantable liberty with the text ; for popular purposes of 'local colour' for exiled Hibernians dwelling in ' God's Own Country ' he added some lines of his own, in which he made Shamus escape and emigrate to America. Instead of retribution descending on Lover for this inartistic piracy he was rewarded by having the authorship of the entire ballad attributed to him : the correct version, as written by Le Fanu, ends with the line, ' And fined like the devil because Jim done them fairly.'

As before stated, Shamus O'Brien had his prototype in Kirby of the county Limerick ; his mother lived in a cottage, about a mile from Abington Rectory, where the outlaw sometimes ventured to visit her. On one occasion an informer gave the police notice of his presence. As it happened, Kirby's sister was absent at a wake. Night fell, the old mother went to bed, but Kirby remained sitting up by the turf fire, with his pistols on a table beside him. Suddenly he heard the sound of horses' hooves approaching the lonely cottage. He sprang up, awoke his mother, seized his pistols, and said he would kill one of his assailants before he was taken. 'Whist, you fool!' replied the mother. 'Be quick! Put on Mary's cap, jump into bed with your pistols, and turn your face to the wall.' The ruse actually saved him. For when the mother admitted the constables, they searched the cottage, but did not presume to disturb the young 'virgin' who was lying, indisposed, in bed. But Kirby met his death not long after, though not by the hands of the law. The alarm being given of the approach of the police, he ran out of the back-door of the cottage, where he was stopping, into a little wood. He had his loaded pistol in hand, and apparently tripped over some undergrowth, for his weapon went off and he was found dead, shot through the heart. William Le Fanu says, 'I do not recollect a larger funeral than his.'

With literary licence, Joseph Le Fanu placed Kirby —Shamus O'Brien's dwelling in the Glen of Aherlow, a picturesque spot he saw under romantic conditions during a walking-tour in the summer of 1838. He and his friends got lost one weird night of moonlight and fog on the Galtee mountains, when there suddenly galloped past them out of the mist a wild chestnut horse, 'the yalla horse,' which Le Fanu hoped was the phooka, the four-footed demon in equine guise, well-known in the superstitions of the south of Ireland. This pleasant belief alarmed the dwellers in a lonely farm-house on the mountain side who later gave the wanderers shelter by the turf fire and warmed them with great mugs of hot goats'-milk. 'Oh, begorra!' cried one; 'they seen the yalla horse! It's a wonder ye all cum down alive and safe; it is few that sees the yalla horse that has luck after.' For it transpired that the phooka was in league with another monster from Erebus : ' had not the night been so calm, we should have been in considerable danger of an attack by the enchanted ' WURRUM,' who had his abode in the dark lake we had passed ; but fortunately for us it is only on wild and stormy nights that, with fearful roars, he emerges from the lake to waylay be-nighted wanderers.'

Again and again, in his short stories particularly, Le Fanu recovered the picturesque traditions of Ireland, and he illumined them with the glowing pictorial colour that was his especial gift—that sense of the subtle affinity between wild scenery and the supernatural. How sombre and powerful, for example, is that presentment in *The Child that went with the Fairies* of the haunted hill of Lisnavoura in the mountain range of Slievefelim, east of Limerick :

' A deserted country. A wide, black bog, level as a lake, skirted with copse, spreads at the left, as you journey north-ward, and the long and irregular line of mountain rises at the right, clothed in heath, broken with lines of grey rock that resemble the bold and irregular outlines of fortifications, and riven with many a gully, expanding here and there into rocky wooded glens, which open as they approach the road. . . . Lisnavoura, that lonely hill-haunt of the " Good People," as the fairies are called euphemistically, whose strangely dome-like summit rose not half a mile away, looking like an outwork of the long line of mountain that sweeps by it. It was at the fall of the leaf, and an autumnal sunset threw the lengthening shadow of haunted Lisnavoura close in front of the solitary little cabin over the undulating slopes and sides of Slievefelim. The birds were singing among the branches in the thinning leaves of the melancholy ash-trees that grew at the roadside in front of the door.'

And then, when her little brothers and sister are missing, the elder girl,

' with an undefined boding looked toward the heathy boss of Lisnavoura, now darkening into the deepest purple against the flaming sky of sunset. Again she listened with a sinking heart, and heard nothing but the farewell twitter and whistle of the birds in the bushes around. How many stories has she listened to by the wintry hearth of children stolen by the fairies, at nightfall, in lonely places.'

The bereaved mother gathers her remaining children in her arms and speaks in that lovely idiom such as Synge used in his later presentation of the Irish peasantry :

' Didn't I lose enough, this night, without lavin' the doore open, for more of yez to go; but first take an' sprinkle a dust o' the holy waters over ye, acuishla, and bring it here till I throw a taste iv it over myself, and the craythurs. . . . Come here and sit on my knees, asthora, come to me, mavourneen, and hould me fast, in the name o' God, and I'll hold you fast that none can take yez from me. . . . '

Even as a boy, Le Fanu became an authority on the superstitions and archaeology of Ireland, as is vouched for by Samuel Carter Hall, who has related :

' I knew the brothers Joseph and William Le Fanu when they were youths at Castle Connell, on the Shannon ; both became famous—one as an author, the other as a civil engineer. . . . They were my guides throughout the beautiful district around Castle Connell, and I found them full of anecdote and rich in antiquarian lore, with thorough knowledge of Irish peculiarities. They aided us largely in the preparation of our book, *Ireland : its Scenery and Character*.'

In May, 1838, the Halls and Sheridan Knowles (a cousin of the Le Fanus) entertained Joseph Le Fanu when he was in London with the idea of entering Lincoln's Inn, for he was now twenty-four years old. But he suddenly abandoned the project of practice at the English Bar. He returned to Dublin at the end of June ; and after taking the B.A. degree at Trinity College,[1] he was called to the Irish Bar in 1839. However, to the disappointment of his relatives, Le Fanu abandoned the Law in Ireland also and gravitated to journalism. About 1841 he became the proprietor and editor of *The Warder*, a

[1] Joseph Le Fanu was one of the best debaters of his time at the Trinity College Historical, and in 1838 was President of the club founded by Burke in 1745.

notable Irish paper, and in the following year he bought *The Protestant Guardian*. He later owned a third share in *The Statesman, The Dublin Evening Packet* and *Evening Mail*, which is now the only survivor of these several journals. Herein he wrote many scathing political skits. Although as editor he advocated High Tory doctrine, at heart, as I have related, his sympathies were ever with the National-ists who suffered in the manner of his Shamus O'Brien and Phaudhrig Crohoore.

In 1844, Le Fanu married Susan, daughter of George Bennett, Q.C., by whom he had two sons and two daughters. Another of Mr. Bennett's daughters, Jane, had married, in 1835, the Reverend Delves Broughton, and became the mother of Rhoda Broughton, the well-known novelist, who was born in 1840. The Bennetts were of The Grange, Birr, King's County, but George Bennett lived at 18 (now 70) Merrion Square, Dublin, and when he died he left this house to his son-in-law, Joseph Le Fanu, who accordingly took up his residence here, which remained his home for the rest of his life and where most of his novels were written. The first was *The Cock and Anchor*, published in 1845, a most excellent ' costume ' romance of old Dublin in the eighteenth century, abound-ing with exciting adventures, highway robberies, murders, and breathless escapes. It was written of course in the prevailing popular mode of Ainsworth and G. W. M. Reynolds, but Le Fanu was able to add his own distinctive original touch by reason of his archaeological knowledge and the Irish setting which the celebrated English writers of his school had not traversed. His scenic descriptions, aided by moonlight and storm, are compact of romance, and here he showed his first evi-dence of clever characterisation. Blarden was an early study of implacable villainy such as later was presented in full blast in the persons of Dangerfield, Stanley Lake, and Silas Ruthyn, while Miss Martha in a way foreran the terrible Frenchwoman in *Uncle Silas*. *The Cock and Anchor* was followed in 1847 by *The Fortunes of Colonel Torlogh*

O'Brien, illustrated by Phiz, a Jacobite story of the time when James the Second was in Ireland, during 1689-1690, and the unhappy days after the Battle of the Boyne. Many of the scenes were laid in the Limerick district so well known to the author, and the tale, despite some faults of style, can hold its own with the best rivals in the same class of romance. Strange to say, these two first books did not meet with much encouragement and success—a matter for regret. For if Le Fanu had continued his series of Irish historical romances, he might have done for Ireland what Scott achieved for Scotland : no writer has ever been more ably gifted to understand and interpret the forces, spiritual and natural, of his romantic native land.

So it came about he abandoned romance writing of an historical nature, and for a long period devoted his energies to journalism. During the next fifteen years his only book was *Ghost Stories and Tales of Mystery*, 1851— now the rarest item in his Bibliography. It included *The Evil Guest* and *The Watcher* (which was later entitled *The Familiar* when reprinted in *In a Glass Darkly*). For sheer terror, the haunting of the unhappy protagonist of this tale has no equal. It is a crescendo of horror. At first he is conscious of footsteps dogging him at lonely spots. They intensify. In time, the malignant Watcher becomes visible. Then the appalling death scene, where the author skilfully leaves to the imagination what supreme terror finally wrested poor Barton's shuddering soul from his body.

It was the sad accident of severe domestic bereavement that caused Le Fanu to turn again to the writing of full-length novels. His wife died prematurely, in 1858, while still a young woman, and her loss was an irreparable grief. From this date he became a recluse and gave up all society save that of a few relatives and intimate friends. It was during this mournful and lonely time that his thoughts reverted to literary composition for solace, and the result was that fine—his finest—romance,

The House by the Churchyard, which is surely one of the greatest romantic narratives in our language. Herein the author conjured up and related with the art of a consummate story-teller all the romantic conditions, legends, and traditions of his native Chapelizod, that village set so picturesquely by the beautiful region of the Phœnix Park. I have never seen the place, but it is as familiar and actual by Le Fanu's printed word as old Paris from the descriptions of Victor Hugo and Italy from the glowing lines of Byron. In *The House by the Churchyard* there is, further, a sense of impending and immutable tragedy that compels attention throughout the long length of this story with all its varied wealth of picturesque detail and scenic description. Light episodes may intervene, but ever the *motifs* of murder and retribution press to the front with a sort of stately inevitableness. At the outset, at the very opening of the first chapter, the right key-note is struck with supreme artistry. The influences of Nature are attune with the atmosphere of menace which is to envelop the story ; thus it begins :

' An awfully dark night came down on Chapelizod and all the country round. I believe there was no moon, and the stars had been quite put out under the wet " blanket of the night," which impenetrable muffler overspread the sky with a funereal darkness.

There was a little of that sheet-lightning early in the evening, which betokens sultry weather. The clouds, column after column, came up sullenly over the Dublin mountains, rolling themselves from one horizon to the other into one black dome of vapour, their slow but steady motion contrasting with the awful stillness of the air. There was a weight in the atmosphere, and a sort of undefined menace brooding over the little town, as if unseen crime or danger—some mystery of iniquity —was stealing into the heart of it, and the disapproving heavens scowled a melancholy warning.'

There is no need for me to point out how powerfully the sombre and dramatic flow of incident continues in this tale and the vivid grim characterisation that gives life to Dangerfield, Sturk, Black Dillon, and many another.   I will only add that in *The House by the Churchyard* I find the most terrifying ghost story in the language. It is in the haunting of The Tiled House, where the evil presence is only manifested visibly by a plump white hand. For long this hand had sought entrance into the house by knocks and scratches at the window, and at last it gains an entry by the door, following a series of loud double-knocks :

' Mr. Prosser, angry, opened the door with his right arm across, cane in hand.   Looking he saw nothing ; but his arm was jerked up oddly, as it might be with the hollow of a hand, and something passed under it, with a kind of gentle squeeze. The servant neither saw nor felt anything, and did not know why his master looked back so hastily, cutting with his cane, and shutting the door with so sudden a slam.'

But alas ! the ghost had obtained its desired entry, and that night the hand knocked gently at the bedroom door, and not long after Mr. Prosser's wife had horrible dreams.   And then one night her husband

' drew the curtain at the side of the bed, and saw Mrs. Prosser lying, as for a few seconds he mortally feared, dead, her face being motionless, white and covered with a cold dew ; and on the pillow, close beside by her head, and just within the curtains, was, as he first thought a toad—but really the same fattish hand, the wrist resting on the pillow, and the fingers extended towards her temple.'

Then the child of this couple, a little boy of three, was assailed by the malignant being.   After being put to bed, the child would often scream with paroxysms of terror. One night the nurse chanced to glance up at the valance over the head of the cot, and there, protruding from its folds, was the hand presented towards the head of the child, who for all the rest of his life was troubled with evil visions.   Though his fate was not so bad as that of the boy in Le Fanu's short story of *Dickon the Devil*, for *he* had been carried off in the arms of a spectre.   When discovered he had become an idiot :

'No one could ever get him to sleep under roof-tree more. He wanders from house to house while day-light lasts . . . and folk would rather not meet him after night-fall, for they think where he is there may be worse things near.'

The House by the Churchyard was succeeded immediately by *Wylder's Hand* in 1863-1864, the story which shows Le Fanu still at the height of his powers, for I place it before *Uncle Silas*, generally regarded as his masterpiece. The plot is more probable and powerful ; the dread secret of sombre Redman's Dell is kept unrevealed until almost the end with infinite art that holds the reader attuned to expectation and excitement ; this is, in truth, one of the few books that compel the reader to sit up till the small hours, for he cannot retire until he has solved the mystery. This is a bizarre tale, and it is told with a raw, jagged power that is suggestive of *Wuthering Heights*, and, indeed, Captain Stanley Lake is of the same implac-able breed as Heathcliff. The scenic descriptions, too, are all in tone—the sad yellow evening light over the dells and wooded slopes of Brandon Park ; the sombre old house whose windows looked ' toward the distant sunset horizon, piled in dusty gold and crimson clouds against the faded, green sky—a glory that is always melancholy and dreamy,' or at night :

' A cold bright moon was shining with clear sharp lights and shadows. Everything looked strangely cold and motionless outside. The sombre old trees, like gigantic hearse plumes, black and awful. The chapel lay full in view, where so many of the strange and equivocal race, under whose ancient roof-tree I then stood, were lying under their tomb-stones.'

It must ever be a matter for regret that Le Fanu's stories were not illustrated by the great contemporary artists who excelled in this kind of work. It is true that Phiz furnished plates for *Ghost Stories* and *Torlogh O'Brien*, but he was not at his best with these drawings. If only George Cruikshank could have drawn Danger-field and Silas Ruthyn as he drew Fagin and Mauger, and have depicted the grim scenes of *The House by the Church-*

yard and Mark Wylder's hand rising in grisly retribution from the peat in Redman's Dell, what pictures of terror we should have ; John Franklin, who supplied the macabre plates for Ainsworth's *Old St. Paul's*, would have been admirable for such a scene as I have quoted above of the hearse-plume-like trees overshadowing a mausoleum ; while for the horrors of *The Watcher*, *Green Tea*, and the Vampire *Carmilla*, Leech would have been the ideal artist, Leech in the phase of his illustrations for *The Ingoldsby Legends* and for Albert Smith's *The Adventures of Mr. Ledbury* and *The Marchioness of Brinvilliers*.

In later years the author's son, Brinsley Le Fanu, executed some excellent illustrations, though not for the three great stories. The best were for *The Evil Guest*, for these have caught the melancholy romance of the narrative. Particularly good is the drawing of the old house, Gray Forest, which, I imagine, the artist must have sketched from the seventeenth century red-brick Kew ' Palace ' as seen from the river-side. This spot is altogether a Le Fanuesque scene when on a misty night the waning moon shines through the avenue of tall poplars and throws the old house in the background into a mass of dark shadows. Brinsley Le Fanu also did a good design for *The Watcher* ; and Cyrus Cuneo's illustrations for this tale and others in the 1905 edition of *Green Tea* also have merit, and so have those by F. H. Townsend and Herbert Cole for the 1903 edition of *Wylder's Hand*. Very weird, too, are the designs by Edward Ardizzone for the 1929 edition of *In a Glass Darkly*.

Wylder's Hand was highly praised by the author's friend, Charles Lever, who wrote to Le Fanu in 1864 :

' I cannot wait for the end of the month, and the end of your story, to tell you of a very serious blunder you have made in it —a mistake perhaps more palpable to myself than to many of your readers ; but which, recognised or not, is still grave. Your blunder was in not holding back your novel some twelve or fifteen years, for you will never beat it—equal it you may, but not pass it. It is first rate, and I feel assured it will have a

high success.   The two women are beautifully drawn, and the
touches of nature in your blackest characters attract the sympathy of the reader to individuals who, if handled by an inferior
artist, would have repelled by their cold rascality.   In this
day of serial deluge, one is driven to hourly comparisons ;
and I tell you frankly, that at my fire-side you carry off the palm
from all competitors. . . .   Though I said it will be hard for
you to beat *Wylder's Hand*, by all means try, at all events.
Write on and write fast.   I am sure that the imaginative
faculty is never the better for lying fallow, and if you be able to
falsify my prediction and do a greater work, none of your
friends will be more rejoiced than myself.'

I agree with Lever that Le Fanu never surpassed
Wylder's Hand, or, I would add, *The House by the Churchyard*, though in general estimation the author's best work
is *Uncle Silas*, which followed in 1864, almost before the
ink of Lever's letter was dry.   In both *Wylder's Hand* and
Uncle Silas Le Fanu laid his scenes in Derbyshire ; in the
first-named book ' Gylingden ' is Buxton and ' Redman's
Dell ' is a picturesque bit of dale scenery in the neighbourhood of that town, where the author had stayed
with his wife soon after their marriage.   So, too, the
fateful house and gloomy domain of Bartram-Haugh in
Uncle Silas could be identified with an estate in the neighbourhood of Buxton.   This book contains some of Le
Fanu's most descriptive writing.   How good is the
account of the long cross-country journey to Bartram-
Haugh and the first glimpse of that foreboding mansion :

' It was a bright, clear morning . . . and so the entire journey
of sixty miles was to be made by the post-road—the pleasantest
travelling, if the mind were free.   The grander and more distant features of the landscape we may see well enough from the
window of the railway carriage ; but it is the foreground that
interests and instructs us, like a pleasant gossiping history ;
and *that* we had, in old days, from the post-chaise window.
It was more than travelling picquet.   Something of all conditions of life—luxury and misery—high spirits and low ; all
sorts of costume, livery, rags, millinery ; faces buxom, faces
wrinkled, faces kind, faces wicked ; no end of interest and
suggestion, passing in a procession silent and vivid, and all in

their proper scenery. The golden corn-sheafs, the old dark-alleyed orchards, and the high streets of antique towns. There were few dreams brighter, few books so pleasant. . . . The slowest part of our journey was the pull up the long mountain road, ascending zig-zag, as sailors make way against a head-wind by tacking. . . . We had just reached the summit when the sun went down. The low grounds at the other side were already lying in cold grey shadow . . . mist was gathering over all by this time. The filmy disk of the moon which was to light us on, so soon as twilight faded into night, hung high in air. . . .

And now we rapidly descended the mountain side. The scenery was wilder and bolder. Our road skirted the edge of a great heathy moor. The silvery light of the moon began to glimmer, and we passed a gipsy bivouac with fires alight and caldrons hanging over them. Two or three low tents ; a couple of dark withered crones, veritable witches ; a graceful girl standing behind, gazing after us ; and men in odd-shaped hats, with gaudy waistcoats and bright-coloured neck-handker-chiefs and gaitered legs, stood lazily in front. They had a wild tawdry display of colour ; and a group of alders in the rear made a background of shade for tents, fires, and figures. . . .

Down we drove, and now I did perceive a change. A great grass-grown park-wall, over-topped with mighty trees ; but still on and on we came at a canter that seemed almost a gallop. . . . . At last the postilions began to draw bridle, and at a slight angle, the moon shining full upon them, we wheeled into a wide semi-circle formed by the receding park walls, and halted before a great fantastic iron gate, and a pair of tall fluted piers, of white stone, all grass-grown and ivy-bound, with great cornices, surmounted with shields and supporters, the Ruthyn bearings washed by the rains of Derbyshire, for many a genera-tion of Ruthyns, almost smooth by this time, and looking bleached and phantasmal, like giant sentinels, with each a hand clasped in his comrade's, to bar our passage to the enchanted castle—the florid tracery of the iron gate showing like the draperies of white robes hanging from their extended arms to earth. Our courier got down and shoved the great gate open, and we entered, between sombre files of magnificent forest trees. . . . The bright moon shining full on the white front of the old house revealed not only its highly decorated style, its fluted pillars and doorway, rich and florid carving, and balustraded summit, but also its stained and moss-grown front. . . . '

What an entry to grim romance and expectant sensation ! In this book it is again the sense of impending
tragedy and horror long drawn out which is almost over-
whelming in its cumulative effect. The imagination is
excited and dilated to such a pitch that when the actual
scene of the murder is reached it is nearly an anticlimax.
In the original short form of the story it was the heroine's
girl cousin who was murdered, and hence its title when
reprinted in *Ghost Stories,* 1851—*The Murdered Cousin.*
In *Uncle Silas* the victim was changed to Madame de la
Rougierre, the weird Frenchwoman who was perhaps
Le Fanu's most powerful creation. She had a prototype
for some of her physical and mental characteristics in the
person of a Swiss governess who had terrorised Le Fanu
in his early childhood.

It is curious that Le Fanu was never attracted by the
dramatic possibilities of *Uncle Silas* and others of his
stories on the stage. He was fond of the theatre and
often attended the performances of the old Theatre
Royal in Dublin, where on one occasion he found himself seated behind an immensely tall man, wearing an
immensely tall top-hat, who completely blocked his
view of the stage. On request, the man removed his
hat, but the view of the play was not much improved
thereby. 'I wish,' said Le Fanu to his young son
Brinsley, who was with him, 'that I could muster up
courage to ask him to remove his head also.' Concerning this point of Le Fanu's neglect of his stage possibilities, Brinsley related :

'I never heard my father say that he thought any of his
novels would dramatise well, and I fancy had he been constructing a plot for a play he would have worked on very
different lines from those he adopted in constructing a plot
for a novel. He had considerable knowledge of the conditions
with which dramatic literature is bounded, as well as a very
keen love of drama itself. Remember, too, that dramatic
authors in his day had no opportunity of reaping the golden
harvest of a *Charley's Aunt* or *Private Secretary.* This may
have had something to do with my father's indifference to this

form of authorship. I feel sure that had he turned his attention to it he could have constructed a play fit to rank with the best of his novels.'

There has been a dramatic version of *Uncle Silas* adapted by other hands—Laurence Irving and Seymour Hicks—which was produced for a matinée performance at the Shaftesbury Theatre on February 13th, 1893, and afterwards on a provincial tour. William Haviland played the part of Uncle Silas ; Holman Clark that of Charke ; Violet Vanbrugh played Maud, and Irene Vanbrugh her cousin Milly ; Laurence Irving and Gordon Craig were in small parts, and Dudley Ruthyn, a dialect part, was taken by Mr. Seymour Hicks, who informs me that one of the critics said he ' spoke one of the seven unknown languages of the stage.' Henry Irving was present at the rehearsal, and perhaps it was the hope of the producers that he would be tempted to assume the rôle of Silas, which, however, in the provincial run was taken over by his son Laurence. Certainly Henry Irving would have made a fine thing of the macabre Silas and his physical characteristics would have been wonderfully adapted to the description in the book :

' A face like marble, with a fearful monumental look, and for an old man, singularly vivid strange eyes . . . his eyebrows were still black, though his hair descended from his temples in long locks of the purest silver and fine as silk nearly to his shoulders. . . . I can't convey in words an idea of this apparition, drawn as it seemed in black and white, venerable, bloodless, fiery-eyed, with its singular look of power, and an expression so bewildering—was it derision, or anguish, or cruelty, or patience ? '

Mr. T. P. Le Fanu, in his *Memoir of the Le Fanu Family*, has made the interesting suggestion that in the character of Austin Ruthyn, the brother of Silas, the author drew a sketch of himself, which Mr. T. P. Le Fanu says coincides with his own recollections of his uncle :

' It was a peculiar figure, strongly made, thick-set, with a face large, and very stern ; he wore a loose, black velvet coat and waistcoat . . . he married, and his beautiful young wife died . . . he had left the Church of England for some odd sect . . . and ultimately became a Swedenborgian.'

And strangely enough the description of the death of Austin Ruthyn from ' one of those fearful aneurisms that lie close to the heart ' prefigured Le Fanu's death from the same cause. Mr. T. P. Le Fanu records another personal touch in the book. At Knowl there was a portrait of Uncle Silas in youth which represented ' a singularly handsome young man, slender, elegant, in a costume then quite obsolete, though I believe it was seen at the beginning of this century—white leather pantaloons and top-boots, a buff waistcoat, and a chocolate-coloured coat, and the hair long and brushed back.' There was an actual picture with these details hanging in Joseph Le Fanu's dining-room in Merrion Square, supposed to be a portrait of George Colman the Younger.

Le Fanu had now in the course of three years produced three sensational stories of murder, and some public comment on his predilection for mystery and bloodshed no doubt caused him to prefix to *Uncle Silas* his able defence of the sensational novel, wherein he pointed out that death, crime, and mystery find a place in all the romances of Walter Scott, even in the apparently placid tale of *The Antiquary*. He held on his own way as a member of what he termed ' the legitimate school of tragic English romance, which has been ennobled, and in great measure founded, by the genius of Sir Walter Scott,' and at once added to his list *Guy Deverell*, an exciting story with clever characterisation. Swinburne, who read Le Fanu, pronounced *Guy Deverell* to be ' too hasty, too blurred and blottesque.' To me, it appears to have two faults, namely that the reader is kept too long in an uncertain state as to what the mystery is, and that the great scene in The Green Chamber, to which fifty-seven expectant chapters have led, is not actually related but left to the imagination. But it has much power, particularly in the sense of presentiment of coming

retribution which ever and anon assails Sir Jekyl Marlowe
—' he had come within the edge of the shadow of judgment, and its darkness was stealing over him, and its
chill touched his heart.' *Guy Deverell* was dedicated to
Charles Lever, who was a very welcome guest at Merrion
Square by reason of his flow of high spirits and good
stories—such as the one relating the occasion when he
was walking in the Park with Archbishop Whately and
two curates.   The Archbishop at this time was interested
in mushrooms and what kinds were edible and what
kinds poisonous.   He picked up a dreadful-looking
fungus, observing : ' Now, Lever, many people would
fancy *that* to be a most poisonous fungus, but I assure
you it is a most wholesome mushroom.'   Breaking off
a piece he handed it to one of the curates, saying, ' Taste
it, and tell us what you think of it.'   ' A very nice fungus,
indeed, Your Grace, and rather sweetish,' replied the unhappy man.   ' And now you, here's a bit for you,' said
the Archbishop to the other curate.   ' If it were nicely
cooked, Your Grace,' replied the second victim, making
a very wry face, ' with a little salt and butter, it would,
I am sure, be delicious.'   ' A piece for you, Lever,' said
the Archbishop, ' try it and say what *you* think of it.'
' I thank Your Grace, but I'd rather not,' replied Lever.
' I am not seeking preferment.   'Tis true I have a brother
in the Church, but he is not in Your Grace's diocese.'
Or that tale of the priest, riding through a remote wild
district of Ireland, who came upon an old woman kneel-
ing in the road outside her cabin, and moaning and
praying in a loud voice.   ' What's the matter ? ' asked
the priest.   ' Oh ! Father, my eldest daughter has been
married for two years and has no child to carry on with
the bit of farm, so I am asking the Blessed Virgin to send
her a son.'   ' Rest assured,' said the priest, ' that your
prayers will speedily be answered.'   About a year later
he was riding that road again, and stopped at the cabin
to see the old woman.   ' Were your prayers answered ? '
asked the priest.   ' Yes, Father,' replied the crone : ' but

the Holy Mother made a bit of a mistake, for She sent the child to my unmarried daughter.'

In the Sixties other guests at Le Fanu's house were his gifted cousins on the Sheridan side, Mrs. Norton and Lady Gifford. Percy FitzGerald was also welcome, though Le Fanu did not care by now to see many people for he was rapidly becoming a recluse. FitzGerald has left a pleasant picture of the nights in Merrion Square, the warm, fire-lit dining-room, on the walls of which hung Sheridan family portraits to the number of a dozen and a pastel portrait of Swift given by that author to a Sheridan. Sometimes the niece of Le Fanu's wife, Rhoda Broughton, would be there, and she would read aloud her early literary efforts—tales of fragile heroines and rugged heroes of the school of *Guy Livingstone*. Le Fanu perceived her promise and printed *Not Wisely but Too Well* and *Cometh Up as a Flower* in 1867 in *The Dublin University Magazine*, which he owned. He said to Miss Broughton : ' You will succeed, and when you do, remember that I prophesied it.' He introduced her to his own publisher in London, Bentley, and by the time *Red as a Rose is She* appeared, in 1872, Rhoda Broughton was famous. Percy FitzGerald says Le Fanu was a very sensitive man and compact of moods, passing from grave to gay, with ever a desire to tell or hear a ghost story. He still, at this time, preserved his predilection for a practical joke, and played quite an elaborate one on Percy FitzGerald. They were discussing the effects of reviews and criticisms, and FitzGerald, who had lately been enjoying some good notices of his books, was discanting on the utter unimportance of such things—the philosopher would be unmoved by them, smile tranquilly if the review was good and contemptuously if it proved to be bad. Le Fanu said nothing, but a few days later FitzGerald received from him a local newspaper which quoted from a London weekly a very stinging notice of FitzGerald's last book which was, indeed, a most bitter attack. FitzGerald rushed round for sympathy to Le Fanu, who condoled and observed : ' Well, the only thing is to summon up your philosophy—and smile when a review is bad : but you are *not* smiling ? ' He smiled himself, however, and owned up to his joke. As the owner of the newspaper, he had been able to have a portion of the type lifted out and inserted in its place this imaginary review of FitzGerald's book which he had composed himself. Only one copy was printed off the introduced type and the original ' make-up ' was then put back.

Another trick Le Fanu played was on one of his contributors to *The Dublin University Magazine*, the antiquarian writer, Patrick Kennedy, who was so ardent an Irish patriot that he frequently claimed famous men of other nationalities as his fellow-countrymen. This amused Le Fanu, who, one evening when he and his friend were discussing race superiority, said, ' I suppose you know that Shakespeare was of Irish extraction ? ' ' Was he ? ' exclaimed Kennedy, very excited. ' Yes, there is hardly a doubt of the fact,' replied Le Fanu ; ' he was descended from a branch of the famous O'Shaughnessys—The O'Shaughnessy-Spears ; but realising in England the awkwardness of the name, the family shortened it to Shaugspeare or Shakespeare.' Mr. Kennedy, much impressed, spent several weeks of research in endeavouring to find the records of The O'Shaughnessy-Spears, but in vain, and he was ashamed to admit that he could not trace Shakespeare to his Celtic source.

More reprehensible was the earlier jest he had practised on William Keogh, later the judge to whom he dedicated *The Wyvern Mystery*. The two were having supper at an old-fashioned tavern in Dublin. Keogh was a nervous, irascible man who eventually committed suicide. He was suspicious of all political opponents, and on this night sat with oysters before him inveighing against some person or movement, when, to continue the story in the words of Brinsley Le Fanu [1] :

[1] Who related this anecdote to Edmund Downey.

'In the course of his philippic he frequently raised his eyes to the ceiling. My father (for some reason which he could not account for except it was the spirit of mischief had suddenly taken possession of him) put a shake of cayenne pepper on Keogh's oysters every time the future judge raised his eyes. "These oysters are rather hot, Le Fanu," he said after the first mouthful. "I don't find them so," replied his friend. "Oh, they're fearfully hot," persisted Keogh. "Nonsense, man!" cried the mischief-maker; "there's nothing the matter with them. It's some trick of your imagination. They are exactly the same oysters I am eating,"—giving them another surreptitious dose of cayenne while Keogh was shooting another glance at the ceiling. Again did Keogh attack the oysters, determined this time not to be daunted by his imagination, though his mouth was like a furnace and his eyes running water. But the ordeal was too much for him, and starting to his feet, his face aflame, he cried : "I know what's the matter. It's that villain Foley" (the proprietor of the tavern). "He has poisoned my oysters!" Le Fanu succeeded in pacifying Keogh ; but to the end of his life the judge was ignorant of the cause of the trouble, and he often spoke of the mysterious fiery bivalves which had turned to live coals in his mouth.'

All through these years Le Fanu was writing novels regularly. *All in the Dark*, 1866, was followed by *The Tenants of Malory*, which describes Beaumaris and Penmon Priory, for at the former place Le Fanu and his family often stayed in summer holidays. *A Lost Name*, as I have mentioned, was the third and full version of *Some Account of the Latter Days of the Hon. Richard Marston of Dunoran* and *The Evil Guest*, though the period of the story is post-dated to the nineteenth century in *A Lost Name*. In the same way, *Checkmate*, 1870-1871, in a nineteenth century setting utilises and reintroduces many of the incidents of the eighteenth century story of *The Cock and Anchor*. The theme of *A Lost Name* and its predecessors, as Dr. M. R. James has pointed out, is the same as that of a once popular sixpenny 'shocker' mentioned by Dickens in *The Guest*, the first section of *The Holly-Tree Inn* (1855) :

'The Road-side Inn, renowned in my time in a sixpenny book with a folding plate, representing in a central compartment of oval form the portrait of Jonathan Bradford, and in four corner compartments four incidents of the tragedy with which the name is associated. . . . Then, I remembered how the landlord was found at the murdered traveller's bedside, with his own knife at his feet, and blood upon his hand ; how he was hanged for the murder, notwithstanding his protestation, that he had indeed come there to kill the traveller for his saddle-bags, but had been stricken motionless on finding him already slain ; and how the ostler, years afterwards, owned the deed.'

But this murder actually occurred, and was related in an earlier form in R. S. Kirby's *Wonderful and Scientific Museum*,[1] 1804, as *Extraordinary Case of Jonathan Bradford who was executed at Oxford for the murder of Christopher Hayes, Esq., in the year* 1736. Bradford kept an inn in Oxfordshire on the high road between Oxford and London. He was of good character. He was found standing by the bed-side of his murdered guest, Mr. Hayes, with his hands covered with blood, and a bloody knife in his hand. He protested his innocence, but was tried and executed, and just before his end admitted to the clergyman, who attended him, that he had indeed intended to rob and kill his guest, but found him already murdered—' he was struck with amazement, he could not believe his senses, and in turning back the bed-clothes, to assure himself of the fact, he, in his agitation, dropped his knife on the bleeding body, by which means

---

[1] Vol. ii. page 321. This reference to the story was pointed out to Dr. M. R. James by Mr. E. H. W. Meyerstein, who also drew attention to the fact that in *The Room in the Dragon Volant* the incident of masqueraders disguised as Chinese arriving at a ball with a figure in a palanquin—subsequently found to be a corpse—was evidently suggested to Le Fanu by a tale related in John Timb's *English Eccentrics* (vol. ii. page 127, edition of 1866). The Rev. Mr. Venables heard of the affair from General Bontourlin at St. Petersburg, in 1834 ; the party arrived at a ball disguised as Chinese, and the figure in the palanquin was later found to have been strangled. The body was never identified, but was supposed to be that of a victim in some gambling fracas. Le Fanu added, of course, the details of one of the masqueraders acting as magician with the corpse as oracle.

both his hands and the knife became bloody.' Hereafter, if Dickens did not err in his memory of the sequel,
this version is different, for it was Mr. Hayes's footman
who confessed to the murder on his death-bed, when it
was too late for justice to invoke the law. The dramatic
story was adapted for the stage by Fitzball, and his
Jonathan Bradford, or the Murder at the Roadside Inn, was
produced at the Surrey Theatre on June 12th, 1833.
Next came a novel bearing the same title, published by
E. Lloyd in 1851, and possibly written by the Prince of
Lurid Shockers, Thomas Preskett Prest.[1] In this story
the landlord is discovered and condemned to death, as
in the earlier versions, but is saved from the gallows by
the timely confession of the real culprit.

The Evil Guest, the scene of which is placed in Cheshire,
may be described as the most bloody of Le Fanu's tales,
and, as in Ainsworth's, there is full measure of bloodshed
and pain in most of them, though in some of the later
books he varied the *motif*. After *Haunted Lives* and *The
Wyvern Mystery* came *The Rose and the Key* (1871), which
deals with the horrors of a private lunatic asylum. Le
Fanu has sometimes been styled ' The Irish Wilkie
Collins,' and in *The Rose and the Key* he does in certain
measure resemble the methods of his great sensational
and contemporary rival who wrote *The Woman in White*.
After he sold *The Dublin University Magazine* in 1869, Le
Fanu contributed to other journals—*Cassell's Magazine*,
Temple Bar, *Belgravia*, *London Society*, *The Dark Blue*, *Once
A Week*, and, most of all, *All the Year Round*, where
among other things first appeared *Green Tea*, that horrific
story of the demon or delusional monkey, with the
red foggy light in its eyes, which haunted to dire death
poor Mr. Jenkins in that sombre, elm-shadowed house
which looked out upon ' the pomp of the then lonely

[1] *Jonathan Bradford* was an anonymous production, described as
' By the Author of *The Hebrew Maiden* and *The Wife's Secret*.' *The
Hebrew Maiden* had appeared in 1841, adorned with fearsome wood-
cuts.

woods of Richmond.' [1]   Here, too, appeared serially *The Rose and the Key* (where twelve years earlier had appeared *The Woman in White*) and Le Fanu's last novel, *Willing to Die*, a strange coincidental title, for he died the year, 1873, the book was published.   This title gave H. J. Byron opportunity for one of his quips : ' I see " Willing to Die " placarded on all the hoardings of London : it should be " Willing to Die ; or Bill Stickers Beware," ' — Willing, of course, being the name of the well-known agent for posters.

In some of his last stories Le Fanu placed the scene in the fells of Cumberland and Lancashire, near a picturesque little town which he called Golden Friars, and three of these tales he grouped together in a volume entitled *Chronicles of Golden Friars* (1871).   The town in question is perhaps Hawkshead, or Ambleside, judging by the description given in another story, *The Dead Sexton*.

' The sunsets were red, the nights were long, and the weather pleasantly frosty ; and Christmas, the glorious herald of the New Year, was at hand, when an event—still recounted by winter fire-sides, with a horror made delightful by the mellowing influence of years—occurred in the beautiful little town of Golden Friars. . . .   A wintry sunset was glaring through a gorge of the western mountains, turning into fire the twigs of the leafless elms, and all the tiny blades of grass on the green by which the quaint little town is surrounded.   It is built of light, gray stone, with steep gables and slender chimneys rising with an airy lightness from the level sward by the margin of the beautiful lake, and backed by the grand amphitheatre of the fells at the other side, whose snowy peaks show faintly against the sky, tinged with the vaporous red of the western light.   As you descend towards the margin of the lake, and see Golden Friars, its taper chimneys and slender gables, its curious old inn and gorgeous sign, and over all the graceful tower and spire of the ancient church, at this hour or by moonlight, in the solemn grandeur and stillness of the natural scenery that surrounds it, it stands before you like a fairy town.'

[1] Le Fanu said he had known of an actual case of a clergyman who had suffered from a belief that he was haunted by a demon in the guise of a monkey.

Surely a Christmas tale of terror never had a more
picturesque introduction, and soon are heard afar off on
the frost-bound roads the clanging hooves of the great
steed bearing a dark, mysterious figure who will carry
off the corpse of the ill-omened sexton, for in this tale
Le Fanu returned to a favourite theme of his youth—the
power of a demoniacal being over a human one.   Probably the grim sexton of the tale, Toby Crooke, was
suggested by Le Fanu's memories of the old sexton at
Chapelizod who had terrified him in his childhood.

I have pointed out the versatility of Le Fanu's work—
how he at different times was a humorist, a writer of
ballads voicing the aspirations and romance of Irish
National Life ; a journalist expressing High Tory views ;
an historical romance writer ; a writer of political satires ;
and a supreme author of ghost stories and novels of
murder and mystery.   He was also a poet as is evidenced
by *The Legend of the Glaive*, and the sad little songs scattered through his novels, such as this :

' The river ran between them
    And she looked upon the stream,
And the soldier looked upon her
    As a dreamer in a dream.
" Believe me—oh believe ! "
He sighed, " you peerless maid ;
    My honour is pure,
    And my true love sure,
Like the white plume in my hat
And my shining blade."

The river ran between them,
    And she smiled upon the stream,
Like one that smiles at folly,
    A dreamer in a dream.
" I do not trust your promise,
I will not be betrayed ;
    For your faith is light,
    And your cold wit bright,
Like the white plume in your hat
And your shining blade."

The river ran between them,
  And he rode beside the stream,
And he turned away and parted,
  As a dreamer from his dream.
And his comrade brought his message
From the field where he was laid—
    Just his name to repeat,
    And to lay at her feet
  The white plume from his hat,
    And his shining blade.'

What simple pathos, but it rings true.

I wish I had space to quote in full that grim ballad of the Ghost of Tim Rooney, who assures his murderer how he will be with him for ever more :

' Up through the wather your secret rises ;
    The stones won't keep it, and it lifts the mould,
An' it tracks your footsteps and your fun surprises,
    And it sits at the fire beside you black and cowld.

    .   .   .   .   .   .

An' when the pariod iv your life is over
    The frightful hour of judgment then will be ;
And, Shamus Hanlon, heavy on your shoulder,
    I'll lay my cowld hand, and you'll go wid me.'

During his last years the mind of Le Fanu became almost entirely pre-occupied with the supernatural, and all the short stories he wrote at this time are of that nature —*Green Tea*, *Carmilla* (the most impressive vampire tale I am acquainted with, for it is written with an artistry that is lacking in the cruder horrors of *Varney the Vampire*, by Thomas Preskett Prest), *Madam Crowl's Ghost*, *The Haunted House in Westminster* (later entitled *Mr. Justice Harbottle*),[1] *The Haunted Baronet*, *The Dead Sexton*, *Dickon the Devil*. His now peculiar habits of life contributed to this obsession, and there can be little doubt but that many

---

[1] Probably Le Fanu had Judge Jeffreys in mind for his Justice Harbottle. Shrewsbury is mentioned in the story : Jeffreys was educated there, and his title was Baron Jeffreys of Wem in the same county of Shropshire, while his London house was in Duke Street (later Delahay Street), Westminster.

of these weird tales came to him in the form of dreams.
His son, Brinsley Le Fanu, gave me a remarkable account
of his father's methods of work. He wrote mostly in
bed at night, using copy-books for his manuscript. He
always had two candles by his side on a small table ; one
of these dimly glimming tapers would be left burning
while he took a brief sleep. Then, when he awoke about
2 a.m. amid the darkling shadows of the heavy furnishings
and hangings of his old-fashioned room, he would brew
himself some strong tea—which he drank copiously and
frequently throughout the day—and write for a couple
of hours in that eerie period of the night when human
vitality is at its lowest ebb and the Powers of Darkness
rampant and terrifying. What wonder then, that, with
his brain ever peopled by day and by night with mysterious and terrible beings, he became afflicted by horrible
dreams, which, as I have suggested, were the bases of his
last stories of the supernatural. Apart from imbibing
much strong tea—which apparently was not of the Green
variety !—he was a most abstemious man, and a non-
smoker. Le Fanu always breakfasted in bed, and at mid-
day went down to the dining-room at the back of the
house, where he would resume work, writing at a little
table which had been a favourite possession of his grand-
uncle, Richard Brinsley Sheridan. This room opened out
to a small garden, pleasant in spring with lilac and flowering shrubs and fruit blossom, and in this small monastic-
like close he took the little exercise he fancied, pacing the
paths with pencil and copy-book in hand, his mind still
and ever with

> ' The dark folk who live in souls
> Of passionate men, like bats in the dead trees ;
> And with the wayward twilight companies.'

During these last years he rarely went out into the city.
Only under cover of the darkness of night would he
venture out, and then generally to the old book-shops in
search of works dealing with demonology and ghost lore.

' Any more ghost stories for me ? ' he would ask with his
pleasant voice and smile,[1] and when the desired volumes
were handed to him he would pore over their contents.
Although he was, of course, deeply learned in the
doctrines of Swedenborg and other exponents of demoniacal possession, he would have nothing to do with
Spiritualism, and despised its ineffectual messages and
mild manifestations.   His mind savoured stronger and
more frightful meat.   He became altogether a recluse,
and would now see no one except his family, and even
his old and congenial friend, Charles Lever, was refused
admittance on the last occasion, as it proved to be, when
he visited Dublin.   Le Fanu soon had cause to regret the
lost opportunity, for Lever died soon after, in 1872 : but
he did not forget the brave days of old, of high romance,
of good friends now gone into the realms of shadow, and
all the bitter-sweets of memory, for he wrote those
haunting lines :

> ' One wild and distant bugle sound
>   Breathed o'er Killarney's magic shore
> Will shed sweet floating echoes round
>   When that which made them is no more.
>
> So slumber in the human heart
>   Wild echoes, that will sweetly thrill
> The words of kindness when the voice
>   That uttered them for aye is still.
>
> Oh ! memory, though thy records tell
>   Full many a tale of grief and sorrow,
> Of mad excess, of hope decayed,
>   Of dark and cheerless melancholy :
>
> Still, memory, to me thou art
>   The dearest of the gifts of mind,
> For all the joys that touch my heart
>   Are joys that I have left behind.'

So entirely had Le Fanu vanished from mortal ken that
he was termed in Dublin ' The Invisible Prince,' which

---

[1] Mr. A. P. Graves in *The Purcell Papers*.

To S.M. Ellis Esq.
From Brinsley Le Fanu.
Oct: 1915.

JOSEPH SHERIDAN LE FANU
From an ink drawing by the novelist's son, Brinsley Le Fanu, 1916

was the last state of one whom Mr. A. P. Graves has described as once ' the beau ideal of an Irish wit and scholar
of the old school.'   And now the chief protagonist of his
literary work, Death, drew near, preceded by a long and
painful illness arising from heart disease.   Long ago he
had pictured, in *Uncle Silas*, the coming of Death as a
dreamless sleep after a weary protest that it is not time
yet :

> ' See how a sleepy child will put off the inevitable departure
> for bed.   The little creature's eyes blink and stare, and it needs
> constant jogging to prevent his nodding off into the slumber
> which nature craves . . . yet he implores a respite, and depre-
> cates repose, and vows he is not sleepy, even to the moment
> when his mother takes him in her arms, and carries him, in a
> sweet slumber, to the nursery.   So it is with us old children of
> earth and the great sleep of death, and Nature our kind mother.
> Just so reluctantly we part with consciousness, the picture is,
> even to the last, so interesting ; the bird in the hand, though
> sick and moulting, so inestimably better than all the brilliant
> tenants of the bush.   We sit up, yawning, and blinking, and
> stupid, the whole scene swimming before us, and the stories
> and music humming off into the sound of distant winds and
> waters. . . . '

But he was not permitted to have this peaceful passing.
Horrible dreams troubled him to the last, one of the most
recurrent and persistent being a vision of a vast and
direly foreboding old mansion (such as he had so often
depicted in his romances), in a state of ruin and threatening imminently to fall upon and crush the dreamer rooted
to the spot.   So painful was this repeated horror that he
would struggle and cry out in his sleep.   He mentioned
the trouble to his doctor.   When the end came, and the
doctor stood by the bedside of Le Fanu and looked in the
terror-stricken eyes of the dead man, he said : ' I feared
this—that house fell at last.'

Joseph Sheridan Le Fanu died at 18, Merrion Square,
Dublin, on February 7th, 1873, at the age of fifty-eight.
He was buried in Mount Jerome Cemetery.

Could he have selected his own epitaph, I think he

would have taken his own lines from *A Doggerel in a Dormant Window* :

> ' And when my glow is o'er,
>   In ashes quenched my fire,
> And its fragrance is no more,
>   And spark and smoke expire ;
>
> O'er me may some one say,
>   As I of you to-day,
> Beneath the nettle and the flowers,
>   Where lies my worn out clay ;
>
> " He did in his allotted hours,
>   What fellows sometimes shirk
> In this enormous world of ours—
>   His halfpenny worth of work." '

The books of Le Fanu have a remarkably wide appeal and apparently are read with pleasure by the most differential types of mind.   He has been, thus, praised by Swinburne, James Payn,[1] Seymour Lucas (the historical painter), and even by the fastidious Henry James, who in one of his short stories, *The Liar*, is describing the arrival of a guest in an English country house, where, in his bedroom, ' There was the customary novel of Mr. Le Fanu for the bed-side ; the ideal reading in a country house for the hours after midnight ' ; and so anxious was Oliver to commence the enthralling tale that he could not forbear to turn the pages, with the result that his dressing was delayed and he was late for dinner—a truly Jamesian situation for analysis.   One must predicate that Le Fanu's readers possess some measure of culture, for he writes with the outlook of a gentleman ; his books attest literary allusion and classical knowledge.   He is indeed an archaeologist, and I think it is his blend of learning with mystery and crime which created romances that

[1] James Payn, in *Some Literary Recollections*, writing of the late Prince Leopold, Duke of Albany, says : ' I had the satisfaction of introducing him to the works of Le Fanu, and his admiration of that author (so strangely neglected by the general public, notwithstanding the popularity of some of his imitators) vied with my own.'

hold the attention of readers who would have no liking for the ordinary sensational novel. For in Le Fanu's work there is something akin to the panoramic pilgrimage of human life, the sunshine and the shadows, the joy and the tragedy, the happy song and the dirge of sorrow, the high lights of the hills of romance and the dark valley through which all must shudderingly pass ere they reach the oblivion of the tomb.

LIST OF WORKS BY JOSEPH SHERIDAN LE FANU

In the course of his literary career, as owner and editor of *The Warder, The Dublin Evening Mail, The Protestant Guardian, The Statesman, The Dublin Evening Packet,* Le Fanu wrote many articles and essays which are, of necessity, not included in the following Bibliography, which deals primarily with his fictional and poetical work.[1]

I. CONTRIBUTIONS TO MAGAZINES

CONTRIBUTIONS TO 'THE DUBLIN UNIVERSITY MAGAZINE.'

1. January, 1838 : *The Ghost and the Bone-Setter.*

2. March, 1838 : *The Fortunes of Sir Robert Ardagh.* (The first short form of *The Haunted Baronet,* in *Chronicles of Golden Friars,* Bentley, 1871.)

3. June, 1838 : *The Last Heir of Castle Connor.*

4. August, 1838 : *The Drunkard's Dream.*

5. November, 1838 : *Passage in the Secret History of an Irish Countess* (this was the original short form of *Uncle Silas.*)

6. April, 1839 : *The Bridal of Carrigvarah.*

7. May, 1839 : *Schalken the Painter.*

8. June, 1839 : *Scraps of Hibernian Ballads* (including *Phaudhrig Crohoore*).

9. July, 1839 : *Jim Sulivan's Adventures in the Great Snow.*

[1] Several book reviews written by J. S. Le Fanu are mentioned in an appendix to Mr. T. P. Le Fanu's *Memoir of the Le Fanu Family,* 1924.

10. October, 1839 : *A Chapter in the History of a Tyrone Family* (this was the original short form of *The Wyvern Mystery*).

11. February, 1840 : *An Adventure of Hardress Fitzgerald, a Royalist Captain* (contains incidents used subsequently in *Torlogh O'Brien*).

12. October, 1840 : *The Quare Gander.*

(All the above were collected and reprinted under the title of *The Purcell Papers*, with a Memoir of the Author by A. P. Graves. 3 volumes. Bentley. 1880.)

13. April to June, 1848 : *Some Account of the Latter Days of the Hon. Richard Marston of Dunoran* (this is the first form of *The Evil Guest*).

14. June, 1848 : *The State Prosecutions.*

15. July, 1848 : *The Irish League.*

16. January and February, 1850 : *The Mysterious Lodger.*

17. June, 1850 : *Billy Malowney's Taste of Love and Glory.* This tale was imitated in later years with the recitation *How Bill Adams won the Battle of Waterloo*, with Cockney dialect instead of Irish.

18. July, 1850 : *Shamus O'Brien—a Ballad.*

19. January, 1851 : *Ghost Stories of Chapelizod ;* (a) *The Village Bully ;* (b) *The Sexton's Adventure ;* (c) *The Spectre Lovers.*

20. December, 1853 : *An Account of Some Strange Disturbances in Aungier Street* (this was the earlier and better form of the story called *Mr. Justice Harbottle* in *In a Glass Darkly*, 1872).

21. December, 1861 : *Ultor De Lacy ;* A Legend of Cappercullen.

(Numbers 19, 20, 21, above, were reprinted for the first time by Dr. M. R. James in *Madam Crowl's Ghost and Other Tales of Mystery*, Bell, 1923.)

Le Fanu purchased *The Dublin University Magazine* in 1861 and owned it until 1869. During that period the following serial stories and ballads written by him appeared within its pages :

22. 1861-2 : *The House by the Churchyard : A Souvenir of Chapelizod.* By ' Charles de Cresseron.'

23. October, 1862 : *Authentic Narrative of a Haunted House.*

24. February, 1863 : *Duan-na-Claev : The Legend of the Glaive.* Ballad. By ' Hyacinth Con Carolan.'

25. March, 1863 : *Abhrain an Bhuideil.* Ballad. By ' Hyacinth Con Carolan.'

26. 1863-4 : *Wylder's Hand.*

27. 1864 : *Maud Ruthyn (Uncle Silas).*

28. March, 1864 : *My Aunt Margaret's Adventure.*

29. April, 1864 : *Wicked Captain Walshawe, of Wauling.* (Reprinted in *Madam Crowl's Ghost,* 1923.)

30. December, 1864 : *A Doggerel in a Dormant Window.* Poem. By ' Hyacinth Con Carolan.'

31. 1865 : *Guy Deverell.*

32. November, 1865 : *Lord Palmerston* : An Obituary Notice.

33. November-December, 1865 : *Beatrice.* A Verse Drama in Two Acts.

34. 1866 : *All in the Dark.*

35. 1867 : *The Tenants of Malory.*

36. 1868 : *Haunted Lives.*

37. 1869 : *The Wyvern Mystery.*

The *Dublin University Magazine* was purchased from James McGlashan's estate by Hurst and Blackett, in 1856, for £750, so it may be assumed that Le Fanu paid some sum in excess of that amount : when he sold the Magazine in 1869 he had greatly increased its value, and he obtained £1,500 from Adams, a printer of Bartholomew Close, London, which moved *Blarney* (4th March, 1871) to observe : ' No doubt that man of many novels, Mr. Le Fanu, was pleased with the Sell. I beg pardon—Sale.'

CONTRIBUTIONS TO ' TEMPLE BAR.'

1. 1867-1868 : *A Lost Name* (this is the final form of *Some Account of the Latter Days of the Hon. Richard Marston of Dunoran* and *The Evil Guest*).

2. January, 1868 : *Squire Toby's Will* : A Ghost Story. (Reprinted for the first time in *Madam Crowl's Ghost*, 1923.)

3. April-July, 1870 : *The Bird of Passage.* (Reprinted as the third story in *Chronicles of Golden Friars*, Bentley, 1871, and as *A Chronicle of Golden Friars* in the book of that name, Downey, 1896.)

4. August, 1884 : *Hyacinth O'Toole.* This unfinished and amusing story appeared posthumously, and was sent to the Editor by Le Fanu's son.

CONTRIBUTIONS TO 'ALL THE YEAR ROUND.'

1. October 23rd-November 13th, 1869 : *Green Tea.* (Republished as the first tale in *In a Glass Darkly*, Bentley, 1872.)

2. November 20th and 27th, 1869 : *The Legend of Dunblane.* (This is not identified, but is possibly by Le Fanu.)

3. February 5th, 1870 : *The Child that went with the Fairies.*

4. April 2nd, 1870 : *The White Cat of Drumgunniol.*

5. April 23rd, 1870 : *Stories of Lough Guir.*

6. October 8th, 1870 : *The Vision of Tom Chuff.* (Somewhat like *The Drunkard's Dream* in *The Dublin University Magazine*, August 1838.)

(Numbers 3, 4, 5, 6, above, were reprinted for the first time in *Madam Crowl's Ghost*, 1923.)

7. December 31st, 1870 : *Madam Crowl's Ghost.* (This was later incorporated in *A Strange Adventure in the Life of Miss Laura Mildmay*, the first of the three stories in *Chronicles of Golden Friars*, Bentley, 1871. *Madam Crowl's Ghost* forms the title story of the volume of collected tales published by Bell in 1923.)

8. 1871 : *The Rose and the Key.*

9. 1872 : *Willing to Die.*

10. July 6th, 1872 : *Sir Dominick's Bargain : A Legend of Dunoran.* (This is a variation of the theme of *The Fortunes of Sir Robert Ardagh* in *The Dublin University Magazine*, March 1838, and of *The Haunted Baronet*, the second story in *Chronicles of Golden Friars*, Bentley, 1871.)

CONTRIBUTIONS TO 'BELGRAVIA.'

1. July-November, 1870 : *The Haunted Baronet*, with illustrations by J. A. Pasquier. (Reprinted as the second story in *Chronicles of Golden Friars*, 1871.)

2. Annual, 1872 : *Laura Silver Bell*, A Fairy Story. With an illustration, 'The Vision of the Fairies,' by E. Wagner.

3. January, 1872 : *The Haunted House in Westminster* / By J. S. Le Fanu / Author of *Uncle Silas*, etc. / With an illustration, 'The Apparition,' by E. Wagner. The title of this story was changed to *Mr. Justice Harbottle* when it was reprinted the same year in *In a Glass Darkly*. The Justice was probably intended for Judge Jeffreys. See page 174.

CONTRIBUTION TO 'CASSELL'S MAGAZINE.'

1. September, 1870-March, 1871 : *Checkmate*. Illustrated by Towneley Green.

CONTRIBUTION TO 'ONCE A WEEK.'

1. Christmas Number, 1871 : *The Dead Sexton*. With an illustration by C. O. Murray, and initial letter design of church tower and bell by Frederick Waddy.

CONTRIBUTION TO 'THE DARK BLUE.'

1. 1871-1872 : *Carmilla*. Illustrated by D. H. Friston and M. FitzGerald. (Reprinted as the fifth story in *In a Glass Darkly*, Bentley, 1872.)

CONTRIBUTIONS TO 'LONDON SOCIETY.'

1. February-June, 1872 : *The Room in the Dragon Volant*. With five illustrations by J. A. Pasquier. (Reprinted as the fourth story in *In a Glass Darkly*, Bentley, 1872.)

2. Christmas Number, 1872 : *Dickon the Devil* by T. (a misprint) Sheridan Le Fanu. With an illustration by H. Wagner. (This story was reprinted for the first time in *Madam Crowl's Ghost*, 1923.)

NOTE.—In the identification of Le Fanu's contributions to magazines I have on several occasions been indebted to discussions with Dr. M. R. James and Mr. T. P. Le Fanu.

II. PUBLISHED WORKS

Many of the following particulars are taken from the fine collection of Le Fanu first editions in the possession of Mr. A. J. A. Symons, of the First Edition Club, to whom I tender my thanks.

1. THE / COCK AND ANCHOR / being / A Chronicle of Old Dublin City / In Three Volumes / Dublin / William Curry, Jun., and Company / Longmans, London / Fraser and Co., Edinburgh / 1845. Boards.

This story, with some alterations, was republished as

MORLEY COURT / Being / A Chronicle of Old Dublin City / By the Author of *Uncle Silas* / New Edition / London / Chapman and Hall, 193, Piccadilly / 1873. Pictorial yellow boards in the series of The Select Library of Fiction.

It was again republished under the original title as

THE COCK / AND / ANCHOR / By / J. Sheridan / Le Fanu / Illustrated by / Brinsley Le Fanu / Downey and Co. / 12 York St. / Covent Garden. (1895.) With pictorial design of ' The Cock and Anchor,' which is repeated in black on the red-brown cover.

Prefatory Note by the author's son, Brinsley Le Fanu, dated London, July, 1895.

2. THE FORTUNES / OF / COLONEL TORLOGH O'BRIEN / A Tale / of / The Wars of King James / With (22) Illustrations by Hablot K. Browne / Dublin / James McGlashan, 21, D'Olier Street / William S. Orr and Company, London / MDCCCXLVII. Green cover with pictorial designs in gold.

This story had appeared in eleven monthly parts, April, 1846, to January, 1847, with a mis-spelling of the name Torlogh on the covers :

THE FORTUNES / of / TURLOGH O'BRIEN / A Tale of / The Wars of King James / James McGlashan, 21 D'Olier Street, Dublin. Pictorial pink paper covers.

The story was republished with all the illustrations by Routledge, N.D., and by Downey and Co., in 1896.

3. GHOST STORIES / AND / TALES OF MYSTERY / With (4) Illustrations by ' Phiz ' / Dublin / James McGlashan, 50 Upper Sackville Street / William S. Orr and Co., Amen Corner, London, / and Liverpool MDCCCLI.

Red cloth cover with design in gold of owl, tombstone, and rising moon, in a scroll. On the back the title is *A Book of Ghost Stories*. This is now a very rare work, and it is not in the British Museum. In addition to my own copy, I know of three others, and a fourth, belonging to Mr. Michael Sadleir, has a different cover, namely morocco grained red cloth, blind blocked on front and back, gold blocked and lettered on the spine : *Ghost Stories / Illustrations*.

The contents of *Ghost Stories and Tales of Mystery* comprise :

A. *The Watcher*. (Reprinted as *The Familiar* in *In a Glass Darkly*, Bentley, 1872, and in subsequent volumes.)

B. *The Murdered Cousin*. (The second early short form of *Uncle Silas*.)

C. *Schalken the Painter*. (Reprinted from *The Dublin University Magazine*, May, 1839.)

D. *The Evil Guest*. (This is the second early short form of *A Lost Name* (1867-1868.)

4. THE / HOUSE BY THE CHURCHYARD / By / J. Sheridan Le Fanu / In Three Volumes / London / Tinsley Brothers, Catherine St., Strand / 1863. Green or blue covers.

William Tinsley, the publisher of this book, stated in his *Random Recollections* (forgetting *The Cock and Anchor*) :

' *The House by the Churchyard* was the only three-volume novel I remember being printed and bound in Ireland. . . . Mr. Le Fanu . . . had had the book printed and part of the edition bound in Dublin before we saw or agreed to publish it ; but when he sent us a specimen copy, we found it was very badly produced indeed. Paper, printing, and binding were all of an inferior quality. We did not alter the printing and paper, but we got our binders to re-bind those sent to us in the binding done in Dublin ; in fact, we made the volumes look as well as we could, and the book sold very well indeed.'

5. WYLDER'S HAND / A Novel / By / Joseph Sheridan Le Fanu / Author of / *The House by the Churchyard* / In Three Volumes / [Monogram] / London / Richard Bentley, New Burlington Street / 1864. Maroon covers.

' To the Hon. Mrs. Norton, whose kindness will overlook its many faults, this Tale is inscribed by the Author.' (Le Fanu and Mrs. Norton were second cousins.)

A later edition of this book, published at sixpence by George

Newnes, 1903, has eight illustrations by F. H. Townsend and pictorial cover by Herbert Cole.

6. UNCLE SILAS / A Tale of Bartram-Haugh / By / J. S. Le Fanu / Author of . . . / In Three Volumes / London / Richard Bentley, New Burlington Street / 1864 (December): the reprint in this form followed in 1865, while in July of the same year appeared the second edition, in one volume, crown 8vo., price 6s. The first edition has maroon covers.

' To the Right Hon. the Countess of Gifford, as a token of respect, sympathy, and admiration, this Tale is inscribed by the Author.' Le Fanu and Lady Gifford were second cousins. She was the eldest of the beautiful Sheridan Sisters, ' The Three Graces,' the other two being Mrs. Norton and the Duchess of Somerset, and she was first married to Lord Dufferin.

The French translation of *Uncle Silas* was called *Mon Oncle Silas.*

7. THE PRELUDE / Being a Contribution towards / A History / of the / Election / for the University / By / John Figwood, Esq. / Barrister at Law, etc., etc. / Dublin / G. Herbert, 117, Grafton Street / 1865 / Price Sixpence.

8. GUY DEVERELL / By / J. S. Le Fanu / Author of . . . / In Three Volumes / London / Richard Bentley, New Burlington Street / 1865. Dark red covers.

' To that writer, so genial, so brilliant, so philosophic, whom all the world reads as Harry Lorrequer and as Cornelius O'Dowd, and to that friend how loved and honoured, known to the privileged as Charles Lever, this story, how unworthy an offering all but he will perceive, is dedicated by the Author.'

9. ALL IN THE DARK / By / J. Sheridan Le Fanu / Author of . . . / In Two Volumes / Richard Bentley, New Burlington Street / 1866. White cloth.

' To my dear brother William Richard Le Fanu, this Tale is inscribed with great affection and admiration.'

10. THE / TENANTS OF MALORY / A Novel / By / Joseph Sheridan Le Fanu / Author of . . . / In Three Volumes / London / Tinsley Brothers, 18, Catherine St., Strand / 1867. Red covers.

11. A LOST NAME / By / J. Sheridan Le Fanu / Author of . . . /

In Three Volumes / London / Richard Bentley, New Burlington Street / 1868. Red covers.

12. HAUNTED LIVES / A Novel / By / J. S. Le Fanu / Author of . . . / In Three Volumes / London / Tinsley Brothers 18, Catherine Street, Strand / 1868. Dark green covers.

' To Mrs. FitzGerald, of Fane Valley, this story is inscribed with kindest regards and many pleasant recollections by the Author.'

13. THE WYVERN MYSTERY / A Novel / By J. S. Le Fanu / Author of . . . / In Three Volumes / London / Tinsley Brothers, 18, Catherine St., Strand / 1869. Brown-maroon covers.

Dedication : ' My dear Judge Keogh, You, who take an interest in all Literature, will not disdain the dedication of these trifling volumes, in testimony of an early friendship, never interrupted, and of an admiration everywhere inspired by your brilliant talents. Ever yours most faithfully, J. S. Le Fanu.' (William Nicholas Keogh was the Judge who tried O'Donovan the Fenian, in 1865, and the Galway Election Petition in 1872. He committed suicide in 1878 after making a murderous assault upon his valet.)

An edition of *The Wyvern Mystery* in one volume, published by Downey and Co. in 1889 contains illustrations by Brinsley Le Fanu.

14. CHECKMATE / By / J. Sheridan Le Fanu /Author of . . . / In Three Volumes / London / Hurst and Blackett, Publishers / 13, Great Marlborough Street / 1871. Green covers.

' To the Right Honourable John Ball, M.P., this Tale is inscribed in memory of an early friendship and many happy hours by the Author.' (John Ball, 1818-1889, politician, traveller, and author, was Under-Secretary for the Colonies, 1855-1857).

15. THE ROSE AND THE KEY / By / J. Sheridan Le Fanu / Author of . . . / In Three Volumes / London / Chapman and Hall, 193, Piccadilly / 1871. Brown decorated covers.

' To Thomas E. Beatty, Esq., M.D., F.R.C.S., a name celebrated in his learned and brilliant profession, a guileless and genial nature, and delightful companion, beloved, admired, and honoured by many friends and by none more than by the Author, these pages are inscribed with much affection.'

16. CHRONICLES / OF / GOLDEN FRIARS / By / J. S. Le Fanu /
   Author of . . . / In Three Volumes / London / Richard
   Bentley and Son / New Burlington Street / 1871. Ma-
   genta covers.

' To the Lady Fanny Cole, these Chronicles are inscribed
with many happy recollections and the kind regards of the
Author.' (Lady Fanny Cole was, presumably, Lady Frances
Monck, daughter of the Earl of Rathdown, who married Owen
Blayney Cole in 1834).

The contents of the book comprise :

Vol. I. *A Strange Adventure in the Life of Miss Laura Mildmay*, in
which is incorporated the story of *Madam Crowl's Ghost* from *All
the Year Round*, December 31st, 1870.

The Haunted Baronet, from Belgravia, 1870, which is based on *The
Fortunes of Sir Robert Ardagh* from *The Dublin University Magazine*,
March, 1838.

Vol. II. *The Haunted Baronet*, concluded.

Vol. III. *The Bird of Passage*, from *Temple Bar*, April-July, 1870.

17. IN A GLASS DARKLY / By / J. Sheridan Le Fanu / Author
   of . . . / In Three Volumes / R. Bentley and Son, New
   Burlington Street / 1872. Brown-maroon covers.

' To Brinsley Homan, Esq., these volumes are inscribed
with much affection by his old friend the Author.'

The contents comprise :

Vol. I.

A. *Green Tea*, reprinted from *All the Year Round*, October-Novem-
   ber, 1869.

B. *The Familiar*, which is *The Watcher*, the first tale in *Ghost Stories
   and Tales of Mystery*, 1851.

C. *Mr. Justice Harbottle*, which is *The Haunted House in Westminster*,
   from *Belgravia*, January, 1872.

Vol. II.

D. *The Room in the Dragon Volant*, reprinted from *London Society*,
   February-June, 1872.

Vol. III.

E. *Carmilla*, reprinted from *The Dark Blue*, 1871-1872.

Green Tea, *The Familiar*, *Mr. Justice Harbottle*, and *Carmilla*
were published in one volume at sixpence, pictorial paper cover,
by George Newnes, London, with four illustrations by Cyrus
Cuneo ; and *The Room in the Dragon Volant* in a separate
volume of similar form with eight illustrations by Herbert
Cole, 1905.

A recent edition notable for its illustrations is :

J. Sheridan Le Fanu / IN A GLASS DARKLY / With Numerous Illustrations / by / Edward Ardizzone / London / Peter Davies / 1929.   Black covers.

18. WILLING TO DIE / By / J. S. Le Fanu / Author of . . . / In Three Volumes / London / Hurst and Blackett, 13, Great Marlborough Street / 1873.   Red-brown covers.
Republished in one volume :
> WILLING / To DIE / By J. S. Le Fanu / Downey and Co. / 12, York Street, Covent Garden.   Green cover.

19. THE / PURCELL PAPERS / By the late / Joseph Sheridan Le Fanu / Author of *Uncle Silas* / With a Memoir by / Alfred Perceval Graves / In Three Volumes / London / Richard Bentley and Son / 1880.   Grey-blue covers.
The contents were all reprinted from *The Dublin University Magazine* :
Vol. I.
A. *The Ghost and the Bone-setter.*
B. *The Fortunes of Sir Robert Ardagh.*
C. *The Last Heir of Castle Connor.*
D. *The Drunkard's Dream.*

Vol. II.
E. *Passage in the Secret History of an Irish Countess.*
F. *The Bridal of Carrigvarah.*
G. *Strange Event in the Life of Schalken the Painter.*
H. *Scraps of Hibernian Ballads.*

Vol. III.
I. *Jim Sulivan's Adventures in the Great Snow.*
J. *A Chapter in the History of a Tyrone Family.*
K. *An Adventure of Hardress Fitzgerald, a Royalist Captain.*
L. ' *The Quare Gander.*'
M. *Billy Malowney's Taste of Love and Glory.*

20. THE WATCHER / AND OTHER WEIRD STORIES / By / J. S. Le Fanu / With 21 Illustrations / By Brinsley Sheridan Le Fanu / London / Downey and Co., 12, York Street, Covent Garden / 1894.   Grey cover with design of bat and silver moon.

The contents were reprints from *The Dublin University Magazine* and *Ghost Stories and Tales of Mystery* (1851) :

A. *The Watcher.*

B. *The Fortunes of Sir Robert Ardagh.*

C. *The Drunkard's Dream.*

D. *Passage in the Secret History of an Irish Countess.*

E. *Schalken the Painter.*

F. *A Chapter in the History of a Tyrone Family.*

21. THE / EVIL GUEST / By / J. Sheridan Le Fanu / With / Thirty Illustrations / By / Brinsley Le Fanu / London, Downey and Co., 12, York St. / Covent Garden / 1895. Dark green-blue cover with design of bats and gold dragon.

This was the fourth story in *Ghost Stories and Tales of Mystery* (1851), an extension of *Some Account of the Latter Days of the Hon. Richard Marston of Dunoran* from *The Dublin University Magazine*, 1848, and the intermediate form of *A Lost Name* (1867-1868). There are some omissions and variations from the original text.

22. A / CHRONICLE OF GOLDEN FRIARS / AND OTHER STORIES / By / J. Sheridan Le Fanu / Author of . . . / Illustrated by Brinsley Le Fanu and John F. O'Hea / Downey and Co., Limited / 12, York Street, Covent Garden, London / 1896.   Green cover.

Contents :

A. *A Chronicle of Golden Friars*, which is *The Bird of Passage*, a story of thirty chapters, reprinted from *Temple Bar*, 1870, and from Vol. III. of *Chronicles of Golden Friars*, 1871.

B. *Jim Sulivan's Adventures in the Great Snow.*

C. *The Last Heir of Castle Connor.*

D. *Billy Malowney's Taste of Love and Glory.*

E. *The Ghost and the Bone-setter.*

F. ' *The Quare Gander.*'

The last five of the above were reprinted from *The Dublin University Magazine.*

23. THE / POEMS / OF JOSEPH SHERIDAN LE FANU / Edited by / Alfred Perceval Graves / With a Portrait of J. S. Le Fanu / London / Downey and Co., Limited / 12, York Street, Covent Garden / 1896.   Green cover.

24. MADAM CROWL'S GHOST / AND OTHER TALES OF MYSTERY /
By / Joseph Sheridan Le Fanu / Author of *Uncle Silas*,
etc. / Collected and Edited by / M. R. James / Author of
Ghost Stories / of an Antiquary / London / G. Bell and
Sons, Ltd. / 1923.

With a Prologue and Epilogue, Bibliographical and Critical,
by Dr. M. R. James. Black cover.

A. *Madam Crowl's Ghost*, from *All the Year Round*, December, 1870.
B. *Squire Toby's Will*: A Ghost Story, from *Temple Bar*, January,
1868.
C. *Dickon the Devil*, from *London Society*, Christmas Number, 1872.
D. *The Child that went with the Fairies*, from *All the Year Round*,
February, 1870.
E. *The White Cat of Drumgunniol*, from *All the Year Round*, April,
1870.
F. *An Account of Some Strange Disturbances in Aungier Street*, from
The Dublin University Magazine, December, 1853.
G. *Ghost Stories of Chapelizod*, from *The Dublin University Magazine*,
January, 1851.
H. *Wicked Captain Walshawe, of Wauling*, from *The Dublin Univer-
sity Magazine*, April, 1864.
I. *Sir Dominick's Bargain*, from *All the Year Round*, July, 1872.
J. *Ultor De Lacy*, from *The Dublin University Magazine*, December,
1861.
K. *The Vision of Tom Chuff*, from *All the Year Round*, October, 1870.
L. *Stories of Lough Guir*, from *All the Year Round*, April, 1870.

EDWARD BRADLEY AND GEORGE LAWRENCE: THE AUTHORS OF 'MR. VERDANT GREEN' and 'GUY LIVINGSTONE'

ON the same day, over a hundred years ago, on March 25th, 1827, were born two boys, one in Sussex and the other in Worcestershire: one was the son of a clergyman and the other became a clergyman. Both were destined some thirty years later to achieve considerable fame as novelists, though neither wrote under his own name. Edward Bradley always used the pseudonym of ' Cuthbert Bede ' ; and to the end of his literary life George Lawrence was only known on his title pages as ' The Author of *Guy Livingstone*,' his first and most famous book, whereby arose much mystery concerning his life and personality. On the other hand, the creator of the immortal Verdant Green was well known to be a genial and popular cleric in the shires.

Edward Bradley came of an ancient Worcestershire family, whose characteristics can be gauged by the phrase ' Land and Liturgy.' The younger sons generally entered the Church, and as far back as 1537 an ancestor, Walter Bradley, was rector of Upton Warren, Worcestershire. The living of Chaddesley Corbet in the same county was held during the eighteenth century by the Rev. William Bradley, D.D., and the Rev. Thomas Bradley, father and son, in direct succession. The son and grandson of the last-named broke the clerical tradition for two generations by entering the medical profession.

This grandson, Thomas Bradley, a surgeon of Kidderminster, married Mary Gower of that town, where their son, Edward Bradley, the future novelist, was born. Another son, Thomas Waldron Bradley, was also a novelist

in future years, the author of *Grantley Grange* (1874)
and *Nelly Hamilton* (1875). The artistic strain in the family
came from the Gowers. The success of *Mr. Verdant
Green* was much aided by the delightful and quaint illustrations drawn by the author.

Edward Bradley was educated at the Grammar School
of Kidderminster, and went as Thorp and Foundation
Scholar to University College, Durham, the patron saints
of which ancient city are the Incorruptible Cuthbert and
the Venerable Bede. Their names were borrowed by the
young *alumnus* for his literary cognomen in years to come.
Although *Mr. Verdant Green* is the most humorous and
characteristic of all novels of Oxford life, the author was
never himself an undergraduate there. But after taking
his B.A. degree at Durham in 1848, he was, during the
following year, for some time in Oxford pursuing various
studies. Then, after helping in the schools at Kidderminster under the vicar, the Rev. T. L. Claughton (afterwards the first Bishop of St. Albans), Edward Bradley
was ordained in 1850, and went to his first curacy at
Glatton, Huntingdonshire. He lodged at the *Woolpack*
inn, a fine old hostelry on the Great North Road by
Stilton, and here he began the sketches which were
to develop into *Mr. Verdant Green*. ' Mr. Bradley's
rooms ' are still pointed out to visitors at the inn. After
a few years he transferred to Leigh, in his natal county of
fruit trees, near Worcester, as curate to the Rev. H.
Somers Cocks.

He had already commenced his literary career, for he
started to contribute to *Bentley's Miscellany* whilst still in
his teens. But it was in the little house, ' The March,'
Bransford, he occupied near Leigh, that he wrote the
greater part of his famous work, *Mr. Verdant Green*, and
in the garden there still survives the old apple tree of
curious angles, forming an orchard seat for two persons,
' provided that they regarded a close proximity as comfortable sitting "—the tree whereon Verdant Green and
Patty Honeywood were seated when he made his first

attempt at the proposal which led to his being 'married and done for.'

As in the case of many other subsequently famous books, there was great difficulty in finding a publisher for *Mr. Verdant Green*. At length the first part appeared in October, 1853, in a series of shilling ' Books for the Rail,' issued by Nathaniel Cooke, Strand. *The Further Adventures* followed in 1854, and *Mr. Verdant Green Married and Done For* in 1856. When the three parts were bound together, more than one hundred thousand copies were sold by 1870, but it is said the author did not receive more than £350.[1] *Mr. Verdant Green* contains, of course, many portraits of Oxford characters in the Forties, including Dr. Plumtre, the Vice-Chancellor, and Dr. Bliss. Mr. Bouncer was drawn from Bradley's great friend, the Rev. J. G. Wood, who later was chaplain to St. Bartholomew's Hospital and a distinguished writer on natural history.

A sequel written many years later, *Little Mr. Bouncer and His Friend Verdant Green* (1873), was not a success. Indeed, Cuthbert Bede never touched again the high mark of his first work, though he continued to write nearly to the end of his life. When *Mr. Verdant Green* made Bradley famous in the literary world he was in fact 'a pale young curate then.' He was introduced to Douglas Jerrold, who, observing his pale complexion, said : ' Mr. Verdant Green ? No ! Surely Mr. Blanco White ? ' At this period, too, he became the friend of George Cruikshank, and his published recollections of the artist are a valuable contribution to the biography of Cruikshank. When Bradley was intimate with him, Cruikshank was in the most eccentric phase of his career as a fanatical advocate for total abstinence and the abolition of what he considered public abuses. Thus he invited

---

[1] There was an imitation of the book in *The Cambridge Freshman, or Memoirs of Mr. Golightly*, by Martin Legrand (James Rice), with illustrations by ' Phiz,' 1871. In *The New Monthly Magazine*, 1852, had appeared *The Recreations of Mr. Jolly Green*, which perhaps suggested the title of Cuthbert Bede's amusing novel.

EDWARD BRADLEY
From an early photograph sent by his son, Mr. Cuthbert Bradley
By kind permission of *The Bookman*

Cuthbert Bede to contribute to *George Cruikshank's Magazine* letterpress for illustrations attacking the evil of the sucking of handles of sticks and umbrellas in the streets and public conveyances. However, Bradley treated the subject too jocularly, and Cruikshank rejected the article. Entitled *Dental Dangers*, it can be found in Cuthbert Bede's *Motley* (1855). Another book of his, published this same year, *Photographic Pleasures*, will amuse those who are interested in the early stages of photography. These books of Nonsense, together with *Medley*, *Love's Provocations*, *Funny Figures*, and other comic works by Cuthbert Bede, are most entertaining ; and his clever, quaint illustrations rank him with Edward Lear and Doyle and Thackeray (as an illustrator of his own literary work). A visit Cuthbert Bede paid in the autumn of 1859 to South Argyllshire caused him to write *Glencreggan, or a Highland Home in Cantire* (1861), which contains some charming illustrations by the author. *The White Wife* (1865) is a collection of legendary and supernatural stories which he heard from the Gaelic-speaking natives of this same West Highland district.

An excellent novel by Cuthbert Bede which deserves resuscitation is *Mattins and Muttons, or the Beauty of Brighton* (1866), a story of social life in Brighton during the town's great decade of popularity sixty years ago. It somewhat resembles Surtees's *Plain or Ringlets* (1860). The odd title was meant to suggest that fashionable life in Brighton was divided into two classes, the carnal who went for gossip and light refreshment at Mutton's famous pastrycook's shop on the King's Road, and the spiritual who resorted to daily services of high ritual at St. Paul's Church, in Queen's Square. A chapter is devoted to a description of this church and its ornaments, for these were the days of ardent Puseyistical agitation. The perpetual curate here was the Rev. A. D. Wagner, who was so prominent at the trial of Constance Kent in 1865. She was an inmate of St. Mary's Home, Queen Square, attached to this church, and confessed to Mr. Wagner the

murder of her brother.   When Mr. Wagner, ' in a whin-
ing tone,' declined to answer any question involving a
breach of the confessional ' there were loud and prolonged hisses in Court.'   Bradley termed the Wagnerites
' Mongrelians,' because they were allied to dog-Latin !

In his later life Cuthbert Bede's literary interests were
of an historical nature.   He wrote an excellent topographical account for *Notes and Queries* (1868) of the flight
of King Charles the Second after the Battle of Worcester
to Staffordshire and the Royal Oak.   He was the first to
trace out the King's route, as Harrison Ainsworth acknowledged in his romance on this subject, *Boscobel* (1872).
Cuthbert Bede's last book, *Fotheringay and Mary Queen of
Scots* (1886), concerned an historical event very close to
his heart.   Like Whyte Melville, he preserved a chivalrous
devotion to the Stuarts.

Cuthbert Bede was a contributor to many and varied
publications—*Punch, All the Year Round, The Field, Once
a Week, The Gentleman's Magazine, The St. James's Magazine, The London Review, The Quiver, The Boy's Own Paper*
and *The Illustrated London News*—wherein he conducted
from 1856 the double acrostics, a pastime he claimed to
be the first to introduce in England.   Who is the claimant
for introducing the infuriating waste-time of ' cross-
words ' ?   If living, he should surely be beheaded like one
of his clues.

Through all his years of literary activity Cuthbert Bede
was also an active parish priest, beloved by a wide circle
of parishioners and friends.   From Leigh he went to his
first vicarage at Bobbington, Staffordshire, 1857.   He
was rector of Denton with Caldecott, Huntingdonshire,
1859-1871, and rector of Stretton, Rutland, 1871-1883.
He raised £2000 for the restoration of his church at
Stretton, partly by giving lectures on ' Wit and the
Humorists ' in the towns of the Midlands.   In 1883 his
friend, Sir Gilbert Heathcote (later first Earl of Ancaster),
presented him to the living of Lenton, Lincolnshire.   Mr.
Bradley died there on December 12th, 1889, but was

buried in the churchyard of his former parish at Stretton.

Edward Bradley married in 1858 Harriet, daughter of Samuel Hancocks, of Wolverley, Worcestershire, and his two sons carry on the loved vocations of his life. The elder, Mr. Cuthbert Bradley, is well known as ' Whipster,' of *The Field*, and an authoritative writer on hunting. The second son, the Rev. H. W. Bradley, is vicar of Misterton, Somerset.

.   .   .   .   .   .

The author of *Guy Livingstone*, George Alfred Lawrence, the elder son of the Rev. Alfred Charnley Lawrence, was born at his father's rectory of Buxted, Sussex. Through his mother, Lady Emily Mary Finch-Hatton, George Lawrence was related to half the peerage. She was the sister of the tenth Earl of Winchilsea and daughter of George Finch-Hatton, of Eastwell Park, Kent (a house rented in later years by the Duke of Edinburgh, and consequently the early home of the present Queen of Roumania), by his marriage with Lady Elizabeth Murray, daughter of the second Earl of Mansfield. Lady Emily Lawrence's grand-aunts included the Duchesses of Cleveland and Somerset and the Marchioness of Rockingham; and her brother, Lord Winchilsea, married a daughter of the third Duke of Montrose. The Rev. Alfred Lawrence was later rector of Sandhurst, Kent, probably a living in the gift of his wife's family.

George Lawrence entered Rugby School in 1841, during the last year of Dr. Arnold's head-mastership, and may have been the original of one of the smaller boys who figure in *Tom Brown's School Days*, for he was the contemporary, though three years their junior, of the Rev. Berkeley Owen Jones (' Slogger Williams ') and the Rev. Augustus Orlebar, who were the boy protagonists of the great fight in that ' noble ' story, as well as of Thomas Hughes himself. I do not think it has been pointed out hitherto that *Guy Livingstone*, in the early scenes, is also a picture of Rugby—that is to say, of the ' muscular ' quality of the school minus the ' Christianity.' Further,

Guy Livingstone appeared in the same year, 1857, as *Tom Brown's School Days*, and it is possible that Lawrence, after reading Hughes's idealised presentment of Rugby, resolved to give his recollections of the school in its harder and more human aspects. The scene in *Guy Livingstone* where Guy as a senior pupil is invited to dine with the Head-master and his bride and flirts audaciously with the latter, finally carrying off as a gage a flower worn by the young lady, with the indignant husband-head-master standing by, was an actual escapade of George Lawrence's, according to his school contemporaries.[1] The lady in question was young Mrs. Tait. Dr. Tait himself was only thirty-one when he succeeded Arnold at Rugby in 1842 ; he married Miss Catherine Spooner[2] the following year. Tait became Archbishop of Canterbury in 1869.

To be ' hard '—more particularly in the physical sense —is the motto of *Guy Livingstone* and the author's succeeding works. So, in a way, these stories, like the ' noble ' youths in the novels of Henry Kingsley, are the legitimate outcome of the muscular cult proclaimed at Rugby eighty years ago. But indeed the model held up for youth in the first two decades of the Victorian era was always muscular. The hero of the virile novel of the period had to be a powerful young demi-god of great stature who could tackle single-handed a band of Chartists or poachers, as the scene in London or country might be ; he had to take in his normal stride on horseback the leaping of disused chalk-pits and ten-barred gates with water-ditch beyond ; and when he joined the army he had perforce to cleave to the chine his Russian or Indian foes with one mighty sweep of his sabre. Even in their lighter moods the muscular young men of the fiction of the forties and fifties were most alarming. Thus, in *Frank Fairlegh*, Harry Oaklands, when annoyed during

[1] These included H. W. Waddington and Professor J. Conington.

[2] Her father was Archdeacon of Coventry and Rector of Elmdon, near Rugby. In *Guy Livingstone*, the head-master's wife is the daughter of a dean.

his pupilage at a private tutor's, ' with a bound like that
of an infuriated tiger,' pitches one of his companions
through the window on to some bushes eight feet below,
and resumes his seat with his legs placed upon the back
of another youth he has sent sprawling.   And Trevanion,
in *Harry Lorrequer*, when he rises, with all his ' gigantic
proportions,' to retaliate the insults of a fire-eating French
officer, wrenches apart the nose and chin of his victim
with ' the force of an ogre,' thereby fracturing the jaw-
bone of Le Capitaine as he spits down his throat.   *Laudator temporis acti* : this breed of young man is extinct in
this our degenerate day ; so it is well we can examine the
type in all its glory in the pages of *Guy Livingstone*.   Guy,
from Rugby to his fatal riding accident, is ever hard—
hard as nails.   At school he knocks a boy senseless with
a brass candlestick.   When *in extremis* he crushes a
silver cup just to prove to his enemy that he could an
he would treat him in the same way.   And he was rough
and masterful with women.   *Guy Livingstone, or Thorough*,
was most amusingly parodied by Bret Harte in his early
volume of literary skits, *Sensation Novels Condensed* (1871),
as *Guy Heavystone, or Entire*.   Therein the hero lays out
his school companions with a piston-rod.   Guy wears a
snaffle-bit in his mouth to ' curb his occasional ferocity,'
and he ends his career, in the manner of Samson, by pull-
ing down the house in his death spasms.   The earlier
novels of Ouida were a direct imitation of the methods of
George Lawrence with their dashing guardsmen and
flamboyant mode of life.   Miss Rhoda Broughton adopted
the idea of the strong, gnarled, silent hero for her earliest
novels, written in 1866-1867.   The later developments
of the ' cave-men ' and tough ' sheiks ' of fiction are thus
in direct descent from Guy Livingstone—' *fons et origo*,'
as Lawrence would have said.

George Lawrence had become the favourite author of
military men, of officers back from the Crimean War and
the Indian Mutiny, and even Lord Dundreary might have
said : ' Here is a novelist a fellah *can* understand.'   But

at the same time Lawrence provided none of the meretricious sops of the ' best-seller ' ; he was a man of culture, wide reading, and classical knowledge. His stories abound with literary and historical allusions and Latin saws—a characteristic Bret Harte did not overlook in his parody. He was entirely a man's author : for women his books were considered ' improper.'

Lawrence followed up his first great success with *Sword and Gown* [1] (1859), wherein the hero, Royston Keene, receives his death wound in the Charge of the Light Brigade at Balaclava. It is strange that with his military predilections, and adventurous, romantic temperament, Lawrence did not himself enter the army.[2] Instead he went as a School Exhibitioner to Oxford, to Balliol, in 1845, where he took his B.A. degree five years later.[3] He became a barrister, and was called to the Bar, at the Inner Temple, in 1852. His younger brother, William Lawrence, did in fact pursue the full career of a Guy Livingstonean hero, for he became a lieutenant in the 9th Lancers and was killed in a regimental steeplechase near Dublin in 1865.

It is strange that eight years previously George Lawrence should have described in *Guy Livingstone* such a similar death and the grief of the hero's mother, Lady Catherine Livingstone, whose bereavement foreran that of her original, Lady Emily Lawrence, the novelist's mother.

However, the even tenor of a barrister's life could not content the restless, roving disposition of George Lawrence for long. He chafed for adventure, and the opportunity came with the breaking out of the Civil War in

---

[1] Both this book and *Guy Livingstone* were published by John W. Parker, West Strand, London, who a few years earlier had issued the *Poems* (1851) of George Meredith.

[2] He was a lieutenant in the Northamptonshire Militia for a time.

[3] He had recited in Rugby School on June 20th, 1845, his long prize poem, fully garnished with Greek quotations, entitled *The Marriage of Marie Antoinette*.

America in 1861. Although he had a wife and a little son of two years, he was resolved to go to the seat of war and offer his services to the South, for whose cause he entertained the most enthusiastic ardour. Before he could reach the Confederate lines he was taken prisoner by the soldiers of the Northern Army, and shut up in a guardhouse. Lawrence managed to communicate with Lord Lyons, the British Minister in Washington, who succeeded in procuring his release, but only on the condition of the knight-errant's immediate return to England. Lawrence's gallant adventure provided him with excellent material for his next book, *Border and Bastille*, which ran into three editions by 1863 ; this was not a novel but a record of his experiences in America. A later visit to that country under more peaceful circumstances he related in *Silverland* (1873).

George Lawrence's other novels were *Barren Honour* (1862) ; *Maurice Dering* (1864) ; *Sans Merci* (1866) ; *Brakespeare* (1868) ; *Anteros* (1871) ; *Hagarene* (1874). Lawrence also had considerable poetical gifts. There is a very scarce little volume, *Songs of Feast, Field, and Fray* (1853), and *A Bundle of Ballads* (1864).[1]

Lawrence lived at Gressenhall, near Old Buckenham, Norfolk, and at 86A, Portland Place, London (where his widow remained until her death in 1893). He was also much abroad and travelled far, and was a most amusing raconteur of his adventures. He died in a nursing home at 134, George Street, Edinburgh, on September 23rd, 1876, at the age of forty-nine, and was buried in that city.

It is difficult to arrive at an estimate of George Lawrence's character, for contemporary reports are very contradictory. His enemies asserted he was lawless and un-

---

[1] One of his poems is an amusing parody of *Young Lochinvar*, relating the exploits of a hunter in Galway :

' He called upon Kathleen—one shout and one spring :
She clove through the air, like a swallow on wing.
He turned in his saddle, " Now follow who dare !
When I ride for my county," quoth Valentine Maher.'

principled.[1] His memory was attacked a few days after his death in a prominent newspaper, and G. A. Sala protested and defended him in *The Illustrated London News*. William Tinsley, who published several of Lawrence's -novels, stated that he was reckless and extravagant and a confirmed gambler. He used to pay Lawrence £1000 for each novel; the author would receive half this amount in advance and rush off to Homburg. In less than a week Tinsley would get a letter saying all the money had been lost at the gaming tables and would the publisher send him some more. He did, and it went the way of the first draft. But Lawrence always finished the novel in hand scrupulously according to contract, although the money for his work had all been received and squandered. Tinsley says, ' He was very honourable,' so let that be the final verdict.

George Lawrence, by his marriage, at St. Mary's Church, Bathwick, in 1851 with Mary, daughter of Patrick Kirwan, of Cregg, Co. Galway, left an only surviving child, George Patrick Charles Lawrence, born in 1859. Mrs. Lawrence was a beautiful woman, but a complete opposite to her husband in character : she has been described to me as ' a Saint, and a strict one too ! ' The son became a brilliant barrister with a considerable practice. He married Hildegarde, daughter of Lord Davey, the Judge, whose third daughter was the wife of General Sir William Gatacre, the commander of the Third Division in the South African War.

George Patrick Lawrence unsuccessfully contested the Guildford constituency of Surrey against Mr. St. John Brodrick (now Earl of Midleton) some twenty-three years

---

[1] How vindictive his enemies could be is evidenced by a note in a copy of Lawrence's *Songs of Feast, Field, and Fray*, which had belonged to the Honourable Percy Feilding, his school contemporary at Rugby :

' These are poems full of merit, yet they were written by as unprincipalled (*sic*) a scoundrel as ever lived, a man utterly devoid of honour or feeling, and it is curious that such a scamp could be capable of such composition.   P. F.'

GEORGE LAWRENCE
From a photograph sent by his niece, Miss Lawrence
By kind permission of *The Bookman*

ago. He died in 1908, also at the age of forty-nine. Thus, by strange fate, George Lawrence, his only son, and his brother, all died early in the prime of manhood—as did the restless, dashing heroes of the tales written by the author of *Guy Livingstone*. The words he wrote of one of his own heroes—

> ' O gallant heart, so early hushed,
> Bear witness from the past . . .
> Life has strange pages we must read,
> Strange riddles none can guess,'—

form the fitting epitaph for brave, reckless George Lawrence.

LIST OF WORKS BY EDWARD BRADLEY—
' CUTHBERT BEDE '

1. THE ADVENTURES / OF / MR. VERDANT GREEN / [Full face portrait of undergraduate]. AN OXFORD FRESHMAN / By Cuthbert Bede, B.A. / With Numerous Illustrations / Designed and Drawn on the Wood by the Author / ' A College Joke to cure the Dumps.' Swift / London / Nathaniel Cooke / late Ingram, Cooke, and Co. / Milford House, Strand / 1853. Paper cover with the under-graduate portrait.

In the series of Illustrated Books for the Rail : One Shilling each.

2. THE FURTHER ADVENTURES / OF / MR. VERDANT GREEN / AN OXFORD UNDERGRADUATE / Being a Continuation of *The Adventures of Mr. Verdant* / *Green, An Oxford Freshman* / By Cuthbert Bede, B.A. / With Numerous Illustrations / Designed and Drawn on the Wood by the Author / ' A College Joke to cure the Dumps.' Swift / H. Ingram and Co. / Milford House, Milford Lane, Strand, London / and by all Booksellers / 1854.

The paper cover has a portrait of undergraduate in profile. The advertisement on back cover states that the First Part of *Mr. Verdant Green* was already in its fourth edition.

3. MR. VERDANT GREEN / MARRIED AND DONE FOR / Being the Third and Concluding Part / of The / Adventures of

Mr. Verdant Green / *An Oxford Freshman* / By / Cuthbert Bede, B.A. / London / James Blackwood, Paternoster Row / 1857.

The paper cover has a design in green of Cupid burning an undergraduate's mortar-board.

The Three Parts were in later years issued in one volume as Mr. Verdant Green / By / Cuthbert Bede, B.A. / (Rev. Edward Bradley) / With sixty-five Illustrations by the Author / London / Chatto and Windus.

4. Motley / Prose and Verse : Grave and Gay / By / Cuthbert Bede, B.A. / Author of *Verdant Green* / With Original Illustrations by the Author / ' Motley's the only wear.' Shakespeare / London / James Blackwood, Paternoster Row / 1855. Pictorial boards.

5. Photographic / Pleasures / Popularly portrayed with Pen and Pencil / By Cuthbert Bede, B.A. / Author of *Verdant Green* / ' Start into Light, and make the Lighter Start.' *Rejected Addresses* / London / 1855 / T. McLean, 26, Haymarket.

Apparently, a few years later, another publisher took over the remaining copies of this work, for in my copy there is a second title-page, much the same as above, but commencing : With Seventy Humorous designs by the Author ; and bearing the imprint : London / John Camden Hotten / Piccadilly / 1859. Dark blue cover with pictorial design in gold.

' To all the light-hearted friends of light painting, these pages of light literature are, with no light regard, dedicated.

' Leigh, Worcester, Jan. 1855.'

Four of the amusing pictures in this book had appeared in *Punch*, and another in No. 1 of *Cruikshank's Magazine*.

6. Love's / Provocations / Being / Extracts / Taken in the most unmanly and unmannerly manner / from the Diary of Miss Polly C—— / By / Cuthbert Bede / Author of . . . . / London / Ward and Lock, 158, Fleet Street / 1855. Pictorial green boards.

This work contains the usual clever illustrations by the author.

7. Medley / By / Cuthbert Bede, B.A. / Author of / *Motley* / *Verdant Green* / &c &c / Hallo my Fancy, whither wilt thou go ? / London / J. Blackwood, Paternoster Row. 1856. In pictorial paper cover with design of jester.

Price One Shilling.   With amusing illustrations by the author.

8. THE / SHILLING / BOOK / OF / BEAUTY / Edited / and / Illustrated by / Cuthbert Bede / 1856 / J. Blackwood, Paternoster Row, London.   Paper cover.

9. TALES / OF / COLLEGE LIFE / By / Cuthbert Bede, B.A. / Author of . . . / London / Charles H. Clarke, Paternoster Row / 1856.   Paper cover.

Contents :

A. *Aeger, or Mistaken Identity.*
B. *A Long-Vacation Vigil.*
C. *The Only Man Left in College on Christmas Day.*

Preface, dated May, 1856, states that these tales were written at various times during the last six years and published in various periodicals.

' The following pages are affectionately inscribed to my brother, T. W. Bradley.'

This work was reissued in 1862 as

COLLEGE LIFE / By Cuthbert Bede, B.A. / Author of . . . / New Edition / London / W. Kent and Co., 23, Paternoster Row.   Boards, in The Shilling Standard Library.

10. NEARER AND DEARER / A Tale Out of School / ' Has she a brother / Has she a nearer one / Still, and a dearer one / Yet than all other.'   Hood / A Novelette / By Cuthbert Bede, B.A. / Author of . . . / London / Richard Bentley, New Burlington Street / 1857.

' With much affection I dedicate this little Tale to my uncle, W. Bradley, who has shown much interest in this novelette, but far more in the Author.   June, 1857.'

This story is illustrated by the Author.

11. FAIRY FABLES / By / Cuthbert Bede, B.A. / With Illustrations by Alfred Crowquill / London / Richard Bentley, New Burlington Street.   1858.   Emerald-green cover with gold design, and rainbow end papers.

Contents :

A. *The Polite Frog.*
B. *The Three Little Kittens.*
C. *The Little Fir-tree.*
D. *The Old Woman and her Parrot.*
E. *The Queen of the Twelfth Cakes.*

' These Fairy Fables are dedicated to Constance May Waldron by her affectionate uncle and godfather, the Author.

Crowquill's illustrations in this volume are delightful.

12. FUNNY FIGURES / By / A. Funnyman / (Cuthbert Bede) /
London / James Blackwood, Paternoster Row.   1858.
Pictorial boards.

One Shilling Plain : Two Shillings Coloured.   In the latter
form there are twenty-four coloured pictures each illustrating
a Limerick in this style :

> ' There were some young ladies named Briggs,
>   Who were horribly frightened at pigs ;
>   If they met in a field,
>   These young ladies squealed,
>   And went off in hysterical jigs.'

13. HAPPY HOURS / AT WYNFORD GRANGE / A Story for
Children / By / Cuthbert Bede / Author of . . . / London / James Blackwood, Paternoster Row / 1859.   Blue
cover with gold design.

Illustrations in colour reproduced by the Dalziel Brothers.

' These pages are affectionately inscribed to my sister, H. M.
Bradley, who has very greatly contributed to my " Happy
Hours." '

14. GLENCREGGAN / OR / A HIGHLAND HOME IN CANTIRE / By
/ Cuthbert Bede / Illustrated with three maps, eight
chromolithographs and sixty-one woodcuts from the
author's drawings / In Two Volumes / London / Longmans / 1861.   Green covers.

15. OUR NEW RECTOR / OR THE VILLAGE OF NORTON /
Edited by / Cuthbert Bede / Author of . . . / London /
Saunders, Otley, and Co., 66, Brook Street, Hanover
Square / 1861.   Purple cover.

This is a very sentimental tale, which concludes with ' Little
Mabel sleeps sweetly under the daisies.'

16. THE CURATE OF CRANSTON / WITH / OTHER PROSE AND
VERSE / By / Cuthbert Bede / Author of . . . / London /
Saunders, Otley, and Co. / 66, Brook Street, Hanover
Square / 1862.   Dark blue cover.

In this volume, the title piece and *Mareli* were printed for the
first time : most of the other items had appeared in *Once a Week,*
The Illustrated News, and *Bentley's Miscellany.*

17. A Tour / in Tartan-Land / By / Cuthbert Bede / Author of . . . / London / Richard Bentley / 1863. Red cover with design.

 ' To my Wife, the dear companion of my tour, this volume is most affectionately inscribed with the earnest hope that, throughout life's journey, we may still be found together. June, 1863.'

18. The Visitor's Handbook to Rosslyn and Hawthorn den, 1864.

19. The White Wife / With Other Stories / Super-natural, Romantic, Legendary / Collected and Illus-trated by Cuthbert Bede / Author of . . . / London / Sampson Low, Son, and Marston / 14, Ludgate Hill / 1865. Blue cover.

20. The Rook's Garden / Essays and Sketches / By / Cuth-bert Bede / London / Sampson Low, and Marston / Milton House, Ludgate Hill / 1865. Green cover.

 Illustrated head and tail pieces. The contents of book were reprinted from various journals.

21. Mattins and Muttons / or, The Beauty of Brighton / A Love Story / By / Cuthbert Bede / Author of . . . / London / Sampson Low, Son, and Marston / Milton House, Ludgate Hill / 1866. In Two Volumes. Brown covers.

22. Charles II's Flight from Worcester.

 This is in *Notes and Queries*, 13th June, 1868.

23. Round the Peat-Fire at Glenbrechy / By Cuthbert Bede / Author of *Verdant Green, Glencreggan, The White Wife*, and other West Highland Stories / With Illustra-tions by the Author. This is in *Oranges and Lemons*, the Christmas Number of *Once a Week*, 1869.

24. Little Mr. Bouncer / and / His Friend, Verdant Green / By / Cuthbert Bede, B.A. / Author of *Mr. Verdant Green* . . . / With Illustrations by the Author / London / James Blackwood and Co. / 8, Lovell's Court, Paternoster Row / 1873. Violet cover with comic de-sign, ' Plucking a goose.'

25. FIGARO / AT HASTINGS, ST. LEONARDS / By Cuthbert Bede /
Author of . . . / With Illustrations by the Author / Abel
Heywood and Son / 56 and 58, Oldham Street, Man-
chester, and 4, Catherine Street, Strand, London. 1877.
Pictorial paper cover.

' To James Mortimer, Esq., Founder, Editor, and Sole Proprietor of *The London Figaro*, the following pages are gratefully inscribed by his friend and fellow-worker writer, Cuthbert
Bede.'

26. HUMOUR, WIT, AND SATIRE / Containing I. *Book of Beauty*,
II. *Motley* / III. *Medley* / By / Cuthbert Bede, B.A. /
Author of . . . / With numerous illustrations by the
Author / London / James Blackwood and Co., Lovell's
Court, Paternoster Row. 1885. Claret cover.

27. FOTHERINGAY / AND / MARY QUEEN OF SCOTS / Being / An
Account, Historical and Descriptive / of Fotheringay
Castle / The Last Prison of Mary Queen of Scots / and
the / Scene of her Trial and Execution / By Cuthbert
Bede / With Illustrations by the Author / and an
original contemporary portrait of Mary Queen of Scots /
now first published / London / Simpkin, Marshall and
Co. / Oundle / Alfred King / 1886. Red cover with
the Queen's monogram in gold.

Dedicated to John Moyer Heathcote, of Conington Castle,
Huntingdonshire, from Lenton Vicarage, Grantham, November, 1885.

This book was an extension, with new illustrations, of three
papers which appeared in *The Leisure Hour*, November, 1865.

28. BETROTHAL RING OF MARY QUEEN OF SCOTS / 1565 / A
Description of the Darnley Ring discovered in 1820 by
a labourer, Robert Wyatt, when digging in the eastern
mound on which stood the Keep of Fotheringay Castle /
Printed for the Tercentenary of Mary Queen of Scots
Exhibition held at Peterborough, 1887.

NOTE.—Cuthbert Bede was a constant contributor to *Notes and
Queries.*

LIST OF WORKS BY GEORGE LAWRENCE

1. THE MARRIAGE / OF MARIE ANTOINETTE / WITH THE
   DAUPHIN / A Prize Poem / Recited in Rugby School /
   June 20. MDCCCXLV / Rugby : Printed by J. S. Crossley,
   1845.
   The copy at the British Museum (Press Mark : C. 57. d.
   10 (10) is bound up with a volume of *The Rugby Miscellany*,
   together with the rare Prize Poem, *Alaric at Rome*, recited by
   Matthew Arnold in 1840 ; *The Longest Day*, recited by Arthur
   Hugh Clough in 1836 ; and others.

2. SONGS / of / FEAST, FIELD, AND FRAY / by Λ / Longman,
   Brown, Green, and Longmans / 1853. Blue cover with
   gold design of vase.

3. GUY LIVINGSTONE / or / 'Thorough' / Ich habe gelebt
   und geliebt / London / John W. Parker and Son, West
   Strand / 1857. Blue cover.

4. SWORD AND GOWN / By the Author of *Guy Livingstone* /
   London / John W. Parker and Son, West Strand / 1859.
   Originally published in *Fraser's Magazine*. Blue cover.

5. BARREN HONOUR / A Tale / By the Author of *Guy Living-
   stone* / In Two Volumes / Originally published in
   Fraser's Magazine / Parker, Son, and Brown, West
   Strand / 1862. Maroon-brown covers.

6. BORDER AND BASTILLE / By / The Author of *Guy Livingstone* / London / Tinsley Brothers, 18, Catherine Street,
   Strand / 1863. Maroon cover.

7. MAURICE DERING / or / The Quadrilateral Novel / by /
   The Author of *Guy Livingstone* / In Two Volumes /
   Tinsley Brothers / 18, Catherine Street, Strand / 1864.
   Scenes in France and India. Maroon covers.

8. A / BUNDLE OF BALLADS / Edited by the Author of *Guy
   Livingstone* / Tinsley Brothers, 18, Catherine Street,
   Strand / 1864. Brown cloth.

9. Sans Merci / or / Kestrels and Falcons / By the Author
   of *Guy Livingstone* / New Edition / Tinsley Brothers / 18,
   Catherine Street, Strand / 1866.   Blue cover.

This is the earliest edition that I have seen.

This story reintroduces the character of Flora Bellasys, from *Guy
Livingstone*, as Lady Dorrillon.

10. Brakespeare / or The Fortunes of a Free Lance / By
    the Author of *Guy Livingstone* / In Three Volumes /
    London / Tinsley Brothers / 18, Catherine Street,
    Strand / 1868.

11. Breaking A Butterfly / or / Blanche Ellerslie's
    Ending / By the Author of *Guy Livingstone*, etc. / In
    Three Volumes / London / Tinsley Brothers, 18,
    Catherine Street, Strand / 1869.   Magenta covers.

12. Anteros / A Novel / By the Author of *Guy Livingstone* / In
    Three Volumes / London / Chapman and Hall, 193,
    Piccadilly / 1873.   Brown covers.

13. Silverland / By the Author of *Guy Livingstone* / London /
    Chapman and Hall / 193, Piccadilly / 1873.   Blue cover.

14. Hagarene / By the Author of *Guy Livingstone* / In Three
    Volumes / London / Chapman and Hall, 193, Picca-
    dilly / 1874.   Brown-orange covers.

Note.—*Guy Livingstone* was twice translated into French : *Guy
Livingstone, ou À Outrance*, translated by C. B. Derosne, Paris, 1877 ;
and *Un Roman de la Vie Moderne*, translated by E. Montègut, 1885.
C. B. Derosne also translated *Barren Honour* as *Honneur Stérile*, 1877 ;
and *Sans Merci* as *Flora Bellasys*, 1872.

THE LITERARY ASSOCIATIONS OF WHITE HORSE HILL: MARY ANN AND THOMAS HUGHES

'Before the gods that made the gods
    Had seen their sunrise pass,
The White Horse of the White Horse Vale
    Was cut out of the grass.'
                                    G. K. CHESTERTON.

APART from their historical interest, there is a peculiar fascination for the imaginative mind emanating from those gigantic figures cut out of the grass of the lofty chalk downs in the west of England long ages ago, and still visible from miles afar when the sun shines upon them. There is the indecent 'Giant of Cerne' in Dorset. He is one hundred and eighty feet high, and is supposed to represent Heil, a god of the pagan Saxons. The peasants of old affirmed human sacrifices had been offered up on the spot, and once in every seven years they cleaned *him* up ; but now he is neglected save by the archaeologist. Above Westbury, in Wiltshire, there gallops for ever on the turf a sturdy white steed with long tail, plainly visible for many miles round ; often in youth I gazed upon him, as a beckoning beacon of romance, across the plains from the causeway of Freshford, near Bath. Most ancient and famous of all these semblances cut in the chalk is the White Horse of Berkshire, for he gives his name to both hill and vale, and, as Thomas Hughes enthusiastically wrote in *Tom Brown's School Days*, 'What a hill is the White Horse Hill ! There it stands right above all the rest, nine hundred feet above the sea, and the boldest, bravest shape for a chalk hill that you ever saw.'

To the north stretches the Vale of the White Horse, which for beauty Drayton, the Poet Laureate, in his *Polyolbion* (1613), compares with the lovely and far-flung Vale of Evesham :

> ' This White-horse all the vales of Britaine would o'erbeare,
> And absolutely sit in th' Imperiall chaire.
> As pure and fresh an ayre upon her face to blowe
> As Evesham for her life : and from her steed doth showe
> Her lustie rising downes.'

Unlike Westbury's normal White Horse, he of Berkshire is a weird anatomical specimen, long and attenuated ; but that is because he is of prehistoric equine shape.   His similitude appears on the British coinage of 50 B.C., where the horse was copied from the design of that animal appertaining to the coins of Philip II of Macedon. Though the White Horse of Berkshire is often assumed to be a commemoration of Alfred's victory over the Norsemen at Ashdown near by, in 871, more meticulous students declare that the figure is one thousand years earlier in date and of Celtic origin, whereby the festival of the Scouring (or cleaning) of the White Horse (which last took place seventy-four years ago) is a survival of a Celtic religious ceremony.   The horse stretches over an acre and is three hundred and seventy-four feet in length. The view from the top of the hill claims to embrace eleven counties.   Close by, on the Woolstone side, is the Dragon's Hill, where St. George, in local legend, killed the dragon, as Job Cork, ' The Uffington Poet,' who was a shepherd for fifty years on White Horse Hill, related in the vernacular :

> ' Ah, zur, I can remember well
> The stories the old volk do tell ;
> Upon this hill which here is zeen
> Many a battle there has been.

> ' If it is true as I heerd zay,
> King Gaarge did here the dragon zlay,
> And down below, on yonder hill,
> They buried he, as I've heerd tell.'

WHITE HORSE HILL

From a drawing by Arthur Hughes

By permission of Messrs. Macmillan and Company

Lord Wyfold, indeed, would have it that the White Horse is no horse but rather the dragon of legend and English heraldry. He says :

' Anybody looking at the beak, the eye, the elongated body and tail of this curious figure must realise that it could never have been intended for a horse. It is surely a representation of one of those prehistoric monsters commonly called dragons. Local tradition supports this opinion, for the hill just below it is called Dragon's Hill, and the story goes that here the dragon was slain by St. George.' [1]

But the suggestion is infuriating, and we cannot at this late day talk of White Dragon Hill and the Vale of the White Dragon, apt title for a fairy tale though it be.

Less than a mile from White Horse Hill on the Rudge-Way (Ridgeway) is the cromlech of sarsen stones known as Wayland Smith's Cave, the burial place, according to tradition, of the Danish chief Bœreg or Baagseeg, who was killed in the battle with Alfred of Wantage afore-mentioned in 871, but the site is probably that of a far earlier burial. In later years arose the picturesque legend that the cave was tenanted by a mysterious being, Weland the Smith, who would shoe the horses of passing wayfarers ; but he was not to be seen by the travellers, who had to leave their steeds by the cave's mouth, whilst they themselves retired out of eyeshot. Eventually the smith disappeared amid a great explosion and flame of fire with a Dark Personage, and so Wayland Smith's Cave became a spot associated with diablerie. On the way down from White Horse Hill to Kingston Lisle is another curious survival, the Blowing Stone, a lump of stone nearly four feet high and perforated with several holes which, when blown into, emit penetrating and awe-inspiring moans such as Bashanic bulls might bellow in Hades. This stone, as the landlord of the adjoining inn

[1] *The Upper Thames Valley*, which also contains many interesting notes on the Icknield Way.

told Tom Brown, was reputed to have been used as a
warning in old times when the enemy was at hand, an
audible beacon or fiery cross heard for a long distance
around.

All these legends of White Horse Hill are alluded to
in either *Tom Brown's School Days* or *The Scouring of the
White Horse*, for Thomas Hughes was born, on October
the 20th, 1823, at Uffington, below the hill, and from his
earliest years had been saturated with all the traditions
and romantic aspects of his native region. He knew all
' the country legends, the stories of the old gable-ended
farm-houses, the place where the last skirmish was fought
in the Civil Wars, where the last highwayman turned to
bay, where the last ghost was laid by the parson.' For
this direction of his literary bent he and we are undoubtedly indebted to his remarkable grandmother, Mary Ann
Hughes, a veritable repository of legend, ghost stories,
and folk-lore, and who sang the old English and Scotch
ballads in a way which charmed both Walter Scott and
Mrs. Siddons.   She came of a family, the Wattses, long
associated with the country of the White Horse.   Both
her father and great-grandfather had been vicars of
Uffington, where she herself was born in 1770.   Her
grandfather, the Rev. George Watts, Master of the
Temple, was that fearless but tactless divine who, when
preaching at the Chapel Royal before King George the
Second and his seraglio, took for his subject the seventh
commandment and as his text 2 Sam. xii. 7 (' Thou art
the Man ').   His determined nature and freedom of
speech were inherited by Mary Ann Watts.   She could
not fill the family living of Uffington herself, but she
married early a clergyman, the Rev. Thomas Hughes,
D.D., one of the Canons Residentiary of St. Paul's
Cathedral ; and in due course she arranged that the valuable living he held in virtue of that office should be ex-
changed for the lesser benefice of Uffington.   Consequently part of each year was spent in her native parsonage
where, in the words of one of her grandsons, she con-

tinued ' the benevolent despotism begun by her there in the days of her father.' In short, if the Canon, her husband, was rector, she was director.

Although beloved by her distinguished literary friends, Walter Scott, R. H. Barham, Harrison Ainsworth, Mrs. Southey, and many another, Mrs. Hughes was a great despot in the family circle. Her only son, John Hughes (1790-1857), was a clever writer [1] and artist, editor of *The Boscobel Tracts*, and in due course destined to be the model of the squire in his son's book, *Tom Brown's School Days*. His relations with his mother were somewhat akin to the case of Ruskin, for even after his marriage (to Margaret Wilkinson) he still remained under the maternal influence and occupied a house [2] at Uffington, close to his parents' parsonage, so that in due course Mrs. Hughes senior had the pleasure of managing her seven grandchildren—without any regard to their individual tastes and desires, not forgetting the worsted socks she knitted continuously for their unwilling little feet. Thomas Hughes (the author) has recorded how a guinea presented to him in childhood by the Duchess of Buckingham was commandeered by his grandmother and expended on a gorgeously bound copy of Milton, which, she said, would be a lasting memorial for him when he grew up, and far, far better than squandering the money on the passing pleasures of tops and sweets ; but, as he adds, ' I owe to my grandmother a dislike for Milton's poetry.' In London, old Mrs. Hughes always did her own marketing, walking very fast to Smithfield and Billingsgate and back to Amen Corner. When her little grandsons were staying with her

---

[1] John Hughes wrote under the cognomen of ' Mr. Buller of Brazennose ' in *Blackwood's Magazine* (where in 1824 appeared his well-known ballad, *The One-Horse Chay* : not to be confused with *The One Hoss Shay* of Oliver Wendell Holmes), and in *Ainsworth's Magazine*, wherein he was the coadjutor of Ainsworth in the famous quarrel with Father Prout (1842).

[2] This house, in which Thomas Hughes was born in 1823, no longer exists. The village schools stand on or near the site.

in London, Mrs. Hughes would take them with her on these shopping expeditions. But as she walked very fast, and never turned round to point out any place of interest to the children, or permitted them to gaze in the shop windows, they had the greatest difficulty in keeping up with her erect little figure almost disappearing in the maze of traffic. Evidently her rule was that children should be neither seen nor heard. The tradespeople called her 'Madam Hughes,' and in her presence the expletives of Billingsgate were hushed.

I have related previously [1] how eventful a friendship commenced when Richard Harris Barham came to St. Paul's Cathedral as Minor Canon in 1821, for it was the stimulus of Mrs. Hughes which suggested to him the right expression of his rare gift of bizarre rhyming. Many of *The Ingoldsby Legends* were based on topographical legends related to him by Mrs. Hughes, and one at least of these, *Hamilton Tighe*, belongs to the Vale of the White Horse, for the alleged event occurred at Faringdon in the person of Hamden Pye, a member of the family of Henry James Pye (1745-1813), most ridiculed of Poets Laureate.

Mrs. Hughes's very memorable friendship with Sir Walter Scott arose in 1806, in Berkeley Square, when they met in the lodgings of Miss Hayman, one of the Ladies in Waiting to the Princess of Wales (Caroline of Brunswick). Mrs. Hughes related :

'Behind her house there was a mews, which opened into Hay Hill, at the entrance of which mews I always saw a half-starved dog. . . . I had such a feeling of compassion for the poor, forlorn, half-starved creature that I always carried in my muff a parcel of bones in a newspaper for him, and as I visited Miss Hayman generally twice a week, the dog was by my gifts kept alive; his gratitude was extreme; I always found him watching for me.'

On the morning Mrs. Hughes met Scott, this incident was related to him :

[1] *William Harrison Ainsworth and his Friends.*

' He made no reply for a minute or two, but leaned back in his chair gazing hard at me under his shaggy brows, but with the most benevolent smile—then thrusting out his hand, he caught hold of mine with a *grip* which I can only compare to a blacksmith's vice, exclaiming, " You and I *must* be friends ! " which, during his remaining life, he verified.'

Dr. and Mrs. Hughes twice visited Scott at Abbotsford, in 1824 and 1828 ; Sir Walter was godfather to one of their grandsons, named Walter Scott Hughes, in 1826. The father of the child, John Hughes, with his wife, stayed at Abbotsford in 1825, and two years previously Scott gave the young man that curious puff advertisement, in the Preface to *Quentin Durward*, of *An Itinerary of Provence and the Rhone*, made during the year 1819 by John Hughes, M.A., of Oriel College, Oxford. Scott, when in London, always dined at the canonical residentiary house in Amen Corner with Dr. Hughes and his wife, and all through the years they kept up an extensive correspondence on the subjects of archaeology, minstrelsy, and legend.[1] Although Scott, when writing *Kenilworth* (1821), had read up Camden for the Berkshire scenes of his novel, it was Mrs. Hughes who supplied him with the picturesque details of the Legend of Wayland Smith's Cave, which he adapted so vividly to his purpose.[2] Few scenes in the Waverley Novels linger more clearly in the mind's eye than Tresilian's adventure with Flibbertigibbet on the lone spaces of the Ridgeway on the Berkshire downs.

In *Jude the Obscure*, by Thomas Hardy, it was from this Ridgeway, by White Horse Hill, that Jude, as a child, obtained his first and distant glimpse of Oxford :

[1] Sir Walter Scott's letters to Mrs. Hughes were published twenty-six years ago under the editorship of Mr. Horace G. Hutchinson. These letters were not seen by Lockhart when he wrote his *Life of Scott*.

[2] See the notes to Chapter XIII of *Kenilworth*. John Hughes made for Scott a drawing of the cromlech which was probably utilised in one of the views of Wayland Smith's Cave to be found in the Abbotsford Edition of *Kenilworth* (1844).

' The track joined the highway by a little clump of trees. Here the ploughed land ended, and all before him was bleak open down.   Not a soul was visible on the hedgeless highway, or on either side of it, and the white road seemed to ascend and diminish till it joined the sky.   At the very top it was crossed at right angles by a green " ridgeway "—the Icknield Street and original Roman road through the district.   This ancient track ran east and west for many miles, and down almost to within living memory had been used for driving flocks and herds to fairs and markets.   But it was now neglected and overgrown. . . . It was waning towards evening ; there was still a faint mist, but it had cleared a little except in the damper tracts of country and along the river courses. . . .   In the course of ten or fifteen minutes the thinning mist dissolved altogether from the northern horizon . . . and about a quarter of an hour before the time of sunset the westward clouds parted, the sun's position being partially uncovered, and the beams streaming out in visible lines between two bars of slaty cloud. . . .   Some way within the limits of the stretch of landscape, points of light like the topaz gleamed.   The air increased in transparency with the lapse of minutes, till the topaz points showed themselves to be the vanes, windows, wet roof slates, and other shining spots upon the spires, domes, freestone-work, and varied outlines that were faintly revealed. . . .   The spectator gazed on and on till the windows and vanes lost their shine, going out suddenly like extinguished candles.   The vague city became veiled in mist.   Turning to the west, he saw that the sun had disappeared.   The foreground of the scene had grown funereally dark, and near objects put on the hues and shapes of chimeras.'

Little Jude also saw the night-glow of Oxford ' at the place of outlook, only just after dusk ; but a black north-east sky, accompanied by a wind from the same quarter, made the occasion dark enough. . . .   No individual light was visible, only a halo or glow-fog . . . making the light and the city seem distant but a mile or so.'   From a somewhat nearer point to Oxford it is possible to see, about sixteen miles away, the actual lights of the city through a dip in these far ranging Berkshire Downs.   I recall a memorable autumn evening, when on the Blewbury Downs, going towards Moulsford, as the last faint gleams of a saffron sky were fading into dun-dusk there could be seen on the horizon the dimly twinkling lights of Oxford.

Dr. Hughes died in 1833, and his widow had at last to resign the management of Uffington, which she had exercised for half a century. Her son removed to Donnington Priory, near Newbury, but she herself remained in the beloved country of the White Horse, taking an old house (now called Thornhill House) with a delightful garden at Kingston Lisle, not far from the picturesque little church, whose surroundings and yew trees have something in common with Mr. Hardy's Stinsford ('Mellstock'). Here she lived for thirteen years, managing her new village, still knitting, still walking fast and alert—always accompanied by her dogs 'Mustard' and 'Pepper,' descendants of the original Dandie Dinmonts given to her by Walter Scott in the long ago. Still beloved, too, by the survivors of her friends, so that she said she thought the society of an old woman was like port wine—the better for keeping.

It was during these last years that her friendship with Harrison Ainsworth provided one of Mrs. Hughes's chief joys. He often visited her at Kingston Lisle, where, under her assiduous maternal care and the culinary skill of her old servant, Mary Hawkes, he finished his romances *Jack Sheppard* and *Guy Fawkes*. The latter work was dedicated to Mrs. Hughes, in a glowing tribute to her many admirable qualities. In his next story, *Old St. Paul's* (1841), Ainsworth placed some of the later scenes in the White Horse country which he knew so well from his visits to Mrs. Hughes. The fugitives from the Plague go to Ashdown Park, and en route Blaize discovers the use of the Blowing Stone, to the alarm of his companions. The view from White Horse Hill is described, and finally the action passes to Kingston Lisle, where Mrs. Hughes and her surroundings are faithfully depicted, though of course the setting is placed two centuries back, and the lady of the house is called Mrs. 'Compton.' Mrs.

Hughes, in a letter to Mrs. Southey (Caroline Bowles), says : ' I had great pleasure in taking Mr. Ainsworth to see Ashdown Park, the old seat (of the Earl of Craven) described in the second volume (of *Old St. Paul's*). It was a strange expedition of ten miles over a down road— so impracticable that we walked as much, and more, than we drove, and had to scramble in and out of the phaeton incessantly ; but we were repaid for our trouble by the interest this singular old place excited. The weather was perfection, the down air delicious, the larks singing, and as we skirted the high down, the whole Vale of the White Horse lay in blue distance before us.'

But the passing years would not be denied, and at the age of seventy-seven Mrs. Hughes found it necessary to remove from her remote Berkshire Downs to Reading, and there she died in 1853, at the house now known as No. 183, Oxford Road. It was in these last days that Ainsworth wrote to her :

' I hope you like your present residence . . . but you must often think of dear Kingston Lisle, and the garden and the old trees, and the little church, and the downs. I often do. It is a picture graven on my heart, as are all my recollections connected with you.'

The tears of things. Even for some of us who never knew these people the eyes may dim in thinking of lives played out long ago, their joys and sorrows, the fine friendships, the beautiful springs they knew before the Eternal Night came. And now all is forgotten, for them nothing remains.

It was sad that Mrs. Hughes did not live to see the publication of her grandson's books, *Tom Brown's School Days* in 1857, and *The Scouring of the White Horse* in 1858, for it would indeed have rejoiced her heart to know that the old stories and aspects of her loved native hill and vale, which she had been the first to tell and point out to Thomas Hughes as he sat a child at her feet, were enshrined for all time in books of which one was destined

to become a classic.[1] Here, too, she herself appears as
'Madam Brown' in those early chapters of *Tom Brown's
School Days*, where the scene is Uffington—its fine old
church and the meadows and the 'Veast' all lovingly
limned as they were a hundred years ago.

The Scouring of the White Horse, with Richard Doyle's
delightful illustrations, perpetuates the festivities and cele-
brations which attended the last cleaning of the equine
stones in 1857, with its great fair, games, races, wrestling,
and sword play. For a century earlier the scourings had
been frequent. They are known to have taken place in
1755, 1776, 1785, 1803, 1813, 1825, 1838, and 1843—at
intervals, it will be observed, of a decade more or less.
But now seventy-four years have gone by and the White
Horse is sadly in need of a thorough scouring, for his front
legs are no longer visible. Writing in 1889 (seven years
before his death) Thomas Hughes, in a preface to a new
edition of his book, realised that the events he had depicted in 1857 were never likely to occur again. But as
to the actual preservation of the Horse, he comforted
himself with the reflection that as the relic had been sche-
duled as an Ancient Monument its future maintenance
was safe. But is it? Parliaments and Lords of the
Manor now seem alike indifferent to the White Horse's
well-being or his ultimate survival.[2]

Tout passe. Even the everlasting hills are in danger
to-day of spoliation by bungalow builders. The merry
jousts and noise attendant on the Scouring of the White

[1] Thomas Hughes commenced his literary career in 1842, as a
youth of nineteen, when his poem, *Milton and the Swedish Lord*,
appeared in *Ainsworth's Magazine*.

[2]   ' The White Horse of the White Horse Vale,
            That you have left to darken and fail. . . .
            Grey twilight and a yellow star,
               Hung over thorn and hill. . . .'
                                    G. K. CHESTERTON.

In 1930 there was an abominable proposal by the Air Ministry to
acquire an area of the Downs near White Horse Hill for bombing
practice : but after public protest the scheme was abandoned.

Horse are no longer heard ; the sparks and glow from Wayland Smith's mysterious forge died out—ah ! so long ago ; the smoke from pagan fires and rites ascended and vanished in far centuries of the dim past. The only smoke that ascends White Horse Hill at evening now is from the wood fires of the gipsies, who frequently camp in the combes below. And yet, who knows ? Perhaps on some Beltane Night, with the moon aghast, strange sights are seen as dark shadows creep from out the long barrows nigh the crest of the hill.

A GREAT BIBLIOPHILE : JAMES CROSSLEY

JAMES CROSSLEY is one of the most remarkable examples of that class of very learned men, such as Porson and Parr, encyclopaedic in their knowledge but who become forgotten by future generations for the reason that they left no hostages to posterity in the form of famous books. Watts-Dunton is of the number, for apart from his idiosyncratic *Aylwin* he produced no creative work of the first importance ; and another instance of our own time is Thomas Seccombe, who from his great stores of learning only evolved such negligible books as *Twelve Bad Men* and *The Age of Johnson*. In Seccombe's case, no doubt, financial reasons decided that he must spend his time in writing articles for *The Dictionary of National Biography* and prefaces for reprints of the classics, or in lecturing to youths at Sandhurst and in Canada, rather than in the composition of fine literary work which might so rightly have proceeded from his pen had assured monetary comfort and leisure been his portion.

And yet who knows : for in Crossley's case it was, perhaps, ease, life-long material comforts, and plethora of good food and old port, that produced a kind of fastidious inertia fatal to the state of prolonged mental and physical travail without which no great book can be born. So it was, James Crossley's long life passed in a state of literary dalliance. He accumulated a vast and wonderful library, and specialised in ancient learning, his knowledge of seventeenth century literature being especially marked. True, there were the working years of his life as a lawyer to set against his time for literary production, but in those days of peace and comfort and easily earned money, amid which his youth and meridian were set, the claims of the solicitor's office did not impinge unduly upon the joys of the library and dining-room.

James Crossley was a native of Halifax,[1] where he was born at The Mount on March the 31st, 1800, the son of James Crossley (1767-1831) by his wife, Anne Greenup (1772-1813), of Skircoat. Young Crossley was educated at the Grammar Schools of Hipperholme and Heath. His father was a merchant and incidentally a bookish man with a fine library, which gave the rein to his son's early developed inclinations. Even as a youth, James Crossley was deeply versed in antiquarian and historical knowledge and the works of the early dramatists and poets. How remarkable his reading had been by the time he was fifteen is related in an autobiographical fragment incorporated in the *Horae Seniles* of his friend, Ainsworth. There Crossley stated :

' Perhaps some of the most agreeable moments in the mind of a scholar are those spent in the retrospection of early studies, in recalling the hours which first opened upon him the treasures of learning, in tracing back his acquaintance with a book to its first commencement in his youth. . . .

A thousand pleasures do me bless,
And crown my soul with happiness,

as I fly back to that period when, uncramped by the restraint of any particular study, and unrestrained by the fetters of academical regimen, the mind was left to traverse the wide domain of literature, and seek amusement in perpetual variety : With what renewed gusto did I range over the contents of a well-fed library, from Rabelais to the Fathers, and from Coryate's *Crudities* to the *Summa* of Aquinas and the theological works of Boëthius ! With what keenness of antiquarianism did I turn over the dusty volumes of Holinshed and Stow, or linger over the uncouth cuts and thrilling details of Fox's and Clarke's Martyrology ! How I delighted to immerse myself in " all such readings as were never read," and neglect the more common and customary paths of every-day study for the huge folios and quartos (which the sons of this

[1] The Crossley family was of Lancashire origin, and for generations resided at Burnley and Colne, a direct ancestor being Edward Crossley De Cliviger, who lived in the sixteenth century.

degenerate age can hardly lift), for the miracles of industry which our forefathers have achieved. How happy was I, when only a boy of fifteen, if I could get into a corner with Hooker's *Ecclesiasticall Politie*, or Sir Walter Raleigh's *History*, and pounce upon the contents as a kite pounces upon a sparrow. The writers of the Augustan Age I left to the perusal of others, for they were read by everybody ; solacing myself instead with the poetry of Claudian, Ausonius, Sidonius Apollinaris, and Prudentius ; and the prose of Aulus Gellius, Macrobius, and Ammianus Marcellinus. To me, the productions of declining Rome were more valuable than the glories of her zenith. How refreshing to my view were those bulky and endless tomes of commentaries, which the era of the Scaligers and Casaubons poured forth. The text of a writer, without its due modicum of annotation, was to me as arid and ungrateful as a plain without a tree. The Fathers were my boon companions ; through them I ranged from Hermes to Saxon Bede, passing ever and anon from the pure Latinity of Sulpicius Severus to the sharp and caustic epistles of St. Isidore, and the hard and embrowned quaintness of Tertullian. How light of heart was I, if at some of those dinners which my father used to give to the reverend sons of the church, I could amaze them by edging in some quotation from the *Cassandra* of Lycophron or the *Dionysiaca* of Nonnus, and procure the appellation of " The Learned Boy."

'*Quas premit atra dies et funere mersit acerbo.* One subject which at one time formed the principal part of my study, and for which I still feel a partiality, which only grows stronger by a lapse of time, was the Old English Drama. . . . I got possession of Dodsley's Collection of Plays, and went through them with most laudable diligence. The most tedious and tiresome of them all did not serve to dispirit my resolution ; and at the age that I then was, I cannot help giving myself some credit for such an exertion. After all this, it is perhaps needless to say what formed the amusement of my boyhood has continued till the present hour a source of unintermitted pleasure.'

And so it was to continue for sixty years more.

At the age of seventeen, in 1817, reasons for his future profession caused Crossley to settle in Manchester, where he remained for the sixty-six ensuing years of his life. He was articled to Thomas Ainsworth, solicitor, of 21, King Street, the father of William Harrison Ainsworth, the novelist, then twelve years of age. The two boys immediately formed a remarkable friendship which continued to the end of life ; they had many tastes in common, and Crossley was a prominent influence in directing young Ainsworth's steps on the path which led to fame and fortune.

Though Crossley himself never reached the same goal, he, at an early age, before he was twenty, was a contributor to the first *Retrospective Review*, *Blackwood's Magazine*, and other journals, and a little later he assisted J. G. Lockhart with biographical articles for *The Quarterly Review*. In fact, when Crossley was twenty-two, Ainsworth reported from Edinburgh that Blackwood, Lockhart, and Croly ' think tremendously highly of you, you are as a god amongst them, an extraordinary genius, a *rara avis*.' [1] And James Browne, the editor of Constable's

---

[1] In this same letter (1822) Ainsworth gives an entertaining description of William Blackwood (1776-1834), who founded *Blackwood's Magazine* in 1817, and his assistant editors, J. G. Lockhart and John Wilson (' Christopher North ') :

' I sallied into Prince's Street. I had not walked far before I saw in monstrous golden characters, " No. 17. BLACKWOOD. No. 17." I entered . . . a spacious kind of room filled round with books of all sorts, and in the midst was a table covered with pamphlets and all the late publications and " odes innumerable " to the King . . . the counter runs all on the left side. . . . Very rusty and beefy fellows keep the shop, which *en véritié* rises above the storm, who is a poor tailor in a cellar below. . . . I saw a man advancing to meet me—" his face was deathly pale, but his nose was beaming bright— this man of the inexpressible visage—for never before saw I such a one, with those funny teeth of his, that queer one eyebrow up and the other down, with gray streaming locks, it certainly looked very astonishing. This, you will suppose, was Blackwood. After a little discourse, for I had contrived by sending a short story or so and a small article to give myself an introduction, he shook me by the hand and led me into his back parlour. Now then for the secret haunt—the recess of Christopher (North). This was a square, small, cold-looking room, with pale, plastery, unpapered walls. Four or five neat chairs thrown up and down, and a table covered with articles, pens, ink, a writing desk, and paper. Here we discoursed long and long. . . . Even while we were engaged in this discourse, enters Mr. Wilson, to whom Blackwood introduced me.

Edinburgh Magazine, was under the impression that his learned contributor in Manchester was ' Dr.' Crossley.

Those were pleasant days for the young literary aspirant of talent, for he was welcomed and praised by polite editors, who instead of returning his manuscript with the fatal slip, ' The Editor regrets ' (as would be his experience to-day if unknown), accepted it with high encomium and begged for more. Here is a letter received by the young man of twenty in 1820 :

' LONDON,

29 July, 1820.

The Editors of *The Retrospective Review* beg to render their thanks to Mr. Crossley for his very excellent Article which is alike valuable for its own intrinsic merit and eloquent writing and for the complete and favourable views it presents of a work so much talked of and so little known as the *Arcadia*. The general reception of *The Retrospective Review* has been flattering, and there is every reason to calculate on its success. The Editors need hardly repeat that the future communications of Mr. Crossley will be received with welcome and respect, and they cannot but lament that his engagements will not allow him to contribute to their next No. Perhaps Mr. Crossley will take the trouble to distribute a few of the prospectuses enclosed.'

The Retrospective Review, which commenced in 1820, had for its object, as the title adumbrates, the reconsideration of famous literary works of the past. It was very ably edited by George Robinson and Henry Southern (1799-1853), who later entered the Diplomatic Service and died British Minister at Rio de Janeiro. Crossley's contributions included essays on Sir Thomas Browne's *Hydriotaphia, or Urn Burial*; Cardan's Life of Himself—*Vita de Propria* ; Fuller's *The Holy State and The Profane State* ; and *The Countesse of Pembroke's Arcadia*,

---

He is a yellow-haired, good-humoured, pleasant, jocund man, and was very talkative. Then directly comes Lockhart—he is a very fine, precise, dandyish young fellow, with black frizzly hair, and quiet, sharp, black eyes . . . very shrewd indeed. Next comes my friend, the Rev. G. Croly. . . .'

by Sir Philip Sidney, based on the eighth edition of 1633. The last named is the article mentioned by the perceptive editors [1] in the letter just quoted, and it is,

[1] Long years after, Crossley contributed an interesting note on *The Retrospective Review* to *The Manchester Guardian*, May 25th, 1874, in the course of which he stated :

' The largest proportion of labour was taken by the two editors, but the list of contributors, when fully given, will embrace several names which are not contained in Lowndes, Allibone, or any of the bibliographical works which have noticed *The Retrospective Review*. Amongst them was that of the present writer, who besides the articles he contributed, furnished, at the request of his friends the Editors, a list of nearly 300 works which appeared to be suitable subjects for articles in the " *Review*," and were accordingly intended to be proceeded with, but from the early discontinuance of the periodical a small number only could find a place in its pages. At the distance of more than half a century, and the writer having survived, it is believed, all those associated with him in the first series of that work, the claims of which to public attention he urged in a contemporary publication (see article on " *Retrospective Review* " in *Blackwood's Magazine*, December, 1821), it is gratifying to call to mind the pleasant intercourse which he then had with his fellow-workers in *The Retrospective Review* and to see how well, through all the fluctuations of taste, it has maintained its place in the estimation of the students and lovers of the literature and *history of the days gone by*.'

C. 2, CAVENDISH PLACE.'

The Editors had preserved a strange secrecy about the names of their contributors as is evident from this letter to Crossley :

' LONDON, 30*th Jan.*, 1821.

SIR,

In the names of the Editors of *The Retrospective Review* I beg to thank you for the article on Fuller's *Holy and Profane States* as well as for your kind endeavours to promote the success of the work, which, I am glad to say, increases in sale and will, I trust, go on prospering and to prosper. The expenses attending and the limited number of the first impression have hitherto prevented our realising any profit, but we shall be able to send you four guineas per sheet for any further contributions you may favour us with. I regret that I do not feel at liberty to disclose the names of different contributors, feeling, as I do, how much the review is indebted to you. If however there are any articles in particular the writers of which you desire to know, I shall have pleasure in communicating their names provided they are gentlemen whom I am at liberty to name. I am glad to learn as a subject of the Republic of Letters

perhaps, Crossley's best piece of criticism. It can claim to be the only book which bears his name as author, for the essay was reprinted thirty-three years later, in 1853, as *Sir Philip Sidney and The Arcadia*, prefixed by a short memoir of Sidney. It formed one of a series entitled 'Reading for Travellers,'[1] published by Chapman and Hall, and had among its companions *Samuel Johnson* by Thomas Carlyle; *Old Roads and New Roads* by W. B. Donne, a now forgotten censor of plays in the Lord Chamberlain's office; an anonymous volume entitled *Magic and Witchcraft*; and *The Village Doctor*, translated by Lady Duff Gordon (the friend of George Meredith). Here is an example of the picturesque language in which Crossley clothed his sympathetic appreciation of Sidney and *The Arcadia* :

'Like the sudden and delightful breathings of an Æolian harp, his overflowings of thought seem to burst forth unstimulated and unexcited, deriving none of their melody from the promptings of a musician's finger, and having in them nothing of earthly aid or human operation. His power does not seem so much to lie in the intellect as in the heart : not so much in the conflicting strife of intellectual prowess, or in the gigantic grasp of mental mightiness, as in the deep-drawn sighings of the soul—as in officiating as the high-priest of its sanctuary— as in exhaling from thence its clouds of imprisoned myrrh and frankincense to heaven. The current of his emotions flows on in unperturbed and imperturbable serenity . . . catching and reflecting all the beauties which expanded nature presents, and receiving splendour and brightness from the silvery

---

that its common stock is about to be enriched by a production from your pen, and take leave to say that if I can be of any service to you in London, or any friend at Cambridge, in the way of reference to authorities or otherwise it will give us great satisfaction to render it.

I am, Sir,

Your obedient servant,

GEORGE ROBINSON.'

[1] It transpires from the Autobiography of Sir Edmund Hornby (published in 1929) that he, as a young man, was the editor of this series. The books were sold at a shilling each, and were very good value for the money.

gleams which his fancy sheds upon it in its course. Around it are all the luxuriant delights of earth, above it is the varied grandeur of heaven, and the voice of sadly pleasing and melancholy inspiration is heard along its shores. He appears indeed to have followed the counsel which he reports his muse to have given him—" Look in thy heart and write " ; and never was that writing unworthy of his character, when he gave utterance to the voice of inspiration within. . . .

' As we read the imaginations of the author of the " *Arcadia*," we can almost fancy him breathing through his own pages, or that we are holding a colloquy with his disembodied spirit : we participate in the distresses of his personages as if they were parts of himself, and therefore to be worshipped,—as if they were the representatives and continuations of his own mind, and therefore to be respected. Our minds are filled with mingling remembrances of himself and his fate, of the promise of his youth and the brightness of his manhood, of the radiant progress of that star, which shed its first beams upon the peaceful glades of Penshurst, and diffused its dying glories over the bloody field of Zutphen. . . .

' The feeling which the perusal of the "*Arcadia*" excites is a calm and pensive pleasure, at once full, tranquil, and exquisite ; not unsimilar to that of meditation by moonlight, when the burning fervour of the day has subsided, and everything which might confuse or disorder our contemplation is at rest. All is peaceful and quiet, and clear as a transparency. The silvery glittering of the language, the unearthly loftiness of its heroes, the ethereality of their aspirations, and the sweet tones of genuine and unstudied feeling which it sounds forth, all combine to imbue the soul with a soft and pleasing melancholy. We feel ourselves under the spell of an enchanter, in the toils of a witchery, too gratifying to our senses to be willingly shaken off, and therefore resign ourselves without resistance to its influence. By it we are removed to other and more delightful climes : by it we are transported to the shady groves of Arcady and the bowery recesses of Tempe—to those heavenly retreats, where music and melody were wafted with every sighing of the breeze along their cool and translucid streams. We find ourselves in the midst of the golden age, with glimpses of the armed grandeur of the age of chivalry. We find ourselves in a period of conflicting sights and emotions, when all that was lovely in the primitive simplicity of the one, and all that was fascinating in the fantastic magnificence of the other, were united and mingled together ; where the rustic festivity of the shepherd was succeeded by the imposing splendour of the tournament, and the voice of the pastoral pipe and oaten reed was joined with the sound of the trumpet and the clashing of the lance.'

William Blackwood also wrote most effusively to young Crossley as an honoured contributor to *Blackwood's Magazine*, wherein, among other papers, appeared his article on Sir Thomas Urquhart's *Jewel*[1] (1820) and the fine appreciation of the Chetham Library (1821) :

'*24th July*, 1821.

MY DEAR SIR,

I wanted much to hear from you, but to-day I have been amply gratified by your favour of the 21st with your most interesting article on Mr. Lamb ; you have really done him in capital style. I have not enjoyed anything so much for a long time. With this I send you novels—*The Abbot* and *Ivanhoe* ; you will recollect that I am still deep in your debt, and I hope you will draw largely on me for whatever books you wish to have. And I beg to assure you that whatever I may send you, I shall still consider myself deeply in debt to you. I cannot repay in any way the gratification your correspondence has afforded me, except by the magazine itself wherein you find work supplied by minds congenial to your own.

I am,

Very truly yours,

W. BLACKWOOD.'

'*26th March*, 1822.

MY DEAR SIR,

We have been obliged again to postpone your articles, for with one thing and another, we have been quite overloaded this month, and notwithstanding yours and many other articles being delayed, I am obliged to give an extra sheet. I hope you will be glad to see you are so well supported. I have had so much to do since I last wrote you that I have neglected *Thomas Browne*. I was so much struck with the beauty and set up of a new brevier type which Ballantyne got the other day that I have made him set up a page, which I enclose you. I think it will look much better on this type and not so commonplace. I also send you a specimen of the paper

---

[1] *Ekskubalauron : or the Discovery of a most exquisite jewel, found in the Kennel of Worcester Streets, the day after the Fight*, 1652.

on which I propose to print the book.   It is not, you will perceive, wire-wove, but made in the old fashioned way, which I
think far better.   Be so good and write me by return of post,
if you approve of this and I will immediately put the work in
hand.   I send you *Conduct is Fate*, which is not very first rate,
but contains some very good things and it is written by the
Right Hon. Lady Charlotte Campbell.

I am,

Yours truly,

W. BLACKWOOD.'

The second letter refers to a reprint of some of Thomas
Browne's rare work which this same year, 1822, Crossley edited for Blackwood, *Tracts by Sir Thomas Browne,
Knight, M.D.*[1]   In the preface, signed ' J. C.', it was
announced, ' To those who are admirers of Browne, it
may be perhaps interesting in some measure to be informed that a full and a correct life of that singular author
is preparing from ample materials, and will shortly be
presented to the public.'   But Crossley, throughout life,
was ever a procrastinator and the great books he meant
to write were never written, just as in later years Theo-
dore Watts-Dunton planned a great book on George
Borrow and another on Swinburne, both destined never
to appear.   Such clever, scholarly, slow men—fastidious
yet diffident, meticulous to the smallest detail—who will
spend an entire morning searching for the verification
and accuracy of some small point of archaeology or date,[2]

[1] In the Catalogue of James Crossley's library appears the copy
of the reprint of these *Tracts* presented by the author to William
Beckford, who had the original boards rebound in russia extra.
It is here stated that only seventy-five copies of the work were
printed for ' private distribution.'

[2] Dr. William Osler has pointed out that this slowness of production of a book—or rather, I should say, the artist's desire to
polish and add, and add, some further detail—has been noticeable
in the work of many great men.   Copernicus delayed issuing his
treatise on Revolution for thirty years, and Harvey postponed for
twelve years the publication of his wonderful discoveries concerning
the circulation of the blood.   Darwin, too, after evolving his
Origin of Species, did not publish his work until twenty years later.

are passed and supplanted in the literary race by more facile writers indifferent to detail and strict accuracy. So it was that Edmund Gosse wrote the Life of Swinburne and Clement Shorter a book on Borrow, and Simon Wilkin produced, in 1835, the Life and Complete Works of Sir Thomas Browne.

But it would seem that Crossley perpetrated a quaint literary revenge upon his rival. He wrote in the authentic style of Sir Thomas Browne, wherein he was saturated, a *Fragment on Mummies*, which he sent to Mr. Wilkin who duly included it in his edition with the note:

'From a copy in the handwriting of J. Crossley, Esq. I have given the fragment on the authority of Mr. Crossley, but have not been able to find the volume in the British Museum which contained it, nor could he inform me; having transcribed it himself, but omitted to note the volume in which he met with it.' By the time, 1852, a new edition of Wilkin's work was issued, the editor realised he had been hoaxed and the *Fragment on Mummies* was omitted. Yet so Brownean was Crossley's *jeu d'esprit* that as late as 1886, Alexander Ireland, writing in *The Manchester City News*, quoted an extract from the *Fragment on Mummies* in illustration of Thomas Browne's style, and in a subsequent letter to Mr. T. Swindells he added, 'I believe the passage to be by Browne from internal evidence alone. No man of this century could have written it.'

Here is an example of Crossley's style, in imitation of Sir Thomas Browne, on Mummies:

'Radzivil hath a strange story of some mummies which he had stowed in seven chests, and was carrying on ship board from Egypt, when a priest on the mission, while at his prayers, was tormented by two ethnic spectres or devils, a man and a woman, both black and horrible; and at the same time a great storm at sea, which threatened shipwreck, till at last they were enforced to pacify the enraged sea and put those demons to flight by throwing their mummy freight overboard, and so with difficulty escaped. . . . Surely, if true, these demons were Satan's emissaries, appearing in forms answerable unto Horus and Mompta, the old deities of Egypt, to delude unhappy men. For those dark caves and mummy repositories are Satan's abodes, wherein he speculates and rejoices on human vainglory, and keeps those kings and conquerors, whom alive he bewitched, whole for that great day when he will claim his own, and marshal the Kings of Nilus and Thebes in dread procession to the pit.   Death, that fatal necessity which so many would overlook, or blinkingly survey, the old Egyptians held continually before their eyes.   Their embalmed ancestors they carried about at their banquets, as holding them still a part of their families. . . .'

Encouraged by his success in emulation of Chatterton, Crossley perpetrated another curious literary deception some five years later, but this time of a different description. John Wallis (1616-1703), the celebrated mathematician, author of *Arithmetica Infinitorum* (1655), castigator of Thomas Hobbes, and Savilian Professor of Geometry at Oxford, made, at a late stage of his life, an excursion into theological controversy and published, in 1692, his *Letters and Sermons on the Trinity*, 'printed for Thomas Parkhurst at the *Bible and Three Crowns*, at the lower end of Cheapside, near Mercer's Chapel.' These tracts (with the exception of one letter) were not included in the collected works of John Wallis, 1693-1699. But James Crossley having purchased, for £13, a copy of the original *Letters and Sermons* with the author's autograph corrections and additions, and original letters from John Howe and the Rev. Edmund Elys (the Royalist rector of East Allington, Devon) to Wallis inserted, there appeared some time after, in 1840, a volume entitled *Eight Letters concerning the Blessed Trinity*, by John Wallis, D.D., published by J. G. and F. Rivington, together with a preface and notes by Thomas Flintoff, dated July 27th, 1840, from Broughton. Thomas Flintoff was a Manchester manufacturer, in business at Back Alley, Union Street, but who resided at Roman Road Terrace, Higher Broughton. He had not hitherto given evidence of any creative literary efforts, and his friends in Manchester were considerably surprised and mystified when he made his appearance as the learned editor and annotator of Wallis's theological disquisitions. Mr. Flintoff died in 1849, and there were rumours that his claims to authorship were dubious. But the matter was not cleared up until nearly forty years later when Crossley's library was sold. Then it was found he had penned a confession less than three months before he died. It was written in his own copy of the 1840 reprint of Wallis's *Eight Letters concerning the Blessed Trinity*. Thus :

' This work, though my friend Thomas Flintoff's [1] name appears as editor, was entirely edited and the introduction and notes written by myself. He undertook the risk of publication, and being myself then in practice as a solicitor, and not wishing to appear prominent in theological controversy, it was arranged that his name should appear ostensibly as the editor. Since his death in 1849 it is no longer necessary that the fact of his having no further connection with the work than as above stated should be kept a secret. Indeed, I do not wish his memory to be held responsible for anything that I have written. He had a high opinion of the merit and value of Wallis's Letters, and his judgment was sound on all literary and theological productions which came in his way. A worthier man never lived or a kinder friend.

JAMES CROSSLEY, 19*th May*, 1883.'

In the introduction to the book, ' Flintoff ' had written he was indebted to the valuable assistance of ' My friend, James Crossley, Esq. Should any pecuniary profit arise, it is intended to be appropriated to the relief of Mr. William Wallis, a lineal descendant of the illustrious author of these Letters, who . . . is now suffering

---

[1] This Thomas Flintoff was presumably a relative of F. E. Flintoff, of Manchester, who married Charlotte Augusta Clough, Crossley's niece. James Crossley had two brothers, Henry (1799-1880), author of *Crichton*, a Tragedy, and George (1806-1880), and an only sister, Charlotte Anne Crossley (1799-1831), who married Robert Clough, of Seacombe, Cheshire; their eldest daughter, Anne Clough, was author of *Cranleigh of Cranleigh* (1873).

in the metropolis all the privations of penury and distress.'
Whether the sales of the book brought about this
estimable consummation I do not know : but the
mysterious volume is now a rarity and of considerable
value.

Throughout his youth Crossley was the coadjutor in
all the literary schemes of his volatile young friend,
William Harrison Ainsworth, so precocious and enthusiastic in everything he did. I have related in my
biography of the novelist how Crossley assisted in the
production of the youthful Ainsworth's dramatic plays
in the basement of the Ainsworths' house, No. 21 King
Street, Manchester. Crossley wrote the Prologue for
the opening of this underground ' Theatre,' 1st October,
1820, and the lines were printed in *Blackwood's Magazine*
for December of that year. They were in the metre of
Pope—and of Pantomime, and were no doubt impressively delivered by the fifteen-year-old manager, Ainsworth, in this style :

> ' High o'er the drama's visionary scene
> The Goddess Fancy rules—its fairy queen.
> Our hearts bewitched, submissive own her sway,
> Beat as she prompts, and, as she wills, obey.
> Called by her power and by her influence led
> The Stage, new peopled, swarms with mighty dead,
> The great of old, a charnel revel keep,
> And Kings and Caesars issue from their sleep. . . .'

In these early days, Crossley, Ainsworth, and another
boy, John Partington Aston, the same age as Ainsworth
and still in his teens, were accustomed to spend many of
their evenings at the *Unicorn* inn, kept by a Mrs.
Fisher, in a short street of ancient picturesque houses
known as Smithy Door, near the Collegiate Church of
Manchester, and now entirely swept away even to the
name. In a little sketch entitled *What Shall I Write ?*,
written apparently in collaboration by Ainsworth and
Aston, and reprinted as *The Theatre* in Ainsworth's early
book, *December Tales* (1823), there is a good description

of Crossley at one of the festal meetings the trio enjoyed in Smithy Door :

' C. (Crossley) is such a man as one would wish to call a friend. Warm-hearted and cool-headed, the impetuosities of his genius are held in due subjection by the clearness of his judgment. Though somewhat reserved in company, it is only needful to overcome his backwardness, to be delighted and surprised by his conversation. To a fund of good sense and correct ideas, called into constant exertion by acute and diligent observation, he adds a facility and aptness of allusion which is astonishing ; the fruit of a deep acquaintance with and recollections of the beauties of the best writers in every department of literature. Among our early authors in particular . . . he is familiar with their times, their manners, their acquisitions in learning and science, he enters into their feelings with a fellowship and congeniality of sentiment unknown to a mere modern man. The result of his studies and acquirements is, that whatever subject he handles, he is always himself ; having always his treasures at command, he can convert them to any use he pleases, and clothes his thoughts in colours which set off their native beauties to still greater advantage. Over whatever he writes is spread a bright gleam of intelligence, penetrating, with acuteness resembling intuition, into the causes of events and phenomena, and seizing with inconceivable rapidity on the links of a chain of reasoning which astonishes while it convinces. His writings are the conclusions of frequent examination and deep research, and everywhere show the mastery and delicate hand of a scholar and a gentleman.

' I dwell with peculiar delight upon the recollection of the dinner I had with C. It was the first time I had been quietly seated in conversation with him. . . . The room was an old-fashioned apartment, with carved oak wainscotting, blackened with age ; a blazing fire roared up the chimney, forming a pleasant contrast to the howling of the wind without (for it was a dull November night). What real comfortable pleasure it was, after dinner to sit by the hearth, and while we discoursed to sip our host's wine, while the rich rough flavour of the Falernian was seasoned by the genuine attic of C.'s conversation. It was impossible not to think of the *dissolve frigus* of Horace. These are the delightful hours that, like good wine, charm not only in present enjoyment but leave a flavour behind them, hours that we recur to again and again with unalloyed pleasure.'

So it was with Crossley, and sixty years later, in conversation with Mr. John Evans, he recalled these meetings in the long ago, the blazing fire in the ancient oakpanelled room, and over the chimney-piece the ' portrait of old Izaak Walton,' given to Mrs. Fisher, the landlady, by Captain Hindley. And, he added, with appreciative gusto, succulent steak and oyster sauce formed no inconsiderable element in the evening's diversion of himself, Ainsworth, and John Partington Aston.

It seemed to be the habit of these three young men in their compositions of a literary nature for Ainsworth to write the major portion, to which would be added contributions by Crossley and Aston. Thus in the *Horae Seniles (Recollections)* which Ainsworth contributed to Constable's *Edinburgh Magazine*, in 1822, it is clearly the fact that Crossley wrote the first part, for he told Mr. Evans that he dictated it to Ainsworth at one of their meetings in Smithy Door; and Ainsworth in the letter to Crossley from Edinburgh, August, 1822, says that James Browne, the editor of *The Edinburgh Magazine*, ' seemed not a little astonished and puzzled, I assure you, to comprehend how I had written *Horae Seniles*, which the poor fellow says are the best things he has had in his Magazine. He says that he thinks that part—the description of Marlowe's *Dr. Faustus*—the finest piece of writing he has seen for some time. Are you not gratified ? '

This was the passage which won the high approbation of Charles Lamb and is discussed by him in the letter to Ainsworth, dated December the 9th, 1823.

Ainsworth gives an inimitable glimpse of Crossley, at the age of twenty-five, at home in Cooper Street, Manchester, engrossed in *The Diary of Samuel Pepys*, which had just, 1825, made its first appearance in print :

' A vision of a man clothed in blue coat and black trousers, with a soiled yesterday's cravat under his ear in place of his chin. This being Sunday his hair is twisted on to the scalp and slightly singed in the bungling attempt of some booby

barber.   He wears a pair of shoes with the heels forced down.
There is a little lather on his ear from the recent effect of
shaving, his eye has a lack-lustre, comical sort of expression,
his right hand is stretched over a book, the other contains a
cup of coffee just raised from a slopped tea-tray—his mind is
full of *Pepys's Memoirs* [1] but I forbear.   Ha ! ha ! ha ! ha ! ha !
oh ! Crossley, this is the picture I would draw for you, but
what I would not permit your enemy to do.'

Crossley became a partner in the firm of Ainsworth,
Crossley, and Sudlow, solicitors, in 1823, and so his future
was set in Manchester, to a life devoted to the law [2] and
library, while the whirligig of Fate carried away his
brilliant friend, Ainsworth, to literary and social fame in
the great world of London.   But Crossley had his part
in all those early triumphs.   He reviewed *Rookwood* (1834)
in *The Herald* and did the author ' right good service.'
Crichton (1837) was aided by Crossley securing for Ainsworth Crichton's rare tracts, *Epicedium on Cardinal Bor-
romeo* and *Gratulatio to Gaspar Visconti*, when also Crossley supplied, by return of post, an English translation of
the old, difficult Latin of the original.   For *Old St.
Paul's* (1841) he provided a rare pamphlet he attributed
to Defoe, entitled *Due Preparations against the Plague both
of Soul and Body*.   Most of all he aided *The Lancashire
Witches* (1848).   He suggested to Ainsworth that *Potts's
Discoverie of Witches* would make a good basis for the
romance his friend had long intended to write around the
wild and impressive scenery of Pendle Hill—the Brocken
of England.   In addition to *Potts's Discoverie of Witches*,
edited by Crossley for the Chetham Society in 1845,
Ainsworth was indebted to *Nicholas Assheton's Journal*,
another publication of the Chetham Society, an institution founded at Crossley's house in 1843 and devoted to

[1] In the first edition the Diary was entitled *Memoirs of Samuel
Pepys, Esq. . . .* comprising his Diary from 1659 to 1669 *. . .* and a
Selection from his Private Correspondence. . . .   In two volumes.
London.   Colburn, 1825.

[2] He retired from his work as a solicitor at the age of sixty.

the archaeology, history, and topography of Lancashire :
Crossley became the second President of the Society in
1848.[1] At this date he was living at No. 4, Booth
Street, Piccadilly, Manchester, and hither came Ainsworth on several occasions when he and Crossley started
off for their visits to Witch-Land—Pendle Hill, Malkin
Tower, Whalley, Hoghton Tower, the Gorge of Cliviger
—where, doubtless, many of the scenes and incidents
which occur in Ainsworth's greatest romance were discussed.   These visits associated with scenery and subjects
so pregnant with interest to both friends ever remained
colourful memories for the twain ; and of course *The
Lancashire Witches* was dedicated ' To James Crossley,
Esq. (Of Manchester), President of the Chetham Society,
and the learned editor of *The Discoverie of Witches in the
County of Lancaster*—The Groundwork of the Following
Pages—This Romance, undertaken at his suggestion, is
inscribed by his old and sincerely attached friend, The
Author.'

This same year the curious rumour circulated that
Crossley was the author of *James the Second* (1848),
which book in its first edition was stated to be
' edited ' by W. H. Ainsworth, but in later issues the
qualifying word was deleted.   Ainsworth wrote to
Crossley :

' I met Harness the other night, and he spoke of you in high
terms ; but would insist that you are the author of *James the
Second*.   Nothing I could say to the contrary would shake his
conviction.   He said it was generally understood so in Manchester, and that you had almost admitted it.   Perhaps you
will enlighten me as to this.'

In *Mervyn Clitheroe* (1851-1858) Ainsworth introduced
two characters suggestive of Crossley, first ' Dr. Foam,'
and later ' Mr. Hazilrigge.'   The latter reflects a clear
picture of Crossley in his library :

[1] This same year, 1847-8, Crossley edited *The Diary and Correspondence of Dr. J. Worthington* for the Chetham Society.

' He took down some of his treasures, and descanted upon them. He propounded the magical oracles of Zoroaster—half fascinated me by the wondrous narratives of Frommannus and Leonard Vair—cited Delancre, Delrio, Cardan, Torreblanca, John Baptist Porta, Psellus, Pererius, Doctor Dee, and other writers on occult philosophy—recounted the history of the three possessed Virgins in Flanders, the Princess of the Sorcerers in Provence, and Martha Brossier—discoursed on the Clavicula Salamonis and the Enchiridion of Pope Leo—flagellated demons and sorcerers with the lashes of Bodinus—revealed the confessions of witches by the help of Binsfeldius—and stunned me with the *Malleus Maleficarum.* . . . At last he took down a large mystic folio, bound in black vellum, and full of blood-red characters and conjurations, and, telling me it was the Grimoire, was about to exhibit to my stupified gaze the veritable sign-manual of the Prince of Darkness, when, luckily, the rumbling of a gong announced that it was time to dress for dinner.'

During all these years Crossley paid frequent visits to London both on business and pleasure. He generally stayed at the *Old Hummums* Hotel in Covent Garden (the building that existed until 1881), and met all the most distinguished literary men of his time. He knew Charles Lamb, William Godwin, William Hazlitt, Leigh Hunt, Thomas de Quincey, and Coleridge. He would enjoy, in his own words, ' Now a little supper with Talfourd and Maclise at the Garrick ; anon a visit to Bulwer at Knebworth ; a breakfast with Disraeli ; a chop with John Forster in Lincoln's Inn Fields ; a snug little dinner with Dickens in Devonshire Terrace; or a gathering at Ainsworth's house at Kensal, on the Harrow Road.'

Lockhart, too, was a friend he always delighted in. Ainsworth would write to Crossley : ' I saw Lockhart and engaged him to dine with you some day on your visit to London. He will be most happy.' ' I enclose you a note from Lockhart and proofs of the review of *Parr.*[1] He wishes you to read them, and make what

---

[1] See *The Quarterly Review,* April, 1829, for this joint review of *The Works of Dr. Samuel Parr, With Memoirs of his Life, and a Selection from his Correspondence,* by J. Johnstone, 8 volumes, 1828.

additions and alterations or annotations you think proper. Pray oblige me, as well as Lockhart, by doing this, as I am sure you can do it excellently.   I am astonished to find how mildly Lockhart has handled the old boy (after the " hoary ruffian," etc.).   Let me see your comments before I return them, and write me privately what you think of the review.   I do not think he has made much of Parr's theological character : the political is decidedly the best.'   ' I think he fails in his editorial capacity. . . .'[1] Pray send your *Terbellia* in time for next number and send it through me.'   ' I was with Lockhart the other day. Would you like to review Croker's edition of *Boswell* for *The Quarterly* ?   If you would, he will send you the volumes as they are printed.   It would be a fine subject for you, and one to talk of hereafter.   Lockhart seemed vastly pleased with the idea of you doing it.' [2]   ' I send you two books and a letter which have found their way from *The Quarterly*.   I presume from Lockhart having sent you Bentley,[3] he wishes you to review that work for him.'   Here is a letter from Lockhart to Crossley at this date :

[1] Lockhart was already failing in health also.   A few years later (April, 1838), Ainsworth told Crossley : ' I met Lockhart the other day looking quite like an old man, and very much shaken with rheumatism.   He is so much altered that I scarcely knew him. . . . I asked Lockhart what he thought of the *Pickwick*.   He said he thought " it was all very well—but "—with one of his usual laughs —" damned low ! " '   Sixteen years later he died, at the age of sixty. Lady Ritchie, in *From Friend to Friend*, gives a vivid glimpse of Lockhart shortly before his death, at Rome, in 1854 : ' He gazed straight before him like some solemn brooding eagle, silent and mysterious.   He was wrapped in cloaks and wore a soft travelling cap, not unlike that hood in which Erasmus is commonly depicted. I only saw his profile and the pale clear-cut features as the carriage rolled away.'   And as Leighton added : ' Could any one forget him who had ever seen him with his beautiful clear-cut features, so pale and so fiery at the same time ; those eyes of jet in a face of ivory ? '

[2] See *The Quarterly Review*, October, 1831.

[3] *The Life of Richard Bentley*, by J. H. Monk, 1830.

24, Sussex Place,
Regent's Park,
May 8th, 1830.

My Dear Sir,

I had not read the *Life of Bentley* when I sent a copy out to you ; I have since done so and found it a work full of interest and information conveyed in a simple and masculine style for which the opening chapter I confess prepared me. It appears to me well worthy of a first rate review, and I earnestly hope you will have later a similar view of the subject. As I am to leave town on the 26th for Scotland, I wish you would give me a few lines soon and say whether you feel disposed to honour *The Quarterly Review* with an article, and when we may expect the manuscript. I should also like to hear what your views and purposes are, on further reflection, respecting the Biography of Dr. Parr.

Very truly yours,

J. G. Lockhart.

Unfortunately Lockhart's idea that Crossley would write a book on Dr. Parr was never carried out (the fate that attended all his big literary intentions), for Crossley must have had personal recollections of Parr who, during his last years, visited his friend, Dr. Holme, at Manchester. Ainsworth preserved similar memories of Parr at this time, for he portrayed him as ' Dr. Bray ' in *Mervyn Clitheroe.*

There can be no doubt that if Crossley had removed to London at this date he could have secured a prominent place in the literary world. Also, both Disraeli and Dickens urged him to settle in London and act as their permanent legal adviser. But Crossley was devoted to Manchester, and would never uproot himself from his life and interests there ; and, indeed, the prospect of packing and removing his vast library of over one hundred thousand volumes—which were piled up in stacks, after the shelves overflowed, in every room of his house—would have deterred any man. He did succeed in removing to two successively larger houses in Manchester, the first upheaval occurring in October, 1869, when after more than thirty years in No. 4, Booth Street,

he took possession of No. 2, Cavendish Place. As Ainsworth wrote to him, ' I rejoiced to learn that you have
got into a new and more comfortable abode, though how
you have made up your mind to leave Booth Street I
cannot conceive—still less, how you could remove your
mass of books. The effort seems superhuman.'

Crossley's travels were bounded by London. I do
not think he ever left England during the course of his
eighty-three years. When he was a young man of
twenty-eight he promised to go to France with Ainsworth, who, delighted at the prospect, wrote : ' I am
infinitely pleased with your promise to be my *compagnon de
voyage*. . . . How we shall ramble over all the delightful
places. The Louvre ! The Luxembourg ! Notre Dame !
Then magnificent, melancholy, gorgeously gloomy
Versailles. . . . I can scarce fancy you in France—how
you will stare at the Cafés and waiters, and blush at the
sight of immodest and immoral chambermaids.'

The chamber-maids were never seen by Crossley, then
or later, for when the time came he would not go to
France ; and so it was all through the years, despite the
seductive visions Ainsworth conjured up for him of
books and wines abroad :

' How you would have enjoyed " learned " Padua and delightful Pavia, where a man might have libraries, books, and
good wine, and all the loveliness of a southern sky for £60 a
year' (1830). . . . ' Vienna is enchanting. *You* would prefer Prague. Such a glorious old Library where you might
revel for a month. There is a Theological Library which
seems to have been undisturbed since the Thirty Years' War.
Such glorious, fat, old calf-skins and such a wonderful old
librarian. You would expire with delight at the sight of him
and his treasures ' (1846). . . . ' What a country is Spain.
You, who are sitting drowsily and dreamily by your fireside,
full of port and prejudice, cannot conceive what worlds of new
ideas are open to you, if you could but quit your jog-trot life
and go abroad for a couple of months. But go to Spain—go
and drink *Val de penas* in La Mancha, and *Xeres* at its own vine-
yard. As to La Mancha, it is unaltered since the days of Cer-
vantes. You see the very windmills that excited the doughty

Knight's ire, and the draw-well by which he watered. And then to pass through the defiles of the Morena, with the chance of being robbed. Would not that excite you ? ' (1849).

Most certainly not. Crossley was content with the noise and such excitement as Deansgate offered. As for wine away from Manchester, he was ever ready to come to London when his best friend desired it :

' When will you come to town. I am quite idle now, and the weather is still fine enough for many a delicious drive. I have excellent hock in my cellar, and venison, and a world of books—new and old—on my table. . . . Let us, now the fogs of October are setting in, and bright, blazing fires beginning to gleam upon our hearths, spend some long talkative evenings together, while we toast our knees at the grate, and sip the fine old bonded wine that gleams like a filmy ruby in our hands.'

In these degenerate days when the habit of whisky drinking has killed the taste for good wine, and it is no longer the hall-mark for a gentleman to tell a vintage claret, it is of interest for the student of manners to note that Ainsworth was only twenty-four years old when he penned the words I have just quoted. Fine wine cemented his remarkable friendship with Crossley throughout their long lives. In 1857, when inviting Crossley to come to Richmond, he wrote : ' The Champagne Cup at the *Star and Garter* is the most delicious beverage ever prepared for a thirsty soul. I had a large flagon of it a short time ago, and found it exquisite. We must drink largely of the Ambrosian cup.' At Christmas, 1869, he said : ' Drink as much old port as you can, while there is yet time, and rejoice as of old.' To celebrate Crossley's seventy-ninth birthday, the two friends stayed with Mr. Harry Wood-Hatton at Penrhos House, Rugby, where they drank ' wondrous port of the finest vintages—1815, 1820, and 1827.' Their host was the nephew by marriage and heir to part of the large fortune of Joseph Hatton, of Hatton, Cheshire, whose celebrated wine-cellar—particularly the bins of Rowley, the Rex or ' Kingly,' port—had been enjoyed in old days by

Crossley and Ainsworth.   Mr. Hatton's hospitable house possessed a wonderful wine fountain or ' wine-fall,' hymned by Crossley in the following lines :

> ' When we meet with a traveller fresh from his journey
> Through Europe in search of its classical views,
> He tells us long tales of the beauties of Terni,
> Of Tivoli's falls and the fount of Vaucluse ;
> But tell me the fountain whose banks you have sat on,
> Of the falls, though made famous by Horace's strain,
> Which can boast, like the wonderful waterfall Hatton,
> An exhaustless supply of Moselle and Champagne ?
>
> Then long may that waterfall, sparkling and gleaming,
> Exult as it sees the deposit below ;
> And long may the fires of the mansion, bright beaming,
> To welcome our coming still cheerfully glow.
> With the best of all hosts, and with Port beyond cavil,
> Be it " Twenty " or " Forty "—I care not for more—
> Let others to seek finer waterfalls travel,
> If they'll give me but Hatton, I'll leave them Lodore.'

Crossley was one of the last of the great wine drinkers —to the end of his life, when over eighty, he would drink an entire bottle of port after dinner—and George Meredith must have had him in mind when writing, in *The Egoist*, his paean to ' An Aged and a Great Wine.'   It is true that his father-in-law, Thomas Love Peacock, was, to a great extent, the original of Dr. Middleton in *The Egoist*, but Peacock and Crossley were much alike in tastes and appearance (even to the shiny black broadcloth and tailed coats that each wore), so let us find both in the picture :

' The classic scholar is he whose blood is most nuptial to the webbed bottle.   The reason must be, that he is full of the old poets.   He has their spirit to sing with, and the best that Time has done on earth to feed it. . . .   Port hymns to his conservatism.   It is magical : at one sip he is off swimming in the purple flood of the ever-youthful antique. . . .   A house having a great wine stored below, lives in our imaginations as a joyful house fast and splendidly rooted in the soil.'

Thus it was at No. 4, Booth Street, and when Ainsworth gave Dickens and Forster and Phiz letters of introduction to Crossley, on the occasion of their visit in company to Manchester, in the autumn of 1838, he did not forget his friend's fine wine cellar.

Ainsworth wrote to Crossley :

'I am sure it will give you pleasure to receive this note, handed to you, as it will be, by my friend, Mr. Charles Dickens ; and I am equally sure that it will give you pleasure to show him any attention in your power during his stay in Manchester. I rather suspect that he is reconnoitreing for character, and perhaps you may aid his researches ; but at all events you can help him to the best glass of wine in Manchester, and that will materially assist his judgment in coming to a favourable conclusion of the habits of my townsmen. I greatly regret that I cannot accompany him. I forgot to mention that Mr. Browne, the artist who illustrates *Nicholas*, will travel with Dickens, so that I must beg you to extend your hospitality to him. Pray let them see the Club, and taste its cookery. I now wish to add a special introduction for my friend Forster. He is Dickens's most intimate friend, as well as mine, and he visits Manchester in order to see it in company with Dickens.'

Ainsworth also provided Dickens and his party with letters of introduction to another old friend in Manchester, Gilbert Winter, who lived at Stocks House in the Cheetham Hill Road, and it was at his suggestion that at a dinner-party here Dickens met William and Daniel Grant, the benevolent merchants of Manchester, who were soon after depicted as the ' Cheeryble Brothers ' in *Nicholas Nickleby*. In ' reconnoitreing for character,' Dickens was also delighted by Gilbert Winter's butler, named Knowles. Writing, later on, to Forster from the New London Inn, Exeter, Dickens said : ' The head waiter is *such* a waiter. Knowles (not Sheridan Knowles, but of the Cheetham Hill Road) is an ass to him.' Gilbert Winter himself was a delightful character, and figures as ' Cuthbert Spring ' in Ainsworth's *Mervyn Clitheroe*. He had a fund of good stories, and John Forster speaks of him as ' Gilbert Winter, one of the kind Manchester friends whose hospitality we had enjoyed with Mr. Ainsworth, and whose shrewd, quaint, old-world ways come

delightfully back to me as I write his once well-known
and widely-honoured name.'

Back in London, 'Dickens and Forster,' Ainsworth
wrote to Crossley, 'called on me on Sunday to give me
an account of their expedition, and to bring me their two
Olivers—*Twist* and *Cromwell*. . . . Dickens is an excellent fellow—I am glad you like him—and so is my friend
Fury-Fire-the-Faggot. The twain expressed themselves
highly, most highly, delighted with your and G. Winter's
attention. . . . Dickens means to bring you a copy of
Oliver Twist.'

So much had Dickens and Forster enjoyed the hospitality and vintages of Ainsworth's Manchester friends
that less than two months later, in January, 1839, they
again visited the northern city. This time they were
accompanied by Ainsworth, and the entire party stayed
with his cousin, Hugh Beaver, at 'The Temple,' Cheetham Hill. There was excellent entertainment here ; a
semi-public dinner given conjointly in honour of Dickens
and Ainsworth took place on the Monday ; on the
Wednesday they dined with Gilbert Winter at Stocks
House ; and on the Tuesday with James Crossley at
No. 4, Booth Street. On the last named occasion, Crossley's dinner-table being triangular in shape, and he himself seated at the apex against the wall, he found his portly
figure very much incommoded and confined. Dickens
noticed this, and when proposing Crossley's health he
remarked : 'During the whole evening, seeing the
peculiar position our host occupied at the dinner-table,
I could not help being reminded of Dr. Primrose's
famous family picture in *The Vicar of Wakefield*, and I
have been wondering all night how ever he should be
got out, but still more amazed how he ever got in ? '

Crossley was a crusted Conservative ; he resented any
change from the old order of things, and consequently
he actively opposed the incorporation of Manchester
with its attendant crop of mayoral officials. However,
the new civic state came into being in 1838 just before

the visit of Dickens and Ainsworth in 1839, and there
can be little doubt but that Crossley wrote or inspired this
paragraph in *The Manchester Courier* :

' We understand that Mr. W. Harrison Ainsworth is visiting
Manchester, accompanied by his friend, Mr. Charles Dickens,
the well-known " Boz." We don't know whether the latter
gentleman has been tempted by our new municipal body to
take a journey northward or not, but we doubt whether he
would find, taking the whole country through, a more copious
harvest than that body presents, including mayor,[1] aldermen,
and councillors, for his inimitable talent of pourtraying the
ridiculous.'

More and more as the years went by, Crossley became
laudator temporis acti, and his regretful retrospection of
the past found its best expression in his admirable gifts
as an after-dinner speaker. Despite his constitutional
shyness and reluctance to assert himself, he excelled in
post-prandial discourse when warmed by superlative port.
It is difficult to recover the full flavour of the spoken
word, and but few reports of his speeches survive. An
example, however, can be given of his style from what
he said at the public banquet given to his old friend,
Ainsworth, at Manchester Town Hall, in September,
1881, when Ainsworth referred to Crossley's social qualities, his learning and scholarship, his varied and extensive
reading. ' It is not an extravagant compliment to say
that he may be compared to the great Dr. Johnson himself.' Crossley, in the course of his speech proposing
the toast of ' The Archaeological and Historical Societies
of the County Palatine of Lancaster,' said :

' I think the aspect of the toast that I am most called to
direct myself to is that which concerns especially my excellent
friend, Mr. Harrison Ainsworth. (Hear, hear.) When,
gentlemen, I look upon that long series of novels which he has
published, extending, in the good orthodox three-volume
form, to somewhere about one hundred volumes, I cannot but

[1] This, the first, Mayor of Manchester was Sir Thomas Potter
(1773-1845), who with his brother Richard Potter (' Radical Dick ')
founded *The Manchester Guardian.*

consider that there is a possibility of the time arriving when his
ample resources may come to an end, for, as the fertility of the
most fertile must have its limit, it may be impossible to have
always at hand plots and subjects and characters. (Laughter.)
When that time does come—when, like the Governors of the
Bank of England, who, seeing bullion going out more rapidly
than is consistent with financial policy and, perhaps, with
financial security, think it necessary to call in some agency
which will rectify and readjust the balance—if ever that does
happen to Mr. Ainsworth, I may say he cannot do better than
direct himself to the societies which are embodied in the toast.
(Laughter.)   Old Mr. Simeon, of Cambridge, used to en-
courage his clerical friends by saying, " My dear sir, whenever
your theological cistern is drawn dry come to me ; I have one
hundred skeletons of sermons which are ready at your service,
and which will keep you on your legs for a considerable time
to come." (Laughter.) The reverend gentleman's metaphors
were rather confused, but still the offer, I have no doubt, gave
great satisfaction—(Laughter)—and must have been a comfort
and consolation to his clerical friends. (Laughter.) Should it
be necessary for our excellent friend, Mr. Ainsworth, to direct
himself to some assistance of that kind, I can, I think, on behalf
of these societies say that we will find him the skeletons of one
hundred historical novels — (Laughter) — which with his
master hand and his creative power can be made instinct with
life, and form a very considerable addition to that long procession of heroes and heroines with which he has made us
familiar, and which are extensive enough almost to form a
literature of themselves, and which certainly will require and
undoubtedly deserve—and I recommend it to the attention of
Mr. Charles Sutton if he happens to be here—an Ainsworth
Bibliography.   (Applause.)   I now will direct myself to
another subject which I think, perhaps, considering the object
of our present meeting, will be rather interesting.   I was very
forcibly struck on coming into this room with the recollection
of another dinner in honour of Mr. Ainsworth which took
place just forty years ago in London, and at which I had the
good fortune to be present.   It was given in celebration of his
popular, and deservedly popular, *Tower of London* ; and if any
one wishes to know how Mr. Ainsworth looked at that time—
for forty years makes rather a difference in a man's personal
appearance—(Laughter)—I cannot do better than recommend
him to look at the fine contemporary portrait by Pickersgill,
Sen., which, through the kindness of Mr. Ainsworth, now

adorns the librarian's room in the Chetham Hospital. (Hear,
hear.) Generally when I go into that room I look up at that
portrait, and it puts me in good humour for the day. (Laughter.) The place where this London dinner was given was one
of those old hotels, spacious and commodious, which had the
reputation of many good dinners. It was in the neighbourhood of Fleet Street, and I have no doubt that at the present
time, in the progress of improvements which are going on, it
is entirely swept away along with Temple Bar and Isaac
Walton's habitation. The inn was a comfortable one, and
excellently adapted for the party, which in number was about
the same that I now see around me. The chairman on that
occasion was Mr. Serjeant (afterwards Mr. Justice) Talfourd,
a man who had no superior that I ever met with, when he had
a fine subject before him, in giving it all the ornament that
could be given to it by beautiful and appropriate language.
(Hear, hear.) He likewise had that gift, which is so admirable
in a chairman, of infusing into his audience a certain portion
of the exuberant kindliness which formed part of his nature.
The party that was congregated on that occasion was a fair and
full representation of those who as authors, as critics, as
artists, as publishers, were in the first rank in the metropolis at
that time. Amongst them was, then in the full bloom of
authorship, delighted and delighting, Charles Dickens—(Hear,
hear)—and with him his friend and subsequent biographer—
I cannot say successful biographer—John Forster ; and a host
of others whom I could particularise, but there is not time on
this occasion to do so. Amongst the party were several of
that group of Fraserians of whom I believe Mr. Ainsworth is
now the sole survivor, but who still sit around their table per-
petuated and pictured by the admirable sketches of Maclise.
(Hear, hear.) Nor was there wanting on that occasion that
artist, whose bark will ever

> Attendant sail,
> Pursue the triumph and partake the gale

with the works of the distinguished authors whom he so
admirably illustrated. Need I say I refer to George Cruikshank? (Applause.) The chairman, in proposing the toast
of the evening, did every justice to the work which had been
the means of calling that party together ; and in his happiest
terms gave his estimate of the literary merits of Mr. Ainsworth.
That estimate was a very high one, and it was enthusiastically
seconded and adopted by the party present. My only regret

is that of that speech and of Mr. Ainsworth's grateful response
there is at present no report.   Horace deplores the want of the
vates sacer, but what is the *vates sacer* to the reporter, without
whom wit, wisdom, and eloquence, are only born and spoken
to perish.   (Laughter and applause.)   The characteristic of the
remaining part of the evening was the grand geniality and the
utter impossibility of everything like a jar.   There were rival
authors present, but they did not quarrel ; there were hostile
critics, but their challenges were limited to champagne ;   there
were men of different schools, but they broke down the parti-
tion in order to make the harmony perfect.   There was a case
of mortal feud, but it was arranged by an armistice which
lasted at all events that evening.   I believe everybody spoke—
(Laughter)—whether accustomed or unaccustomed to public
speaking, who was able and capable in his turn of assisting that
grand social exhibition.   Amongst the gentlemen who were
present was one of the name of Swift, who lived to a very advanced age.   He was the keeper of the regalia of the Tower,
and a collateral relative of the great Dean of St. Patrick's.   All
that could be expected of him was the usual stereotyped
speech of an official, but had the Dean of St. Patrick's himself
been resuscitated from the dead he could not have given
utterance to a speech more admirably appropriate than that
which was spoken by Mr. Swift.   (Laughter.)   You said at
once, " The man who could make such a speech as this deserves to keep the regalia of England."   (Laughter.)   The
good fortune of the speakers extended even to the humble
individual who now addresses you.   (Hear, hear.)   I happened,
when called upon, to mention that twenty years before I had
the pleasure of co-operating with the Chairman in contributing
to a publication which is now, I believe, not forgotten, and
that was *The Retrospective Review*.   That seemed to touch some
pleasant chord in the Serjeant's mind, and he in his usual impulsive manner, left the chair and gave me a most cordial
greeting.   (Laughter.)   More than that, he invited me, not to
see his library—(Laughter)—for he thought, possibly, I had
seen libraries enough—(renewed laughter)—but invited me to
examine and to taste that unique collection of specimens of the
fine historical vintage of Oporto—(laughter)—extending in
chronological series from 1790 to 1830—which at great trouble
and great expense he had collected for himself and well affected
friends—(Laughter)—and which ultimately—I say nothing
about *Ion*, or his Parliamentary and forensic eloquence—most
deservedly placed him upon the judicial bench.   (Loud

laughter.) I accepted the learned Serjeant's invitation, and I made it my business, as far as I could, to assist him in those historical investigations—(Laughter)—of which he had supplied the material at his hospitable table. (Laughter.) Gentlemen, I may say further, and I must really conclude the matter by the observation, that the proceedings were carried out with admirable spirit and success to the end. (Laughter.) I cannot tell you—I have referred to my diary, but it does not assist me —at what time we broke up ; but from inquiries I made I ascertained that every guest present awoke a wiser and a better man in the morning, but without the disagreeable headache which generally accompanies that discovery. (Laughter.) . . .'

Commenting on this speech a few days later in *The World*, Edmund Yates, who had been present at the banquet, observed :

' The presence of Mr. James Crossley, President of the Chetham Society, a portly gentleman recalling the portraits of Coleridge, served as a pleasant link with the past.'

As his long years drew to an end, Crossley's quaint figure was indeed a remarkable link with the past in Manchester, the city he had witnessed grow from a friendly town of ancient picturesque houses of black and white timber, mingled with buildings of mellow Georgian red brick, to the sombre Colossus of factory and mean street which has destroyed the old town and devoured the lovely country that once lay at the doors of Manchester. The cut of his black broadcloth suit was that of his youth ; and when he walked abroad he was enveloped in a long, dark-coloured cloak, and from beneath a wide-brimmed hat his long silvery hair fell to his shoulders. His creed was old times, old friends, old books, old wine.[1] He attributed his longevity to port, celibacy, and never indulging in snuff or tobacco. He never had to use spectacles for reading. He might have added his old age was indebted to constitutional good health, for, unlike other inveterate drinkers of port, he

[1] The maxim of King Alphonso of Castile, according to Mr. Oldbuck in *The Antiquary* : ' Old wood to burn, old books to read, old wine to drink, and old friends to converse with.'

seems to have been free from gout, blood-pressure, and
such-like unpleasant danger signals of Nature in the guise
of Temperance Advocate.   Most of all he was indebted
to a singularly placid and equable temperament, a never
failing *joie de vivre*, a delight in the daily joys of *living*,
reading, and dining.   When he was seventy-six years old
he wrote to a friend of ' the many agreeable reminiscences with which May Day is accompanied in my mind.
I have been looking back to see how and when I spent it
during each of the last forty-five years, and it has certainly
done its duty in the general complement of the happiness
of my life.   I have had to chronicle no misfortune, no
pain mental or physical on that day, and whether the
temperature was balmy or chill, whether Phoebus shone
out or was obscured, the soul's clear sunshine was never
overclouded or disturbed.'   Such a happy retrospect of
life has been the fortunate fate of but a very few men.

His good health was in no way attributable to exercise.
In his youth, of course, it had been the fashion and
necessity to ride as a means of getting about ; and he was
no doubt strong and active, for there survives a strange
document, dated December, 1824, discharging him from
all liability to serve in parish or ward offices in the parish
of West Ham, Essex, as a reward for that ' Patrick
Collins was convicted of feloniously and burglariously
breaking and entering the dwelling house of James
Crossley in the night of the 20th day of September last
at the parish of West Ham in the county aforesaid and
stealing therein goods value nine pounds, eight shillings,
and that it doth appear unto me [Sir James Burrough]
that the said James Crossley was the person who did
apprehend and take the said Patrick Collins and did
prosecute him so apprehended and take him until he was
convicted as aforesaid.' [1]

---

[1] Crossley's activities as a thief-taker must have occurred when he
was in London in 1823-1824 to complete his legal training.   The
house at West Ham was probably the residence of his father, who
was living in the neighbourhood of London at that date.

JAMES CROSSLEY
From a drawing by W. G. Baxter, 1880, for *Momus*

But for the greater part, Crossley's life was entirely a sedentary one ; he played no games, except bowls, and his interest in that ' sport ' probably arose from its Elizabethan associations rather than pleasure in its backbreaking attitudes and rotatory triumphs. He was secretary of the Cheetham Hill Bowling Club (founded in the sixteenth century). The members met once a week in the summer on the green of the Kersal Moor Hotel. After playing bowls for a few hours, they dined at seven, made speeches, and sat over their excellent wine until midnight.

In other directions, Crossley was President of the Manchester Athenæum,[1] 1847-1850 ; and he took a prominent part in the formation of the Free Library, 1851, when he helped to select the many thousands of books. He was a member of the Abbotsford Club, and of the Surtees and Philobiblon Societies, and President of the Spenser Society, founded in 1866. Most of all he was interested in the Chetham Society, and the venerable institution in Manchester after which it was called. In 1816, when he first came to Manchester as a boy, and for years after, he spent part of each day reading at the sixteenth-century table in the oriel window recess of the Reading Room of Chetham's. As far back as 1821 he had described The Chetham Library and Hospital in *Blackwood's Magazine* ; in 1855 he became one of the

---

[1] Disraeli wrote to Crossley in 1845 :

' *Private*.

My Dear Sir,
            A fortnight ago I forwarded a copy of *Sybil* to the Athenæum, the receipt of which has not been acknowledged. I presume it may not have reached its destination. I don't like to enquire of the Secretaries, because it might look as if I was anxious to receive a letter of thanks, whereas I really only want to ascertain whether they have got the book. Be pleased to enquire as to this, and have the kindness to let me know.
                        Yours faithfully,
                                    B. Disraeli.

Grosvenor Street,
     May 23rd, 1845.'

Feoffees, and Governor in 1860 ; in 1875 his portrait was presented and placed there ; and in 1877 he acted as honorary librarian.   It was strange, indeed, that he did not bequeath his own great library to this fitting haunt of ancient peace, where it would have been preserved intact for all time in those cloistered rooms of the fifteenth century, with their lovely Jacobean panels and furniture, and the portraits of bygone worthies, all so dear to Crossley's heart.   As he said, so deeply interested was he in the place, ' Sit anima mea cum Bibliotheca Chethamensis.'

In his earlier life he occasionally took part in politics. He spoke at meetings for Gladstone in 1837, that curious episode in the politician's career when, despite his candidature for Newark and his refusal of the invitation to stand for Manchester, the Tories of the latter town nominated him and assured the electors that Gladstone ' was the most promising young statesman of the day.'   However, Gladstone was at the bottom of the poll for the three candidates ; and in view of his subsequent change to ultra-Liberal politics, it is strange to think he was once the approved young Tory of the ultra-Conservative Crossley.   In one of the rhyming letters Crossley used to send to his friends, he thus on January 1st, 1879, addressed William Bleackley, of Prestwich (father of Mr. Horace Bleackley) :

> ' I know a man—if he were knighted,
> How all good folks would be delighted.
> Because on earth there does not live
> A truer staunch Conservative.
> Nor, what to find in vain you'd labour,
> A heartier friend, a kinder neighbour.
> He is not only great in Kersal—
> The deep respect is universal.
> Just see him at a public meeting—
> What orator receives such greeting ?
> All Gladstone's false, long-winded proses
> As clear as day-light he exposes ;
> Each fallacy he puts his hand on,
> And leaves him not a leg to stand on.

At Bowling Dinners when presiding
His eloquence we take a pride in ;
So well the healths and toasts he passes,
We all fill bumpers in our glasses.
His Myrtle Grove—full well I know it—
Beats that of any classic poet ;
And rather there I'd take my Tippy,
Than quaff the streams of Aganippe.
One only of his fine quotations
Is worth a score of Whig orations ;
A feast of Scripture texts to dish up,
I'd put him against Dean or Bishop ;
As a Concordance you may view him :
Old Cruden's self is nothing to him.
Such then he is—the opening year
Shall bear to him the wish sincere—
Long may he bowl ; Long may he live
With all the blessings life can give.
                New Year's Day, 1879.' [1]

But politics were but a very subsidiary interest :
Crossley's real life was in his library.   As I have indicated
earlier, he commenced his collection as a boy, but he was
ever a very careful and cautious purchaser.   The story
is told that as a youth of seventeen he was examining an
old book, Bull's *Defensio Fidei Nicenæ*, at one of the stalls
in Manchester, and hesitated over the price asked, five
shillings, when a rough Lancashire voice behind him
said : ' Buy it, lad ; t' book is cheap, and you ought to
buy this one with it—Outram's *De Sacrificiis*—they ought
to go together : the Unitarians, if they were to write till
Doomsday, can never answer them.'   The adviser proved

---

[1] William Bleackley died suddenly, from apoplexy, in September
of this year, aged sixty.   Though much younger than Crossley he
was a very valued friend, and for several years he always entertained
Crossley in honour of his birthday, when the veteran would drink
the best part of two bottles of vintage port without any discomfort.
Crossley was greatly grieved by William Bleackley's death, for they
had been united by the bonds of Toryism, bowls and port, a sense
of humour, and a faculty for quoting the Scriptures.   It is related
that after his friend's death, when his name was mentioned his eyes
would mist and his voice falter.

to be the eccentric Joshua Brookes (1754-1821), who
from humble origin rose to be a chaplain of Manchester
Collegiate Church and a fine scholar. With the passing
years Crossley's quality as a bargainer increased more and
more. Mr. T. Swindells relates in his *Manchester Streets
and Manchester Men* :

' He was one of the last of the book lovers of our city who
systematically haunted the book stalls, examining with a keen
eye their contents, and bidding down the price asked by the
stall-keeper for some volume or volumes. This bidding down
was a well known feature of " Old Crossley," as he was called by
booksellers and stall-keepers; and it was said by some who knew
him well that he was never known to pay the price originally
asked for a second-hand book. It was that custom of running
down of prices that caused him to miss a *Wynkyn de Worde*, now
to be found amongst the treasures in our Reference Library.' [1]

At the age of seventy-eight, Crossley transported his
enormous library and his portly self to Stocks House, the

----

[1] James Crossley in old age much resembles Jonathan Oldbuck,
and in style and content he might have written such a passage as
this from *The Antiquary* where Oldbuck narrates the joys of the
book-collector :

' How often have I stood haggling on a halfpenny, lest, by a too
ready acquiescence in the dealer's first price, he should be led to
suspect the value I set upon the article. How I have trembled, lest
some passing stranger should chop in between me and the prize,
and regarded each poor student of divinity that stopped to turn
over the books at the stall as a rival amateur, or prowling bookseller in disguise. And then, the sly satisfaction with which one
pays the consideration and pockets the article, affecting a cold indifference, while the hand is trembling with pleasure. Then to
dazzle the eyes of our wealthier and emulous rivals by showing
them such a treasure as this—(displaying a little black smoked book
about the size of a primer)—to enjoy their surprise and envy, shroud-
ing meanwhile under a veil of mysterious consciousness our own
superior knowledge and dexterity—these, these are the white
moments of life, that repay the toil and pains and sedulous attention
which our profession, above all others, so peculiarly demands.'
Crossley was the worthy successor of David Wilson—' Snuffy
Davy '—mentioned in *The Antiquary*, who bought *The Game of
Chess*, 1474, the first book ever printed in England, at a stall in
Holland for two groschen, or twopence of our money.

fine old house in Cheetham Hill Road where his friend, Gilbert Winter, had lived at the time Dickens visited Manchester forty years earlier. The Stocks estate was originally the property of the Rydings family, and the house with its numerous outbuildings, ornamental gardens, and lake-like ponds, dated from the eighteenth century. All these landed accessories placed old Crossley in a new light, and Ainsworth wrote, in July, 1878, that he must ' have a look at you in all your grandeur at Stocks House . . . and discuss a bottle of old port—or better still in this hot weather, a bottle of claret. . . . I have no doubt you will like the Stocks exceedingly—better than any previous residence—and I sincerely hope you may long live to enjoy the place. For me it has many pleasant associations. I am truly glad the old house has come into your hands.'

But alas ! the years could not be denied ; the horizon of life was darkening for both the friends, and the time fast coming when old books and old wine and existence itself would vanish from their happy consciousness. Ainsworth died some three years later : Crossley survived him for rather more than a year. He was failing in health, but he paid a visit to London. A fall at Euston Railway Station [1] hastened his end. He died on August the 1st, 1883, at the age of eighty-three.

Long, long years before, in the days of youth, at one of those ambrosial nights in Smithy Door, Crossley had written some words from an imaginary play to serve as a motto for the romance, *Sir John Chiverton*,[2] J. P. Aston

---

[1] He was knocked down by a porter wheeling a truck of luggage.

[2] This was the romance mentioned by Walter Scott in his Diary, October the 17th, 1826 :

' I read with interest, during my journey, *Sir John Chiverton* and *Brambletye House*—novels, in what I may surely claim as the style—

    " Which I was born to introduce—
      Refined it first, and showed its use."

They are both clever books.'

was writing with the help of Ainsworth. This book
described the picturesque old timber mansion, Hulme
Hall, then still standing on the high, rocky banks of the
river Irwell near Manchester. In that work can be seen
the meteor gleam of romance that shot athwart those
young lives, lighting up all things with the golden glow
of imagination : the solicitor's office vanished, and the
old historic, colourful past lay spread out before their
eyes. Crossley's motto for *Sir John Chiverton* ran thus :

> ' *Merrie Daies, or Hie Away for Hulme Hall.*
>
> *Eustace.*—" Is that the merrie old hall ? Doth its table still
> groan with the chyne—and its tankards foam as they were
> wont ? Doth old Badge, the servitor, still sit at the porch ;
> and Sir John telleth he at his third cup, how he hunted the boar
> at Furness ; and of his merrie pranks with the Keeper's
> daughter at Bowland ? Talketh Master Hugh, the parson, still
> of Beza and Whitaker, and the New Doctrines—and goeth the
> Steward forth at Martinmas with his staff, to call the tenants to
> suit and service—and to drink their Lord's health in a hum-
> ming cup of the best—Are these still as heretofore ? "
>
> ' *Lancelot.*—" Lord help thee, Eustace ! Have thy thoughts
> gone a wool-gathering ? Sir John and the Parson and the
> Steward sleep soundly enough under an *hic jacet* this many
> longsome years. Little of festivity seeth the old Hall now.
> Its courts are grass grown, and its floors are mottled with mud.
> Clean gone are its old faces. . . ." '

Sad and true words. So, too, Stocks House is demolished and gone, like the old faces and jollity it once
knew ; and James Crossley lies under a neglected grave
in Kersal churchyard, for Manchester has almost forgotten [1] one of her most remarkable and most learned
citizens—her ' local Doctor Johnson.'

The year following his death, a portion of James

---

[1] I can, by personal knowledge, exempt two inhabitants of Manchester from this indictment : Mr. J. H. Swann, of the Public
Library, and Mr. Sidney Barton, of Cheetham ; to both I tender my
thanks for assistance in transcribing documents for this article.
Mr. Barton endeavours to keep tidy Crossley's grave in Kersal
churchyard.

Crossley's great library was sold in Manchester, in May, 1884. The more valuable books and manuscripts were removed to London and sold at Sotheby's, during seven days in July. In the following June, 1885, there was a further sale, occupying nine days. The two sales in London comprised 5943 lots. It is therefore impossible to do more than glance at a few of the exceptional items.

Here, then, were Ben Jonson's copy of *The Faerie Queen* (1617), with his signature and numerous marginal notes in his holograph ; also his copy, with many manuscript notes, of Joachim Camerarius's *Commentarii Utriusque Linguæ* (1551). . . . An exceedingly rare edition of Sir Thomas Browne's *Religio Medici* (Printed for Andrew Crooke, 1642), being the surreptitious impression of which Sir Thomas Browne complains in the Preface and Letter to Sir Kenelm Digby in the subsequent editions. . . *Les Effects Pernicieux des Meschants Favoris* (1653), with the bookplate of Horace Walpole and this manuscript note : ' This book, of which I never saw another copy, was given to me by Mr. James Bindley, Dec. 15, 1775. Horace Walpole.' Also Walpole's copy of *The Court Beauties*, a Poem (1718), with the names filled in by him. . . . King James the First's copy of Camden's *Britannia*, with the Royal Arms stamped in gold and originally presented by the author to F. Godwin, Bishop of Llandaff ; and King Charles the First's copies of M. Griffith's *Bethel* (1634) and Scioppius's *Scaliger Hypobolimæus*. . . . The very rare second edition of Coleridge's *Poems* (Bristol, 1797), and the even rarer *Lyrical Ballads* of Coleridge and Wordsworth (London, 1798). . . . Two Satires on Davenant, written by Sir J. Denham, Donne, and others, relating to his *Gondibert*. . . . *The Established Government of England* (1687) by Fabian Philipps, of which, according to Crossley's note, there is no copy in either the British Museum or Bodleian libraries. . . . Many first editions of Butler's *Hudibras*, of Fielding, Keats, Sterne (including his own copy of *Tristram Shandy*, with Sterne's autograph in two of the volumes); Boswell's signed copy of Aubrey's *Miscellanies*; the excessively rare first edition of Shelley's *Queen Mab* (1813), and Byron's *Hours of Idleness* (Newark, 1807), apparently a large paper copy.

Crossley's collection of Defoe was marvellous, extending to over nine hundred volumes. It included all the rare tracts and nine volumes of *Review of the Affairs of France and of all Europe* (1712-1713) : only six volumes of this work were in the British Museum, and Crossley's ninth volume was, apparently, the only copy in existence. He also possessed Defoe's autograph manuscript of *The Compleat Gentleman*, believed to be unpublished. Crossley bought it for £75 18s. at the Dawson Turner sale.

Equally remarkable were the hundreds—nay thousands —of tracts, broadsides, trials, old novels, and plays of the sixteenth and seventeenth centuries. For example : the very rare satire on James the First written by Scioppius in the assumed name of Casaubon, 1615,—Legatus Latro, with the note : ' This violent attack is so scarce that I never saw another copy. The " Legatus " referred to, was John, first Baron Digby '. . . C. Hotham's *Ad Philosophiam Teutonicam Manuductio* (1648). . . . An early novel, *English Adventures*, by the Earl of Orrery, ' In the Savoy, 1676,' and apparently unknown to all Bibliographers.

Crossley's numerous Black Letter books included a splendid Froissart, *Chronycles of Englande, Fraunce, Spayne, Portyngale, Scotlande, Bretayne*, translated by John Bourchier, Lorde Berners, two volumes in oaken boards, 1525. . . . R. Holinshed's *Chronicles of England, Ireland, and Scotland*, an extremely large and fine copy of the second edition, 1586. . . . *The Anatomie of Abuses*, by P. Stubbes, published by Richard Iones, 1583. . . . *Cardanus Comforte*, by the Earle of Oxenforde, 1576. . . . J. Darrell's *Narration of the Possession, Dispossession, and Repossession of William Sommers*, 1598. . . . *The Discoverie of Witchcraft*, by R. Scot, 1584.

Witchcraft was a subject of especial interest for Crossley, and largely represented in his collection. Here were R. Baddeley's scarce *Boy of Bilson . . . expulsion of the Divell out of a young boy named W. Perry, in the County of Stafford,* 1622. . . . *De la Demonomanie des Sorciers,* by S. Bodin, 1580. . . . Delrio's *Wierus de Præstigiis Dæmonum, ac Incantationibus,* 1577. . . . Cotton Mather's *Wonders of the Invisible World : Tryals of several Witches lately executed in New-England,* 1693. . . . H. Hallywell's *Melampronœa,* 1681. . . . *Observation of Witchcraft practised by J. Samuel, of Warboise, upon the five daughters of R. Throckmorton,* 1589.

Crossley possessed many valuable manuscripts. He owned Robert Barret's unpublished work, *The Sacred Warr, a Poem Epike,* 1613, which formerly belonged to Southey. Crossley wrote in it : ' There is no unprinted Poem of the same period in English in existence, that I know, which is philologically of such value. When I met Southey in Manchester, some years ago, he spoke of this volume as the great poetical treasure of his library.'

Another rarity was *Troilus and Creseid,* ' written by the most-famous Prince of Poets, Geofrey Chaucer, done into Lattine by Sir Francis Kynaston,' 1629. Here, also, were two hundred letters addressed to George Selwyn by his famous contemporaries, and the papers concerning the prosecution of Selwyn for having, when he was a student of Hertford College, ' impiously ridiculed and profaned the sacrament of the Lord's Supper.' Here, further, were accounts of witchcraft in the Fairfax family, 1621-3, accompanied by most curious drawings ; the Poems of Dr. John Donne, Dean of St. Paul's ; the Journal of William Upcott, 1803-1807 ; the Autobiography of Dr. John Trussler ; the Mitford manuscripts ; and these lines addressed by Burns to Mr. Fergusson :

' The king's poor blackguard slave am I,
   And scarce dou spare a minute ;
But I'll be wi' you by and by,
   Or else the devil's in it.
                              ' R. B.'

Crossley owned practically all the manuscripts of Roger North (1653-1734), including his Lives of Lord Keeper Guilford, Sir Dudley North, and Dr. John North. Most valued of all was the manuscript Autobiography of Roger North himself, running to over three hundred closely written pages. Crossley noted : ' I gave Mr. Dawson Turner in hard cash the sum of One Hundred and Fifty Pounds, in the year 1838, for this volume.' He intended to edit and publish it, and consulted Ainsworth, who wrote in October, 1838 :

' I saw Colburn on Saturday and am sorry to say that the interview was not attended with the success I could desire. He did not positively decline the proposal—in fact, he wished the matter to be kept open (for he is a sad shuffling fellow), that if you would put the work in order, and when complete offer the MS. to him, he thought he *might venture* to print one edition of 750 copies, for which the utmost he could give would be £150. This I told him I was sure you would not listen to. . . . Your safest and best plan will be to publish it on your own account. . . . I have no doubt that I might by dint of bullying Colburn get you £200 for an edition of 1000, but such remuneration is inadequate and absurd.

' The copyright is a very valuable one and not to be hastily parted with. I really think, judiciously managed, you ought to make £1000 by it. Now, if you think proper, I will do this for you, and I am so sure that I am right that I strongly urge it as a means of repaying, in some degree, the obligations I am under to you. I will, I say, undertake the whole arrangement of the matter for you with the Longmans or some other equally influential house, and I will engage to say you shall have £500 in your pocket before the end of 1839, and the copyright of the work into the bargain. . . . I will make bargains for you with paper makers, printers, boarders, etc., so as to relieve you of all trouble; I will give directions about advertising, and will, moreover, use all my influence with reviewers. I mentioned the subject on Saturday to Forster, and he is of the same opinion as myself.' . . . ' Forster is anxious to see you. He has spoken to Colburn, since I last wrote, on the subject of North's Diary and will tell you what he has heard. It appears that Colburn is now not unwilling to undertake the book. You will find Forster able to give you the best practical advice on the subject. .... At the beginning of December I shall be wholly at your service, and will put you to press if you are ready.'

That was the end of the matter, for Crossley was never ready. The books he meant to produce were never published : nevertheless, he was a great bibliophile.

MRS. J. H. RIDDELL: THE NOVELIST OF THE CITY AND OF MIDDLESEX

CHARLOTTE RIDDELL was truly what is called a born story-teller. In the course of half a century she produced over fifty books, novels and tales, and there are probably many short stories from her pen still hidden away and unidentified in the pages of forgotten magazines. She lost all count of her works, possessed very few copies of them herself, and often forgot where certain stories had appeared or what had happened to her rights in them. Thus, on one occasion, I wrote to ask her where I could find what I consider her best tale, in its special category, and one extremely rare from a bibliographical point of view—*The Haunted River*. She answered:

'In reply to your kind note, I think *The Haunted River* was sold with several other stories to a company who bought the right of reproduction. I never saw this story amongst others in volume form, but will endeavour to ascertain. . . . I have made inquiries, but am sorry to say so far without success. When any information reaches me (or rather if any should), I will write at once. Meanwhile, will you accept the accompanying little booklet in which there is one story, *So Near, or the Pity of It*, that has been liked a little. Kindest wishes. I am still far from strong.'

She died in the following year, 1906, and she never traced the whereabouts of *The Haunted River*, though she wrote to several editors and friends in the endeavour to help me. I mention this little incident at the outset, as it illuminates her charming character—her kindness, her alacrity to assist others : though ever she was carelessly indifferent to her own rights or would not trouble to claim them by reason of her Irish insouciance. For

fifty years she wrote stories of three distinctly different
categories—stories of commerce and City life ; most impressive stories of the supernatural, with the authentic
thrill of the inexplicable, without which such tales are
vain and tiresome ; and, above all, clever and observant
but sad stories of real life, sad because any story that
truly reflects human life must possess that quality at
times and not omit pictures of terror and death : our
happiest paths are all over-shadowed by the inevitable
End. Charlotte Riddell was pre-eminently equipped
by Fate to present with personal knowledge the sadness
of human things in literary form, for her own life was one
of sorrow and sacrifice, hard work with but passing
monetary reward, and at the last many lonely years termi-
nated by a terrible and painful disease.

Charlotte Elizabeth Lawson Cowan was the youngest
daughter of James Cowan, of Carrickfergus, High Sheriff
for the county of Antrim, but her mother, Ellen Kilshaw,
was English. Her paternal grandfather was in the Navy,
and a great-grandfather fought at Culloden on the right
side, so she mixed the blood of the three kingdoms.
From her father, Mrs. Riddell said,[1] ' I think I got the
few brains I possess. Undoubtedly he was a very clever
man, but *I* never knew him at his best, for as far as my
memory goes back he was always more or less a sufferer,
blessed with the most tender and devoted wife man ever
had. . . . On most subjects people have two opinions,
but I never heard a second opinion about my mother.
Even amongst those who only knew her in later life,
when stricken with disease, and changed by long years
of sorrow, she stands out a distinct personality, as one of
those possessed of the manners, appearance, and ideas
that we associate with the highest bred women of the
past. And she was good as she was beautiful.'

Charlotte Cowan was born on September the 30th,
1832, at The Barn, Carrickfergus, a long, low house—

[1] To Helen C. Black for her excellent sketch of Mrs. Riddell in
Notable Women Authors of the Day, 1893.

somewhat in the Italian style as was often the case with houses in Ireland built early in the nineteenth century. It was set in lovely gardens, with terraces, conservatories, and vineries.   As I have said, she was a born tale-teller, for she has related : ' I never remember the time when I did not compose.   Before I was old enough to hold a pen I used to get my mother to write down my childish ideas. . . .   In my very early days I read everything I could lay my hands on, *The Koran* included, when about eight years old.   I thought it most interesting.'   By the time she was fifteen she had written a full-length novel— ' It was on a bright moonlight night—I can see it now flooding the gardens—that I began, and I wrote week after week, never ceasing until it was finished.'   It was never published : but success was lurking many years ahead.

The happy home life at Carrickfergus all too soon came to an end.   Mr. Cowan died when his daughter was scarcely of age, and, owing to reasons connected with the family estate which have not transpired, Charlotte and her mother were at once reduced from comfort, if not affluence, to very limited means—in fact, merely the amount of Mrs. Cowan's jointure.   They had to depart from the pleasant house and gardens, and went to live at Dundonald, in the adjoining county of Down.   It was a charming village, and thirty years later Mrs. Riddell fully described it as the setting for her story, *Berna Boyle* (1884), which also presents some account of Belfast.

It is curious that Mrs. Riddell only occasionally re- turned to her native Ireland for the scenes of her many books.   In *Maxwell Drewitt* (1865) she gives an excellent picture of life in Connemara, including all the excitements of an election and an unforgettable glimpse of how the sombre interior scenery of the country suddenly changes to all the emerald loveliness of the islands in the bays :

' Connemara, where, beside lonely lakes, the plover whistles, and the bittern cries, where desolation reigns supreme, where there is a solitude which may be heard, a silence which has a voice. . . . Away to the left were hills without end ; to the right the blue conical mountains reared their heads towards heaven . . . far as the valley extended, nothing met the eye save lonely lakes and swiftly-flowing streams, thousands of acres of bog land, thousands more of moor . . . when suddenly, the road taking a sharp curve, the view changed—the bogs and the lakes and the mountains were left behind, and the sea burst upon the view. How shall words ever give even the faintest idea of the exquisite beauty and peace of that summer's evening scene ? How can pen and ink ever tell how green looked the grassy knolls that lay down by the shore ; how fair were the islands in Duranmore Bay ; how soft, and rich, and mellow the golden light that lay on wood and water, that steeped the trees and fell in great patches on the hill-sides ? With what a glad sound of welcome the " sweet chimes of the waves " sung their low song in the stranger's ear. . . .'

The book is full of scenes of Irish life and character and amusing stories, such as that of the drunken wife of the squireen of Castle Cronac. He went to the doctor to ask for a remedy to cure the lady of her failing. Could not Mr. Murphy mix her up something ?

' If we could mix up anything to cure that disorder,' says Murphy, ' we should be made men : but I tell you what, take home a gallon of whisky, and let her drink as much as she likes, and I will be round with you before night.'

It was in the summer-time, but not moon-light, and when the woman was thoroughly drunk, Murphy and the husband carried her down into the vaults of that old castle and laid her down on some boards till she should come to. . . . When she woke about twelve o'clock she began calling out and asking where she was. 'Well, you are in the vaults underneath Eversbeg Abbey, ma'am,' Murphy says. ' And how long have I been here ? ' she inquired. ' A matter of ten or twelve months,' he answered. ' Then I'm dead, in course ? ' she says. ' As a door-nail,' wound up Murphy. ' And are you dead too ? ' ' Yes, ma'am.' ' And how long have you been here ? ' ' Somewhere about five years,' he said. ' Then we are all dead ? ' ' Yes.'

She sat down on the floor and thought the matter out a bit. Murphy said he could not imagine what she would say next, when she began : ' You must know the ways of this country a good deal better than me. Where can you get a drop of good whisky now, reasonable ? ' ' That floored me,' Murphy finished. ' Squire,' said he, ' you'd better take your wife home ; if she thinks there are whisky-shops in Hades, it is of no use trying to frighten her with death. Take her home and let her live.' And he let her live ; but she ruined him and died a beggar in Spanish Place, Galway.

Again, in *The Nun's Curse* (1888) Mrs. Riddell paints the wild beauty of far Donegal, when with a few broad touches this gifted author conjures up all the mystery of Irish scenery so interlocked, as it is, with the mentality of the race—as exemplified at its best in the work of J. M. Synge. Thus Mrs. Riddell conveys the spirit of a night of storm :

' Given a wild winter's night, when the storm spirits are abroad, howling among the hills and shrieking out at sea, the land seems one abandoned by its Maker, and given over to utter desolation and destruction. . . . Walking along a *boreen*, over which distant but ubiquitous Muckish frowned heavily, was a man who paused from time to time, and looked around as if in search of some landmark or dwelling where he might make inquiry. Not even a glimmer of light rewarded his scrutiny. . . . There was not a sign—the roaring of the wind over the waste of rock and turf, the dash of water not far distant, were the only sounds that met his ear—and he was about to make the best of a bad business, when he caught the faint echo of footsteps coming down the old coach-road. At times they were lost, swept inland by the wind, but in the lulls of the gale he could hear them approaching nearer and nearer. . . .'

How skilfully is here created a Le Fanuesque atmosphere of mystery and the stage picturesquely set for a romantic tale. Mrs. Riddell again reminds one of Le Fanu in a short story entitled *The Last of Squire Ennismore* (in *Idle Tales*, 1888), a legend of the supernatural and satanic possession with a setting on the coast of Antrim. *The Earl's Promise* (1873) is a full-length Irish story, of Ulster, and in several of her shorter tales, such as *The Rusty Sword* (1893) and those which form the volumes entitled *The Banshee's Warning* (1894) and *Handsome Phil*

(1899), Mrs. Riddell dealt with various aspects and traditions of her native land.

But, for the greater part of her work, Charlotte Cowan was destined by Fate to be the pre-eminent novelist of far-distant and entirely different scenes—the City of London and its nearer suburbs, and to find her inspiration in old City mansions and courts and the melancholy but attractive scenery of Middlesex and the Thames Valley. In after years Mrs. Riddell realised that it was all for the best, in the sense of her future literary career, that she had removed, when still a young girl, with her mother from Ireland, though it was with grief at the time that the decision was made to leave Dundonald. She has stated :

' I have often wished we never had so decided, yet in that case I do not think I ever should have achieved the smallest success, and even before we left, with bitter tears, a place where we had the kindest friends, and knew much happiness, my mother's death was—though neither of us then knew the fact—a certainty. The illness of which she died had then taken hold of her. Coming as strangers to a strange land, in all London we did not know a single creature. During the first fortnight, indeed, I really thought I should break my heart. I had never taken kindly to new places, and, remembering the sweet hamlet and the loving friends we had left behind, London seemed to me horrible. I could not eat ; I could not sleep ; I could only walk over the " stony-hearted streets " and offer my manuscripts to publisher after publisher.'

Thus it was, she arrived in London—the City she was to learn to love and interpret with that rare sympathy which is only acquired by personal sorrow leading to understanding—friendless and unknown, conscious of literary gifts she did not know how to utilise, but burning with anxiety to earn sufficient to keep a mother, dying from cancer, in necessary comfort. Her manuscripts, unsupported by any recommendation or introduction, were rejected again and again by unperceptive publishers —as will be the case with future famous authors and other publishers until the end of Time. The desolation and pain and devastation of this period were deeply

etched on Mrs. Riddell's sensitive nature, and were the
cause of much of the sadness that found a wistful echo
in her books. So the weary trail to publishers' offices
went on ' o'er moor and fen ' of the stony book-world—
little wonder that she called one of her earliest books *The
Moors and the Fens*, for it was written amid ' encircling
gloom ' when she was about to lose a face she had ' loved
long since.'   But the publishers, though they would not
at this date accept her books, were nice to her.   ' Looking back,' she observed, ' I *must* say they were all very
kind to me.   I was too ignorant and heartsore to understand how gracious they were to my simplicity, even
more than to my youth. Yet I shall never forget how
charming Mr. George Bentley's manner seemed the first
day I saw him.   His father—the kindest, most impulsive,
most sympathetic of men [1]—was alive then, and for many
a year afterwards ; but it so happened that Mr. George
Bentley was the partner whom I saw, and, though he,
like every one else, refused my work, still I left his
office not unhappy, but thinking much more about how
courteous and nice he was than of how entirely the wrong
person in the wrong place I seemed to be. . . .   I have
now known three generations of Bentleys.'

At long last, a publisher was found willing to risk a
little money in the production of a story by Miss Cowan,
and the credit for perceiving her future promise as an
author attaches to Thomas Cautley Newby, of 30, Welbeck
Street, Cavendish Square, an old-fashioned publisher,
who for some years back had issued the voluminous
works of the King of Best Sellers, G. P. R. James. Mr.
Newby had a cosy office and house, and if he was old-

---

[1] Richard Bentley (1794-1871) was originally in partnership with
Henry Colburn. In 1832 he became a publisher on his own
account.   The firm flourished for over sixty years and was eventually amalgamated with that of Macmillan. Bentley was associated
with the early work of Dickens and Ainsworth, and these impatient,
hot-blooded authors have conveyed the impression that their publisher was a hard man to deal with : Mrs. Riddell's pleasant tribute to
Bentley perhaps restores the balance of fair judgment.

fashioned, in another direction he was a pioneer, for he employed a female factotum or manager of his business, Miss Springett, and a woman in such a capacity in those days of publishing was, I imagine, unique. The winter when the Cowans arrived in London was a terribly severe one—the Black Winter of January, 1855, which decimated our troops fighting in the Crimean War. In London, Charlotte Cowan was shivering in bonnet and shawl as she tramped the cold streets and courts in vain visits to publishers, and she was truly glad to reach this friendly haven. ' I could always,' she says, ' when the day was frightfully cold—and *what* a winter that was when I first came to London—turn into Mr. Newby's snug and warm office in Welbeck Street, and have a talk with him and his " woman of business," Miss Springett. She was a lady, always kind, nice, and capable ; she remained with him until her death, I believe.' The book by Miss Cowan which Newby published was entitled *Zuriel's Grandchild* (1855-6) and in this form, should any copies survive, it is the rarest item in her bibliography : years later, when the author was famous, it was reprinted with the title *Joy After Sorrow* (1873). The scene is Stor Court, Lancashire.

More lasting success was at hand when, in 1856, *The Moors and the Fens* was accepted by a leading firm, Smith, Elder, the publishers of Thackeray and Charlotte Brontë. Following the example of the Brontë sisters and that of another popular author whose works were published by this firm, Harriet Parr—' Holme Lee '—Charlotte Cowan adopted the *nom-de-plume* of ' F. G. Trafford.' By a cruel blow of Fate, Mrs. Cowan died at Christmastide, 1856, long before *The Moors and the Fens* appeared in 1857-8, and the sorrowing daughter devoted the first cheque, £20, she received from this work to a memorial for the mother she had loved so dearly. She recorded thirty-six years after :

' As for me, the grief of her death seems sharp and present as on that sixteenth of December when she left me. . . . She had always a great horror of pain, mental and physical ; she was keenly sensitive, and mercifully before the agonising period of her complaint arrived, the nerves of sensation were paralysed ; first or last, she never lost a night's sleep the whole of the ten weeks during which I fought with Death for her— and was beaten.'

Charlotte Cowan was now alone and, after the struggle, was on the threshold of fame.   Much of the story of these sad days she afterwards told in *A Struggle for Fame* (1883).   She was not destined, happily, to be alone for long, for in 1857, at the age of twenty-five, she married Joseph Hadley Riddell, of Winsor Green House, Stafford-shire, but he, being professionally a civil engineer, was generally resident in London.   Mrs. Riddell's first home as a wife was in the City, in Scott's Court, Cannon Street, demolished when the railway station and hotel of the latter name were built in 1866.   It was a typical bit of old London—a sombre Court containing a few trees, a few houses where of yore had dwelt prosperous citizens, and a melancholy burial ground—probably the grave-yard of the now demolished church of All Hallows the Great—where, mouldering, they occupied their final home.   Without doubt, Mrs. Riddell's plastic and imagi-native mind thus early took the impression of the grim fascination of such a spot, for again and again in her books she returned to picture a scene of this kind—a great gloomy house o'er-hung by trees, and the relent-less rain falling alike on the quick and the dead—

' Shuddering from far away,
    Like dead, white fingers tapping on a tomb,
    The pitiless song of the cold Autumn rain.'

And in later years she always chose to live in some-what melancholy houses, tree-shadowed, and with sluggish water near.   This old house in Scott's Court had a hall ' paved with diamond-shaped blocks of black and white marble.'   Many years later when Mrs. Riddell came to write *The Haunted River*, the hall of the Mill

House was paved with blocks of black and white marble,
and the dismal reason why one of them was cracked across
can be read in that macabre tale.   Scott's Court and her
house there she fully described in *Austin Friars* (1870) :

' She looked out into the night, a wild, dreary night, with
the rain pelting down in torrents, and the wind howling
among the bare branches of the churchyard trees. . . .   There
were but few houses in Scott's Yard ; the last one, on the right
hand side, as a person entered the Court from Bush Lane was
only No. 5, but this was a large dwelling, with two windows
on each side of the hall door and one very wide window at the
gable end, which last over-looked the graveyard . . . the
kitchens were awful places below the level of the graveyard,
and probably, indeed, built over a portion of it, where the
moisture from the rank, foul earth outside makes its way
within, and drips slowly down the walls—places where meat
will not keep, where silver gets dulled, where myriads of small
black flies—flies belonging to no honest and healthy breed—
cover the dressers. . . .   Where the bones of the citizens
crumbled into dust, cinders from innumerable engines now
strew the ground.   Where men and women had their homes,
other men now crowd the railway platform.   The Quaker
Boarding-house, the lawyer's office, the whilom Lord Mayor's
chambers with their entrance in Turnwheel Lane, the few trees
growing in the graveyard, the blackened, unregarded monuments, the high iron railings, the parish ladders hung against
the wall, the wretched patch of grass, the whole of Turnwheel
Lane, are gone. . . .'

Here, and in many another passage from her books,
Mrs. Riddell has topographical value by preserving the
aspect of long vanished portions of London.   It was
owing to her residence in Scott's Court that she acquired
that peculiar knowledge of the City of London and City
life which brought her success and fame when presented
in her City novels, *We Two Alone*, *City and Suburb*, *George
Geith of Fen Court*, *The Race for Wealth*, *The Senior Partner*,
Mitre Court, *The Head of the Firm*, and others, despite the
fact that at first her publishers did not at all like this
choice of subject by a young Irish writer.   With the
topography of the City she became intimately acquainted,

and knew every court, winding lane, and historical building, when much remained as rebuilt after the Great Fire
and before 'progress' had transformed the ancient parts
of London into Americanised mammoth blocks of buildings.   The City offices she knew so well were in the old
residential houses of the merchants.   'In all the old City
churches and graveyards,' Mrs. Riddell said, 'you could
take no better guide than myself; but alas ! many of
the old landmarks are now pulled down.   All the pathos
of the City, the pathos in the lives of struggling men,
entered into my soul, and I felt I must write, strongly as
my publisher objected to my choice of subject, which he
said was one no woman could handle well.'

This publisher was Charles J. Skeet, of 10, King
William Street, Strand, and his objections proved to be
ill-founded.   His portrait can be found in *A Struggle for
Fame* under the guise of Mr. P. Vassett, antiquarian publisher, of Craven Street, Strand :

'Mr. Vassett's ideas were modest, his notions perhaps a
little old-fashioned, his views somewhat circumscribed.   He
was doing a very safe trade, and stood very well.   If he could
not claim to be a Murray, no one could speak of him as a
disciple of the Minerva Press.'

Skeet had published Miss Cowan's third story, *The
Rich Husband* (a title of his own choosing), which probably appeared anonymously early in 1858, and it is
doubtful if the author received any financial profit from
the book.   After she became famous it was reprinted in
1867 with the same title and with her name given as the
author.   *The Rich Husband* is apparently the earliest of Mrs.
Riddell's literary efforts that survives, for it was commenced soon after her arrival in London.   The scenes
in Wales she saw in the course of the journey from Ireland,
while in the character of Alice Crepton she depicted her
own painful struggles in London to get her stories
accepted and how she wrote through the night hours
with Death about to summon her mother :

' The clock had just chimed one quarter to eleven, but still the young aspirant for literary honours was sitting writing ; she never dreamt of weariness. Night was the time when phantoms born half of reality and half of ideality in that mysterious world lying dimly in the brain of poets, authors, musicians, and painters came forth from their hiding-places, walked across the narrow apartment, talked, looked, moved, and felt as they might have done had they been natural persons, and not the mere dream-like memories of experience, the spectres of fancy, or the ghastly forms of that awful shadowy train lengthening at every step, which we all bear after us—the innumerable but never-forgotten departed.'

It was curious that Smith, Elder, did not arrange to publish Mrs. Riddell's novels succeeding *The Moors and the Fens*, which presumably was successful (though the author had never seen the sombre fens of Lincolnshire she described in her story), because these publishers issued other editions, that of 1876 being illustrated by Walter Crane. However, the author's fourth book (the second written under the name of 'F. G. Trafford') was also accepted by Skeet. This was *Too Much Alone* (1860), which has for its setting an old City mansion near East-cheap and the wastes of Bow. The story was much talked about, although only four copies had been sent out for review ; Shirley Brooks, in *Punch*, ventured the opinion that it was written by a man ; while Mr. Riddell was highly amused when a City acquaintance mentioned the book and said he knew Trafford, 'who was a good sort of fellow.' *City and Suburb* (1861), a story of engi-neering, the suburb being West Green, Tottenham, was followed by *The World in the Church* (1862), a tale laid in Staffordshire—Swarston Royal being evidently intended for Winsor Green, the family home of Mr. Riddell and where his ancestors had long been established. Both these works were also issued by Mr. Skeet. As I have indicated, he was old-fashioned and more a seller of old books than a publisher of new ones. Consequently he did not respond to Mrs. Riddell's suggestion that she ought to receive better terms than he had hitherto paid

her, so she, in view of the attention and praise lately
bestowed upon *Too Much Alone*, resolved to offer elsewhere the manuscript of her new novel, *George Geith of
Fen Court*.   She decided to go to the Tinsley Brothers,
who were publishing many of the wonderful sensational
novels of the Sixties by Miss Braddon and other famous
authors.   In after years Mrs. Riddell used to tell the story
how, towards the end of 1863, she arrived at No. 18,
Catherine Street, hard by the old Gaiety Theatre, or,
rather, the Strand Music Hall as it was in those days.   She
found one of the publishing brethren, Edward Tinsley,
in his shirt-sleeves, behind the counter of his shop, and
duly introduced herself as ' F. G. Trafford.'

' *What ?* ' shouted the publisher.   ' *Here !* Bill ! ' he
bawled to his brother in the back sanctum ; ' here's *Too
Much Alone* ! by God ! I have been wanting to find her.'
Immediately a conclave of three took place, and within a
couple of hours ' the charming young Irish lady,' as
William Tinsley describes her in his *Recollections*, had in
her hand a contract for £800 for *George Geith of Fen
Court*, together with £50 on account, very much to her
surprise.   The terms were exceedingly liberal for that
period, and Mr. Skeet, when he heard the unpleasant
news that he had lost his rising author, said the Tinsleys
would never get their money back : but, in the words of
William, ' the book was a success, though we had given
the clever lady quite five times as much money as she
had received for any work up to that time.'   *George Geith
of Fen Court* (1864), indeed, was the most famous and
successful novel ever written by Mrs. Riddell, and in
after years she was always described as its author by way
of definition, in the same way as one of her celebrated
contemporaries, George Lawrence, was described as
' The Author of *Guy Livingstone*.'   Some of its success
was probably owing to the fact that Lady Geith of the
story in certain respects reminded readers of the protagonist of *Lady Audley's Secret*, the most popular romance
of the day ; but apart from the Braddonesque flavour

MRS. J. H. RIDDELL
Drawn from a photograph (Elliott and Fry) by W. F. Thomas

George Geith has very distinctive merits of its own, for it is an engrossing and moving tale, and Beryl is a very real creation of a lovable if capricious girl, an earlier Clara Middleton. The country scenes of the story are laid in Hertfordshire, some seven miles from St. Albans, while Fen Court, of course, still exists, though entirely changed in aspect, between Fenchurch Street and Leadenhall Street, for it was originally the graveyard of the church of St. Gabriel Fenchurch, which until the Great Fire of London had stood in the swamp and fen of what is now Fenchurch Street. For those who have read this powerful story of sacrifice, sorrow, and death, the figure of poor Beryl must ever rise in memory as they pass Fen Court and Austin Friars.

George Geith of Fen Court most deservedly and definitely established Mrs. Riddell in her peculiar position as the novelist who could present with pathos the lives and aspirations of City men and make interesting the details and hectic excitements of business affairs, stocks and shares, and Company promoting, and for this quality she was equipped with a personal liking for men and a sympathetic understanding of the masculine mind. As she expressed it to Raymond Blathwayt[1] : ' I fancy I must have a certain sympathy with City men, their lives and hopes and struggles, for they have always spoken freely to me about their affairs, and so, to a great extent, I have learned a great deal from them. . . . I understand men well, I have much in sympathy with them, and I always find them easier to describe than women. Men, especially young men, doctors and others, come and talk to me about their work and their life. I am more in harmony in describing City people . . . or amongst clergymen, who to me are a well-known class. Of the grandees of the West End I know but little and with whom I have the smallest sympathy. . . . I always find that when a City man once begins my novels he reads the whole of them, and many business people in the country

[1] Interview in *The Pall Mall Gazette*, 18th February, 1890.

write to me about them. . . . I have known a good deal about City Companies. . . . I usually take up one phase of City life for each novel.' Many of her details of Company promoting, engineering, and business ways were supplied by Mr. Riddell, who in these days was prosperous and full of hope. He was of an inventive turn of mind, and a student of literature, medicine, science, and mathematics. It was well for him and his wife that the latter continued her literary work assiduously after marriage, for otherwise the future would only have held complete ruin for both. It was her unusual choice of the subject of commerce and the lives of City people that brought her success in the first place—for the theme was new for popular novels in England, though Balzac had employed it to a certain extent in France— but she was to suffer the nemesis of financial ruin and wearing trouble arising from City affairs and speculation in the coming years. The City was both her blessing and her bane.

But now, in 1864, and for several years to come all was well, and she could command good terms for her books. There was even a market now for her early and forgotten stories, and finding a publisher willing to reissue *Zuriel's Grandchild* (under a new title, *Joy After Sorrow*) she resolved to go to Mr. Newby for a copy of her old tale, for she no longer possessed one herself. Newby had only known her as Miss Cowan when he published this and another story, and, as I have said, being old-fashioned he did not keep up much with the history of modern fiction. And, further, after her marriage, Mrs. Riddell no longer found her way passing by Welbeck Street with its warm welcome and cheerful fire which she had so much appreciated in earlier days. Mrs. Riddell used to tell the tale of how she returned, at a time of financial anxiety, to Newby's office in pursuit of *Zuriel's Grandchild* thus :

' Nothing looked much changed, and no one seemed much older, except myself, who had lived many lives in the interval. Of course both Mr. Newby and Miss Springett had a vague

memory of me, when I reminded the former that he had published *Zuriel's Grandchild*.   What I wanted was a copy of the
book.   He feared he had not one, but promised to ascertain.
I can see them both now in that warm, comfortable back room,
into which, as a girl, I had often gone shivering.   He took a
seat on one side of a large table, she on the other.   I sat facing
Mr. Newby—a most anxious woman, yet amused.   " Have
you," he said delicately, " gone on at all with literature ? "
" Oh, yes ! " I answered.   " Have you—published anything ? "
—with great caution, so as not to hurt my feelings.   " Several
books," I replied.   " Indeed ! ! ! "—*amazed*.   " Might I ask the
names ? "—tentatively.   " Well, amongst others, *George Geith*."
A dead silence ensued, during which I had the comfort of feeling that they both felt sure I was saying what was not true.   I
sat quite quiet, and so did they.   If I had not been so burdened
with care I must have laughed out loud.   As it happened,
I comported myself, as I have often done since in many difficult and humorous positions, with decent gravity, and then
this came from Mr. Newby, the while the ribbons on Miss
Springett's cap were tremulous :   " If you *really* wrote *George
Geith*—*then* indeed you have achieved a Success." ' [1]

Following the publication of *Phemie Keller* (1866), a
story of sacrifice, with scenes laid in the Cumberland hills,
Norfolk, and Hastings, and *Maxwell Drewitt*, the author
resolved to write under her own name.   Accordingly *The
Race for Wealth*, after a serial appearance in *Once a Week*,
was issued in 1866 as by Mrs. J. H. Riddell, for as a true

---

[1] The success of *George Geith* was long and lasting.   Thirteen
years after the publication of the book, the story was dramatised as
a play in four acts and a tableau by Wybert Reeve, a provincial
actor-manager.   He played the part of George Geith when the drama
was produced at the Theatre Royal, Scarborough, on August 6th,
1877, with Ada Lester as Beryl Molozane ;   William Blakeley as
Tillett, the lawyer ;   J. Bannister as Bemmidge ;   and Jane Coveney
as Mrs. Bemmidge.   Wybert Reeve and Ada Lester continued their
success in this play when they took it to Australia.   Like the
modern film version of a successful novel, the dramatic version of
George Geith was very different from the original, for Beryl, instead
of dying, was provided with a new lease of life as wife and mother !
George Geith, or Romance of a City Life was revived at the Crystal
Palace on October 30th, 1883, with F. H. Macklin as the hero,
supported by Mrs. Macklin, Albert Chevalier, E. W. Gardiner, and
Miss Coveney.

Victorian woman she was willing to merge her identity
with that of her husband, and this description she nearly
always used as an author on her title-pages rather than her
own Christian names of Charlotte Elizabeth, despite the
clouds that overwhelmed Mr. Riddell in his closing years,
when his name could be of no possible service, but entirely
the reverse, at the launching of a book. It had proved difficult to find the right title for *The Race for Wealth*; many
suggestions had been made, when Mrs. Riddell said to
Edward Walford, the editor of *Once a Week*, 'I am not
particular about the name of the book so long as it gives
a notion of a race for wealth,'—and so the title was found.
The scenes of the story are laid in Stepney and Grays,
Essex. *The Rich Husband* was reissued in the following
year, 1867.

Some years before this date the Riddells had removed
from the City to St. John's Lodge,[1] Hanger Lane, Tottenham, a large house with extensive and well-wooded
grounds situated in a district then really countrified. But
the growth of London began to threaten its rural charms;
by 1872 Hanger Lane had been rechristened St. Ann's
Road, and its hanging woods destroyed, and in the following year Mrs. Riddell fled before the devastating advance
of the speculative builder. How delightful Tottenham,
West Green, and Harringay had been a few years earlier she
has pictured in many of her books of this period. Thus
in *Above Suspicion*, writing in 1874, she says :

'Sixteen years ago no more rural village could have been
found within five miles of the General Post Office than West
Green. It was as utterly in the country as though situated a
hundred miles from London, and by a natural consequence it
was country in its ways, habits, and manners. The various
lanes leading to it from Stamford Hill, Tottenham, Hornsey,

[1] St. John's Lodge, which was long ago demolished, stood
exactly opposite to Black Boy Lane on a site which now forms part
of the extensive premises and grounds of the North Eastern Fever
Hospital. Fortunately the grounds of another old mansion called
The Chestnuts still survive in the form of a public park bearing that
name, adjoining Black Boy Lane.

and Southgate were rural, which they certainly are not now. . .
As for Hanger Lane, no one had yet dreamed of the evil days
to come, when mushroom villas should be built upon the
ground that not long before was regarded as an irreclaimable
morass—when at first a tavern and then a church (the two
invariable pioneers of that which, for some unknown reason,
we call civilisation) appeared on the scene, and brought
London following at their heels . . . when, in a word, Hanger
Lane should be improved off the face of the earth and in the
interest of speculative builders . . . called, as it is at present,
St. Ann's Road, it has only taken sixteen years to change West
Green from an extremely pretty village to an eminently unde-
sirable suburb.'

Like all imaginative writers, she was strongly imbued
with the sense of topography, historical association, and
scenic beauty ; consequently such writers, if they be also
of a romantic and sentimental turn of mind, must always
regret the spoliation of rural beauty and quiet, and the
destruction of old houses, by the growth of a neighbouring city or large town.   Owing to the happy associations
of her married life and the pinnacle of her literary fame
with this district of Middlesex, with the famous Seven
Sisters trees for its centre, Mrs. Riddell again and again
in her books looked back regretfully to the deep, winding
lanes and spreading sylvan prospects she had known and
loved in Tottenham, Enfield, Southgate, and by the quiet
beauty of Izaac Walton's river Lea as it flowed to the
marshland.   Thus in *Far Above Rubies* (1867), in the
main a story of the Northaw and South Mimms (here
called South Kemms) district, she wrote :

' To the north of London there is still a perfect tangle of
narrow country lanes, in some of which Lamb assured Barton
he " made most of his tragi-comedy."   There are several not
far from the churchyard where he sleeps so well.   Close to his
old home they wander away from Chase Side, up hill and down
dale ; they strike out of the Southgate Road, they wind in and
out from Angel Lane to Bury Street, and thence by devious
routes to Winchmore Hill and Enfield.   Some of the loveliest
lanes on earth, perhaps, are those on the opposite side of the
Lea, leading from Higham Hill to Chingford and Woodford.

Utterly still, utterly quiet. There the bee hums, and the wild roses bloom, and there is no sound heard, no din or sound of that great city which lies so near at hand.'

Alas ! for the spoliation is now at hand of Winchmore Hill and Southgate, as earlier disappeared the charms of Tottenham, Acton, Chiswick, Willesden, Twickenham, Greenford, Heston, Kingsbury, and many another once pretty rural suburb. It is indeed amazing to reflect what changes a few years now bring to the country near London. To make a brief personal digression, I purchased for twopence, not long ago, at a bookseller's stall, a presentation copy of the Poetical Works (once praised by Tennyson) of Edmund Peel (1817-1885), Colonel of the 11th Hussars, a nephew of Sir Robert Peel, Prime Minister. His youth had been passed at Southgate, and in a letter to a friend, inserted in this volume, he says of one of his poems :

' The scenery of *The Return* is in the neighbourhood of Southgate, Middlesex, between Southgate and Hornsea, a grass country, well-timbered, watered only by the New River and a Brook ; what the sneerers might call Cockney ; yet, I trust, not described in a Cockney manner, whatever that may be. Keats was born in Moor Fields, at the Livery Stables where my Father's horses were put up when he came into the City, about four days in the week. Well, Keats resided, mostly, either in London or the neighbourhood : yet I am not acquainted with any poetry more graphic and picturesque.'

The Return is a long piece of forty-one printed pages, and I will only quote a few lines to give an idea of what the scenery between Southgate and ' Hornsea ' was like a hundred years ago :

> ' Once more the river windeth into view,
> 'Mid fields of verdure flowing to the west,
> Till checked by pastoral hills of gentle slope
> The waters turn to the meridian beam
> Between our path and that Hesperian hill
> Dark-browed, with bosom open to the south.
> The wavy lawn and level ground alike
> Are rich in herbage, grazed of goodlier kine . . .

Dear unto me the landscape early lost
And long lamented, redolent of May
New-blown, 'mid flowering hedge-rows interspersed,
And elms wide-branching, whence the village smoke
Emerging, curleth round the grey Church tower.
Peace, smiling, filleth all the land with light . . .
Blithe voices warble round the village-green,
And Echo . . . sings of love and joy. . . .'

Mrs. Riddell knew the same scenes, still little changed,
seventy years ago, and though she was successful and
happy during this brief period, I think she read in the
gentle yet melancholy beauty of the Middlesex landscape
some wistful presentiment of the changes and sorrow and
financial ruin that, storm cloud-like, were already massing
on the horizon of her life.   Else why should she write :

' Through the meadows the rivulet of her life had flowed
peacefully and monotonously.   Vaguely she understood that
there were different existences, that there were other lands,
through which swept rivers, broad and deep and dark, in the
depths whereof lay wrecked hopes and terrible memories ; she
had heard of existences lost on those great streams, of corpses
which the currents carried down to the vast ocean ; she vaguely
comprehended that there were rapids and pools, contrary
currents, cruel storms, to be encountered by some human ships,
but it was all vague to her.'

This was in 1867.   In April of the following year she
became editor and part-proprietor of *The St. James's
Magazine*, and the Struggle for Fame (but not wealth and
happiness) was won.   For she was now a power and
influence in the literary world, and humble aspirants to
that realm of mingled joy and bitterness sought entrance
to her salon at St. John's Lodge, Tottenham, and at
Leyton, where it would seem she was living in 1873-1875.
It was then a charming rural district in the midst of cornfields, for though, to the south, lay the dreary wastes of
Stratford and to the west the great expanse of Hackney
Marsh, so impressive as the sun sets and the mists rise
to veil the last angry gleams of a brick-red sky, to the
north and east stretched the lovely woodlands of Epping

Forest. Mrs. Riddell described the scenery of this district again and again in her books. Particularly in her powerful story of a murder case, *A Life's Assize*, did she picture the Essex marshes ; and in Essex she found the right drear setting for the haunted house of *Fairy Water*, so admirably depicted by Randolph Caldecott's sombre drawing, when late on an autumn day ' the eyes of man never beheld a picture of more utter desolation,' where beyond the fated house and ruined garden lay the belt of pine trees and ' the lake of the dismal swamp, which had furnished Crow Hall with no less than two trage-dies.' Best of all of her Essex stories is *Alaric Spenceley* (1881), which again has topographical value, for she described Poplar, West Ham, Bromley Marsh and Abbey Marsh (now Canning Town) as she saw them when she first came to London :

' There were foot-paths in all directions—foot-paths across greens where the children could gather daisies and dandelions, and their elders, walking out from Shadwell and Limehouse and Stepney, take the air on Sundays. . . . Taking the locality as a whole, it was quite in the country, and the houses . . . were set in flower and kitchen gardens, full of fruit trees, on the borders of the wide-spreading marsh. . . . Between banks of brightest green the steely blue waters of the Lea flowed gently onward. There were sheep feeding on the marsh beyond. The birds were twittering and flying on swift wings hither and thither ere seeking their accustomed haunts for the night. There was a great peace and a great loneliness all around.'

Among the literary or artistic aspirants who sought the help of Mrs. Riddell when she was a power in the world of letters was the subsequently successful cartoonist, Harry Furniss, when he arrived from his native Ireland at the age of nineteen and his fortune to seek. He has left an amusing account of his visit, partly contained in a letter dated August 11th, 1873, and partly in later comments :

' I like London very much indeed. . . . Having an intro-duction to a Mrs. Riddell, an authoress. . . . I called on her, and had the honour and real pleasure of her company for several hours. I took lunch with her at her rural seat at Leyton, Essex, and came away with a note of introduction to Mrs. Ross Church,[1] Editor of *London Society*. . . . Mrs. Riddell is not a pretty woman. She is a " fine " woman, and not altogether young, but her " get-up " is thoroughly authoressish. [In those Victorian days most of the poetesses and authoresses affected the long flowing black velvet gown, low cut bodices, lace and jewellery. Even such a practical authoress as Mrs. J. H. Riddell was so attired. On her writing-table an ordinary cup and saucer answered the purpose of an ink-stand, the cup was half full of ink and half a dozen feather pens lay diagonally across the saucer—these little affectations were a survival of the literary lady Thackeray described so well a generation before in his *Character Sketches* as " The Fashionable Authoress."]

' Mrs. Riddell gave me several " tips "—woman's " tips " I ought to add—about literary circles. She is to ask me to some of their Bohemian parties, and take me with her to be introduced to all the " big-wigs." As you might expect, she is very severe on her sex's endeavours in writing. Mrs. Henry Wood " is simply a brute, she throws in bits of religion to slip her fodder down the public throat." She says there is not a magazine in London paying, the libraries destroy the sale. [Mrs. Riddell had made a great reputation with her " prize novel," *George Geith*, but she was unhappily married, at least, I believe her husband through some queer way in business was resting somewhere at his country's expense. This led Mrs. Riddell to work desperately hard. . . .']

Mr. Furniss's mischievous suggestion that Mr. Riddell was in prison was entirely indefensible and, I am assured by those who knew Mrs. Riddell, false. It is true that at this date Mr. Riddell was involved in grave financial difficulties, with which, by temperament, he was quite unfit to cope. But that he committed any malfeasance leading to imprisonment seems highly improbable, for Mr. Arthur Hamilton Norway, C.B., who was Mrs. Riddell's most intimate friend, has stated to me :

' I did not ever hear from her, or any of the numerous friends of hers who were kind to me in my youth, a single word that could suggest such a thing. I do not think she knew that

[1] Florence Marryat (1838-1899), novelist and spiritualist, daughter of Captain Marryat, the naval novelist.

Furniss had said this, for she would have resented it fiercely : [1] yet she always spoke of Furniss with friendship, though she saw little of him.   The suggestion does not square at all with what she used to tell me of her husband, of whom she certainly was very fond, though she made no secret of the fact that his great abilities—as she regarded them—were not of a practical kind.   And I think she regarded him as ill-fitted to struggle with the world.   But she spoke of him often to me, without hesitation or reluctance, and always as a man of high character. Had it been otherwise, I think I must have had reason to suspect it.'

Mrs. Riddell regarded her husband as one who was very early in life overborne by a weight of business cares too heavy for his nervous nature to sustain : ' Courageous and hopeful, gifted with indomitable energy, endowed with marvellous persistence and perseverance ; modestly conscious of talents which ought to have made their mark he, when a mere lad, began his long quest after fortune, one single favour from whom he was never destined to receive ' ; and in her story, *Mortomley's Estate* (1874), she added, she ' but told the simple story of what, when in ill-health and broken in spirit, he had to encounter before ruin, total and complete, overtook him.   In spite of harassing trouble and continuous misfortune, our twenty-three years of married life were happy as few lives are, simply by reason of his sweet, patient temper, and his child-like faith.' [2]   Mr. Riddell

---

[1] Mrs. Riddell had been dead seventeen years when Mr. Furniss first printed his assertion in 1923, in his *Some Victorian Women*.

[2] In *Mortomley's Estate* she said of her husband's prototype : ' Mortomley was an experimenter.   When ruin has marked a family for her own, she usually endows the last of the race with some such form of genius, which clings about and lends a certain picturesque grace to his decay, as ivy climbing around an almost lifeless tree clothes it with a freshness and a beauty it lacked in the day of its strength.   And the form of genius of the first Mortomley who engaged in trade had, with every condition of existence altered, reappeared in this later, weaker, and more sensitive descendant. Even in his father's time he had introduced processes and combinations into their laboratory hitherto unthought of. . . .'

died in 1880—' Suddenly and unexpectedly, the end came, and the crowning sorrow of a much-tried life was laid upon the devoted wife when death claimed her gifted husband.' It was a sorrow which was ever keen in her remembrance. Her financial troubles only increased with the death of Mr. Riddell, for quixotically and without any legal obligation, she took upon herself to pay off liabilities due to her late husband's relatives. For many years she struggled valiantly to cancel the debt of honour, and succeeded—by crippling herself financially, for she paid away money necessary for ordinary comfort in her later years when her books were no longer highly remunerative. As Mr. Norway so truly says : ' Her embarrassments were not of her own creating—in no degree—for she was simple in her mode of life and generous only to others. She grew poorer and poorer, but lived to discharge fully and honourably the liabilities assumed to her husband's people. She was always brave, humorous and cheerful, contemptuous of parade or insincerity, a very warm true friend, wiser for others than for herself, since she would have counselled any other person, out of her rich experience, to reject the burdens which she assumed and which crushed her.'

After the financial crash, when great retrenchments became necessary, Mrs. Riddell resolved to leave the pleasant northern suburbs, where she had held a literary court since the success of *George Geith* ten years earlier, and settle in quite another district. She decided upon the then quiet and remote village of Addlestone, near Weybridge, in Surrey. She took, in 1875, an old-fashioned house, Raglan House,[1] whose surroundings, rather melancholy and most remarkably aquatic, were exactly what she liked. Through the heavily-wooded garden ran, or more correctly crept, a sombre stream called the Bourne, which a little lower down joined the Wey, as the latter river flowed through the Ham Haw

[1] Raglan House is now divided into two houses known as ' Bourneside.'

Meads on its way to mingle with the near-by Thames.
From the Bourne, past the main front of the house, ran a
tributary little stream, crossed by a rustic, rose-covered
bridge leading to another part of the garden, and this
rivulet went under the high road to the New River Wey
(a continuation of the Basingstoke Canal). Here, immediately in view of Mrs. Riddell's house, on the bank
of the canal stood a ruinous old water-mill belonging to
the timber-yard of the Liberty family, owners of most of
the adjoining property. To the left, the canal was
crossed by one of the little high, round bridges, peculiar
to canals, which led to a picturesque old red-brick and
red-tiled farm-house and to the rich, lush water meadows,
bounded by the rising woodland heights of Chobham
and Pyrford. The view is impressive even to-day, when
the water-mill has disappeared and ugly modern buildings
have taken its place. It is one of the curiosities of coincidental nomenclature that the little canal bridge opposite
to Mrs. Riddell's house at Addlestone was called Black
Boy Bridge and that her house at Tottenham, St. John's
Lodge, stood opposite to Black Boy Lane.

Raglan House, Addlestone, had, in fact, an island
situation, and in its almost sinister setting (for there is
always something sinister about dark trees shadowing
slow moving water, and mill-pools and weirs—perhaps
because we remember the deaths of Eustacia and Wildeve)
and the prospect of the water-mill and deep canal Mrs.
Riddell found the inspiration for her most impressive
story of *The Haunted River*, though, of course, with a
novelist's licence she changed or enlarged some of the
aspects of the sombre scene. But in the main her descriptions are exact. Thus, the setting of her house :

'A square edifice only two stories high, with a broad
verandah shading the lower rooms upon two sides. . . . Water,
water everywhere—gardens sloping down to a clear glassy
river—lawns reflected in the limpid mirror. Roses hanging
over the stream. . . . Willow trees dipping their branches in
the flood . . . As for the mill, it was closed ; falling to decay,

THE HAUNTED RIVER
Cover design of Routledge's Christmas Annual, 1877

in parts roofless—in all places rotten—silent, neglected. Still and useless was the broken wheel . . . an uprooted willow-tree lay across the stream, and from the opposite bank some solitary pines, their crests twisted northward with the force of the south winds, looked sombrely upon the desolation which had been wrought.'

It is not possible to give a lengthy quotation here illustrating the supernatural element of this best of ghost stories, but a brief scene by Black Boy Bridge may be cited. Ike, a bargeman, is taking his horses over the little bridge on the last night of the year. It is a mild winter with no snow or frost, that night, when suddenly he hears the sound of ice cracking :

' There was no frost ; it was a dull, heavy winter's night, with but a glimmer of starlight . . . he listened, and then he heard another tremendous crack and splashing and struggling under the yew-trees at the back of the Mill House. . . .   Then all in a minute, as he tore on, the moon shone out—mind this, there was no moon at all that night !—and he saw the river lying before him one sheet of ice, white and glittering—all white and glittering, except just in one place, where there was a hole, and the water looked dark and threatening. . . .   " I came out all over in a sweat," he said, " for I knew there was no ice nor no moon ; and while I was standing, too frightened to move, I see a hand and arm rise out of the water where the hole was—a hand with a gold ring on one of the fingers which clutched hold of the ice, and then the ice gave and broke with the weight, and I heard a great cry, and the ice closed all over the hole again, and the moon disappeared : and I fell on my knees and prayed " . . .'

Despite the simplicity of the language, the episode is strangely vivid and appropriate to the actual spot, where the canal flows so silently and sinuously under the picturesque little bridge :

' . . . the white stars a-shiver.
" Here is your resting-place, here by my side
      For ever, for ever,
And they shall forget that you lived or died."
      Thus sang the river.'

But *The Haunted River* is not all ghosts and gloom. Mrs. Riddell's sense of humour would always peep out, as in the olfactory description of the young railway porter from Addlestone station : ' Jim, shod in very heavy boots, tramping on in front, and leaving behind for our benefit a number of odours in which those of an ill-kept farm-yard, corduroy, tobacco, and mortar were most promi-nent.'

In addition to *The Haunted River*, Mrs. Riddell wrote two other ghostly tales in similar vein at Raglan House— *The Uninhabited House* (1875) and *The Disappearance of Mr. Jeremiah Redworth* (1878)—which also depict her sinister surroundings at Addlestone : ' The sombre pines, the dark canal, the murmuring reeds, the rustling rushes, the stunted oak trees, the sorrowful sobbing of the water as it oozed through some broken lock-gates higher up the disused canal.'

Mrs. Riddell did not reside many years at Addlestone, for by the time *The Haunted River* was published (1877-9) she had removed to Kingston Hill. The story was dedi-cated to her friends and late neighbours, the Misses Liberty, of Ham Moor, Addlestone, ' in recollection of much kindness and many pleasant days.' A few years later Mrs. Riddell wrote a novel, *Daisies and Buttercups* (1882), which fully preserved her memories of the district, for Weybridge is described under the name of ' Reed-bourne,' and Addlestone as ' Hampsfield.' She delighted in picturing all the rich, green beauty of the Surrey country-side, with its wealth of flowers and foliage in May, and then by way of vivid contrast the same scene when the winter floods are out :

' When the Thames is four miles wide at Chertsey, it is some-thing to look out on that waste of waters, and listen to the lonely soughing of the spreading flood, which is like unto no other sound that ever falls on the ear of man. . . . Choose a gloomy winter's afternoon, with a pallid sun going down behind the Egham hills, the blackness of night travelling fast from the east, casting darksome shadows before it—no man or

woman, no dog, or horse, or animal of any description to
bestow one touch of life on the desolate landscape—and the
spectator sees before him a scene he will remember when he
has forgotten many a fair outlook, many a brighter view."

Such a prospect, indeed, was after the very heart of
Mrs. Riddell, and if the lurid winter's sunset, fading
behind the wooded heights of St. Ann's Hill and Chobham Heath, was succeeded by the advancing cohorts of
storm and rain clouds she was the better pleased, for one
of her personal characteristics was that she liked walking
in the rain and the wind, and through the wet woods, a
trait she shared with George Meredith, who often was
moved by similar wondrous experiences in Surrey :

> ' For lo, beneath those ragged clouds
> That skirt the opening west, a stream
> Of yellow light and windy flame
> Spreads lengthening southward, and the sky
> Begins to gloom, and o'er the ground
> A moan of coming blasts creeps low. . . .
> A crow flies from the yellow hill,
>   And in its wake
> A baffled line of labouring rooks :
> Steel-surfaced to the light the river looks . . .
> Pale the rain-rutted roadways shine
>   In the green light
> Behind the cedar and the pine ;
>   Come, thundering night ! '

George Meredith had lived at Weybridge, and described the Chertsey and Shepperton reaches of the
Thames in *The Ordeal of Richard Feverel.* In that story,
Raynham Abbey is Woburn Park, near Addlestone, and
Farmer Blaize's Farm is Ham Haw Farm ; and the old
lock at Shepperton and its meadows inspired the famous
passage, ' Golden lie the meadows ; golden run the
streams.'

Despite the winter floods, Mrs. Riddell pronounced
Weybridge to be a wonderfully healthy place—' worthy
to compete with that Yankee town where they had to kill
a man to start a new cemetery.' *Daisies and Buttercups*

is one of the most entertaining of the author's tales, and probably many of the characters were drawn from local inhabitants of that time. Thus, in a passing reference, the Reverend Thomas Spyers, D.D., Headmaster of Weybridge Grammar School, who had an interrogative trick when preaching of saying ' What saith St. John ? ', and so on, was not forgotten :

' Walk over and listen to the clergyman there trying to prove that two and two made five, and enlivening his discourse at intervals with the remark, which he really put in the form of a conundrum—" What saith St. Paul ? " . . . There is one benefit, however, I derive from all these discourses. Were I inclined to turn infidel, I could not do it. Nothing which was not true could ever survive the sermons that are preached about it.'

And there was a dissenting preacher who was in doubt what name to give his house :

' Poor dear, he were going to call it " The Retreat," but he feared the name might be regarded as Papistical. He were always so careful not to give offence ; and though he had no ill-will to the priests and such like, remembering they could not help their ignorance, still he could not abear anything like following of the Pope.'

And there was a tactful local doctor :

' " What is your name, sir ? " " Smith." " Oh, indeed," said the doctor, as if pleased to make the acquaintance of any gentleman possessed of so distinctive a cognomen.'

About 1879 or 1880 Mrs. Riddell went to live in London for a few years. She took an old-fashioned house, No. 75, on the west side of South Lambeth Road. The house was demolished long ago, but, as always the case with this author, her books of the date reflect her surroundings, for no novelist was ever more personally topographical or more strongly influenced by the Spirit of Place. So it is, in Mrs. Riddell's *Weird Stories* (1884) will be found descriptions of certain old mansions then still standing in the locality. One gives the title to the story, *The Old House in Vauxhall Walk*, and another, in *Walnut-Tree House*, is presented with all the sombre suggestiveness of Le Fanu :

' Many years ago there stood at the corner of a street leading out of Upper Kennington Lane a great red-brick house, covering a goodly area of ground, and surrounded by gardens magnificent in their proportions. . . . One very wet evening, in an autumn the leaves of which have been dead and gone this many a year, Walnut-Tree House, standing grim and lonely in the mournful twilight, looked more than ordinarily desolate and deserted. There was not a sign of life about it ; the shutters were closed—the rusty iron gates were fast locked—the approach was choked up with grass and weeds—through no chink did the light of a single candle flicker. For seven years it had been given over to rats and mice and blackbeetles ; for seven years no one had been found to live in it ; for seven years it had remained empty, while its owner wore out existence in fits of moody dejection or of wild frenzy in the madhouse close at hand. . . .'

Weird Stories comprise some of the best ghost tales ever written. There is real terror in *The Open Door*, while *Nut Bush Farm* achieves the difficult success of a supernatural appearance in the open air, for the usual *mise en scène* of a ghost requires an oak-panelled chamber, or tapestry, long corridor, or wide staircase with oriel window. As may be supposed, Mrs. Riddell was an admirable verbal raconteur of ghostly tales around the fireside, for she told such stories with all the added wealth of her Irish imaginativeness and sense of drama and humour. She loved the Christmas season, and there is a passage in *George Geith* lyrical of Christmas joys that rivals Dickens in the same vein—picturing one of those good, comfortable, Leech-ian Yule-tides of the Mid-Victorian time :

' In the year of grace of which I am writing, Christmas came to every home in Britain in the garb which all Christmasses, if they were properly minded, would don for the gratification of Englishmen and Englishwomen. Crowned with holly, from amidst the polished leaves thereof shone scarlet berries ; arrayed in frosted snow, which glittered and glistened in the light of the winter's sun ; with icicles for his jewels, with white and glorious robes of state, Christmas, surrounded by his minstrels and singers, by his bards and story-tellers, by fair girls and happy children, by grey-beards, and stalwart men and smiling women, came sweeping through the City streets and along country lanes, flinging largesse as he travelled—alms to the poor, rest to the weary, mirth to the young, contentment to the old, comfort to the broken-hearted, hope to the despond-ing. " In remembrance," Christmas fed the hungry, clothed the naked, sheltered the homeless, visited the fatherless and widows in their affliction, and beautified with his beneficent hand careworn and suffering faces. Free from earthly mists, with the glories of his radiant apparel undimmed by rain, un-obscured by gloom, Christmas arrived, bringing with it en-chantment to George Geith. . . . Walking through the City streets, he seemed as though treading on air ; he could have greeted every man he met like a brother ; he entertained no contempt for the groups who were holding endless arguments as to what it would be best for them to buy for the to-morrow's dinner. There was a beauty to him in the prize-meat, in the laurels and hollies that decorated the butchers' shops, in the decorations of the grocers' windows, in the long lines of turkeys, in the parti-coloured ribands that were tied round the necks of the sucking-pigs. There was a life in the scene he had never noticed before, a meaning in the merriment and excitement that pervades the streets of London on a Christmas Eve which he had never previously grasped . . . the happiest day in all the year. . . . What a beauty he found likewise in the white country roads ; what refreshment in the cold, crisp air ; what quietness in the eyes of the bright shining stars ; what exquisite loveliness in the laurels laden with frosted snow, in the great black trees, whose branches were half-clothed with white. How picturesque Wattisbridge Church looked as he passed it by, lighted up, doubtless, for the finishing touches to be put to the decorations for the morrow ; what a Christmas look the earth wore. . . .'

During the years in South Lambeth Road, Mrs. Riddell wrote many excellent stories—*The Mystery in Palace Gardens* (1880), which she liked best of her many books ; *The Senior Partner* (1881) ; *Daisies and Buttercups* (1882) ;

Three Wizards and a Witch (1883); *A Struggle for Fame* (1883); *Berna Boyle* (1884); and *Mitre Court* (1885). She had disagreed with Tinsley and the books of this period were mainly published by the famous house of Bentley, which had by now long repented former refusals of her work. Time brings its revenges. Mr. Richard Bentley, the second, has told me of Mrs. Riddell's curious method of writing a novel. On one occasion he asked her how she was progressing with a story his firm was to publish. 'It is finished,' she replied. 'Good,' said Mr. Bentley, 'then may we have the manuscript to-morrow?' 'Oh, NO!' returned Mrs. Riddell; 'what I meant was that the tale is completed in my head, to the last conversation; but I have now to write it down on paper, and that will take a considerable time.' So great was Mrs. Riddell's power of concentration and memory, and control of her material, that she invariably composed the end of her stories first. The situations and characters of her books were, as I have demonstrated, often drawn direct from actual places and people. At other times the influences were unconscious. She ever observed things closely; then later on, when between the border land of sleeping and waking, scenes, people, words, that she had noticed seemed to be photographed on her brain; sentences formed themselves, together with vivid episodes, and in the morning she was able to reproduce and detail them in her narratives. According to another of her publishers, Mr. Edmund Downey, she wrote very slowly, and said that she would like to take two years over a book. Her motto was slow but sure, and her stories were written with infinite care. So were the books of her contemporaries, the women novelists of her school, Miss Braddon, Rhoda Broughton, 'Holme Lee,' Mrs. Alexander, Mrs. Hungerford, Florence Marryat, and many others, for all were ladies of culture and knowledge, with the result that novels of this class were of far higher merit and interest than those of the present day which are often the product of young misses ignorant alike of the world and literature, but who can turn out a serial of a typist's love idyll for *The Daily Shock* in less than six weeks.

After her husband's death in 1880, Mrs. Riddell's life was a sad and lonely one, and none too prosperous, for though her books were still selling well, she did not find writing lucrative despite, or owing to, the fact, in her own words, that ' I *must* put as much good as I have in me into my books'; and as already related, there was a quixotic and heavy drain on her financial resources. Things were more cheerful for her when, in 1883, a family friend, Mr. Arthur Hamilton Norway, then a young man of twenty-three, occupied rooms in her house after he came to London to take up an appointment in the Secretariat of the Post Office.[1]   She always had a profound sympathy with young men alone in London and with their way to make in the world.   Mr. Norway remained with her for three years ; in 1884, at a time when Mrs. Riddell was badly over-worked and worried, and sadly in need of a change, he persuaded her to go off with him on a sudden trip to Germany and through the Black Forest.   Their adventures abroad she fully and amusingly described in a book entitled *A Mad Tour, or a Journey undertaken in an insane moment through Central Europe on foot* (1891), wherein it may safely be concluded Mr. Norway figures as ' Bobby.'   He also went with Mrs. Riddell to Ireland in 1885, when they visited Londonderry, and on to Donegal and Horn Head—scenes she described in *The Nun's Curse* (1888).   At Dunfanaghy, Mrs. Riddell ' went Irish ' again, for seeing some hens of her native country she promptly fell in love with them, bought them, and conveyed them in a crate for the rest of her tour as an item of her luggage, thereby causing much confusion and

[1] Mr. Norway in later years became Secretary to G.P.O., Ireland. He is the author of *A History of the Post Office Packet Service*, 1793-1815 (1895) ; *Byeways in Devon and Cornwall* (1897) ; *Highways and Byeways in Yorkshire* (1899) ; and *Naples, Past and Present* (1901).

profanity of language at hotels and among ' bootses ' and railway porters until home was reached. There, fortunately, she was now living in the country, for it was in this year, 1885, that Mrs. Riddell, with Mr. Norway, removed from South Lambeth Road to The Cottage (now known as Old Farm Cottage) at Upper Halliford, near Shepperton, for she had resolved to return to the Middlesex river scenery that she loved better than the most magnificent prospects other parts of the world could offer. Here, from the upper windows of the cottage, she looked across her large meadow to a wide expanse of flat green country bounded by the distant heights of the enchanted land of Windsor Forest. The Cottage, covered with trellis work, clustering white roses and clematis, was a delightful old-fashioned place with low-ceiled rooms leading one from the other, quaint cupboards, and odd little steps cropping up in the most unexpected situations. Mrs. Riddell wrote in the pleasant bow-windowed room to the right, from which a glass door led into the really beautiful garden—bounded by a great holly hedge, originally thirty-two feet in height. It was this old-world garden with its roses, japonica, lavender, rue and other herbs, which was Mrs. Riddell's particular joy, for as Helen Black related in her pen-portrait of Mrs. Riddell at the age of sixty :

' It was chiefly the tranquillity and privacy of this delightful garden with its grand old hedge of holly, now bright with red berries, which attracted Mrs. Riddell, and decided her to settle down, away from the world, after long and fierce buffeting with the stormy seas of sorrow, disappointment, losses, and bereavement, of which she has had so large a share. The gentle, quiet face tells its tale of early struggles, heavy burdens, severe trials ; yet time has not laid its ruthless hand over-harshly on the author. Not a silver hair is visible on the soft brown hair, which is simply rolled into a neat coil, high on the back of her head, and fastened by a large tortoise-shell comb. The deep grey eyes are undimmed, and wear a look of peace and resignation, nobly won ; while " ever and anon of griefs subdued, there comes a token " which recalls the past. But

Mrs. Riddell can still smile sweetly, and when she smiles, two—yes two—absolutely girlish dimples light up the expressive countenance. She is tall, has a good carriage, and is dressed in black ; she has worn no colours for over ten years.

'The little room is very simply but prettily furnished. Soft white rugs lie here and there on the dark red carpet, and an old-fashioned bookcase contains the works of her favourite authors. There are no particular curiosities or decorations to be seen, save one valuable bit of old Dresden china, two or three plates of ancient Crown Derby, together with a couple of quaint Delhi-work salvers, and a few pictures hanging on the walls. Of these last, two are particularly attractive. One is the head of Christ crowned with thorns, beautifully painted on copper ; the other, over the fire-place, represents the Castle of Carrickfergus which, though built nearly a thousand years ago, is still strong enough to hold a troop of soldiers.

'In the garden, a turn round the last walk leads to the poultry yard, which is a great delight to Mrs. Riddell. She has several fine breeds of fowls and geese, amongst which last are two handsome but noisy specimens from Japan. One little peculiarity of interest must be noticed. The wall which supports the granary steps is pierced by two holes for dog kennels, an arrangement of great antiquity.'

Mrs. Riddell had an old gardener who was quite a character. When she took possession of The Cottage, she found a cupboard full of decaying medical stores, medicines, pills, and lotions, left by some former tenant. She instructed her old gardener to wheel the lot away in his barrow and burn them. Some weeks later, on her asking the old man how he was in health, he replied, ' Well, mum, better, I hope, since I've been taking all them things you gave me.' ' What things, Richards ? ' ' Why, all them lotions and medicines and pills, mum. I've been taking some of 'em in turn every day. They done me a rare lot of good, though some of them stings me up, and no mistake.' This old Adam of eighty must have been eager to utilise a strange article of furniture he had in his cottage, a legacy from his predecessor in the situation of gardener. This other old man, taking Death by the forelock, so to speak, desired to make his own coffin, so a friendly neighbour gave him enough elm for his purpose. The grim shell was duly finished, but Death still tarried, so the future tenant, getting tired of waiting and finding his coffin much in the way, converted it into a useful upright corner cupboard.

Mrs. Riddell always liked walking, so by choice she attended Littleton Church some two miles away, a quaint building filling one side of the village Square. Littleton Park once possessed a great Wren mansion, long the seat of the Wood family. Mrs. Riddell described Littleton in *For Dick's Sake* (1886). At that date, as she said, the village had ' stood still for over two hundred years. There is no resident rector or squire, or doctor, or lawyer, or farrier, but it is a sweetly peaceful spot, and the woods in primrose time are a sight to behold ; whilst at Sunbury, to show you how little change may take place, in one hundred years there have been only two vicars, and one of them is alive now.' Shepperton and Lower Halliford form the setting of her story, *A Terrible Vengeance*.

It is a pity that Mrs. Riddell was not, apparently, acquainted with her not very distant literary neighbour at Teddington, R. D. Blackmore, for he fully shared her love for the quiet West Middlesex scenery, so lovely in spring-time with its wealth of orchard blossom ; and he, too, described the Sunbury and Halliford district in his *Kit and Kitty* (1890). Mrs. Riddell had several friends in her neighbourhood, however, and one she valued very much indeed, Miss Victoria Matthews, of 21, Manchester Square, who, with her parents, had a country place, Lawn Cottage (now called ' Frith Grange '), Upper Halliford, where they spent part of each year from 1886 to 1890. They were kind neighbours to Mrs. Riddell, who corresponded with Miss Matthews when the latter was in London. These letters tell much of the author's life at this period and her views on contemporary books. By the courtesy of Miss Matthews, I give the following extracts, by which it will be seen that even the quiet annals

of village life were related with Mrs. Riddell's characteristic humour :

'1886.

Here is *Little Lord Fauntleroy* with many thanks. I am
very glad indeed to have read it. The story is pretty, but I
quite fail to see the reason for such a fuss as has been made
about it. In every respect, Mrs. Ewing's books are better.
I have been reading the Bishop of Ripon's extraordinary utter-
ances about novels. It seems a little hard that in order to be
popular a Bishop must say or do something foolish. Nowadays
one feels quite thankful to those Church dignitaries who have
sense enough to hold their tongues. Never was there a time
when silence seemed so golden as now, and surely never was
there a time when we had so little of it. . . . A testimonial is
being got up by the Secretary of the " Incorporated Society of
Authors "—whatever that may be—for Mrs. Burnett. Subscription limited to £2 2s.

It is so much easier to praise than to blame : one need give
no reason for praising, that I cannot wonder at the reluctance
people seem to have to express an adverse opinion. Besides
it is more amiable to praise, and one doesn't like to seem un-
amiable : but yet, when a book is lauded as *Lord Fauntleroy* has
been, it is only natural to enquire why the public are so taken
with the story. I have no hesitation in saying it is because the
book is a cross between a tract and a play. It appeals to
mothers, and the sentiments are those which " bring down the
galleries." Long, long ago, one of the first small band which
made *The Saturday Review* such a brilliant success told me that
every author ought to test his plot to see if it would act. I
thought then he was wrong ; I am *sure* now that he was,
because the very best novels that have ever been written won't
act at all : but *Lord Fauntleroy* would act,[1] and the very qualities
in it which would make a good play spoil it to my notion as a
story. Further, I do think an author ought to avoid poaching
on another's manor. If you have *Jackanapes*[2] by you, re-read
it and you will see what I mean. In *Nancy*[3] also, when her

[1] *Little Lord Fauntleroy*, by Mrs. Hodgson Burnett, had just been
published this year, 1886. When dramatised the story brought to
the author over £20,000.

[2] *Jackanapes*, by Juliana Horatia Ewing (1841-1885), was published in 1883.

[3] *Nancy*, by Rhoda Broughton (1840-1920), had appeared in 1873.

lover asks her what she would wish for if she were rich, she
tells him all the good things she would like to have for others.
It is possible Mrs. Burnett may not have read her Broughton
or Ewing, but if she has not, the "jumping of wits" is very
extraordinary.

In a play we do not enquire too closely into probability, but
in a story we have a right to demand it.   Now Lord Fauntleroy
is not a probable—indeed, I may go further and say he is not a
possible—child.   The reformed old Earl isn't a possible old
Earl out of a tract, and the whole episode of the false heir is as
clumsy as it can well be.   I know we ought not to judge little
things by a big standard, but the public has elected to make so
big a thing of *Lord Fauntleroy* that one is compelled to criticise
it seriously.

What is needed now in literature is a GREAT writer.   When
I look back and consider the authors there were even in my
time, and think of those who immediately preceded them, I feel
the century is getting so old as to be doting, and I can only
hope that in some public place—looking with bright young
eyes on the stream of London life, or taking a lesson from the
mountains and the silent moors and the lovely lakes—there are
lads who will arise as prophets in 1900,[1] teaching the world
that money is not all and success is not all, that to an author his
Art ought to be as near and dear to him as his God.   It is
strange to think that somewhere there are boys growing up
who will do all this, for it is impossible Literature can go on
sinking as it has been doing within the last twenty years and
especially within the last ten.   Forgive this lengthy protest.

It is my own fault that you misunderstand me a little, for I
was so busy with my brief against the poor boy Lord that I
omitted to say how good in many respects I think the story is.
The dialogue is often capital, the tale moves on rapidly and
easily, the contrast suggested between the real old Earl and the
boy's imaginary nobleman is very humorous, and *Lord Fauntleroy* is altogether a good wholesome book, but I cannot see
anything to—as the lower orders of Irish say—" make such a
song about," as has been sung.   The worst of everything
nowadays is that people go to such extremes.   Think of how

[1] The boys of 1886 whom Mrs. Riddell envisaged as prophets in
1900 do not seem to have materialised.   Messrs. Shaw and Wells
though writing of course, thirty years ago, were of the previous
generation and already well known in 1900.

they raved over *Called Back*,[1] and in that case not a soul could have given a reason for the faith that was in him. Think how long it was on the other hand before *Lorna Doone* made the smallest impression, and then it was not on its merits but because it got mixed up in the stupid public mind with the Marquis of Lorne.[2] There ought to be " sense in the roasting of eggs," and there is no sense in the way a book gets praised at present. You are right. We do not resent weakness in our friends because " we but love them whatever they are," and we do not resent weakness in our acquaintance either if they do not request us to admire them as something very extra-ordinary. But we *are* asked to look upon Lord Fauntleroy as a creature really too beautiful, and that provokes criticism and so—you must forgive me.

I do not fancy I know enough of modern American authors to pass an opinion on their works. Howells I do know a little, and think a book of his might be held up to any young writer as an example of what mere command of words can do. Give him a pat of good butter, and I think he could spread it over miles of bread. But then we must remember that making much out of little is a tendency of the time. On the principle that " an empty cask when tipped over makes the most noise," so people make up for paucity of original thought by talking a great deal about thoughts which are not original. When I take up one of the old authors I can but be struck by the " grip " of his subject he displays in even the shortest sentence. It is as when a master lays his hand upon the piano.

This would be a weary world if the children were not generous and loving, if they had not big thoughts in their little bodies for benefitting those dear to them. There is many a ragged Lord Fauntleroy running over the London pavements, giving out of his poverty, in fact as well as in imagination, as much as any millionaire. I will send you a true story of one of these.

[1] *Called Back*, by Hugh Conway (whose real name was Frederick John Fargus), had a tremendous success in 1883. The story originally appeared in *Arrowsmith's Christmas Annual*. Conway also wrote *Dark Days* of which there were several burlesques, such as Andrew Lang's *Much Darker Days*, by A. Huge Longway, ' Author of *Scrawled Black, The Mystery of Paul Targus*,' etc. (Long-mans, 1884) ; and in *Punch*, November 22nd, 1884, appeared *Bright Nights*, by the Author of *Hauled Forward*.

[2] See page 125.

You are most good to me in every way, and help me more than I can tell you. The little words of pleasantness you forget, perhaps, as soon as they are spoken. Your hundred kindnesses have fallen on my heart like the seeds of sweet flowers borne by the wind. And they are growing in my heart where some day you may find them again, as Longfellow did his song.

I won't come up to-day, for I am " taking care " of my cold, and am moreover hard at work on my novel,[1] which is great happiness. I found a verse the other day which just describes what I am doing :

> " I often think of the beautiful town
> That is seated by the sea,
> Often in thought go up and down
> The pleasant streets of that dear old town,
> And my youth comes back to me.

> " And a verse of a Lapland song
> Is haunting my memory still :
> ' A boy's will is the wind's will,
> And the thoughts of youth are long, long thoughts.' "

If you could send me a few autumn flowers I should be so grateful. Only a few—marigolds and mignonette.

Yours affectionately,
CHARLOTTE E. L. RIDDELL.'

'*December* 8*th*, 1886.

I went up to the Mission, and it may gratify you to know the attendance was good, the music so awful the schoolmaster had to change the chant for the *Gloria*, after which Mr. Langworthy told us he had arrived at the conclusion that " the Day of Judgment would be a great surprise to many people." '

'*June* 27*th*, 1887.

I wish I felt stronger, so as to be of more use, but I find it hard to fight against a constant weariness, which is as great when I rise as when I go to bed.'

[1] This book was *Miss Gascoigne* (1887), which seems to describe Carrickfergus, Mrs. Riddell's early home, for it pictures a town by the sea. Mr. Edmund Downey, who published the novel, stated to me : ' I always felt that she was the heroine of *Miss Gascoigne*. She hinted at something of the kind.' It is the story of the love of an older woman for a young man. Mr. Downey added ' She was a *very* attractive woman, notwithstanding her strong (somewhat masculine) voice. She was not a blue-stocking.'

'*December 6th*, 1888.

Hitherto there have been two books which I shall always think of with the same sort of horror as I should of a bad nightmare—one, Forster's *Life of Dickens*, the other Froude's *Carlyle*. To these I fear I must now add Besant's *Eulogy*,[1] which indeed I have only skimmed, but which I mean to procure hereafter and read very carefully, because I want to obtain a closer knowledge of Jefferies [2] as a man. As an author, I think I took his measure long ago pretty accurately after reading *The Gamekeeper at Home*. It seems to me a great pity that revelations of a man's mistakes and sorrows should be published even to help his widow and children (I hope and believe Besant means to give them the proceeds of his *Eulogy*). Even in the hardest and most unsuccessful literary experiences, there are compensations the world wots not of, and if any author fails to find them I say quite unhesitatingly the fault is in himself. I imagine the fault was in Jefferies's nature, but also I think the mischief lay deeper than in any suggestion made by Besant—viz., that he quite over-rated his own capacity. Before receiving Besant I had begun a letter to you concerning quince jam which perhaps I may send on to you some day when my spirits have a little recovered from the depressing effect of *Jefferies's Eulogy*.'

'*January 11th*, 1889.

It was not because I desired to make the fowls tipplers that I bought the beer, though I do think the spectacle of fifty hens going up to *The Goat* for half a pint of ale each evening would be irresistibly funny. The fact is I lost so many last year that when I found this year promised to be as disastrous unless I could combat roup, I was forced to consider why it happened : I never formerly proved so unfortunate. I tried everything to stop the plague, but still the creatures went on dying ; then suddenly I remembered I had been in the habit of having a pail-full of the thick beer grounds from Chambers at a nominal cost, say once a fortnight or so. All last year I could not get any, and my consequent loss has been at least £10 in stock, to say nothing of the deprivation of profit. They were all *very*

[1] *The Eulogy of Richard Jefferies*, by Walter Besant, 1888.

[2] Richard Jefferies (1848-1887), naturalist and novelist. The son of a farmer, his *The Gamekeeper at Home* first appeared in *The Pall Mall Gazette* in 1877, and *Wild Life in a Southern County*, in 1879. *Wood Magic* was published in 1881, and *The Story of my Heart* in 1883.

tipsy the other day—sleepily drunk, but woke up next morning quite ready to begin again like hardened old topers. I think they will be all right now if they have a dose of beer and bran once a week. In former days I have seen a hen so tipsy she has stood in a corner to support herself; this is a favourite device with animals.

Have you read *Rogers's Life*—the " Hang Theology " man? I am delighted with it.'

'*February* 27*th*, 1889.

Did you read Sala's delightful letter to-day in the *Telegraph* about Piggott? [1] I roared over it, my only sorrow being I had nobody to roar with. I consider Piggott charming. In my own acquaintance, however, I know two who could successfully enter into competition with him—both being as great liars, quite as impecunious and much more humorous. One is from north of the Tweed and one, alas! Irish. . . . Am I not a foolish woman? Perhaps as a matter of courtesy you may think it right to say " No." All I can say is that whether foolish or wise, busy or idle, I am yours affectionately,

CHARLOTTE E. L. RIDDELL.'

'*March* 8*th*, 1889.

In a fable, which no doubt you read when a good little girl, we are told how a traveller wrapped his cloak closer around him and strode on in the teeth of a bitter wind (I should imagine the East when at its worst on the way back from Shepperton station). The fable goes on to tell, however, that when the sun shone and milder airs prevailed the same gentleman cast aside his wraps and succumbed to the heat. It is a long time since that fable was written, but history repeats itself. History *has* repeated itself in my person at Upper Halliford. Save for a small ailment which I mentioned to you as having at once grappled with and defeated, I got splendidly through a wrestle with the cold which tried most people severely, but the very first morning of the thaw I woke with as many pains as Caliban. By the way, was it Caliban or somebody or everybody else who had pains? Perhaps Mr. Irving will inform you if you feel curious on the point. Anyhow,

[1] The Special Judicial Commission to investigate Richard Piggott's allegations made in his *Parnellism and Crime* had been held the previous year, 1888, when he broke down under cross-examination, and fled to Madrid, where he committed suicide in 1889.

I had pains bad enough to have ensued from all the curses of
all the people on Prospero's isle.   Just as some folks have an
eruption of spots or boils or blains, so I had a rash of aches.
When I opened my eyes the conviction came to me that my
bed had been made on rocky hillocks and that I had been
sleeping on one, but when I felt the surface, behold, it was flat
as a pancake.   In addition to the aches I had a sore throat, and
I literally exhausted conjecture in wondering what sort of a
sore throat it might be.   Not being able to come to any satisfactory conclusion, I remembered the friend in need—Tur-
pentine, and used it so generously I felt afraid to go near the
fire lest I should ignite.   Putting all the foregoing into
moderate and sensible language, I have not been well, but now
to quote the phrase of a simple and kindly Irishman of my
acquaintance, I am " on the mend."

Do you know that Mrs. Henry Wood is to have a tomb
erected to her in Highgate Cemetery after the model of Scipio
Africanus bearing the text, " The Lord Giveth Wisdom."
Can you explain the conundrum ?   It can't be a joke, for it
appeared in *The Rock*, which never was guilty of such a thing.' [1]

'*April* 16*th*, 1889.

My loss is your gain, as religious people say when some
one for whom they do not care in the least shuffles off this
mortal coil.   The parallel does not quite hold, as I care for
you very much indeed, but Upper Halliford at present, I am
bound to confess, is looking its very worst.   Even a partial
eye—mine for instance—finds it difficult to trace those
beauties we both wot of, and so, as I before remarked, you
will be better at St. Leonards—a place I humbly hope I may
never see again.

I want to send you an Easter Egg in the shape of one of my
books it is unlikely you have read, and which I hope you may
like.   And so God bless you and give you many a happy
Easter time in the future with those you love.

I should like to see *A Glorified Spinster*, though I have some
misgivings that she would closely resemble any other bore.
It is a beautiful name.   Did you ever—apropos of nothing—
read *Mother Rigby's Pipe* ?   I send it with this.   It is rather
grimy, having during the past fourteen years been much read
by all sorts and conditions.   If you see Mrs. Hancock, do

---

[1] Mrs. Henry Wood had died in 1887.   It is not clear why Mrs.
Riddell disliked her work so much.

apologise to her for my stupidity in sending her a goose's egg to-day with nothing to cover its nakedness, not even a fig-leaf.

No, I think I must not read James's novel [1] now. I must stick to my own, such as it is. If you ever meet with Jerrold's (Douglas) *St. Giles's and St. James's*, read it. I have not seen the book for years and years. Somehow one rarely comes across the good old books, yet they must be somewhere.

There is nothing of which I feel more sure than that every village and parish ought to have its own playground. I hear the cricket field at Shepperton is now fenced in and kept solely for ladies and gentlemen. If this be so, I can imagine nothing so likely to engender bad blood between the classes. Baal [2] has been amusing himself with rubbing his nose against my pen while I have been writing, which will not make this note easier to read.

You must have thought me very ungrateful for not answering your letter before this, but I have been running about from editor to printer and publisher till quite fagged out. I had to go to bed the other night at 8, and am not rested yet. It is impossible for me not to understand your most kind suggestion and equally impossible to help thanking you for it with all my heart. But I am not short of money now. I have had this week £136. 17. 1.—to be quite precise, and shall have more I expect before Christmas. I earn enough to supply all my own wants if I wanted twice as much as I do. But I must spend nothing it is possible to help spending if I am to pay what I have to pay and do what I have to do. Probably also I am the slowest author in England, and I certainly believe there is no other author of any standing who gets so little for her or his work. Please understand I am not complaining in the least : only I have never hit the popular taste, being behind the age instead of abreast of it. Then I am as much burdened as if I had a family of my own to keep (more), and so to cut a long story short, I feel it is right for me to stop at home and attend to my business, and that it would be wrong for me to go gadding just now. You see what a rigmarole you have brought on yourself. Do not propose a kindness to any one again. Emily's mother is here to-day doing a great scrub, and I am very miserable, as I always am when a great cleaning is going on.'

[1] *A London Life.*

[2] One of her five cats.

'*April 24th*, 1889.

The name of Rackstraw seemed so familiar to me that I used it in a story I wrote for an Editor (*Cassell's Saturday Journal*). The story has come back to go through the " cutting down " process with which I am so painfully familiar, and I shall alter the name, as it would be nasty to put the future tenant of Lawn Cottage in a cheap periodical. I can use it at some future period if the negotiations fall through.'[1]

'*February 7th*, 1891.

There is in to-day's issue of *The Lady's Pictorial* an interview with Miss Edna Lyall, which is really very nice. . . . Interviews generally are detestable, but I do think you will say Miss Bayly makes a very pleasant picture. . . .[2] Have you seen what Rudyard Kipling says about the American twang ? viz., that when the Yankees stole English books their snort of triumph is fixed for ever in their nostrils by a just Providence. This, however, strikes as a case of the pot calling the kettle black, for surely we are not so honest in the matter of copyright as to be able to throw stones across the Atlantic. . . . Did I tell you how delighted I was with Froude's *Two Chiefs of Dunboy*, and have you read *Pax Vobiscum* ? I don't like it quite so well as *The Greatest Thing in the World*. . . .'[3]

'*September 14th*, 1891.

My thoughts are continually with you in your trouble, and you were so close to me in my dreams last night that I cannot help just a line saying how heavy the great sorrow you are enduring lies on my heart. Sometimes it almost seems to me that though so far apart you must feel me sometimes press your hand and bid you be of good courage. May He who knows all the human heart can suffer give you strength to bear this sore trial.'

[1] The name was changed to Backstraw when the story was published on July 6th, 1889, as *Bertie Evering's Experience*.

[2] Ada Ellen Bayly (1857-1903) had already written her most successful novels, *Donovan*, *We Two*, and *In the Golden Days*.

[3] *Pax Vobiscum* and *The Greatest Thing in the World* were both written by Professor Henry Drummond, F.R.S.E., and appeared in 1890.

'*February 22nd*, 1890.

Herewith the "Interview,"[1] which is supposed to have taken place *here*—wherefore the "low-ceilinged room" the "charming" Mr. Blathwayt evolved out of his own "internal consciousness." The editorial scissors have I fancy been used so freely that my statements have got a little mixed, and the result reminds me of Frank Lincoln's story about the American child who told his mother he had met a young man on the stairs of the Langham, "and he said Washington's father would rather George had told a hundred lies than cut down one cherry-tree." However, it was very good of *The P.M.G.* to put it in at all when their paper is so full, and I am greatly obliged to Mr. Blathwayt for taking so much trouble in writing so kindly about me.'

'*April 20th*, 1890.

Is it not strange the impression joy makes on us. Have we so little of it in our pilgrimage? I do not think so. Perhaps it is only a merciful provision that we remember happiness longer than sorrow.'

'*July 16th*, 1890.

I fancy the wrench from Lawn Cottage must have caused a great difference in your life. . . . Indeed I shall be very glad to know you have found some compensating interest and that your memory of the dear old place is growing a little hazy. Upper Halliford has never looked better than it does this season—everything is so rich, so luxuriant. I could but think as I walked to church last Sunday evening what a peaceful quiet place it is to be so near London. I shall never walk with you to Littleton Church again I suppose. . . . The Allens are gone from Charlton Court. Poor Mr. Vigne![2] Roman Catholics at Sunbury Court, Wesleyans at Lawn Cottage, and Jews at Charlton. It only needs Agnostics at The Lodge to complete the charm.'

'*July 23rd*, 1890.

Like you, I never care to see a remembered house in a new dress. Better to leave it now and for ever keeping the memory

[1] In *The Pall Mall Gazette*, February 18th, 1890, wherein Raymond Blathwayt describes Mrs. Riddell at the age of fifty-eight as a 'cheery and pleasant lady, light-haired and middle-aged.'

[2] The Reverend H. Vigne had been Vicar of Sunbury since 1842.

of the dear old place as it was. . . .   If the Suffolk air be anything like the Norfolk air you ought to get well. . . .   I was
ailing when I went down to Stansfield Rectory in the bygone
days, but the first night I slept there I felt better and soon got
strong again. . . .   My *five* cats are thinning the rodents.'

                                        '*August 9th*, 1890.
   With all my heart I wish I could go to you, but I must not.
I have done so little work for the last two years that my only
hope is now to let nothing come between me and my writing.
You *know* how I should like to go to you, and may imagine
what it costs me to refuse.   Halliford has been a noisy, noisy
place this summer with the pea pickers.   I shall be thankful
when the quiet autumn time comes.   Talk of Missions to the
Heathen !   If some clergyman would kindly walk into the
field behind *The Goat* orchard he would find plenty of work
without the trouble of crossing the ocean ! '

                                        '*August 21st*, 1890.
   You will be interested to hear that at this present time of
writing the School Treat for the Upper Halliford Chapel
children is in full swing on the opposite side of the road, so for
the first time during my tenancy the meadow wears an attractive not to say rakish appearance.   I confess I am amazed at
the amount of dissenting festivity.   Before breakfast was over,
a " deputation," consisting of one member, came to ask
whether a clothes line might be attached to a nail in Palmer's
attic, as they wanted to pass it across the road.   We tied this
cord to the balusters, and from it many flags now hang—an
unusual spectacle which a few minutes ago caused one of the
brisk cart horses to think it might be a nice thing to run away.
   By nine A.M. the youth of Upper Halliford had assembled in
great force and lined the fence.   It was exactly like a scene
from one of the Christmas papers.   There were children of
all sizes, and frocks of all colours, the wearers being dirty
enough for perfect happiness—playing at " Lemons and
Oranges," pretty children most of them, and so tattered and
torn as to be quite artistic.   One might have thought we lived
in a country where needle and thread were never so much as
seen, to say nothing of soap and water.   A stout individual,
by name Day, who seemed to direct the proceedings, told
Sarah the Upper Halliford children much shocked him.   He
had belonged to the Church of England, but went over (or

back) to the Wesleyans, and is reputed to be the part author of a little book in which it is stated a clergyman could not take his " flowing robes " into Heaven with him. This seemed to stagger Sarah a little till I said, " But neither can Mr. Day take his Sunday trowsers." She then, full of her new learning, proceeded to inform me he meant there " would be no sects in Heaven." " But he need not think they will all be Wesleyans," I thought it only right to observe, which statement produced such an effect that she has arrived at the conclusion if the givers of the feast were properly minded they would allow the whole tag, rag, and bob-tail of Upper Halliford to join in the games, which they won't (as I think very properly), so we have tried to solace the Church outcasts by giving them apples.

I have just been asked to distribute the prizes, but declined on the ground of " being unaccustomed to public speaking." Mrs. Pease is to be asked therefore to oblige the company. I wonder if she will. They have hired a piano-organ and two strong-armed youths who grind by turns, but the field is wide and the noise not so great as might be imagined. Flags of all nations are floating in the breeze. There is a swing in the oak tree. Races and football have been proceeding, but the greatest success of the entertainment has been provided quite accidentally by the newly-mown hay (Mrs. Strean rented the field from me for early grazing). After their mid-day meal, the children who were not invited, or wanted, appeared on the scene clean and clothed, with shoes and stockings on, and with hair combed and made beautiful. They stood like Peris at the Gates of Paradise till on Sarah's earnest intercession they were allowed inside, though expected to keep at a respectful distance. I could not help wondering whether Mr. Day was not thinking it was all like the final Judgment Day, the sheep being gathered under the oak tree and the goats straying wild near the palings. By degrees, however, the goats edged up and up till all distinction was temporarily lost and the whole of the children tossed the hay alike and were covered with it. Christianity went even so far as this, that when the Wesleyans had finished their tea, the Church sinners had quite a little feast and a real good time.

I wish I could say the brickfield lads and the field girls showed themselves grateful, but they—the bigger sinners—behaved simply abominably, till Day said next time they, the Wesleyans, must have a policeman to protect them. Indeed, when the youth of Upper Halliford get together their manners lamentably lack repose. They do not in the least resemble those of Vere de Vere. After all, I distributed the prizes, value say 10/. When it was growing dark a deputation, again of one, attended, saying there was no other person to be found, Mrs. Pease having presumably declined, with great sense, to oblige. I did not see then and I do not see now why Mr. Day could not have performed this function himself. We all gathered under the oak tree—the Saints, those who were not Saints, the badly-behaved boys and girls, a gipsy carrying a baby, and many camp-followers. With great difficulty Mr. Drinkwater made his little speech, which was well-nigh drowned by the noise made by the " brickers." He referred to me as " this good lady," and requested three cheers, which as the cheers meant an unearthly row pleased the naughty boys vastly, but they laughed more than they cheered—alas!

Then the prizes were given, and the neighbourhood has resounded with the " hoot-tooting " of tin trumpets ever since. We then had three more cheers and " again," after which I enquired if they would not sing a hymn before they separated. The question arose *what* they could sing, but at last we had three verses of the Evening Hymn. Standing almost in the dark—such a singular collection of human beings—the hymn struck me, badly as it was sung, as very curious and plaintive.

Mr. Day was good enough to see me " across the road," but I had immediately to retrace my steps as the " Sinners" began to pitch the hay out of the field. Sarah dispersed them gallantly, all her Christian feelings towards the outcasts being by that time scattered to the winds, and we stood guard till the hurdles were replaced. Some of the lads had stolen the bolts. Peace and Silence reigned once more. I would not write all this to any one else, but I feel sure it won't bore you. I know how that kind heart of yours yearns over Upper Halliford.'

I think it will be granted that seldom have the simple incidents of a village school treat been presented with such reality and sense of humour as in the above letter; and it is of interest to observe how the imagination of the practised story-teller seized on the picturesque touches of the gipsy with a baby and the singing of the hymn in the dusk under the oak tree (which still stands though the meadow is now a cultivated garden).

In October, 1889, Mrs. Riddell paid her final visit to Ireland, when, she said, ' such of our old friends as were left I found as kind as ever.' During 1891 she was writing *The Head of the Firm*, published by Heinemann in the following year, which had some of its scenes laid at Teddington. Always by choice a slow writer, she was no longer able to produce books regularly, for she was now suffering from bodily weariness and weakness, and about this date she had an unpleasant experience over a story to which she had devoted a good deal of labour. It was entitled *Grays Point* (and presumably depicted the Essex reaches of the Thames). It was commissioned by Edmund Downey, who was to pay her £400, and the tale was announced in the publisher's list of forthcoming works. Mrs. Riddell wrote the story in batches which she would bring to the office and receive a cheque on account in return. After about £300 had been paid, Mr. Downey's partner was dissatisfied with the arrangement and thought the terms were too high. Mrs. Riddell on hearing of this at once resigned her contract, took back her manuscript, and with her usual quixotic sense of honour paid back the £300 she had received, though of course there was no legal obligation for her to act in this manner. She was left with the novel on her hands, and apparently it was never published. In telling me this account, Mr. Downey concluded : ' I could never find whether the novel was published or not. I lost touch with Mrs. Riddell for some time then. I think she was fed-up with novel writing and she was not getting younger. She used to call to see me when I was managing *T.P.'s Weekly*. She was obviously ageing then. I have nothing but pleasant memories of Mrs. Riddell.'

It was probably in 1892 that Mrs. Riddell became aware that she was the victim of the same terrible disease, cancer, which had killed her mother in the far back years of her early literary struggle. Henceforth she was a sad and lonely woman, for with the acute sensitiveness of her imaginative temperament she shrank from any observation or discussion of the malady that threatened her. The symptoms were kept in check for some years by means of drugs, but the gloom and depression of the future made her restless and unable to settle long in any one place.   So it was she decided to bring to a close the pleasant years in Halliford, a period which had certainly been one of the happiest of her not too happy life.   Ere the old landmarks were torn up and she left Halliford for ever, her thoughts must have recalled that poignant passage she had written in *George Geith* :

'Who does not grieve, who does not sorrow, for that passing away which is, after all, the misery of life ?   Friends, youth, beauty, fame, happiness—hours when the sun is streaming on us, moments when in the moonlight we look at faces which we love, days which are full of such happiness that they seem scarcely to have been spent on earth ; all these we touch, to feel they are but part of a procession which is ever moving from us, ever passing away.   Why should we grieve ?   Good heavens !   how could we do otherwise, when we know so well that after the sunshine comes gloom—after the day, night ?   Is it marvellous that, feeling the darkness creeping on, we should linger to the last in the light ? that, feeling the waves of the cruel ocean we have breasted licking our feet, we should stretch out our hands after the groups that are walking away over the pleasant sands we shall never tread more ? Life's days are so gloomy when the summer is gone, its streets are so deserted when the gallant cavalcade is past, its ways are so stony when we have to tread them alone, that it is no wonder we grieve when the hour comes for parting, and the sad good-byes are spoken.'

During the winter of 1892-1893, while she was looking out for another country house, Mrs. Riddell stayed at 135, St. Mark's Road, Notting Hill, a district she depicted in a later story, *A Rich Man's Daughter* (1897).   From here she wrote to Miss Matthews on December 22nd, 1892 :

'You have it no doubt remarked that authors are rarely able to judge of the effect their work produces on others.   For instance, an actor can see at once how he affects an audience, and in like manner singers and musicians may be said to feel the pulse of their hearers.   An artist hangs his picture, and

sees hundreds fascinated by its beauty, but it is not so as a rule
with us. We think our thoughts and write down our ideas
in silence and solitude, and it is only now and then, after years
may be, some voice comes across the stillness to bid us be of
good cheer because words spoken long before have touched
another heart and awakened an echo in it. You were that
voice to me about *Alaric Spenceley*,[1] and I thank you for its
loving message with all my heart.'

In February, 1893, she moved to her new home, The
Elms, at Harlington, in her favourite county of Middlesex
of course. It was a pleasant, trim, low house such as the
builders in the early part of the nineteenth century so
often put up, with French windows opening on to a wide
verandah, such a trim villa and garden, in fact, as Mr.
Pickwick retired to at Dulwich. Harlington is a scattered village lying on both sides of the Bath Road, and
set in a wide stretch of flat country planted with fruit
orchards which made it lovely in blossom time : I say
' made,' because the advent of by-pass roads with consequent building developments are fast ruining what was,
less than forty years ago, a lonely and remarkable bit of
country though so near London. The great plain of
absolutely flat meadows and orchards reaching from
Southall to Staines, and Old Windsor, intersected by the
river Colne, the Old River, the King's River, with
numerous tributary streams and canals, is much like
portions of the flat water-lands of Lincolnshire, and like
Lincolnshire it has magnificent sunsets. As at Addlestone and Upper Halliford Mrs. Riddell's distant views
were bounded by the heights of Egham and the enchanted ranges of Windsor Forest and Herne the Hunter,
so also were they at Harlington, with the added glory of
seeing the sun set behind the magic Castle rising high on
its hill. Given a misty eve of autumn, and the setting
sun bursting through dark clouds and lighting up the
noble towers as with torches of blood-crimson light,
Windsor is a veritable Gnomes' Castle such as Wagner

[1] *Alaric Spenceley, or a High Ideal,* was published in 1881.

dreamed of and conceived with strains of immortal
melody.   Here indeed is visible Romance, here indeed

'The splendour falls on castle walls . . .
O hark, O hear . . .
O sweet and far, from cliff and scar,
The horns of Elfland faintly blowing.'

And yet how few people seem to have seen at their own
doors what they rush to see on the Rhine and in Touraine.
However, it is quite certain that the beauty of this English
scene was perceived by one sad and lonely and doomed
woman who had come to Harlington for a space, accompanied only by one old servant and the last survivors of
the cinque-company of cats at Halliford, and these, like
their mistress, were growing old.   Mrs. Riddell, writing
on October 4th, 1893, to Miss Matthews when sending
her a present of quinces gathered from the garden of The
Elms, related of her life at this time, so quiet and changed
from that she had led a quarter of a century earlier, when,
as a leading author and editor of a popular magazine, she
had been a forceful influence in the World of Letters :

'When, dear friend, did you ever not give to me since the
happy day when I first knew you.   And what have you not
given me ?   Love, encouragement, strength.   If ever I forget
your kindness, I shall have forgotten most things—all worth
remembering certainly.   Often—often I think of you all and
wish—vain things.   My poor black cat, The Baroness, is dead ;
picked up some poison, no doubt, and came back to die—at
home.   The other old cat is the last animal I have left from
the Halliford days, and since The Baroness's death he is so
changed I don't think he will last over the winter.   I have a
few hens, a few ducks and a *kid*—the tamest and greediest
creature that ever drew breath.   There are some nice old
Churches round about, which I hope one day to say something
concerning in print.   I think I told you the Rectory people are
Irish and very kind.'

The three churches in question, Harlington, Harmonds-
worth, and West Drayton, are all remarkably interesting
buildings, and similar in style, being of the Gothic Per-

pendicular period.   All three Manors, too, had originally
been held by the Pagets, Earls of Uxbridge, now the subsidiary title of the Marquises of Anglesey.   Harlington
churchyard is remarkable also for an ancient yew tree
(said to be over seven hundred years old, and whose
annual clipping, until the year 1825, was attended by
jocund festivities such as took place at the Scouring of
the White Horse in Berkshire), and a magnificent cedar.
Mrs. Riddell was very fond of the quiet beauties of Harlington both in summer and winter.   In a sketch entitled *A Personal Experience*, she wrote :

' Even on that February afternoon, how lovely the country
looked, how fresh the wind, how pure the air . . . our pretty
village had quite a spring-like appearance.   Sunshine glinted
across the pond still half-sheeted with ice, rested tenderly on
the grassy mound clustered around the old church of St. Peter
and St. Paul, touched the great cedars with shafts of gold . . .
an enormous wood bon-fire kindled in the orchard.'

She was getting poorer and poorer as her health declined, for though the remuneration for her books became
less and less, her voluntary payments in settlement of
claims against her late husband's estate continued with
quixotic regularity until the debt of honour was wiped
out.   But she was now often suffering pain, ever to a
greater extent, as her terrible malady gained ground.   In
October, 1893, she was grateful to accept some temporary
assistance from Miss Matthews, to whom she writes :

' Thank you again and again for your kind note and en-
closure which I should have acknowledged at once had I not
been in the agonies of finishing a story [1] which was promised
to go by the last post.   It is quite impossible for me to say how
grateful I feel or to tell you the relief your kindness is to me.
The money will be a great help, but in one way I think your
note is even more of assistance.   If you knew how I hesitated
about writing and how after my request was posted I longed to
recall it.   For the first time almost I omitted to insert a clause
in my agreements for this year that I should receive some

---

[1] Presumably *The Rusty Sword* (1893).

money as the work progressed, with the consequence that I have had to neglect bigger and really profitable work in order to write short things that the pressing claims might be met. I could pay all I have to pay without much difficulty at the end, say, of six months or a year, but my worry is that I have to send cash each month so that I never really seem to get my breath. But I don't want to grumble when I only feel grateful. . . .

I never forget my dear friends who made Upper Halliford " blossom like the rose." How far away that time seems when I used to see you so often. This has been a year of trouble, loss, and anxiety to most people, I think. Publishers, at all events, have not known so bad a time for many a long day, but no doubt the reaction will set in ere long. . . .'

In 1895 Mrs. Riddell moved to another house in Harlington, for what reason is not apparent except that her increasing illness made her more and more restless and that the change of home diverted her mind for a time. The Cedars, however, a comfortable white house on the other side of the Bath Road, was also a secluded house, screened from observation by trees and clumps of thick shrubberies, a melancholy house such as she had ever delighted in for the setting of her stories and which now was attune with her own mournful condition. Though she led a retired life here, she kept in touch with a few friends and preserved an interest in their affairs. Thus she wrote to the Rev. Richard Free, then a clergyman working in North Kensington and desirous of publishing a novel he had recently written :

'The Cedars,
Harlington,
Middlesex,
September 20th, 1895.

Indeed I should be sorry if you ever could think of me save as your friend. Your joys and sorrows must always interest me, and till life's tale is told I should love to hear of your happiness and success, and to be allowed to sympathise with you when trouble comes, as it is sure to do even in the most prosperous career. Since I wrote I have been trying to find some letters from a literary man who was kind enough to take an

interest in my future—long, long ago.   He was dying at the
time, but though ill with a mortal disease he gave me advice
which I never profited by as I ought.   I wanted to find his
letters because I thought they might contain some hint useful
to you, but it was impossible for me when moving from The
Elms to see to the packing, and I have never been able to
arrange my papers since, so I have failed.   There is one suggestion he made, however, which I venture to repeat : " Do
not put any restraint on your pen while writing, but *blot freely
afterwards.*"   Now this seems to me a weighty piece of advice,
because it is so easy to blot, and so hard to write in.'

She advised Mr. Free to write a novel dealing with the
lives and mentality of the clergy, and proceeded :

' Often when listening to a sermon I cannot help wondering
how matters stand between the preacher and his God.   I have
marvelled and longed to know what was troubling him.   I
have exhausted myself in fact wondering about the mortal who
felt himself privileged to speak of immortality.'

And later she continued :

' See Downey *himself*.   He is a nice little fellow who will I
believe help you if in his power.   My novel is approaching
completion.   Wish me good luck with it, for indeed I sorely
want a little " clapping ".'

The novel mentioned was presumably *The Ruling
Passion*, published in 1896 by Hutchinson.   Mrs. Riddell's
literary career was now nearing the end.   *Did He Deserve
It* and *A Rich Man's Daughter* both appeared in 1897 ; in
The Footfall of Fate, 1900, she once again described the
Thames scenery near Chertsey ; and her last book was
Poor Fellow, published in 1902.   By this date she had
removed to her last home, Elmdale, Witham Road, in
Spring Grove, that very pleasant part of Isleworth.   It
was merely a small and quite new red-brick villa, such a
house as one could never picture as congenial to Mrs.
Riddell.   Here were no haunted rooms whose dark,
leaded panes were touched, as with shuddering fingers,
by the over-shadowing branches of elm and cedar tree,
here no dank ivy and screening hedge of yew, here no

creeping water and sinister mill-stream. But the windows of the house looked west over open land to the sunset, and still on the horizon lay the enchanted realm of Windsor. Mrs. Riddell was still in Middlesex and in the midst of orchards, lovely in blossom time. Spring Grove at that date led to a really charming stretch of placid, green country near Wyke Farm : but now all is ruined and destroyed by the Great West Road, along which rushes a never-ceasing Juggernaut of noise and fume, while small suburban villas now press upon and overlook the once secluded and High Aristocratic Privy Privileges of Osterley Park. Shade of Sarah Countess of Jersey. . . .

I will not dwell on Mrs. Riddell's last years, so sad a record it would be of 'genteel' poverty, loneliness, depression, and terrible pain, though at times the old Irish humour and somewhat impatient wit would break through the gathering shadows. But release was at hand from both bodily and spiritual weariness. In her own words, written in the long, long ago, in *George Geith* :

'She had come, at last, to that page of human existence at the bottom whereof Finis is written, and for her there was to be nothing more, whether of joy or of sorrow, added to the volume for ever. The short day was drawing to its close— that day which had been lived so fully ; the book was written, the tale told, the story ended.'

The end came on September 24th, 1906, a few days before her seventy-fourth birthday. She was buried on the west side of the churchyard of Heston, which was then still a village church, filled with the monuments of the Jersey family of Osterley Park. The service was taken by Mrs. Riddell's friend, the Rev. Richard Free (now Vicar of St. Clement's, Fulham). Tennyson's *Crossing the Bar* was read at the graveside. The simple stone bears the words : 'Charlotte, widow of J. H. Riddell, Esq., Born 30th Sept. 1832. Died 24th Sept. 1906. Author of *George Geith*, *The Senior Partner*, and

many other novels.' It will be observed that there is no
text. As she was a woman who had a deep sense of
religion, knew her Bible exceedingly well, and went to
church frequently, if not regularly, the omission cannot
have been due to indifference or accident. It may be
concluded that in a moment of wracking pain and extreme weariness towards the end, realising the futility
and falsity of words proclaiming peace and comfort and
joy, she impatiently gave the direction, ' Let there be no
texts above my grave.' There was no occasion to proclaim publicly what her beliefs or future hopes might be,
and that she was one who had sorrowed and suffered
very pitifully was, and is, well known to her friends.
She would be satisfied to be remembered just for her
books, and it is fitting that the resting place for her body
should be in the Middlesex she loved so well and so
admirably described.

LIST OF WORKS BY MRS. RIDDELL

1. ZURIEL'S GRANDCHILD, published about 1855 by T. C.
   Newby, 30, Welbeck Street, Cavendish Square, London.
   The book probably appeared anonymously. It was
   republished some eighteen years later under the title of
   JOY AFTER SORROW / By / Mrs. J. H. Riddell, and again
   reissued in this form by Hutchinson and Co., 1892.
   Red cover. The scene is laid in Lancashire.

2. THE MOORS AND THE FENS / By / F. G. Trafford / In
   Three Volumes / London / Smith, Elder and Co., 65,
   Cornhill / 1858. Olive-green embossed covers.
   Republished in one volume :
   THE MOORS AND THE FENS / By / Mrs. J. H. Riddell /
   Author of . . . / A New Edition with four illustrations
   (by Walter Crane) / London / Smith, Elder & Co., 15,
   Waterloo Place / 1876. Red cover.

3. THE RICH HUSBAND was originally published, in three
   volumes, probably in the early part of 1858, and anony-

mously, by Charles J. Skeet, 10, King William Street, Charing Cross, London. It was republished some years later as

THE / RICH HUSBAND / A Novel / By Mrs. J. H. Riddell / Author of . . . / New Edition / London / Tinsley Brothers, 18, Catherine Street, Strand / 1867. Light brown cover.

The Preface, dated November 1st, 1866, states : ' Many years have elapsed since *The Rich Husband* was written—nearly nine since it was first published. The original three volume journey having proved moderately successful, it has been thought desirable to reproduce the book in a cheaper form. . . . With the exception of some slight curtailment and the correction of typographical and grammatical errors, no alteration has been attempted. The title, which is not mine, was suggested by Mr. Charles Skeet, through whose courtesy I am permitted once again to make use of it.'

The scenes of the story are laid in Wales and London.

4. TOO MUCH ALONE / By / F. G. Trafford / Author of *The Moors and the Fens* / In Three Volumes / London / Charles J. Skeet, Publisher / 10, King William Street, Charing Cross / 1860. Brown-sepia covers.

Scenes laid in Eastcheap and Bow.

5. CITY AND SUBURB / By F. G. Trafford / Author of . . . / In Three Volumes / London / Charles J. Skeet, 10, King William Street, Charing Cross / 1861. Green covers.

Some of the scenes are laid at Tottenham and West Green.

6. THE WORLD IN THE CHURCH / By / F. G. Trafford / Author of . . . / In Three Volumes / Second Edition / London / Charles / J. Skeet, 10, King William Street, Charing Cross / 1863. (The first edition probably appeared in 1862.) Green covers.

Scene laid in Staffordshire.

7. GEORGE GEITH OF FEN COURT / A Novel / By F. G. Trafford / Author of *Too Much Alone* / In Three Volumes / London / Tinsley Brothers, 18, Catherine Street, Strand / 1864. Brown covers.

' To Alexander Johns, Esq., of Sunnylands, Carrickfergus, in thankful remembrance of kind advice, of cordial encouragement, and of valuable assistance, this book is dedicated by his old friend, the Author.'

Although the Tinsleys continued to publish Mrs. Riddell's books after the date in question, it is of interest to note that an early edition of *George Geith* was issued by another firm :

GEORGE GEITH OF FEN COURT / By Mrs. Riddell, Editor of *The St. James's Magazine* / New Edition / Frederick Warne and Co., Bedford Street, Covent Garden / 1868. Frontispiece by F. W. L.

There is a Tauchnitz edition in two volumes.

GEORGE GEITH, OR ROMANCE OF A CITY LIFE, a Drama founded on Mrs. Riddell's novel by Wybert Reeve, was published by Richard Bentley and Son, 1883.

8. PHEMIE KELLER / A Novel / By F. G. Trafford / Author of . . . / In Three Volumes / London / Tinsley Brothers / 18, Catherine Street, Strand / 1866. Brown covers. This book must have appeared in the autumn of 1865, as it is mentioned on the title page of *Maxwell Drewitt*, 1865.

A second edition of *Phemie Keller* was published in 1867 (1866).

9. MAXWELL DREWITT / A Novel / By F. G. Trafford / Author of *George Geith*, *City and Suburb*, *Phemie Keller*, *Too Much Alone* / In Three Volumes / London / Tinsley Brothers, 18, Catherine Street / Strand / 1865. Brown-sepia covers.

MAXWELL DREWITT / By the Author of / *George Geith of Fen Court*, *City and Suburb*, etc., etc. / New Edition / London / F. Enos Arnold, 49, Essex Street, Strand / 1869. With three illustrations of Ballyhinch Lake, Inland, and Off the Coast. Green cover.

There is a Tauchnitz edition.

10. THE / RACE FOR WEALTH / A Novel / by / Mrs. J. H. Riddell / Author of . . . / In Three Volumes / Tinsley Brothers / 18, Catherine Street, Strand / 1866. Terra-cotta covers. The scene is laid at Stepney and Grays.

This story also appeared serially in *Once a Week* during 1866. There is a Tauchnitz edition.

11. FAR ABOVE RUBIES / A Novel / By / Mrs. J. H. Riddell /
    Author of . . . / In Three Volumes / Second Edition /
    London / Tinsley Brothers / Catherine Street, Strand /
    1867.   Dark puce covers.
New edition 1868.   Scene laid in Hertfordshire.
There is a Tauchnitz edition.

12. THE MISERIES OF CHRISTMAS appeared in *Routledge's
    Christmas Annual* for 1867.

13. A STRANGE CHRISTMAS GAME, a Ghost Story, and COULEUR
    DE ROSE appeared in *The Broadway Annual* for 1868.

14. MY FIRST LOVE comprised *The St. James' Christmas Box*
    for 1869, ' Profusely Illustrated and Richly Bound in
    GOLD and COLOURS, forming a very handsome Present.'
    This was the Christmas Number of *St. James' Magazine*,
    edited at this date by Mrs. Riddell, and published by
    F. Enos Arnold, *St. James' Magazine* Office, Strand,
    W.C.

    MY FIRST LOVE and MY LAST LOVE, A Sequel, were both
    printed in *Frank Sinclair's Wife and Other Stories*, 1874,
    and were republished by Hutchinson and Co. in 1891,
    as a single volume.

15. AUSTIN FRIARS / A Novel / By Mrs. J. H. Riddell / Author
    of . . . / Reprinted from *Tinsley's Magazine* / In Three
    Volumes / London / Tinsley Brothers, 18, Catherine St.,
    Strand / 1870.   Blue covers.

16. A LIFE'S ASSIZE / A Novel / By Mrs. J. H. Riddell /
    Author of . . . / In Three Volumes / London / Tinsley
    Brothers, 18, Catherine Street / Strand / 1871.   Brown
    covers.
' To Frederick C. Skey, C.B., F.R.C.S., Late President of the
Royal College of Surgeons, in Admiration of his genius, as a
token of esteem, in acknowledgment of kindness that for thirty
years has never varied, and of skill the exercise of which has
never been asked in vain, this story, which is not all fiction, is
dedicated by his Friend, the Author.'
    This story had appeared serially in *St. James' Magazine*, April, 1868,
to February, 1870.   It is a powerful story of murder, in Nithsdale,
and later scenes are laid in the Essex marshes.

17. THE EARL'S PROMISE / A Novel / By / Mrs. Riddell / Author of . . . / In Three Volumes / London / Tinsley Brothers, 8, Catherine Street, Strand, 1873. Green covers.

A story of Ulster. There is a Tauchnitz edition.

18. HOME, SWEET HOME / A Novel / By / Mrs. Riddell / Author of . . . / In Three Volumes / London / Tinsley Brothers, 8, Catherine Street, Strand / 1873. Brown covers.

' To Mrs. Frederick Nolan, as a slight token of the Author's regard and esteem this Book is affectionately dedicated.'

A second edition, in one volume, also appeared this year, 1873.

A story of professional musicians.

19. FAIRY WATER / a Christmas Story / by Mrs. J. H. Riddell / Authoress of *George Geith*, etc. / comprised the whole of *Routledge's Christmas Annual* for 1873. With six illustrations by R. Caldecott, engraved by E. Evans, and pictorial paper cover. A ghost story with scene laid in Essex. It was republished as a book, with stiff pictorial paper cover, but without the six plates :

FAIRY WATER / By / Mrs. J. H. Riddell / Authoress of *George Geith* / London and New York / George Routledge and Sons / 1878.

Also issued in illustrated boards, 2s., by Chatto and Windus.

20. MORTOMLEY'S ESTATE / A Novel / by Mrs. Riddell / Author of . . . / In Three Volumes / London / Tinsley Brothers / 8, Catherine Street, Strand / 1874. Dark brown covers.

' To Emma Martin, of Wadesmill, Herts, this story is dedicated as a token of the Author's respect and affection.'

There is a Tauchnitz edition.

21. FRANK SINCLAIR'S WIFE / AND OTHER STORIES / By / Mrs. Riddell / In Three Volumes / London / Tinsley Brothers, 8, Catherine Street, Strand / 1874.

Vol. I. FRANK SINCLAIR'S WIFE.

Vol. II. Ditto, concluded. The story had appeared in *Cassell's Magazine*, January-June, 1871, with illustrations by F. J. Slinger.

MY FIRST LOVE.

Vol. III. MY LAST LOVE, a sequel to *My First Love*.
FOREWARNED, FOREARMED
HERTFORD O'DONNELL'S WARNING. (Reprinted from *London Society*, Christmas Number, 1867, and republished in later years as *The Banshee's Warning*.)
   The one volume edition of *Frank Sinclair's Wife* only contains in addition the dream story, *Forewarned, Forearmed*.

22. HOW TO SPEND / A MONTH IN IRELAND / By / Sir Cusack P. Roney / New Edition revised by / Mrs. J. H. Riddell / Author of *George Geith, Too Much Alone*, etc., etc. / Embellished with eighty illustrations and a map / London / Chatto and Windus, Publishers / 1874.

23. LITTLE JANE / By / Mrs. J. H. Riddell / A story of ten pages, with illustrations, appeared in The Christmas Number, 1874, of *London Society*.

24. THE UNINHABITED HOUSE / By Mrs. J. H. Riddell / With (six) illustrations by A. Chantrey Corbould / comprised *Routledge's Christmas Annual* for 1875. It was republished, without the illustrations, a few years later in the Two Shilling Novel series :

THE UNINHABITED HOUSE / and / THE HAUNTED RIVER / By / Mrs. J. H. Riddell / Author of *George Geith, Fairy Water*, etc. / London / George Routledge and Sons / Broadway, Ludgate Hill / New York, 9, Lafayette Place.
   Pictorial cover showing a woman knocked down by a hansom cab and with the title given as ' *An* ' *Uninhabited House*.
   The Uninhabited House is also listed by Chatto and Windus at two shillings, in pictorial boards, in 1885-1921.

25. ABOVE SUSPICION / A Novel / By / Mrs. J. H. Riddell / Author of . . . / In Three Volumes / London / Tinsley Brothers, 8, Catherine St., Strand / 1876. Brown covers.

   The period of the story is about 1858. It appeared serially in *London Society* during 1874-1875.

26. HER MOTHER'S DARLING / A Novel / By / Mrs. J. H. Riddell / Author of . . . / In Three Volumes / London / Tinsley Brothers, 8, Catherine St., Strand / 1877.
   ' To Eliza Charlotte, Harriette Lois, and Constance Margaret Greene, This Story of a Young Girl's Life which, from sympathy, will have an interest for them outside their own happier

experience, is in remembrance of many a loving word and kindly token, Dedicated by their attached cousin, The Author. Weybridge, January, 1877.' Dark slate covers.

27. THE HAUNTED RIVER / A Christmas Story / By Mrs. J. H. Riddell / Author of *George Geith*, etc., etc. / London and New York / George Routledge and Sons / formed the whole of *Routledge's Christmas Annual* for 1877 (or 1879). It was in twenty chapters, with six illustrations by D. H. Friston, engraved by Edmund Evans.

' To the Misses Liberty, of Ham Moor, Addlestone, in recollection of much kindness and many pleasant days, this little story is dedicated by The Author. Kingston Hill, Surrey.'

The story was republished a few years later, without the illustrations, together with *The Uninhabited House*, see No. 24 above.

28. THE DISAPPEARANCE / OF / MR. JEREMIAH REDWORTH / By Mrs. J. H. Riddell / formed the whole of *Routledge's Christmas Annual* for 1878. A Ghost Story with six illustrations by D. H. Friston.

29. THE / MYSTERY IN PALACE GARDENS / A Novel / By Mrs. J. H. Riddell / In Three Volumes / London / Richard Bentley and Son / 1880.

The action of the story also passes to Forest Gate and Epping. It appeared serially in *London Society*, volumes 37-38.

30. ALARIC SPENCELEY / or / A HIGH IDEAL / By Mrs. J. H. Riddell / Author of . . . / In Three Volumes / Charles J. Skeet, 10, King William Street, Charing Cross / 1881. Red covers.

Scenes in the story are laid in West Ham and Abbey Marsh.

31. THE SENIOR PARTNER / A Novel / By / Mrs. J. H. Riddell / Author of . . . / In Three Volumes / London / Richard Bentley and Son / 1881. Green covers with ivy band.

Scene is mainly in an old house in a court off Basinghall Street. The story appeared serially in *London Society*, volumes 39-40.

32. THE CURATE OF LOWOOD / or / EVERY MAN HAS HIS GOLDEN CHANCE / By Mrs. J. H. Riddell, Author of . . . Illustrated / London / Office of *London Society* / 22, Exeter Street, Strand / 1882 (date not given). On the green pictorial cover the title is EVERY MAN HAS HIS

GOLDEN CHANCE / by Mrs. Riddell / With (3) other Proverb Stories for Boys and Girls. This is a volume of The Golden Acorn Series.

33. DAISIES AND BUTTERCUPS / A Novel / By / Mrs. J. H. Riddell / Author of *George Geith, The Senior Partner*, etc. / In Three Volumes / London / Richard Bentley and Son / 1882. Pale brown covers.

A story of Weybridge and Addlestone. ' To my cousins, Colonel and Mrs. Kilshaw Irwin (Mobile, Alabama), I dedicate this Book, in the hope that to one of them it may recall a pleasant memory of the green fields and softly gliding streams of Surrey. Charlotte E. L. Riddell. London, 1882.'

A later and cheaper edition was published by Sampson, Low, Marston, Searle, and Rivington, St. Dunstan's House, Fetter Lane.

34. THE / PRINCE OF WALES'S GARDEN PARTY / AND OTHER STORIES / By Mrs. J. H. Riddell / London / Chatto and Windus, Piccadilly / 1882.

A. THE PRINCE OF WALES'S GARDEN PARTY (scene at Chiswick House).

B. LADY DUGDALE'S DIAMONDS.

C. FAR STRANGER THAN FICTION.

D. CAPTAIN MAT'S WAGER ⎫
E. MARGARET DONNAN ⎬ Stories of Carrickfergus.

F. MISS MOLLOY'S MISHAP.

G. MRS. DONALD.

35. THREE WIZARDS AND A WITCH appeared in *London Society*, volumes 43-44, commencing in January, 1883. It was issued in the following year as

SUSAN DRUMMOND / A Novel / By / Mrs. J. H. Riddell / Author of *The Senior Partner* / *George Geith* / In Three Volumes / London / Richard Bentley and Son, New Burlington Street / 1884. Pale blue covers.

Prefatory Note states : ' As this story may seem familiar to some readers, it may not be out of place to state here that it originally appeared in *London Society* under the title of *Three Wizards and a Witch*. New Burlington Street, Jan. 15, 1884.'

This story of London and Hertfordshire in 1873 was ' Dedicated to Mr. and Mrs. Colin Campbell Wyllie, of Walden, Chislehurst, in Remembrance of Days gone bye.'

36. A / Struggle For Fame / A Novel / By / Mrs. J. H. Riddell / Author of *The Mystery in Palace Gardens*, *George Geith*, etc. / In Three Volumes / London / Richard Bentley and Son / 1883. Light blue covers.

' To Mrs. Skirrow, 20, Sussex Gardens, in remembrance of staunch friendship and tender sympathy.'

37. Weird Stories / By / Mrs. J. H. Riddell / Author of . . . / appeared originally, I believe, in 1884, in cloth, crown 8vo, published at 3s. 6d. by Chatto and Windus. The only edition I have seen is A New Edition / London / Chatto and Windus, Piccadilly / 1885, with pictorial yellow cover.

A. Walnut-Tree House.

B. The Open Door.

C. Nut-Bush Farm.

D. The Old House in Vauxhall Walk.

E. Sandy the Tinker.

F. Old Mrs. Jones.

38. Berna Boyle / A Love Story of the County Down / By / Mrs. J. H. Riddell / Author of . . . / In Three Volumes / London / Richard Bentley and Son / 1884. Green covers.

It was reissued by the same publishers in the following year, 1885, in one volume, black cover.

39. Mitre Court / A Tale of The Great City / By / Mrs. J. H. Riddell / Author of . . . / In Three Volumes / London / Richard Bentley and Son / 1885. Lavender covers.

The scene is an old house in a court off Botolph Lane, Eastcheap. The story appeared serially in *Temple Bar*, volumes 73-75.

40. For Dick's Sake / By / Mrs. J. H. Riddell, author of *George Geith*, etc. / Society for Promoting Christian Knowledge / London / Northumberland Avenue, W.C. . . . 1886. This story, in eight chapters, was one of the tales in The Penny Library of Fiction, each consisting of 32 pages, and pictorial paper wrapper, price one penny. Some were illustrated. Several well-known writers had their works published in this series of cheap novels, including Grant Allen (*The Sole Trustee* and *A Living Apparition*), G. Manville Fenn, Katharine

Macquoid, the Rev. P. B. Power, and Mrs. L. B. Walford.

41. MISS GASCOIGNE / A Novel / by / Mrs. J. H. Riddell / Ward and Downey / 12, York Street, Covent Garden, London / 1887.

42. IDLE TALES / By / Mrs. J. H. Riddell / Author of . . . / In One Volume / London / Ward and Downey / 12, York Street, Covent Garden / 1888. Red cover with floral design.

A. THE RUN ON CONNELL'S BANK.

B. ONLY A LOST LETTER.

C. HE LOVED AND HE RODE AWAY.

D. PRETTY PEGGY.

E. A SLIGHT MISAPPREHENSION.

F. THE MISSES POPKIN.

G. THE LAST OF SQUIRE ENNISMORE.

H. A STORM IN A TEA CUP.

Dedicated ' To Mrs. Whittle, In Remembrance of Many Happy Days spent by the Author long ago at Larchmount, Co. Londonderry.'

43. THE NUN'S CURSE / A Novel / By Mrs. J. H. Riddell / Author of . . . / In Three Volumes / London / Ward and Downey / 12, York Street, Covent Garden / 1888. Green-blue covers.

' To Dr. and Mrs. George Harley, with the affectionate regards of their friend, the Author.'

A new edition was issued by the same publishers in the following year, 1889, in one volume with pictorial yellow cover.

A similar edition published by Chatto and Windus before 1898.

44. PRINCESS SUNSHINE / AND OTHER STORIES / by / Mrs. Riddell / In Two Volumes / London / Ward and Downey / 12, York Street, Covent Garden / 1889. Red covers.

Vol. I. PRINCESS SUNSHINE.

  Scene is at Kingsland Gate and Stamford Hill.

Vol. II. PRINCESS SUNSHINE, concluded.

  A TERRIBLE VENGEANCE. (A ghost story. Scene laid at Shepperton.)

  WHY DR. CRAY LEFT SOUTHAM.

45. A Mad Tour / or / A Journey Undertaken in an
      Insane Moment Through Central Europe on Foot /
      by / Charlotte Elizabeth Riddell / London / Richard
      Bentley and Son / 1891.

   'Dedicated to Arthur Hamilton Norway, Esq., by his
Friend, the Author.   Upper Halliford, 1891.'

46. The Head of the Firm / A Novel / By / Mrs. J. H.
      Riddell / Author of . . . / In Three Volumes / London /
      William Heinemann / 1892.   Light green covers.

   'Dedicated to my kind neighbour, Mrs. J. Gibson Bennett,
Clock Towers, Upper Halliford.'   Scenes are laid in Battersea,
Borough Market, Cannon Street, and Teddington.

47. The Rusty Sword / or / Thereby Hangs A Tale / By /
      Mrs. J. H. Riddell / Author of . . . / London / Society
      for Promoting Christian Knowledge / Northumberland
      Avenue, Charing Cross, W.C. / 1894.   With illustra-
      tions by J. N. (Nash).   Salmon pictorial cover.

   This story had appeared serially in *The Dawn of Day*, 1893.

48. A Silent Tragedy / A Novel / By Mrs. J. H. Riddell /
      Author of . . . / In One Volume / London, F. V. White
      and Co. / 31, Southampton Street, Strand, W.C. / 1893.
      Boards.

49. The Banshee's Warning / and Other Tales / By / Mrs.
      J. H. Riddell / have been published several times.   The
      second edition, issued by Remington and Company, 15,
      King Street, Covent Garden, in 1894 comprised 277
      pages in grey-blue boards ; the reissue by Routledge in
      1905 comprised 125 pages ; while the edition published
      by John Macqueen, 49, Rupert Street, London, 1903,
      has 120 pages in pictorial paper cover.   The contents
      are :

A. The Banshee's Warning. (This story, originally entitled
      Hertford O'Donnell's Warning, had appeared in *London
      Society*, Christmas Number, 1867, and was reprinted under that
      title in *Frank Sinclair's Wife*, Volume III, 1874.

B. Mr. Mabbot's Fright.

C. A Vagrant Digestion.

D. Bertie Evering's Experience. (This story, somewhat cur-
      tailed, had appeared in *Cassell's Saturday Journal* for 6th July,
      1889.)

   The scene is laid at Shepperton and Kempton Park.

E. LITTLE JANE. This story had appeared in *London Society*, Christmas Number, 1874.

F. SO NEAR; OR THE PITY OF IT.

50. DIARMID CHITTOCK'S STORY / By Mrs. J. H. Riddell / Author of *George Geith* / in six chapters, appeared in the August, September, and October, 1894, numbers of *The Lady of the House*, published by Wilson, Hartnell, and Co., Commercial Buildings, Dublin. An Irish story of mystery and death, written in the style of Sheridan Le Fanu. In Dublin one of the characters ' chancing to pick up Le Fanu's *House by the Churchyard*, he explored Chapelizod reverently and with a deep feeling of sadness.'

51. THE RULING PASSION / A Novel / By / Mrs. J. H. Riddell / A New Edition / London / Hutchinson and Co. / 34, Paternoster Row / 1896. Embossed maroon cover.

I have not seen a copy of the first edition of this book. The Preface of the 1896 edition states : ' The Author wishes it to be understood that the following work is a revised edition of a story originally published several years ago.'

52. DID HE DESERVE IT ? / by / Mrs. J. H. Riddell / Downey and Co., Ltd., 12, York Street, Covent Garden, London/ 1897.

' To my dear young friend, Annette Haddock, Harlington Rectory, Middlesex.' The scene is partly at South Lambeth.

53. A RICH MAN'S DAUGHTER / by Mrs. J. H. Riddell / London, F. V. White and Co. / 1897.

' To Mrs. Helen C. Black, Capable, True, Kind, who has devoted long years to the Relief of Suffering Humanity, this book is dedicated by her friend, the Author.'

This story of North Kensington was republished in the following year, 1898, in crown 8vo cloth, by Chatto and Windus, at 3s. 6d.

54. HANDSOME PHIL / AND OTHER STORIES / By / Mrs. J. H. Riddell / London, F. V. White and Co., 14, Bedford Street, Strand, W.C. / 1899.

A. HANDSOME PHIL.

B. DIARMID CHITTOCK'S STORY. (This had appeared in *The Lady of the House* in 1894, see No. 50.)

C. OUT IN THE COLD.

D. MR. POLZOY'S LITTLE KATEY.

E. IN DEADLY PERIL.

F. CONN KILREA. (A Ghost Story.)

G. DR. VARVILL'S PRESCRIPTION. (This had appeared in *The Chemist and Druggist*, July 28th, 1894.)

H. A PERSONAL EXPERIENCE.

55. THE FOOTFALL OF FATE / By Mrs. J. H. Riddell / Author of . . . / London, F. V. White and Co., 14, Bedford Street, Strand, W.C. / 1900.   Green cover.

A Thames-side story of ' Abbotsmead ' (Chertsey).

56. POOR FELLOW. / By / Mrs. J. H. Riddell / Author of . . . / London / F. V. White and Co., Ltd. / 14, Bedford Street, Strand, W.C. / 1902.   Red cover.

A story of an unsuccessful man who ends his career by suicide.

Mrs. Riddell, it is believed, also wrote stories entitled QUITE TRUE and LONG AGO, but I have not succeeded in tracing these in any form.

I am indebted to my friend, Montague Summers, for indicating the serial appearance of some of Mrs. Riddell's stories and for the loan of some of her books from his collection.

INDEX